Khobar Towers
Tragedy and Response

Khobar Towers
Tragedy and Response

Perry D. Jamieson

Air Force History and Museums Program
United States Air Force
Washington, D.C. 2008

Library of Congress Cataloging-in Publication Data

Jamieson, Perry D.
  Khobar Towers : tragedy and response / Perry D. Jamieson.
    p. cm.
  Includes bibliographical references and index.
  1. Dhahran Military Housing Facility Bombing, Dhahran, Saudi Arabia, 1996. 2. Terrorism—Saudi Arabia. 3. Bombing investigation—Saudi Arabia. [1. Dhahran Military Housing Facility Bombing, Dhahran, Saudi Arabia, 1996. 2. Terrorism—Saudi Arabia. 3. Saudi Arabia—Relations—United States. 4. United States—Relations—Saudi Arabia.] I. Air Force History and Museums Program (U.S.) II. Title.

  HV6433.S33J36 2008
  363.32509538—dc22
  ISBN 978-1-78039-283-7   2008010703

They came from Pineville, West Virginia, from Cambridge, Minnesota, and from other small towns. In many ways, they were ordinary young Americans: they liked music, cars, and a laugh with their friends. But in one way, they were extraordinary young Americans: they gave their lives for their country.

This book is for them.

Foreword

America's mind's eye carries all too many painful pictures of terrorist actions against her: the collapsed Marine Corps barracks in Beirut, a gaping hole at the waterline of USS Cole, and shocked, bleeding casualties sitting in the streets of the U.S. embassy in Kenya, as well as fire blossoming from New York City's Twin Towers. Another enduring image is the shredded walls of Khobar Towers where nineteen airmen gave their final full measure on June 25, 1996.

This account of the Khobar Towers bombing, so eloquently narrated by Dr. Perry Jamieson, tells the story of the horrific attack and the magnificent response of airmen doing their duty under nearly impossible circumstances. None of them view their actions as heroic, yet the reader will marvel at their calm professionalism. All of them say it was just their job, but the reader will wonder how they could be so well trained to act almost instinstively to do the right thing at the right time. None of them would see their actions as selfless, yet countless numbers refused medical attention until the more seriously injured got treatment.

Throughout this book, the themes of duty, commitment, and devotion to comrades resoundingly underscore the notion that America's brightest, bravest, and best wear her uniforms in service to the nation.

This book is more than heroic actions, though, for there is also controversy. Were commanders responsible for not adequately protecting their people? What should one make of the several conflicting investigations following the attack? Dr. Jamieson has not shied away from these difficult questions, and others, but has discussed them and other controversial judgments in a straightforward and dispassionate way that will bring them into focus for everyone. It is clear from this book that there is a larger issue than just the response to the bombing. It is the issue of the example set by America's airmen. Future airmen who read this book will be stronger and will stand on the shoulders of those who suffered and those who made the ultimate sacrifice.

No matter what conclusions the reader might reach, one continues to return to the magnificent actions of young Americans far from home working in grueling conditions, who just do their duty. A duty they do without equivocation and for the love of their country and their service. Ultimately, then, this is a story of victory, because the Air Force learned from Khobar Towers. It learned about a ruthless enemy, and all airmen will learn, too, that even under the most devastating conditions, they can fight back and win, a lesson that the world's terrorists have yet to learn. But learn they will.

C. R. Anderegg, Director
Air Force History and Museums Program

Preface

For some Americans, the catastrophic events of September 11, 2001 may have overshadowed the Khobar Towers bombing of June 25, 1996. Yet as horrific as the attacks on the Pentagon and World Trade Center were, the bombing in Dhahran—terrible in its own right—should still command our attention. There is no distinguishing of the importance among these, or any other terrorist events, to those who lost their loved ones in them. That the Khobar Towers tragedy was followed by ones even larger in scale does not diminish its importance: it furthers it. The "Bleeding Kansas" of the 1850s prefigured a far bloodier Civil War in the 1860s, and the blasted facade of Building 131 anticipated the yet more deadly terrorism of the twenty-first century.

This history is based largely on tape-recorded oral history interviews conducted by the author and held by the Air Force Historical Studies Office, on Bolling Air Force Base, Washington, D.C. Other historians contributed a few more of these sessions and those sources are identified in the endnotes and backmatter. Where I conducted the interview, the endnotes describe it as an interview "with" the participant; where another historian asked all or most of the questions, the notes call it an interview "of" the participant. In the endnotes which have shortened citations, the use of one of these prepositions or the other tells the reader whether the interview cited was conducted by the author or another historian. In every case, the AFHSO holds copies of these taped interviews.

Many of the interviewees offered painfully vivid accounts of the Khobar Towers bombing and its aftermath. Their stark honesty made it difficult to quote some parts of their interviews. I tried to describe accurately the horrors of a terrorist attack and at the same time to respect the feelings of those who survived the bombing that night and of the families of those who did not.

Another difficulty raised by these oral history interviews was that they sometimes contradicted one another. When two or more witnesses disagreed about a small point, I did not, except in a very few cases, try to reconcile the competing versions. It is not surprising that under the stressful circumstances of a terrorist attack, some people recalled certain details differently than others; the remarkable fact is that, in the great majority of cases, these oral accounts verified one another.

In addition to the oral history interviews, many documents were quoted or otherwise used to prepare this work. Wherever possible, I have cited in full these sources. The text never quotes classified or "for official use only" documents, but in two or three instances, it makes indirect use of open portions of them. In these few cases, the notes describe the source, but do not give a formal citation. This methodology protects the identification of closed documents, while offering some help in retrieving them in the future, if they are declassified and released. The AFHSO retains the documents, classified and unclassified, that are cited or described in the endnotes.

The Khobar Towers story cannot be told without encountering controversies, and most of the people best informed about these were on active duty with the United States Air Force when this manuscript was written. In the instances where these airmen were quoted by the press, they are identified by name and the relevant source is cited in the endnotes. In some cases, where an oral history interview provided sensitive information, the speaker is not identified. All of these interview tapes, held by the AFHSO, have been assigned a number. In the instances where the witness is not identified by name, the endnotes cite one of these numbers. This reserves the identity of the speaker, while ensuring that future researchers eventually will be able to confirm the quotations and to read or hear them in their full context.

Unit designations can be confusing. It would have been more accurate to identify the Air Force units deployed to Southwest Asia by their provisional designations, but these four-digit numbers would have cluttered the narrative. Where reasonable in both the text and notes, I used the more familiar, stateside designation of these units. In a few cases, the text does not make it clear that the speaker in an interview or the author of a document had served in Saudi Arabia and that the value of their evidence should be credited accordingly. In these instances, their unit's provisional designation is given, to alert the reader that the speaker or author had been in Saudi Arabia.

Stating the ranks of officers and airmen proved less confusing than identifying units. The largest issue here was that many Khobar Towers veterans received promotions after the attack, and before they were interviewed, or before this manuscript went to press. I have identified them with the rank they held on June 25, 1996. The notes acknowledge the cases where colonels at the time of the bombing later were promoted to generals.

I followed the convention of telling when an event took place by citing the local time. Military documents often use "zulu" time, equivalent to Greenwich Mean time. I converted these to the local a.m. and p.m. modifiers, which are familiar to general readers.

The nomenclature of local geography raised a few problems. The name "Khobar Towers" itself can be misleading. To avoid cluttering the narrative with repeated qualifiers, I followed the Air Force practice of using this name when only the USAF area of the larger compound is meant, a refinement which is detailed in chapter two. A similar case involved the Ministry of Defense and Aviation (MODA) complex on the King Abdul Aziz Air Royal Saudi Base, which included the King Abdul Aziz Air Base Hospital. Air Force personnel generally used the term "MODA Hospital" to mean specifically the King Abdul Aziz Hospital. Again to simplify the text, and to follow the useage familiar to Air Force readers, I refer to the King Abdul Aziz Air Base Hospital as the "MODA Hospital." "King Abdul Aziz Air Base" itself introduces another issue: the text usually refers to it, as Americans did, as Dhahran Air Base.

Beyond this particular case, it sometimes proved difficult to identify and locate the Dhahran hospitals that treated the wounded Americans. Air Force documents, prepared quickly in the aftermath of a terrorist attack, and airmen who suddenly found themselves patients in a foreign city in the dead of the night, weren't able to answer every question a historian could ask. Doctors in the medical section of the Royal Saudi Embassy in Washington, D.C., and at King Abdul Aziz Air Base, Saudi Arabia, identified in the backmatter, gave me valuable information about the Dhahran hospitals. Saudi Embassy personnel also clarified other points of local geography and history.

Finally, a word about the personal stories included in the narrative. It is fair to ask why they, and not others, were used. Some veterans judge a work of military history by narrow criteria: Does it tell the story of their particular unit? How closely does its narrative match their own memory of events? The Khobar Towers bombing affected thousands of Americans, Saudis, and others. No single volume can do justice to the experiences of all the Air Force personnel, let alone the many others, who were touched by this terrible event of June 25, 1996. British Field Marshal W.J. Slim wrote in the preface to his memoirs of World War II's Burma campaign: "I am very conscious that for every [individual, unit, and formation] I mention there were a hundred others whose doings were just as worthy of record." And so it is with the Khobar Towers episodes told here; many others were just as worthy of record.

This narrative tells the story, based on their own accounts, of only a few of the hundreds of airmen who were at the Khobar Towers that night. It recounts what they were doing just before the bombing and what happened to them immediately afterward. The sample is intended to give an idea of the activities of airmen on a summer night during Operation Southern Watch. Moreover, it was chosen to convey the experiences of people across the area affected by the attack, from the mechanics on the flightline at King Abdul Aziz Air Base to the security policemen on the roof of Building 131 at the Khobar Towers.

This sample necessarily had to be kept small enough that a reader could keep track of individuals and events. In addition to the few airmen mentioned in the narrative, the stories of hundreds of others could just as well have been told. There was no intention to slight the experiences of any of the many veterans of the Khobar Towers attack.

While this selection process posed a dilemma, it also underscored one of the strongest themes of the Khobar Towers story. The bombing did not produce three, or six, or ten heroes or heroines, whose stories stood out from all the others.

Instead the blast left in its wake, as one officer later said, a thousand stories of people helping people. No account can do justice to them all. If this one *begins* to give its readers an appreciation of how American military men and women responded to the Khobar Towers tragedy, it has done its job.

Perry D. Jamieson

Acknowledgements

So many people helped me tell the Khobar Towers story that it's difficult to account for all of them. I've made my best effort here, and apologize to those I've failed to remember.

The most fundamental contributors were the many officers, airmen, and civilians who gave me and other historians oral history interviews about their experiences with the Dhahran bombing. A list of them appears in the Sources.

A number of chiefs of the Air Force History Program and heads of the Air Force Historical Studies Office (under its various names over the years) supported this project. They include Dr. Richard P. Hallion, Mr. William Heimdahl, Col. (ret.) C.R. (Dick) Anderegg, Col. George Williams, Col. Christine Jaremko (Hallion), Col. Leonard Maggio, Col. George (Barney) Ballinger, and Col. Carol Sikes.

Three senior officers read drafts of this work, and their suggestions greatly improved it: Maj. Gen. (ret.) Daniel M. (Dan) Dick, Brig. Gen. (ret.) Terryl J. (Terry) Schwalier, and Col. (Dr.) Douglas J. Robb.

Every book like this one depends on the valuable work done by the airmen and civilians of the Air Force History field program. In this case, three historians deserve particular credit. SrA. Ronald J. Biggs, Jr. greatly helped my research at Nellis Air Force Base and also gave me a fine oral history interview about his own experiences as the historian of the 4404th Composite Wing (Provisional) at the time of the bombing. SSgt. Eric O. Grzebinski wrote a valuable history of the unit, covering the crucial period May 1–July 31, 1996. SSgt. Yancy Mailes made a tremendous contribution to my research at Eglin Air Force Base. As this book's Sources shows, he also conducted a number of significant oral history interviews. The names of several other conscientious field historians who helped me appear in the next paragraph.

Many other people contributed to this book, in a wide variety of ways. Some of them are listed here, with their ranks as they were at the time they assisted me: Ms. Sharon Adamoyurka, Dr. Feher S. Alsharif, U.S. Army Brig. Gen. (ret.) David A. Armstrong, SSgt. Ronald (Beetle) Bailey, CMSgt. Robert Beggs, Mr. Lawrence (Larry) Benson, Mr. Dennis Case, Mr. Joseph Caver, Mr. Mark Cleary, Ms. Diana G. Cornelisse, Dr. Richard G. Davis, Brig. Gen. Daniel M. (Dan) Dick, Col. Gary R. Dylewski, Col. Thomas R. Friers, Maj. Phillip G. (Slick) Gibbons, SSgt. Ken Goss, Dr. Rebecca Grant, Mr. Grant Hales, Dr. Daniel Harrington,

SSgt. Gregory Henneman, Mr. Bruce Hess, Maj. Roy Houchin, Capt. Robert L. (Bob) Jones, Lt. Col. Donald Jozayt, Ms. Yvonne Kinkaid, Col. (ret.) Thomas A. McCarthy, Maj. (Dr.) Pat Merrill, Ms. Debra Moss, Ms. Toni L. Petito, U.S. Army Capt. Erik R. Pohlmann, Dr. Diane Putney, TSgt. Tracy Reed, Lt. Col. (Dr.) Douglas J. Robb, Dr. Frank N. (Mickey) Schubert, Brig. Gen. (ret.) Terryl J. (Terry) Schwalier, Maj. John (Irish) Setter, Lt. Col. Thomas H. Shafer, Dr. Kamal Shahab, Dr. Fred Shaw, Ms. Marie Shaw, SSgt. C. Michael Sibley, MSgt. William Sine, Maj. Beverly Sloan, CMSgt. William (Ed) Stevens, Dr. Wayne Thompson, Dr. Jeffery Underwood, Mr. John D. (Jack) Weber, Mr. Herman S. Wolk, and Mr. William T. (Tom) Y'Blood.

The Author

Perry D. Jamieson earned a B.A. from Michigan State University and an M.A. and a Ph.D. from Wayne State University. Dr. Jamieson taught American military history at the University of Texas at El Paso and has worked for the Air Force History Program since 1980. He has contributed to the annual histories of the Strategic Air Command, Air Force Systems Command, Air Force Space Command, and Headquarters United States Air Force, as well as to many special projects. Dr. Jamieson is the author of *Lucrative Targets: the U.S. Air Force in the Kuwaiti Theater of Operations*, a volume in *The USAF in the Persian Gulf War* series. He has also written four books on the U.S. Army during and after the Civil War.

Contents

Foreword vii
Preface ix
Acknowledgements xiii
The Author xv

Tragedy

1 Approaching 10 P.M. 5
2 Operation Southern Watch 15
3 Stay Alert, Be Observant 23
4 The Attack 43
5 In the Wake. 53

Response

6 Golden Hour. 71
7 Accounting 89
8 Wednesday: At Khobar Towers. 109
9 Wednesday: Elsewhere. 129
10 Three Departures from Dhahran 151
11 Honoring and Remembering. 161
12 After the Attack 177

Epilogue 199

Appendix: Biographical Sketches. 203
Notes 213
Sources 259
Index 263

Illustrations

Maps and Diagrams

Middle East xix
T-Building Typical Floor Plan. 8
U.S. Section Khobar Towers 11
Dhahran Area 100

Photographs

Building 131 dirt parking lot 36
Main gate 36
View southwest from Khobar complex 36
Saudi residential towers 37
Saudi residential towers after installation of barriers 37
Mosque east of building 131 37
Parking lot north of building 131; location of tanker truck with explosives . . 37
"Jersey" barriers and concertina wire 38
Sepentine entrance to main gate 38
Barriers at at main gate 38
Roof-top security police post 38
Truck inspection 39
Inside entrance bunker 39
Bunker at entrance to complex 39
Truck for emergency blocking at entrance 39
"Jersey" barrier installation 39
North end of complex after explosion 40
Security policemen SSgt. Alfred R. Guerrero, SrA. Corey P. Grice, and
  A1C. Christopher T. Wagar receive Airman's medal from Air Force
  Chief of Staff Gen. Ronald R. Fogelman 40
Buckled northeast corner of building 131 after explosion 40
Explosion crater 41
Close-up of north face of building 131 after explosion 41
Humvee remains after explosion 41
Room interiors after explosion 42
Chaplain Aleson speaks at departure ceremony 140
Casket loaded into C-5 aircraft 140
C-5 bay with all caskets laded 140
Dr. Robb with patients aboard medical evacuation aircraft 141
General Ryan with patients aboard medical evacuation aircraft 141
Landstuhl Regional Medical Center 141
C-141 and C-9 on Eglin runway 142
Ambulances waiting for patients at Eglin 142
General Cranston and Dr. Treadway visit patients aboard medevac aircraft . 142
Patients assisted from medevac aircraft 143
Patients carried off medevac aircraft 143
Khobar returnees speak with the media at Eglin 144
Colonel Dylewski, General Cranston, and President Clinton 144
F-15 missing man formation 144
Eglin hangar ceremony 145

Colonel Dylewski and President Clinton speak at Eglin ceremony........ 145
Dedication ceremony for Khobar memorial at Patrick.................. 146
Khobar memorial at Patrick.. 146
HC-130 flyover during Patrick dedication ceremony.................... 146
Khobar memorial at Eglin.. 147
Memorials at Gunther's Enlisted Heritage Hall....................... 147
Khobar memorial at Gunther.. 147
Khobar memorial at Prince Sultan Air Base.......................... 147
Generals Schwalier and Anderson................................... 148
Maj. (Dr.) Steven P. Goff receives Airman's medal from Air Force
    Chief of Staff Gen. Ronald R. Fogelman......................... 148
Secretary of Defense Perry 148
Secretary of the Air Force Widnall and Colonel Cochran............... 149
Dr. Treadway with patient 149
Col. Thomas R. Friers.. 149
Acting Secretary of the Air Force Peters 150
Secretary of Defense Cohen and Chairman of the Joint Chiefs of Staff
    General Shalikashvili.. 150
Maj. Gen. Daniel M. Dick.. 150

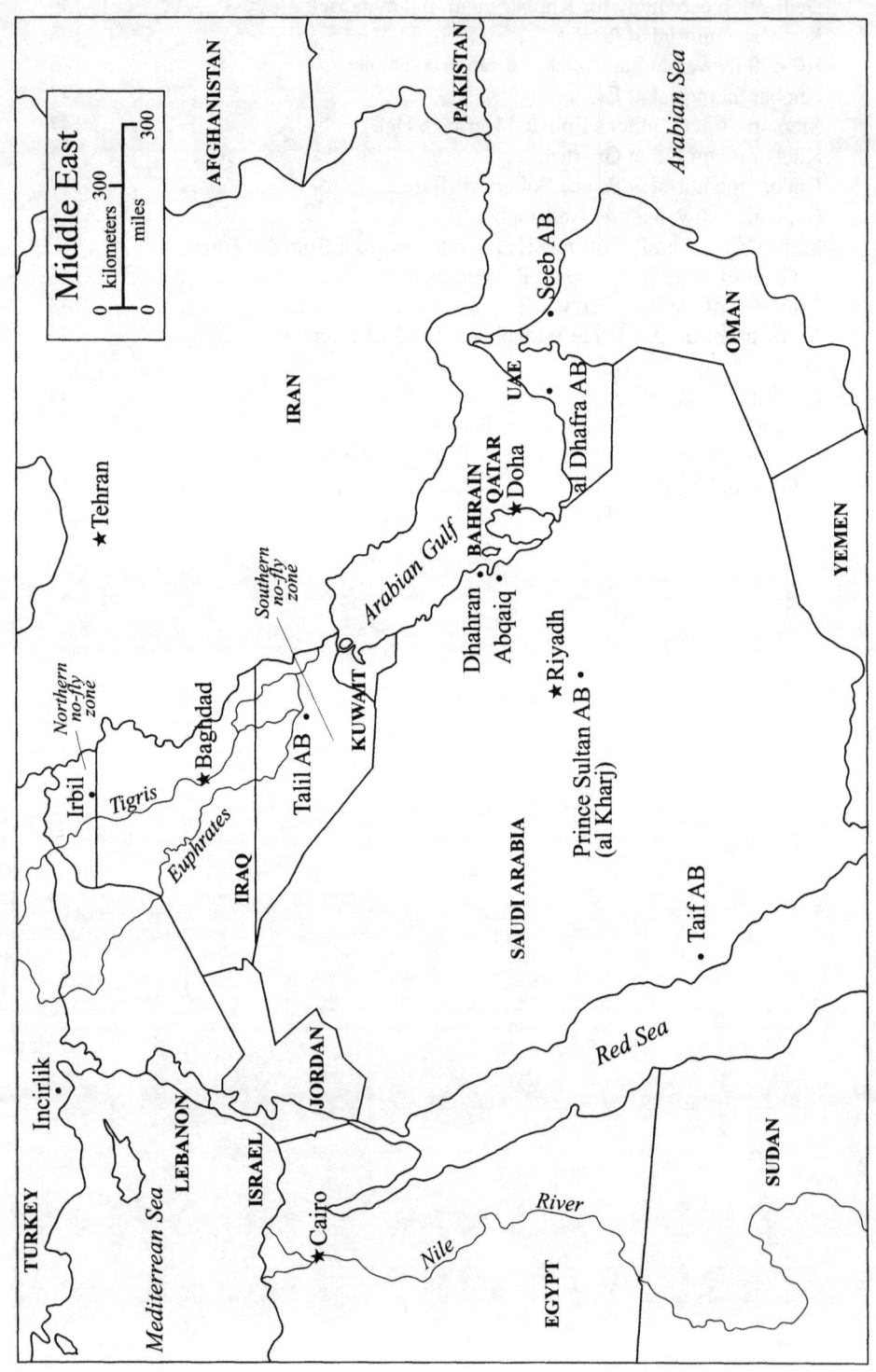

There are a thousand little stories out there, about people taking care of people.

> Colonel Gary R. Dylewski
> Commander, 33rd Fighter Wing

Khobar Towers
Tragedy and Response

Tragedy

Their best efforts were simply overcome by the speed with which the event developed and the sheer magnitude of the blast.

Major Brian G. Fillmore
Air Force Office of Special Investigations

Chapter One

Approaching 10 P.M.

The HC–130P came home early. This Combat Shadow tanker, tail number 0986, had launched at about 3 p.m. on Tuesday, June 25, 1996. The aircraft had flown from King Abdul Aziz Royal Saudi Air Base, Saudi Arabia, a facility that Americans usually called Dhahran Air Base. The HC–130 was scheduled to return about eight hours later, but sometime before 6:30 its crew saw a fuel-correction light begin flickering on and off, alerting them to a discrepancy in their number one engine. They returned to base and briefed the problem to the team of eight maintenance airmen who worked during the dayshift.[1]

The aircrew started back to their living quarters, which were a few miles east of Dhahran Air Base's military flightline. If their HC–130 hadn't encountered its difficulty, at 10 p.m. that night they would have remained airborne. Instead, by that hour the crew were in their dormitories, in the American sector of the Khobar Towers housing complex.

The tanker's early return also meant that the nightshift engine mechanics would relieve the dayshift sooner than usual. At 7 p.m., the seven NCOs of TSgt. Donald Herlacher's maintenance team came on duty and began troubleshooting the problem. A1C. Ken Smith of the dayshift, wanting to improve his skills, stayed to work with them.[2]

The HC–130's engine problem, as one officer commented later, had created "a trade-off. The aircrew that was back in the dorms shouldn't have been there, [and] the maintenance guys that would have been back in the dorms weren't at the dorms, because they were at the airplane."[3]

The maintenance airmen continued their efforts into the night, beyond 9 p.m., beyond 9:30 p.m. MSgt. Joel Schaeffer drove over from the Khobar Towers compound and picked up Airman Smith. They headed east, back to their dorm. By then, it was nearing 10 p.m.[4]

At that hour, the unrelenting heat from a June day in Saudi Arabia had left the Khobar Towers compound. Late night offered the best time to exercise before going to bed. "You can't run in the day," as one officer put it, "unless you're just really obsessed or have a death wish, really." After dark, many of the airmen who had been on duty during the hours of brutal heat came out of their dorms to walk, jog, or head for the gym. This facility, more formally called the recreation and fitness center, occupied a converted parking garage near the middle of the compound's western edge.[5]

On that day, June 25, workcrews had just finished refurbishing the gym. The main improvement was the addition of a room for aerobic workouts. It featured about twenty televisions that circled the exercise equipment, so an airman could watch TV while using a rowing machine, stationary bicycle, or stair-stepper. The sparkling new mirrors that circled the walls contributed another highlight to the remodeling. Late that morning, Brig. Gen. Terryl (Terry) J. Schwalier, commander of the 4404th Composite Wing (Provisional), had cut the ribbon on this renovation and the airmen celebrated with a small party.[6] That evening, a bench-pressing contest was held in the facility.[7]

Among the many regulars at the gym was MSgt. Dwayne R. Berry, an administrator and deployed first sergeant of the 71st Rescue Squadron, from Patrick Air Force Base, Florida. Sergeant Berry arrived at the recreation center later than usual, that night of the twenty-fifth. In two days his tour in Saudi Arabia would end, and he had promised his wife he would get in a final round of shopping for her in Dhahran before he returned home. Ordinarily, he and TSgt. Arthur Bisby, his workout partner, would get to the gym about 6 p.m. That evening, they shopped downtown and didn't reach the rec center until 9 p.m.[8]

Dressed to exercise, the two NCOs went through the heavy door that led from the brand-new aerobic area into the weight room. Sergeants Berry and Bisby started into their dumbbell routines. Nine thirty went past, nine forty-five. Berry looked at the mirrors and realized that something was wrong: they were cracking.[9]

While these two NCOs pitted themselves against the equipment in the Khobar gym, several hundred yards to the northeast, the senior officers of the 58th Fighter Squadron, deployed from Eglin Air Force Base, Florida, were contending with another kind of challenge. They lived on the seventh floor of Building 127, which faced Eighth Street, the eastern perimeter of the Khobar compound. It was an eight story structure, consisting of a ground level with seven numbered ones stacked above it. About half of the squadron's pilots had rooms on the sixth floor, about half on the seventh, or top, one.[10] Like the other T-shaped dormitories in the complex, each floor had three suites—each suite contributing one arm of a building's T. All of the eight-story dormitories accordingly had twenty-four suites. One of these on the seventh floor of Building 127 was the "command module," the residence of the deployed 58th Fighter Squadron's commander, Lt. Col. Douglas R. Cochran; the operations officer, Lt. Col. Thomas A. McCarthy; and the project officer for the deployment, Lt. Col. William Miller.[11]

The officers of the 58th were busy that night. The squadron had all but finished its tour in Saudi Arabia. The fighters would fly just four more sorties, and then their tour would end. In two days, the squadron would be going home, and its officers were dealing with, as one of them later summarized: "all the turmoil that comes with [getting] diplomatic clearances, with making sure our people [will be] getting home, making sure their equipment [will be] getting home, making sure the trans-

Approaching 10 P. M.

ports, the fuel, the airborne fuelers—everything—the jets are ready to go, and the pilots are ready to go."[12]

The biggest issue bubbling during the night of the twenty-fifth was the need to secure a diplomatic clearance for one of the transports that would carry some of the squadron's weapons and cargo back to the United States. There was mundane housekeeping to be done, too: preparing for the departure, Lt. Col. Cochran had cleaned his bathroom that night. Then he gave his attention to the items on his desk, the paperwork necessary for the return home. Beyond the door to Colonel Cochran's room, Lt. Cols. Thomas McCarthy and William Miller had taken up stations in the day room, the common area of the suite. They were helping him get the clearance issue resolved and, expecting a call, they had the telephone bracketed between them.[13]

The two lieutenant colonels watched a movie on the television, Paramount's 1976 *Marathon Man*. As 10 p.m. approached, the film reached one of the most harrowing scenes in cinema history. Christian Szell, a former Nazi portrayed by Laurence Olivier, used a dental drill to torture Thomas Babbington (Babe) Levy, a Columbia graduate student played by Dustin Hoffman.[14]

Not far from Cochran's suite stood Building 131, at the northeast corner of the Khobar Towers complex. It was configured like 127 and all the other T dormitories: it had eight floors; three suites per floor, twenty-four suites per building. That night the residents of Building 131 were busy packing up and cleaning their rooms. The next day's inspection, just before they departed, would be a demanding one. The first sergeants would check the rooms closely, making sure the airmen left them in good order for the next occupants.[15]

On the first floor of Building 131, a minor mob scene developed in the kitchenette of TSgt. George Burgess's suite. Sergeant Burgess, who was an assistant flight chief, and his suitemates had cleaned their rooms thoroughly. But one problem area remained: the refrigerator. A senior airman had cleaned it, but his effort hadn't satisfied his suitemates. They all crowded into the small kitchen, working on the refrigerator, and indulging in some good natured criticism of the E–4. Burgess pitched in with the others, crammed together in the limited space. While he jostled with his suitemates, a stray thought crossed his mind: it was the only time during their ninety-day tour that all four of them had been in the kitchenette at the same time.[16]

Down the hall from Sergeant Burgess and his suitemates, SSgt. Eric D. Ziegler and his roomates also were making their apartment "spick and span" for the next day's inspection. For his part, Sergeant Ziegler offered to clean the bathroom. He finished the task and decided to visit A1C. Brent E. Marthaler. While Airman Marthaler was sprucing up his room, Ziegler entertained him with some conversation.[17]

Leaving Airman Marthaler to his work, Sergeant Ziegler joined the rest of his suitemates, who were in the day room. Their conversation was good spirited that night. Like the other members of the 58th Fighter Squadron, these airmen had been in Dhahran since April and were glad to be going home.[18]

Sergeant Ziegler handed TSgt. Patrick P. Fennig, his roomate, two Southwest Asia service medals. To raise their souvenir value, "Z" wanted them flown on one of

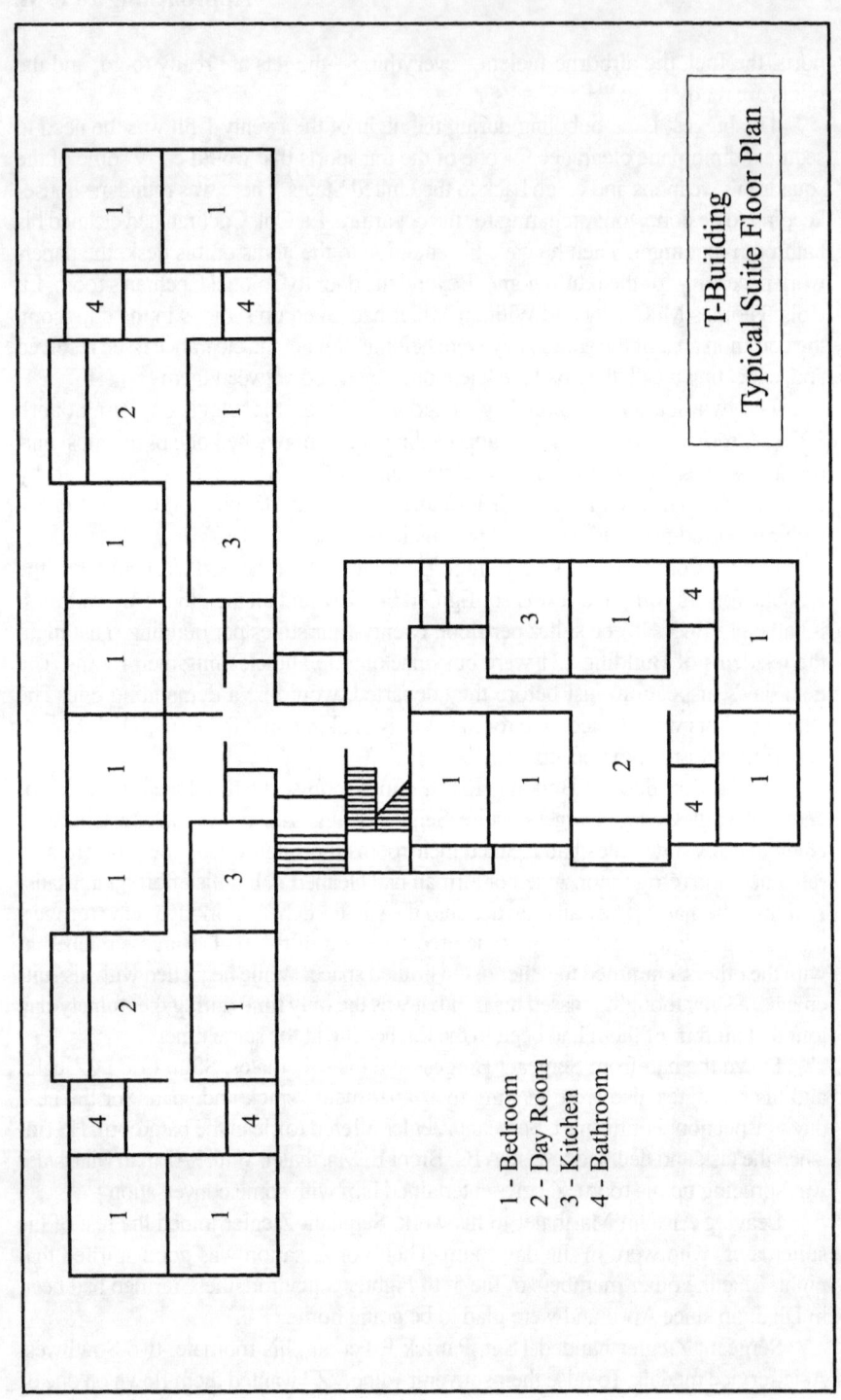

Approaching 10 P. M.

the Operation Southern Watch F–15 missions. Sergeant Fennig, a flightline expeditor, assured his roomate he would get them out on a sortie the next morning.[19]

The group watched some television and at about five minutes before 10 p.m., Sergeant Ziegler headed for bed. The staff sergeant checked his digital alarm clock and realized that at some point during all the cleaning, it had gotten unplugged. Ziegler had to monkey with it a bit to get it reset. Two nights before, he had broken the clock and, this late in his tour, he didn't want to spend the money on a new one. With a little tinkering, the NCO set the current time and the wake-up one that he wanted. Then he tested his "snooze" button.[20]

Six floors above Sergeant Ziegler, SSgt. Alfredo R. Guerrero, a ten-year veteran and an instructor in antiterrorist training, checked the security police post on top of Building 131. Two "SPs," SrA. Corey P. Grice and A1C. Christopher T. Wagar, were assigned to the roof of this dormitory. These young men were among the 169 personnel assigned to the security police squadron then stationed near Dhahran.[21]

The watch was passing quietly at the rooftop security post and the weather at the time was normal. On most Saudi nights in late June, at about 8 p.m. the air began to give up some of the daytime's broiling heat. Around 9 p.m. the temperature usually would fall again, but even after this drop the thermometer typically remained in the nineties and the humidity stayed high. On the night of June 25, 1996, there was nothing remarkable about the weather, the visibility, or the level of activity around the Khobar Towers complex.[22] "The nights over there were all pretty quiet, pretty much," Sergeant Guerrero commented later, "because that was everybody's 'down' time. You'd have joggers in the area, and people 'recreating' around."[23]

Sergeant Guerrero had come on duty at 6 p.m. In the normal course of things, the twenty-nine year old airman on temporary duty from Edwards Air Force Base, California, would have been on a patrol in the area himself, rather than making a supervisor's check of the posts of other security policemen. As it happened, two supervisors had ended their tours on Sunday, June 23, and for the full week to follow, he and another staff sergeant were to pick up the supervisory responsibility. On the night of Tuesday the twenty-fifth, the assignment fell to Guerrero.[24]

Ordinarily, too, the NCO would have begun his post checks sooner and arrived on the roof of Building 131 earlier in the night. That evening an agent of the Air Force Office of Special Investigations had found a Saudi national engaged in suspicious activity and detained him. The AFOSI officer brought this man to Guerrero's police desk, while the sergeant was making out the duty schedule for the next day. "So we were doing the report on that," Guerrero recalled, "and we had to call in a Saudi lieutenant, to come [and] take him. That put me a couple hours behind schedule, because normally I did the roster [for the next day] and I still had to go over the roster, before I started checking the posts." And so it was after 9:30 p.m. when Guerrero set out, on foot, to check the security police posts. "I wonder what would have happened," he mused later, "if I'd gone up [on the roof of Building 131] even five minutes earlier."[25]

Sergeant Guerrero began his rounds by going directly to the roof of this dormitory, at the far northeastern corner of the Khobar Towers compound, and checking

Khobar Towers: Tragedy and Response

on Senior Airman Grice. Then he walked across the top of the building to its northern edge, where he stopped to talk with Airman First Class Wagar. Guerrero had not spent five minutes on the roof: the time was approaching 9:50 p.m.[26]

Sergeant Guerrero and Airman Wagar had a good view of the area around them. The weather had been normal that day, and continued so that night. Eight floors below the two security policemen, Thirty-first Street ran east to west across the front of Building 131 and marked the northern end of the Khobar Towers complex. The north side of this avenue—the northern perimeter of the compound—was protected by a staggered double row of concrete "New Jersey" barriers and a ten-foot chain-link security fence, topped with concertina wire.[27] Beyond this border of the Khobar Towers stood the large parking lot of al Khobar Park, a public area. This carpark was covered by three inches of asphalt and shaded by ornamental trees. Just north of it, Guerrero and Wagar could see the buildings of al Khobar, a well-settled community of Dhahran. For about seven miles to the west and northwest, the taller structures of this urban area stood out over the flat landscape.[28]

The distance, as a bird would fly it, from where Sergeant Guerrero stood on the roof of Building 131 down to the southern end of this open parking lot, was only about thirty-five yards. While the staff sergeant stood talking with Airman Wagar, a white four-door Chevrolet Caprice drove south along the western edge of the parking lot, toward the northwest end of the Khobar Towers compound. Then it made a left hand turn and headed east.[29] At about 9:50 p.m. Sergeant Guerrero spotted this sedan and, slowly following it, a second vehicle: a Mercedes-Benz fuel or sewage tanker, with a capacity of 3,500 to 4,000 gallons.[30]

The car and the truck drove east along the southern edge of the large parking lot, just beyond the northern perimeter of the compound. When the Caprice reached a point opposite Building 131, it made another left hand turn and headed away from the perimeter fence and pulled a very short distance into the carpark. The overhead lights in this part of the parking lot were out; the area was dark.[31]

Standing next to Airman Wagar on the roof of the dormitory, Sergeant Guerrero paid less attention to the Caprice than to the much larger vehicle that followed it. The tanker continued a bit further east than the car. Then it, too, turned left and rolled a short distance away from the fence and into the parking lot. Both vehicles came to a stop in the darkness.[32]

The security policemen riveted their attention on the large truck. With its headlights off, it began backing up toward the hedges that grew along the north side of the security fence. Both airmen immediately knew that something was very wrong. It was not unusual to see big trucks in the area around the compound; what *was* unusual, Sergeant Guerrero explained later, was "the type of vehicle, the position it was in." "It was quite clear," he added, "that they wanted to leave it in a certain spot."[33]

Two men got out of the tanker truck and ran to the white Caprice. Months later, Sergeant Guerrero recalled exactly what went through his mind, during those seconds on the roof of Building 131: "When they jumped out, we just couldn't believe it happened. You could see it happen, but it seemed, 'This isn't happening.'"[34]

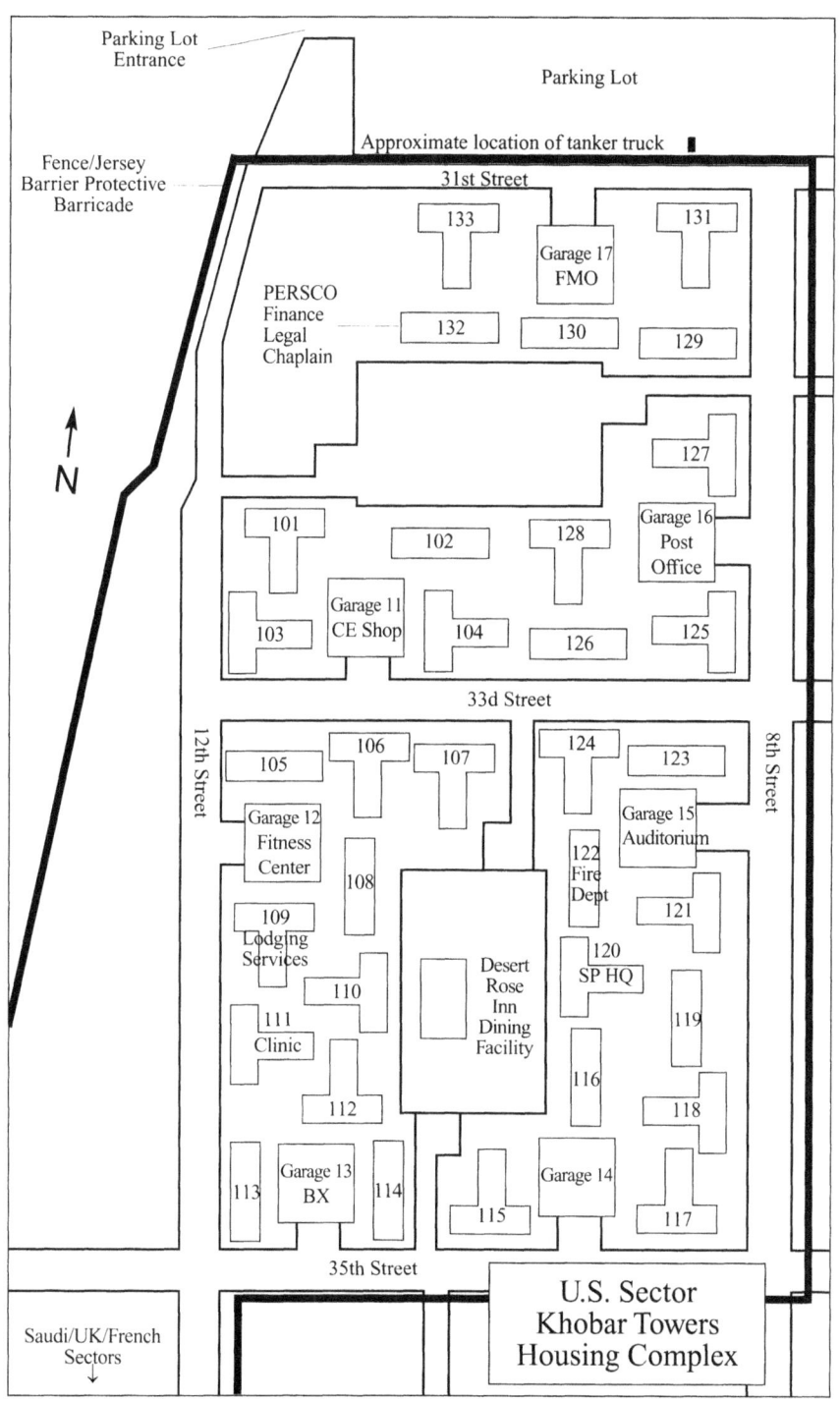

Khobar Towers: Tragedy and Response

The Caprice sped off into the night and instantly the two security policemen were certain that the tanker truck was a bomb. Both men stepped back from the three-foot lip at the edge of the building. The racing departure of the white sedan, Sergeant Guerrero later stated, "was the clicker. They were in a hurry. I felt something was going to happen very soon."[35] He did not know it then, but "very soon" turned out to be less than four minutes.[36]

The security policemen might have put their own lives ahead of others and fled. They did not do that. Instead, Guerrero got on his "brick" radio and alerted the SPs at the compound's main gate and all others who were on patrol that night. He then called Mr. Marwan Darwish, who was the 4404th Wing's liaison officer, serving as an interpreter of Arabic for the Americans and advising them on Arabian affairs. In performing these jobs, Mr. Darwish worked closely with the base security police and was well acquainted with their operations and procedures. Lt. Col. James J. Traister, commander of the 4404th Wing's security police squadron, said of this liaison officer: "Without him we would be hard pressed in working with our counterparts. He is the hardest working individual I have ever worked with."[37]

That night Mr. Darwish, who routinely carried a pager and a cellular phone, had gone into Dhahran to eat dinner and do some shopping with Maj. Kevin C. Greenfield, the 4404th Wing's judge advocate general; Capt. Lisa A. Winnecke, Major Greenfield's deputy; and Lt. Col. Christomer Dooley, the United States Military Training Mission's JAG, who worked out of its offices in Riyadh and Dhahran.[38] Within the first minute after Sergeant Guerrero spotted the truck, he paged Darwish at a downtown mall. The interpreter used his cell phone and quickly reached the security policeman on the roof of Building 131. Guerrero told him about the threatening vehicle and his intention to evacuate the dormitory.[39] Darwish rang off on the SP and immediately called the Saudi military police, the "Red Hats." The line was busy. The interpreter tried several calls, making his way up the Saudi military police chain of command. Every line was busy; something was very wrong. Darwish told his companions, We need to get back to the Khobar Towers.[40]

While Mr. Darwish tried to reach the Saudi MPs, the security police on the roof of Building 131 had taken action. Airman Wagar ran for the access to the top floor of the building, where he would begin spreading the alarm. Sergeant Guerrero sprinted across the roof and called to Senior Airman Grice, "Let's go!"[41]

Not far from Building 131, SrA. Craig J. Dick was patroling in a "humvee," a military vehicle that blended the features of a jeep and a three-quarter ton truck. Senior Airman Dick had heard a security alert on his radio and sped to the scene, warning some joggers out of the area along his way. He pulled up near Building 131, jumped out from behind the wheel, and headed for the rear, or southern, entrance of the dormitory at a dead run.[42]

Eight floors above Senior Airman Dick, Sergeant Guerrero and Senior Airman Grice got off the roof and found that Airman Wagar, who had left ahead of them, already was carrying the word along the top, or seventh, floor. Guerrero ran on down the stairwell to the sixth floor, and Grice to the fifth. An officer assigned to the

Approaching 10 P. M.

Khobar Towers that night later praised the three security policemen for their "remarkable" job of starting an evacuation of the building. "It was amazing," he said, "what they were able to accomplish in three minutes [before the explosion]."[43]

The three security policemen raised the alarm the same way that Roman sentries would have: yelling and pounding on doors. They found most people still awake, sitting in the day rooms of their suites, watching television or engaging in conversations. The SPs moved rapidly from one apartment to the next, spreading the word. Wagar recalled: "I was yelling, 'Get the hell out of the building.'" "When we would knock," Guerrero said, "we would ask, 'Is there anybody else in here?'"[44]

The urgency in the speech and actions of the security policemen immediately convinced the dorm residents that this was *not an exercise*. Like many others that night, two pilots of the deployed 71st Rescue Squadron, Capts. Michael D. Morelock and Matthew Winkler, were watching television. Captain Morelock sat in a chair and Captain Winkler on a couch across from the set, which was wedged in a corner in front of the sliding glass doors of their day room. Their suite, numbered 7-1, was on the top floor of Building 131, and their rooms directly faced the park and the truck bomb. Morelock had gotten up and headed for bed, when an SP knocked loudly and burst through their unlocked door. Months later, he quoted the policeman: "We have a situation with a fuel truck. You need to get out of the building now."[45]

Captain Winkler also remembered vividly the intense seconds that followed the SP's appearance. In Winkler's experience, security policemen always had their M–16s in "the right place at all times." The pilot recalled a telling detail: the SP had his weapon "slinged over his shoulder and it was kind of getting in his way because he was trying to hurry so much."[46]

Captains Winkler and Morelock, like many others on the top floors of Building 131 that night, did not ask any questions or make silly remarks. The dormitory residents responded like military professionals. Sergeant Guerrero said of the people he alerted: "They immediately jumped up and started running, they didn't hesitate."[47]

Although Captains Winkler and Morelock left their suite promptly, neither felt any sense of immediate danger. Winkler said later that he had no fear for his life and Morelock had the passing thought that perhaps someone simply had parked in the wrong place and triggered a false alarm. Winkler went into his bedroom and picked up his brick radio and beeper from the nightstand, and put his shoes on. Morelock got his radio, too, and shuffled through his flightsuit to find his identification card. The security policeman asked them if there was anyone else with them. Their third resident, Capt. Thomas F. Edman, a navigator, was in the bathroom at the front of the suite. The pilots called to Captain Edman and the SP also knocked on the latrine door and told him that he would have to leave the building immediately.[48]

Captain Winkler gained a small lead on Captain Morelock, who checked at the neighboring suite to make sure that Lt. Col. Thomas H. Shafer, commander of their deployed squadron, and Captain Christopher J. Adams, a pilot and the deployment operations officer, had gotten the word to evacuate.[49] Morelock learned that these two officers had heard the warning. Captain Adams had roused Lieutenant Colonel Shafer, already asleep for the night, with the news. They had started to run out of their suite when Adams noticed that the squadron commander was not wearing any shoes and suggested he go back for a pair.[50]

Having checked on Lieutenant Colonel Shafer and Captain Adams, Captain Morelock followed Captain Winkler down the stairs. The two made it as far as the first landing, half way between the seventh and sixth floors. Winkler turned to his right, toward the next flight down. Each of the stairwell landings had a large glass window, and unfortunately for the two officers, they were now near one. All of the compound's dormitories had been built on the same pattern. So the large windows featured on every stairwell landing proved dangerous that night, not only to Morelock and Winkler, but to others as well.[51]

Lieutenant Colonel Shafer later praised the security police for their rapid warning of the residents on the top floors of Building 131. He noted that Captains Winkler and Morelock and others who were evacuated from their suites by the SPs doubtless were safer in the interior of the dormitory, in the elevator lobbies and stairwells, than they would have been in their rooms, which directly faced the bomb. But Colonel Shafer also pointed to two other aspects of the night's tragic events. First, not one person got out of Building 131 before the detonation. Second, it may well have been for the better that they did not: large numbers of people might have run out of the dormitory and directly into the explosion. Captain Winkler agreed: "If I'd got to the ground floor, I might have been killed. You can't 'what if?' it." Lt. Col. Thomas A. McCarthy, operations officer of the 58th Fighter Squadron, and no doubt others, thought the same thing.[52] These two considerations raised by Colonel Shafer do not diminish the alert work done by the security police that night, but they underscore the fact that terrorist attacks, like other acts of violence, have a capricious quality.

Captains Winkler, Morelock, and many others responded promptly to the warnings from the security policemen. Sergeant Guerrero and the SPs with him had done as well as possible, within the few minutes they had to raise the alarm. Now only a matter of seconds remained. Guerrero had almost finished spreading the word along the sixth floor. He ran to the door of the one remaining suite. People moved past him rapidly, leaving the building as they had been told. It was 9:53 p.m.[53]

Chapter Two

Operation Southern Watch

The terrorist bombing of the Khobar Towers killed nineteen United States Air Force personnel and injured hundreds of others. With the loss of these casualties, the American press and much of the public began asking questions about the nation's military presence in Dhahran. How many Air Force officers and airmen served there and elsewhere in Saudi Arabia? Why were they there? How long had they been there? What were the "Khobar Towers"?

Uniformed Americans had been on duty in southwest Asia since World War II, but for decades their numbers remained small. When the United States sent its first military training mission to Saudi Arabia, in 1944, it consisted of just twelve members. During the next year and into 1946, Americans had helped the Saudis build King Abdul Aziz Air Base, in Dhahran. In 1951, the two nations began negotiating formal agreements that resulted two years later in the establishment of a United States Military Training Mission. Working in cooperation with the Saudi Ministry of Defense and Aviation, the USMTM assisted the kingdom's regular military forces. Beginning in the 1950s, the United States helped build several air bases in Saudi Arabia. The Office of Program Management-Saudi Arabian National Guard, a United States Army program manager's office that helped modernize the kingdom's National Guard units, was established in Riyadh in 1965. Throughout the Cold War, the number of uniformed Americans stationed in the oil-rich Saudi nation, ruled by a royal family that was wary of non-Islamic foreigners, stayed well under 1,000.[1]

This remained the case until 1990. On August 2 of that year, Iraqi units under the orders of dictator Saddam Hussein invaded Kuwait, Saudi Arabia's small neighbor to the north. Faced with more than 200,000 soldiers and over 2,000 tanks beyond the northern border of his kingdom, King Fahd bin Abdul Aziz then took the unprecedented step of inviting thousands of military personnel from the United States and other non-Islamic nations to help defend his country.[2]

Saddam Hussein did not invade Saudi Arabia, but he remained in Kuwait, which he claimed to have annexed as an eleventh province of Iraq. The Air Force and the other military services carried out Operation Desert Shield, an enormous defensive deployment that protected the large Saudi kingdom. President George Bush mobilized an international coalition against Saddam Hussein, but the Iraqi dictator stubbornly refused to leave Kuwait. The United Nations set a deadline,

Khobar Towers: Tragedy and Response

January 15, 1991, for Iraq to end its occupation of its southern neighbor. When Saddam ignored this final warning, a coalition of nearly forty nations contributed to the military effort designated Operation Desert Storm, commonly called the Gulf War. A stunningly successful forty-three day air campaign and a four-day ground offensive rapidly ended the Iraqi dictator's occupation of Kuwait. Aerospace operations provided the centerpiece of this dramatic military victory. By the end of the Gulf War, Saudi Arabia hosted a vastly larger foreign presence than ever before in its history. More than 54,000 Air Force personnel were assigned to southwest Asia, and most of them served in that Islamic kingdom.[3]

The Gulf War ended initially with a temporary, and later a permanent, cease-fire. On March 3,1991, Lt. Gen. Sultan Hashim Ahmad of the Iraqi army agreed to the terms of a temporary cease-fire dictated to him by Gen. H. Norman Schwarzkopf, the commander in chief of the United States Central Command (USCENTCOM), at Safwan airfield in southern Iraq. A month later, on April 3, the United Nations Security Council adopted Resolution 687, which stated its conditions for a permanent cease-fire. The UN called on Iraq to destroy its nuclear, biological, and chemical weapons and established inspections to see that it did so. Resolution 687 also directed the Baghdad dictatorship to scrap all but its short-range missiles and to renounce international terrorism.[4] Saddam characterized the Security Council's terms as "one-sided and unfair," but on April 6 he accepted them and a permanent cease-fire went into effect.[5]

The American-led coalition had expelled Saddam from Kuwait, but he then lashed out in other directions. In the wake of the 1991 Gulf War, the Kurdish people of northern Iraq, an ethnic minority within their nation, rebelled against the dictator in Baghdad. Saddam dispatched several divisions to crush their uprising. By mid-April 1991, hundreds of thousands of Kurdish refugees had fled their country through the mountain passes into Turkey and Iran.[6]

Another tragedy developed in southern Iraq, where the Shi'ite sect of Muslims rebelled against Saddam's government and army, dominated by Sunni Muslims. Here, too, the Iraqi autocrat moved quickly and brutally against the insurrection. His Hip and Hind helicopter gunships and his ground troops killed hundreds, perhaps thousands, of Shi'ite men, women, and children.[7]

Although the international community denounced Saddam's supression of these rebellions, it took no further military action against him. On the night of April 5, the United Nations Security Council adopted Resolution 688, which contended that the wave of Kurdish refugees into Turkey and Iran threatened "international peace and security," and rejected Saddam's claim that this was an internal issue. UNSCR 688 called on the Iraqi government to end its repression of the Kurds and "to ensure that the human and political rights of all Iraqi citizens are respected." Having made this declaration, the United Nations took no steps to enforce it. Nor did the United States support either the Shi'ite or Kurdish rebellions. In "a feckless abdication of a victor's power and responsibility," one historian contended, "the [George Bush] administration turned a blind eye."[8]

Operation Southern Watch

President Bush did take action to get humanitarian aid to the Kurds. On April 5, before the UN adopted Resolution 688 that night, he ordered Operation Provide Comfort, an airlift of food and supplies to the Kurdish refugees in northern Iraq. Three days later, Air Force MC–130s began air dropping food, tents, and other supplies into the mountainous region near the Turkish border. Operating from Incirlik Air Base, Turkey, the 7440th Composite Wing (Provisional) provided a variety of aircraft—fighters, special operations helicopters, and transports—in support of the air portion of Provide Comfort.[9] On April 10, President Bush established a "no-fly" zone above 36° north latitude. The United States, other nations, and international organizations would begin delivering aid to the Kurdish refugees, and the American president served Saddam notice that the USAF would shoot down any Iraqi aircraft attempting to interfer with the relief effort. The Air Force continued the Provide Comfort mission, and by early May, most of the Kurds had left their refugee camps and returned to their homes.[10]

In the case of the Shi'ites, President Bush on March 14 took the position that Saddam should not use his helicopters against his own people within Iraq. The chief executive said he was "warning" the Iraqi government: "Do not do this." The president did not, however, direct any military measures against Saddam's gunships. His fundamental premise, expressed in early April, was that the coalition that had won the Gulf War "did not go there to settle all the internal affairs of Iraq."[11]

President Bush stood by this assumption, but as months passed and as Saddam persisted in his brutalities, the chief executive decided that the United States must protect the Shi'ites and ensure that Baghdad did not further its military position in southern Iraq. In late July 1992, reports multiplied that the Iraqi air force was sending military aircraft from Talil Air Base against hapless villages in that region. The United Kingdom and France expressed support for an American proposal to patrol southern Iraq and shoot down any fighters or helicopters that Saddam sent against the Shi'ites.[12]

On August 26, 1992, President Bush announced that the United States, the United Kingdom, and France would enforce a no-fly zone over southern Iraq, similar to the one previously established to protect the Kurds. It would cover the airspace over Iraq south of 32° north latitude, an area roughly the size of Iowa. The chief executive cited Saddam Hussein's "harsh repression" of the Shi'ites and the need to enforce the UN's April 1991 Resolution 688.[13] Later, in October 1994, the Security Council also would adopt Resolution 949, which limited the Baghdad government's right to deploy military forces in southern Iraq.[14]

The three Western allies gave various names to their military enforcement of the no-fly zone. The British called their effort "Operation Jural," and the French "Operation Alysse." The Americans designated theirs "Operation Southern Watch," and assigned it to the Joint Task Force Southwest Asia (JTF-SWA), a component of USCENTCOM. This unified command had southwest Asia as its area of responsibility and MacDill Air Force Base, Florida, as its headquarters. U.S. Army Gen. J. H. Binford Peay III had been the USCENTCOM commander since August 1994. The

Khobar Towers: Tragedy and Response

Air Force component of General Peay's unified command was U.S. Central Command Air Forces (CENTAF), provided by the Ninth Air Force, headquartered at Shaw Air Force Base, South Carolina. CENTAF was commanded by Lt. Gen. John P. Jumper from August 1994 until June 1996, when he was succeeded by Lt. Gen. Carl E. Franklin. The unified command's JTF-SWA operated from a headquarters in Riyadh, Saudi Arabia, and was commanded by Air Force Maj. Gen. Kurt B. Anderson. From January to July 1993, Major General Anderson had commanded Operation Provide Comfort's Combined Task Force and was thoroughly acquainted with the southwest Asian theater.[15]

The 4404th Composite Wing (Provisional) was the only Air Force unit in the southwest Asian area of responsibility and contributed the air component of JTF-SWA, which flew Operation Southern Watch. It had been activated as an Air Combat Command unit on June 1, 1992, and its Tactical Air Command predecessors dated back a bit earlier, to March 1991. During the Gulf War, the 4th Tactical Fighter Wing had been assigned to al Kharj Air Base, and after the war, the 4404th Composite Wing succeeded it at that facility.[16] In July 1991, the wing headquarters moved to King Abdul Aziz, or Dhahran, Air Base, in Ash Sharqiyah, or the Eastern Province, of Saudi Arabia. The 4404th Wing had been stationed near Dhahran four years when, in July 1995, Brig. Gen. Terryl J. (Terry) Schwalier became its thirteenth commander. General Schwalier, who had entered the Air Force in 1969, was a pilot with combat experience in RF–4Cs and F–16Cs. The 4404th represented his second assignment as a wing commander.[17]

A provisional wing, the 4404th was made up of a command element and five provisional groups. The command element consisted of (with its personnel as of June 25, 1996) the wing commander, Brig. Gen. Terry Schwalier; vice commander, Col. Wayne L. Schultz of the Colorado Air National Guard; senior enlisted advisor, CMSgt. Paul K. Ayers; the commander's executive officer, Capt. Bradley K. Burhite (three other executive officers served General Schwalier during his thirteen months as wing commander); and an administrative staff that supported the wing commander. There were eight staff agencies: comptroller, Maj. Andre Burgess (Maj. David V. Raths succeeded him on June 26); chaplain, Lt. Col. Dennis E. Aleson (Lt Col. Wayland M. Hartsfield, June 26); historian, SrA. Ronald J. Biggs, Jr.; staff judge advocate, Maj. Kevin C. Greenfield; manpower, Capt. Andrew Baker; public affairs, 2d. Lt. Laura Koury; safety, Col. Kurt B. Dittmer (Lt. Col. Allan L. Mink II, June 26); and a wing operations center.

The five provisional groups, and their commanders as of June 25, 1996, were the 4404th Operations Group, Col. Jonathan S. (Scott) Gration; 4409th Operations Group (stationed at Riyadh), Col. Dale F. Bible; 4404th Logistics Group, Col. Peter R. Mooy; 4404th Support Group, Col. Gary S. Boyle; 4404th Medical Group, interim commander, Lt. Col. (Dr.) Douglas J. Robb.[18]

A composite unit, the 4404th Wing employed a variety of aircraft to enforce the no-fly zone over southern Iraq. While it was heavy in fighters, it flew airframes as diverse as the EF–111A, F–4G, and C–130. The wing's large number—and variety

Operation Southern Watch

of types—of aircraft offered "wonderful" opportunities to a commander, as General Schwalier observed. "You got to deal with every aspect of air power. You had fifteen, sixteen types of aircraft over there, at any one time."[19] Most of the 4404th's assets were based at Dhahran Air Base, and from there, the unit launched 100 or more Southern Watch flights each day. "We would fly seven days a week," General Schwalier recounted. "It was intense, is the best way to describe it." Working at this high tempo of operations, by 1996 the wing had flown more than 100,000 sorties over Iraq. On the day of the terrorist bombing, the unit flew all 118 of its scheduled sorties, and 81 of them were Southern Watch operations.[20]

The 4404th Wing had more than 5,000 personnel assigned, at eleven locations in four countries.[21] The largest concentration of them were the 2,300 airmen stationed in the American sector of the Khobar Towers compound, just east of Dhahran Air Base. (Second to this Dhahran group were the 1,500 personnel deployed to Riyadh, where the 4404th Wing's 4409th Operations Group flew its tankers and reconnaissance aircraft.[22]) No relatives of these active-duty members of the USAF, or any other service, accompanied them to Dhahran.[23]

The Air Force manned the 4404th Provisional Wing largely by rotating officers and airmen through southwest Asia on temporary-duty assignments. Although entire *units* of some aircraft—including HC–130s, C–130s, A–10s, and tankers—served in the theater 365 days a year,[24] nearly all of the more than 2,300 *individuals* in Dhahran served there on 90-day rotation tours. Only nineteen of the 4404th Wing's billets were permanent ones.[25] The rotation manning policy meant that about 10 percent of the unit's personnel, 200 or more airmen and officers, turned over every week.[26] Like the Air Force, the Army rotated its personnel through Dhahran. Its Patriot Task Force crews served six-month tours.[27]

There were few exceptions to the Air Force's standard 90-day assignments. In June 1996, some security policemen, who belonged to a relatively small career field whose members were critically needed on deployments overseas, were serving in Dhahran on 45- and 65-day rotation tours, as well as the typical 90-day one.[28] Members of the 71st Rescue Squadron generally served 60-day rotations.[29] When Brig. Gen. Terry Schwalier took command in July 1995, he began a one-year assignment. He then became the first wing commander to serve a full-year tour. Nine other senior positions of the 4404th also represented one-year assignments.[30] Beyond these few cases, exceptions to the standard 90-day tour were extremely rare. An assignment of more than 179 days in the theater required a waiver signed by the Secretary of the Air Force.[31]

As for unit deployments, the one made during the spring of 1996 by the 58th Fighter Squadron, whose F–15s provided the wing's primary air-to-air unit,[32] represented a typical case. A component of the 33d Fighter Wing, it consisted of 18 aircraft, about 40 officers, and roughly 300 airmen, and it deployed approximately 260 personnel to Dhahran. Each squadron of the wing usually went to Saudi Arabia about every eighteen to twenty-four months, and its officers knew a year or so in advance about their next Southern Watch tour, and would spend about a month

Khobar Towers: Tragedy and Response

preparing for a deployment.[33] The 58th left the United States on April 14, 1996, served the usual rotation of about ninety days, and was scheduled to return to Eglin Air Force Base, Florida on June 28. This return date, as events developed, fell just two days after the Khobar Towers bombing.[34]

Both Saudi Arabia and the United States favored the ninety-day temporary duty tours. The Saudi government, driven by Iraq's 1990 invasion of Kuwait, had accepted foreign troops, but the Islamic kingdom remained sensitive about military forces from other countries taking permanent station within its borders. In consideration for this sensivity, the vast majority of uniformed Americans in Saudi Arabia after the Gulf War served in brief rotation tours like those of the 4404th Wing. The short-term deployments also were consistent with the foreign and military policies of the United States in southwest Asia. When President Bush had directed the Desert Shield deployment in defense of Saudi Arabia in 1990, he had stated that the American forces would leave when their mission was completed. The United States sought no bases or continuing presence on the Arabian peninsula, and it did not consider Southern Watch a permanent operation.[35] And yet by the time of the Khobar Towers bombing, American airmen had been patrolling the skies over Iraq for half a decade. After the terrorist attack suddenly drew attention to Operation Southern Watch, as Brigadier General Schwalier commented, "The fact that we had been there for five years came as a surprise to many people."[36]

Those airmen who deployed to Dhahran for Southern Watch lived in the American sector of the Khobar Towers compound, a complex named for al Khobar, the community of eastern Dhahran where it was located. (Arab translators usually rendered the name "al Khubar"; English ones nearly always made it "al Khobar.") The Arabic words that transliterate to "Khu-bar" or "Kho-bar" translate in English to "small settlement." This phrase suggests the origin of the community's name, because as late as the 1940s Khobar was no more than a small fishing village on the Arabian Gulf.[37]

The economic rise of Khobar dated to 1936, when the Arabian American Oil Company had dug the Dammam No. 7 well and confirmed that Saudi Arabia held a vast supply of the hydrocarbons that were so valuable throughout the world. The history of Dhahran, the area around it, and the entire kingdom, changed fundamentally. During the late 1940s and into the next decade, ARAMCO discovered new oil fields south, west, and north of Dammam. As the company expanded and its exports and revenues increased, al Khobar began developing from a small fishing village into an urbanized community. During the 1950s and 1960s the mudbrick huts of the fishermen gave way to modern residences, multi-lane highways, and handsomely landscaped streets.[38]

In 1979 contractors working for the Saudi government finished building the Khobar Towers. The kingdom's leaders intended the facility, as they had Eskan Village outside Riyadh, to house Bedouin tribesmen. These nomadic people, however, preferred their own tents and traditions to the government's apartments and a new lifestyle, and both compounds went unused for years. The buildings of Khobar

Towers stood empty until Americans began quartering there during the Desert Shield deployment of 1990 and the Gulf War that followed.[39]

The complex originally intended for the Bedouins was large, taking in about fourteen residential blocks. The Air Force and U.S. Army occupied only about two of them. When USAF airmen in the 1990s spoke about "Khobar Towers," they usually were referring to just the American sector, secured within its own perimeter, as opposed to the larger, fourteen-block Khobar area, which featured both Saudi military and civilian housing.[40]

Most of the U.S. Army personnel who lived within the American perimeter worked on Lucky Base, a small facility about five miles south of the Khobar Towers. These "green suiters" belonged to the 6th Battalion, 52d Air Defense Artillery, a Patriot missile unit from Fort Bliss, Texas, and to the 54th Signal Battalion, from Fort Huachuca, Arizona. South of the Army and Air Force facilities, yet still within the secured compound, French and British personnel occupied four buildings.[41]

The American sector of the compound was bounded on the north by Thirty-first Street, on the east by Eighth Street, on the south by Thirty-fifth Street, and on the west by Twelfth Street. Press accounts stated that the complex was a mile in circumference; resident joggers, who took an interest in such things, put it at the same distance or a little less, perhaps nine-tenths of a mile.[42]

Within this perimeter stood forty-one buildings. Twenty of them were tall, T-shaped structures that served either as dormitories or as a combination of housing and offices. These high-rise buildings gave the "Khobar Towers" complex part of its name. The "Khobar" came from the local community, and "Towers" was a useage similar to "tower" apartments in the United States.[43] In addition to these twenty tall buildings, the compound also featured seven partially underground parking garages that had been converted to storage or services facilities, including a shopette, post office, and a furnishings management office. The buildings of the Air Force complex ranged from four to eight stories, each floor divided into two or three suites. Within the dormitories, each floor had three suites, each housing as many as ten people, or thirty per floor.[44]

By 1996, the appearance of the Khobar Towers suffered from the sustained use of the facilities. A number of airmen—from general officers down through the ranks—expressed honest opinions about this. General Schwalier said that when he arrived at the Khobar Towers, the conditions reminded him of something out of "*M*A*S*H**." "I remember thinking," he stated in 1999, "I would not let my son live in some of these barracks, they were in such disrepair." His successor, Brig. Gen. Daniel M. Dick, commented that by 1996 Khobar Towers had gained the appearance of "a TDY [temporary duty] hang out." One airman contrasted the quality of the Air Force facilities with those enjoyed by the Arabian American Oil Company, less than five and a half miles to the west, which he openly envied.[45]

The 4404th Wing's May 1996 Five-Year Facilities Improvement Plan included $500,000 for repairing and upgrading 432 dormitory rooms. "If this renovation is

Khobar Towers: Tragedy and Response

not accomplished," the report stated, "Khobar Towers quarters will continue to deteriorate, eventually to the point of condemning the only living quarters available to the GIs in Dhahran. In addition, repair calls will increase, tasking our civil engineers beyond their resources."[46]

The area around the Air Force's Khobar Towers compound was well populated. South of it was the Saudi military housing complex, whose tall buildings mirrored the USAF dormitories. These structures continued beyond the eastern border of the Air Force compound and then gave way to civilian housing, open fields, and a mosque. Not much further east lay the Arabian Gulf: airmen could smell the sea air and could see the Gulf water from their dormitory balconies. The northern perimeter of the Air Force compound was Thirty-first Street and just beyond it stood al Khobar Park. Across from the northern part of the compound's western border, there were private residences and south of them, open areas.[47]

Less than a mile west of the Khobar Towers was the eastern portion of Dhahran Air Base, which featured an air defense reservation and the civilian runways of Dhahran International Airport. The western part of the base, with its military runway, was about another five miles from the Khobar Towers. The King Fahd expressway, a limited access highway that connected the city of Dhahran with a causeway to Bahrain, ran north-and-south between King Abdul Aziz and Khobar.[48]

This Saudi Arabian base was one location among many where, in June 1996, about 12,000 Air Force people were serving in deployments around the world.[49] Few Americans knew anything whatever about Dhahran Air Base and the housing complex at the Khobar Towers. A sudden tragedy dispelled this ignorance.

Chapter Three

Stay Alert, Be Observant

There had been violence in the Dhahran community of al Khobar before June 1996, and there would be afterward. During the Gulf War, on February 25, 1991, an Iraqi Scud missile killed twenty-eight Americans and wounded ninety-eight others when it hit an Army barracks. This facility, a converted warehouse near Souk's Supermarket, stood a little less than six miles from the Khobar Towers.[1] After the June 1996 bombing, the community returned to the news in 2001. Not long after the September 11 attacks on the World Trade Center and the Pentagon, on the night of October 6, a bomb exploded on a crowded al Khobar street. One American and several other foreign nationals were killed.[2]

After the Gulf War had ended, tensions remained in Saudi Arabia. Iraqi dictator Saddam Hussein's persisting belligerence had prompted President George Bush to direct "Operation Southern Watch." Another source of tension was created by militant Islamics within Saudi Arabia. During the 1991 Gulf War, these religious fundamentalists began to build a popular following by denouncing the presence in their country of Americans and other foreign "infidels." The militants also criticized the Saudi royal family, alleging that its extravagant living and corruption betrayed a lack of fidelity to Islam.[3]

During the early 1990s, very few violent acts were aimed at Westerners. Americans, civilian and military, generally believed themselves safe in Saudi Arabia, particularly so in the quiet Eastern Province. Doubtless most of them felt more secure in Riyadh, and certainly in Dhahran, than in the large cities of the United States.[4]

Then on November 13, 1995, a deadly event changed this pattern. Terrorists exploded a car-bomb in Riyadh, at the Office of Program Management-Saudi Arabian National Guard, the training facility for the Saudi National Guard the U.S. Army had operated since 1965.[5] An Islamic fundamentalist group claimed responsibility for this explosion of the equivalent of 200 pounds of TNT, which killed seven people, five Americans and two Indians, and wounded sixty others. Immediately after this bombing, the U.S. State Department alerted the embassies, consulates, and military units in the region that "threats have been made against American citizens in Saudi Arabia. The American Embassy in Riyadh is informing the local community to exercise caution, keep a low profile and limit travel within Saudi Arabia."[6]

Khobar Towers: Tragedy and Response

Despite the Riyadh bombing, the Saudi government minimized the numbers and strength of the dissidents who opposed the rule of the royal family and the presence of Americans. In a May 1996 interview, a senior Saudi official estimated that his country harbored no more than 300 hard-core militants, whom he compared to the American extremists who had held law officers at bay in Montana earlier that spring. "Basically, these are our Freemen," he stated. "They say the same thing—that they do not recognize the government." About the same time as this interview, the Saudi defense minister played down the threats against American installations, calling them "boyish acts," stressing that "the Kingdom is not influenced by threats."[7] The Saudi ambassador to the United States told American reporters: "Islamic radicals are very, very small, and looked upon in this country as outcasts.... Islamic extremists are not a threat to the stability of the country." Saudi authorities seemed to regard the Riyadh bombing as an aberration.[8]

Americans responded much differently to the November 1995 attack. Immediately following the bombing, the State Department began a study of its facilities in Riyadh. At the same time Gen. Joseph W. Ralston, Air Combat Command commander, and Lt. Gen. John P. Jumper, commander of the Ninth Air Force, which provided the air component of the United States Central Command, toured the southwest Asian theater and reviewed the measures taken to protect the forces there.[9]

These general officers were in no way alone in their concerns about the security of Americans in the region. After the Riyadh bombing, airmen of all ranks in Saudi Arabia believed they were in dangerous surroundings. Many shared the view of Maj. Bennie L. Umstead II, the JTF-SWA commander's executive officer, who often drove past the Saudi Arabian National Guard building during the weeks after the attack. "We saw the bombing site there," Major Umstead said later. "We knew there was, of course, always the potential for violence. There was a carefulness in the air."[10]

Airmen in Dhahran, more than 200 miles from Riyadh, were equally concerned. After the Khobar Towers bombing, SSgt. Anthony Overbay, who had lived in Building 131 on the compound, told the press: "This building we were in, we constantly joked that we were a fine target, out in this corner, right next to the park." Another NCO directly acknowledged: "I didn't feel comfortable about this tour."[11] Still another airman commented, referring to a series of five suspected reconnaissance incidents reported by the security police between April 1 and 25, 1996: "We knew that people were watching us. We had people stopping and looking at the area and leaving."[12]

None of these airmen were any more concerned than their own senior officer, the commander of the 4404th Composite Wing (Provisional). Brig. Gen. Terry Schwalier himself stated: "We realized there were people out there who were serious about hurting Western interests."[13]

After the Riyadh attack, General Schwalier immediately issued a Battle Staff Directive that raised the alert status of the Khobar Towers from "Threatcon Alpha" to "Threatcon Bravo."[14] At the time General Schwalier made this decision, the official USAF guidance on "threatcons," or threatening conditions, was stated in Air Force Instruction 31-210, which had been in effect since July 1, 1995. Like its predecessors, this AFI used the phonetic alphabet to designate four levels of threatcons, which might develop against any installation. Each of these letters represented a warning against a range of potential threats from terrorists or others, and each required a base to take certain security measures. As the threatcon advanced through the alphabet, it reflected an increased threat to the installation and it usually meant that the intelligence about that threat became more specific. At each level of warning, an installation took all of the security measures required at the earlier, lower ones, and additional ones as well.[15]

Air Force Instruction 31-210 defined Threatcon Alpha as a general alert of possible terrorist activity, whose exact nature or full extent could not be predicted. Security measures taken at this level included increasing overall vigilance, reviewing bomb threat procedures, checking deliveries of packages, and reducing the number of entrance points to a base. Threatcon Bravo represented an increased and more predictable threat of terrorist activity, without any specific target being identified. A commander declared this level of warning when he or she had information that terrorists were actively preparing for an operation in the general area of their installation. At Threatcon Bravo, personnel took all the measures of Threatcon Alpha and additional ones such as moving vehicles, trash dumpsters, crates, and other large objects at least twenty-five meters (about eighty-two feet) from buildings; routinely locking vehicles and checking them for tampering when unlocking them; reviewing security plans; and maintaining a low profile.[16]

The Khobar Towers remained at Threatcon Bravo on June 25, 1996. After determining a threat condition, commanders sometimes modified the security measures taken at its level. In the case of Khobar Towers, by June 25, 1996, Brigadier General Schwalier had implemented so many of the measures associated with Threatcon Charlie that some of its residents believed that the compound stood at that higher level, rather than at Bravo.[17]

When the Khobar Towers moved to Threatcon Bravo after the Riyadh bombing, the security police responded accordingly. Three days after this change in alert status, General Schwalier noted in a private letter: "Our cops are on 12-hour shifts—having doubled up on the gates and increased their patrols." The security police tightened their checking of identification cards at the compound's main gate. At Threatcon Bravo, as one security policeman put it, the SPs became "more vigilant in [their] normal duties."[18]

In addition to raising the threatcon level, General Schwalier directed a number of measures to improve the protection of the Khobar Towers perimeter. Thousands of sandbags were used to build two M–60 machine gun bunkers that covered the main gate and seven similar defensive positions on Dhahran Air Base. A formidable line of concrete "New Jersey" barriers in double rows fortified the western, northern, and eastern perimeters of the complex. After the November 13 bombing, work crews reinforced these large obstacles with others like them that had been left scattered along the road to the installation. "We immediately started to check and reinforce our barrier," General Schwalier stated. "We worked straight for three or four days bringing in barriers that were strewn along the highway. We got very serious about completely surrounding our area with these Jersey barriers." Eventually, eight hundred of these obstacles protected the Khobar perimeter.[19]

The 4404th Composite Wing took other steps as a result of the Riyadh bombing. General Schwalier directed that a "serpentine," or staggered, pattern of barriers be installed in front of the compound's entry points, which forced all vehicles to slow down before they reached a security checkpoint. The wing commander also restricted off-base travel, and he directed that trash dumpsters and parked vehicles be moved at least twenty-five meters away from buildings. Non-essential commercial deliveries into the complex were suspended. "I wouldn't let vendors come on base" right after the Riyadh attack, General Schwalier stated. "We tried to make sure we really got a grip on everything that was going on within the compound." He summarized the wing's view of force-protection issues, before and after November 13: "We were aware of security before, but we got hyper about it as a result of the Riyadh bombing."[20]

During the next month, December 1995, the 4404th Wing began a vigorous training program for its Disaster Control Group. Headed by the wing's support group commander and made up of representatives from key functional areas, the DCG would restore the unit's communications and manage its recovery, in the event of an attack, an aircraft accident, or other contingency.[21] It was also during December that General Schwalier initiated an ongoing series of weekly security review meetings, which were attended by the Air Force Office of Special Investigations (AFOSI) detachment commander, the wing's support group commander, its civil engineering squadron commander, security police squadron commander, intelligence officer, and others when required. During the same month, too, General Schwalier directed the 4404th to conduct a tabletop terrorist bombing exercise.[22]

On January 8, 1996, the AFOSI presented General Schwalier with a Vulnerability Assessment.[23] Twice a year OSI officers, as a routine part of their responsibilities, submitted a document like this one to the senior officer in Dhahran. They gave the commander of the Khobar Towers, and of other such facilities worldwide, their observations of possible vulnerabilities of their installation to terrorists and a list of recommendations on how to strengthen these potential weaknesses. No one could state definitely which, if any, of the points identified in any AFOSI assessment would ever be exploited by attackers, but these semiannual reports helped senior leaders focus their efforts against the greatest threats.[24]

When Brigadier General Schwalier had taken command of the 4404th Wing in July 1995, the AFOSI had a vulnerability survey underway. It provided this report to the commander in September and he directed the 4404th to begin work on its recommendations. Before the wing could implement the suggestions of this AFOSI vulnerability survey, the Riyadh car bombing took place. The OSI began a new report, which would take into account the concerns raised by this November 1995 terrorist attack. It was this vulnerability assessment that General Schwalier received on January 8, 1996.[25]

The AFOSI team identified a number of potential vulnerabilities at the Khobar Towers, and their January 1996 assessment listed thirty-nine "action items." These included recommendations about cutting vegetation from the compound's perimeter fences, protecting radio transmissions, monitoring the activities of the third country nationals who worked at the Khobar Towers, improving parking arrangements, strengthening the security of the senior members of the wing's staff, and other issues.[26] By the time of the June 25, 1996, attack, the 4404th Wing had implemented thirty-six of the OSI's thirty-nine recommendations.[27]

The AFOSI's January 1996 vulnerability assessment listed five terrorist scenarios: driving into the Khobar Towers to make a suicidal car-bombing, parking and abandoning a vehicle with a bomb in it, carrying a human-portable explosive device into the compound and leaving it there, entering the base wearing a body charge to make a suicidal man-pack bombing, or posting a package or letter bomb to the facility. Given the experience of the Riyadh attack, preventing a car-bomb from penetrating the Khobar Towers became the top priority.[28]

After the January 1996 assessment, the wing took further steps. To prevent a speeding vehicle from penetrating the compound, Brigadier General Schwalier directed that dumpsters be positioned at key locations. After the Riyadh attack, each Khobar gate had serpentine barriers that forced all incoming traffic to approach at slow speeds, and after the January assessment, the security at these entry points was further improved. Although the staggered obstacles slowed vehicles and reduced the chances of a suicide car bombing, they also could delay the traffic legitimately entering the compound. Vehicles carrying Air Force passengers might back up and become a target for terrorists. After the January assessment, the security police accordingly set up two checkpoints at each gate, and directed military vehicles into the second, more guarded one while they completed their identification checks.[29]

In addition to vehicle security, General Schwalier also remained concerned about off-base travel. The limitations he put in place after the Riyahd bombing continued in various forms throughout the winter and spring of 1996. For airmen with a few hours leave, Bahrain beckoned as a popular destination. It was a forty-minute drive from the Khobar Towers, across the fourteen-mile King Fahd causeway and through its six security checkpoints, to the U.S. Navy, Central Command facility, which featured a post exchange and a beach club. Here, in contrast to the Saudi kingdom where Islamic law prevailed, the Khobar airmen could buy alcoholic beverages.[30]

During December 1995 and early 1996, a series of terrorist bombings took place in Bahrain. Although their pattern suggested they represented local criminal activity, rather than attacks aimed at Americans, General Schwalier saw no reason to take risks. On February 21 he stopped all unofficial travel to Bahrain. "My concern," he stated later, "was that [the terrorists] were starting to choose places Americans might frequent." One Air Force officer later praised the travel restriction, in candid terms: "I think the commanders there [at Khobar Towers] did a pretty darn good job of keeping the security as tight as it was, when all us 'Joes' over there were going, 'Hey, I'd like to go to Bahrain and have a whiskey.'"[31]

In an irony of dates, the Bahrain restriction would have ended on June 26, 1996. The new travel policy took effect on the twenty-fifth, the day of the bombing, and on that Tuesday airmen began signing up for passes that would have allowed them to return in civilian clothes to the popular NAVCENT facility. The terrorists struck that night, and all such trips were canceled.[32]

The Bahrain travel restrictions represented only one example of the tense situation around the Khobar Towers during the spring of 1996. Saudi security forces took an action that no doubt prevented a terrorist attack when, on March 29, they intercepted a late-model Chevrolet Caprice being smuggled into their country from Jordan. Border guards searched the car and found eighty-five pounds of plastic explosives. As ominous as the large quantity of deadly material was the fact that it had been expertly concealed within the Caprice's engine compartment. Saudi press reports connected this smuggling attempt with the November 1995 Riyadh bombing.[33] Before this episode and after it, continuing into early April, some Saudi newspapers ran a series of anti-American articles that increased the mood of tension.[34]

On March 14 a new commander of the 4404th Wing's security police squadron, Lt. Col. James J. Traister, reported to the Khobar Towers.[35] Lieutenant Colonel Traister had a strong background in antiterrorism, and one Air Force report said of him: "He was considered to be a superb squadron commander."[36] He met with General Schwalier and discussed the issues related to his new assignment. While the two officers talked about a range of possible threats to the installation, the wing remained focused on preventing the penetration of the compound, particularly by a car-bomb. Colonel Traister later summarized the strategy: "The defense of Khobar Towers is to stop and eliminate any threat (human bomber or car bomber) from getting [past] 12th Street [the western perimeter] into the main compound. This is with the assumption that all personnel perform their jobs and everything falls into place with lots of luck." He also stated: "This plan is not designed to stop stand [off] type weapons, RPG [rocket propelled grenade], mortar attack, or sniper fire. Our intent is to make the base as hard a target to hit as possible to force the enemy to go elsewhere."[37]

In April Brigadier General Schwalier, Lieutenant Colonel Traister, and Col. Gary S. Boyle, the wing's support group commander, implemented additional counterterrorist measures. Airmen trimmed back vegetation growing on the interior of the perimeter fence and put seven miles of concertina wire along the top of the double Jersey barriers. The security police increased their patrols and worked twelve-hour to fourteen-hour shifts, six days a week.[38]

In another of these April 1996 measures, General Schwalier and Colonel Traister established sentry observation posts on the dormitory roofs at each of the four corners of the Khobar Towers. From the top of Building 201, between Thirty-seventh and Thirty-fifth Streets, the security police had an excellent view of the main gate and the west side of the compound. It was manned around the clock.[39] Another dormitory, Building 101, stood just east of Twelfth Street and south of Khobar's softball field, and complemented Building 201 as an observation post for the western perimeter. The roof of Dormitory 101 also overlooked the northwestern part of the compound, an area that included the offices of the 4404th Wing. The security police manned this post during the midnight shift. Building 131, located at the northeast corner and manned by the midnight shift, was destined to gain the greatest notoriety of these four observation posts. SPs were stationed there, like Building 101, on the midnight shift. The fourth, Building 117, stood in the southeast corner of the compound and complemented 131's view of the eastern perimeter. It would be manned when threat conditions increased.[40] General Schwalier had taken an extraordinary step: neither the British, nor the French, nor the U.S. Army Forces, Central Command (ARCENT) buildings had any rooftop sentries.[41]

On April 22, there was a dramatic development in the Riyadh bombing case. The Saudi government announced it had arrested four of its own nationals for this crime and televised these suspects making confessions. During this broadcast the prisoners stated that they had been influenced by Islamic groups outside their country and admitted that they had planned more attacks. On May 15, with these men under a death sentence, the American Embassy issued another advisory: there were threats of "retaliation against Americans in Saudi Arabia" if the condemned were executed.[42]

In late April and into May, the Defense Department, Federal Bureau of Investigation, and Central Intelligence Agency sought permission to question the four prisoners. The American agencies wanted, among several things, to investigate whether the Riyadh bombing and other attacks were the work of Saudi militants acting alone; of terrorists from Iran and other countries; or, what one Saudi official called "the most dangerous possibility," a combination of the two. The Saudi government denied the American requests and the U.S. Embassy in Riyadh renewed the question on behalf of the FBI. After this approach was refused, the State Department raised the issue with the Saudi Embassy. As the end of May approached, the Americans had received received no reply.[43]

While the State Department waited for a response, an odd incident took place at the Khobar Towers: a car rammed one of the Jersey barriers that stood along the compound's eastern perimeter, toward its northern end. The vehicle approached very slowly, ran into the solid concrete at a low speed, four to six miles per hour, and moved it two or three feet. The driver then backed up and drove away.[44] Airmen living in Building 127, a dormitory in the northeastern part of the complex, promptly reported the episode to the security police. "The dorm residents," General Schwalier noted, "did as we asked. They reported it." After this episode, the wing's civil engineering squadron staked down all of the Jersey barriers around the perimeter. The incident was reported up the chain of command and an official Air Force report of

Khobar Towers: Tragedy and Response

April 1997 stated: "The incident was fully investigated.... The investigation was inconclusive, with explanations ranging from the possibility of an accident to the more serious concern that it may have been a test of the perimeter."[45]

Between May 26 and 31, Chairman of the Joint Chiefs of Staff Gen. John M. Shalikashvili toured the Arabian Gulf and on the morning of the twenty-ninth he visited Dhahran. General Schwalier escorted the Chairman around the military side of Dhahran Air Base. "I put in front of him as many of my people as I could," General Schwalier later related. "I had groups waiting for him at the operations area, the logistics areas, [and elsewhere], probably a couple hundred, three hundred people each place."[46]

Addressing the Dhahran airmen, General Shalikashvili emphasized the importance of their Southern Watch mission. "And the work that you do," he said, "each and every day, here on the flightline turning wrenches, or performing admin functions, or myriad other tasks that make the 4404th so outstanding, and make your mission run so smoothly—every task is vital, and every one of you is indispensable." At the end of his remarks, the Chairman twice exhorted the airmen to "be safe." "So let me tell you that I am proud of you," General Shalikashvili declared, "your families are proud of you, and the Nation is proud of you. And I ask a few things of you: keep up the magnificent job you're doing over here, and do what only you all can do, which is to take good care of your equipment and of each other, and be safe." Then he closed: "Good luck to you all, be safe, and God bless you."[47]

General Shalikashvili's emphasis on safety was already firmly in the minds of his audience, as an attitude of caution had prevailed that spring. The travel restrictions remained in force. Wing personnel were not to go into downtown Dhahran, unless the AFOSI had advised them it was safe, and then, under a long-standing rule, they were to move in groups of at least two but no more than four. An article in the *Gulf View*, the wing newspaper, alerted readers in mid-April: "So next time you go downtown, remember [terrorists] look for targets of opportunity like Westerners in groups larger than four, or one person alone (that's the reasoning behind the two to four rule)."[48] Air Force members also were advised to check their cars for bombs.[49]

In addition to the travel restrictions, General Schwalier stressed security awareness to his subordinates during his weekly "stand ups" of the 4404th's staff, at force protection meetings, and on other occasions. At the wing's staff meetings, his officers discussed at length what the appropriate threat condition should be for the week ahead.[50] General Schwalier coordinated this setting of the threatcon level with the JTF-SWA and ARCENT and with the British and French. The 4404th Wing and the JTF-SWA convened a large number of meetings of military officers representing Saudi Arabia, the United States, and other nations participating in Southern Watch and its counterpart operations, to discuss security issues.[51] There was, an AFOSI representative later commented, "excellent cooperation from all parties involved."[52]

The security efforts of the 4404th Wing also extended to the 200 to 300 new arrivals it received each week. Like all such deployed units, it conducted a series of

Stay Alert, Be Observant

"Right Start" orientation briefings for its newcomers. The 4404th held its sessions for incoming personnel in one of the Khobar compound's seven converted garages. The northern side of this building featured an auditorium, used for the Right Start briefings, USO-type shows, and other sizeable gatherings. (The southern portion of the structure was the home of the "Khobar Konnection," where dances, attended by Air Force and Arabian American Oil Company personnel, were held.) Brigadier General Schwalier directed that the Right Start briefings be held every Friday, roughly tripling their frequency. The commander personally gave a forty to forty-five minute presentation at the opening of each session, reviewing the wing's standards and rules. He urged each group of arrivals to view their temporary duty at Khobar Towers as an opportunity to improve the combat capability of their unit, to represent America well by being good guests in the Kingdom of Saudi Arabia, and to better themselves and their installation during their tour. General Schwalier stressed to each week's audience the importance of protecting the forces in the theater.[53] "I would talk about the threat," the wing commander recalled, three years later, "about things we had seen [happen], particularly the Riyadh bombing.... I said, You'll probably be mad at me because of the force protection measures that I have instituted." At the Right Start program on June 21, five days before the bombing, he emphasized to the newcomers that the wing was operating under a heightened threatcon and that it was *not* conducting an exercise—it was responding to an actual threat.[54]

During a wing "stand up" meeting, on May 31, the dramatic news arrived at Khobar Towers that the Saudis had executed the four Riyadh bombers. General Schwalier later commented that his unit learned about this development very promptly, "through the Saudi community," because of the positive relationships he and his officers had established with their hosts. "I think [we received the news] before anybody else knew about it. The Saudis don't generally say anything about these executions." This news indeed represented an abrupt turn of events: when the executions took place, the State Department was still waiting for a reply to the FBI's request to question the prisoners. The AFOSI believed that the death sentences would not be carried out until June 17.[55]

When General Schwalier received this sudden news, he immediately deployed additional security police patrols and took further measures to protect the complex. Two vehicles drove a surveillance route around the perimeter roads of the compound, which were, beginning on the northern side and moving clockwise: Thirty-first, Eighth, Thirty-fifth, and Twelfth Streets. The security police also walked two foot-patrols, one covering the half of Khobar Towers that lay north of Thirty-third Street, and the other covering the area south of it.[56]

After the executions, Brigadier General Schwalier issued a Battle Staff Directive that "locked down" the Khobar Towers: all residents were to remain within the compound, except for traveling to their duties at nearby Dhahran Air Base. (From gate to gate, the distance from the Khobar Towers to the air base was six tenths of a mile, or about a three-minute drive. The trip to the base's military flight-

Khobar Towers: Tragedy and Response

line, which took a curving route, was about five miles.) Under the lock down, personnel were required to sign in and out of log books when they entered certain buildings on the Khobar compound, and telephone security was tightened.[57]

With the Khobar Towers locked down, all traffic in and out of the compound moved through the main gate, and this single entry point received concentrated attention. Lieutenant Colonel Traister implemented a number of security improvements. Since the Riyadh bombing, two bunkers with M–60 machine guns had covered the traffic entering and leaving the main gate. After the executions, Colonel Traister directed that a pair of two-and-a-half ton dump trucks be positioned to close the gap between these two bunkers, and the security police kept two more of these vehicles on stand-by. In the event of an attack, the SPs could use these trucks to close the roadway, and fire from behind them. Emergency vehicle lights, so bright they could be seen day or night, were mounted behind the main gate. These beacons, a back up to the radios of the security police, could be used to alert other security posts if any trouble developed at the main entry point.[58]

The security police manning the main gate, always vigilant, were particularly so during the lock down. Six SPs served there, making identification checks on every vehicle entering the compound and conducting extensive searches. A seventh professional, a French military policeman, joined them between 8 p.m. and midnight, the nighttime hours when the volume of traffic at the main gate ran high. Two teams of security police dogs trained to detect explosives also served at this entry point during the day, and at least one team at night.[59]

The Khobar Towers remained locked down for five days, until June 5, and military facilities in Riyadh for even longer. In the case of the latter, Brigadier General Schwalier praised Col. Dale Bible, the commander of the 4409th Operations Group in Riyadh, for acting in "lock step" with the actions that he himself had taken in Dhahran. The wing commander characterized Colonel Bible as "one of my real good ops group commanders."[60]

It was evident to every resident of Khobar Towers, and every visitor to the compound, that security had tightened during the late spring of 1996. An assistant crew chief pointed out that, in addition to the machine gun bunkers at the main gate, "There was a bunker on the British building. You could tell security was getting tighter. There were a lot more checks; you had to show your ID." A civil engineering officer, who had served a Dhahran tour during June–September 1995, was surprised at the high level of security she found when she returned a year later: "There were vehicle searches in place.... There were no trips to Bahrain, and very limited trips to downtown [Dhahran]." An NCO who made many rotations to Dhahran had a similar experience. He returned in February 1996 to find that "security was stepped up a lot" and that "towards May... the base got super tight."[61]

Khobar Towers airmen commended the security measures that had been taken before June 25, 1996. "They had machine gun nests at the front gate," a pilot of the 71st Rescue Squadron recalled months after the bombing. "They had put up a double set of barriers. They were doing a lot heavier checking [of vehicles at the gate]."

"I watched those security guys at Dhahran," Capt. Jeff Prichard asserted, "and I know how good they are. There is no question in my mind that security was as tight as it could be."[62]

Mr. David Winn, the United States consul general in Dhahran and a veteran of twenty-five years service in the Middle East, found out first hand how tight it was, when he drove on the compound one day that spring, intending to make a quick shopping foray at the commissary. The diplomat went in to buy some razor blades and returned to find the security police were preparing to tow his vehicle. Mr. Winn had parked too close to the commissary and had violated the minimum safe distance, had his consul-general's car turned out to be a mobile bomb. He paid the SPs a compliment when he told General Schwalier: "My God, Terry, you know they really gave me a shakedown." On another occasion, Winn stated that General Schwalier's force protection measures "were so stringent, so draconian, so professional that I thought he almost had overreacted."[63]

This emphasis on security and readiness remained strong throughout the days just before the attack. About two weeks before the Khobar Towers bombing, Lt. Col. (Dr.) Douglas Robb arrived in Dhahran to serve a one-month interim assignment as the commander of the 4404th Wing's medical group. At Dr. Robb's first meeting with his staff, he asked about the unit's preparations to deal with a disaster involving mass casualties. The medical group's readiness officer already was updating the unit's contingency plans and the new commander accelerated that review, so that it was completed before the bombing. During the week before the attack, Robb conducted what he later called a "'mass cal' logistical supply exercise." His medical professionals checked first hand—not on paper—the availability and quantities of the supplies they would need in the event of a disaster. If, for example, their paperwork said a closet held fifty cots, they located the key to that storage area, opened it, and counted the cots. In the few cases where they discovered shortages, MSgt. Luis Madrigal, the unit's supply sergeant, filled them. On June 20, about the same time that the medical group was making these first-hand checks, members of the 4404th Wing's transportation squadron conducted an emergency-response exercise.[64]

General Schwalier commissioned a series of articles on security awareness and antiterrorism in the *Gulf View*. On June 20, the same day the transportation squadron ran its exercise, one of these feature stories appeared in the wing newspaper. It occupied nearly a half page and carried the headline: "Terrorism: Real threat exists... stay alert, be observant." At about the same time, Gen. J. H. Binford Peay III, U.S. Central Command commander, told a general officer who visited his MacDill Air Force Base, Florida headquarters that he was concerned terrorists would attempt to make a "catastrophic hit" somewhere in southwest Asia.[65]

In the hindsight available after the attack, the security of one particular part of the Khobar Towers compound, the northern perimeter, became an issue. The fence here, running along the north side of Thirty-first Street, stood less than 100 feet from the Building 131 dormitory and other structures at this end of the complex. In November 1995 and again in March 1996, Colonel Boyle asked his counterparts in the Saudi security forces for permission to extend this perimeter. During interviews a few days following the bombing, Brigadier General Schwalier told journalists about these two occasions when the Americans had approached the Saudis about moving the border from 100 to 400 feet. "We asked them," he stated, "to move it outside of the parking lot." The wing commander explained to the press that "the pace [of decision making] is different in Saudi Arabia" than the United States. "We did as much as we could," he said, "given the environment."[66]

The Saudi security forces had replied that moving the compound's perimeter farther north would interfere with access to the parking lot next to al Khobar Park and to a mosque that stood to the east. They stated that they had no authority to approve the American request, without the approval of the government ministries that owned the property. The Saudi security officers contended that the existing perimeter was sufficient against a car-bomb attack on the scale of the Riyadh one. The host government offered to increase its own security patrols inside and outside Khobar Towers and, in response to American concerns about suspicious vehicles, to run checks on license plates.[67]

The Saudi government never denied the American requests to extend the northern perimeter; it refused to act on them. As Secretary of Defense William J. Perry characterized it, "the answer was not now, not yet." General Schwalier told reporters: "The answer was, 'Not at this time.'" U.S. Navy Capt. Michael Doubleday, the Defense Department's press briefer, stated that "it was not a matter of refusal, it was a matter of ongoing discussions."[68] "It's an ongoing process of negotiation with the Saudis," one senior American military officer explained. "Requests are not made and satisfied in a day.... It was reasonable for the Saudis to take time [with the request to expand the perimeter] because it would affect their road network." During a June 27, 1996, press conference, Maj. Gen. Kurt B. Anderson, the JTF-SWA commander, pointed out: "We are on Saudi Arabian soil. We will coordinate our security measures with them. They will help us. But we do not own this country." Major General Anderson reminded the journalists of the fundamentals of the relationship: "We are here living on the facilities they have provided us. That sets up certain constraints that our security measures must operate within."[69]

After the magnitude of the Khobar Towers bomb became known, many knowledgeable observers concluded that the location of the northern fence was a moot point. "We're dealing with a huge bomb," General Anderson emphasized, one that caused so much destruction over so wide an area that some Saudis thought there had been more than one explosion. General Peay stressed the same point to reporters, soon after the attack: "Frankly, you could have moved that blast a number of yards farther out and you probably would have had similar results. So this was an act of exorbitant degree of capability... that you don't normally see [in terrorist cases]."[70]

Some relevant findings came from a survey of the Khobar Towers bomb damage that experts from the Defense Special Weapons Agency and the Army Corps of Engineers conducted soon after the explosion. This team projected what the explosive effects might have been had the terrorist truck been parked 400 feet north of Building 131, the perimeter the Americans had requested. They concluded that in this case "the blast would likely have produced damage comparable to that which actually occurred at Building 133," which stood west of dormitory 131 and *was* about 400 feet from where the bomb actually had been located. The damage survey team projected there would have been "significant structural damage and shattering of most or all glass windows and doors. While deaths from blunt trauma might be reduced in this scenario, severe injuries and death from glass fragmentation would likely occur."

Underscoring the obvious importance of keeping terrorist bombs at a distance from facilities, the team's report then pointed to some hard realities, which applied directly to the case of the Khobar perimeter. "For large threats," it stated, "represented by truck bombs... these standoff distances quickly become extremely large, and often extremely difficult to implement. For example, for a blast equivalent to 20,000 lbs of TNT, concrete structures would still suffer damage at a standoff of over 400 feet and there would be significant glass shattering at over 1,000 feet."[71]

The survey echoed Lieutenant Colonel Traister's realistic observation that were limitations on what could be done to protect Khobar Towers against standoff weapons. Securing the compound's perimeter was another matter and in that regard, many believed that General Schwalier, Colonel Traister, Colonel Boyle, and others had succeeded. One junior officer asserted in February 1997 that, were it not for the force-protection improvements made during General Schwalier's tenure, "half of us wouldn't be here today." The general's successor later offered this assessment: "If [the terrorists] could have gotten that truck into the middle of Khobar Towers and set it off beside the dining hall... then the death toll would have been tremendously worse. It was the great work of Terry Schwalier that the tragedy was as contained as it was."[72]

Immediately after the Khobar Towers attack, an AFOSI officer stated: "As tragic as this event is, it should be recognized that personnel responded in a professional manner, as trained, to attempt to counter the threat that was immediately perceived when the explosives laden vehicle parked outside the perimeter fence. Their best efforts were simply overcome by the speed with which the event developed and the sheer magnitude of the blast."[73]

Dirt parking lot southwest of Building 131 where some of the wounded were initially taken; Building 130 is at center left, 127 at top right (*top*). Looking across an underground garage at the main gate (*center*). View southwest from Khobar complex, Dhahran Air Base is just beyond the highway at the top right of the picture (*bottom*).

Opposite page, top to bottom: Saudi residences similar to Khobar Towers' buildings, looking southeast across 8th Street from Building 131. Same intersection as above, but with additional "Jersey" barriers installed. Mosque east of Building 131, the Arabian Gulf is visible in the distance. Parking lot north of Building 131 before the bombing, the tanker truck would park just off the picture at bottom right. (See map on page 11.)

"Jersey" barriers and concertina wire at the corner of 12th Street and 31st Street (*top left*). The serpentine entrance to the main gate (*top right*). Barrier at the main gate (*center*). A roof-top security police post (*left*).

Opposite page: Truck inspection (*top left*). Machine gun inside bunker (*top right*). Bunker on road into complex (*center top*). Dump truck behind bunker for blocking entrance in emergency *(center bottom)*. Installation of additional "Jersey" barriers (*bottom*).

Khobar Towers complex, with Building 131 at left, after the attack (*top*). Security policemen SSgt. Alfredo R. Guerrero, SrA. Corey P. Grice, and A1C. Christopher T. Wagar each receive the Airman's Medal from Air Force Chief of Staff Gen. Ronald R. Fogleman (*center, left to right*). The panels on the northeast corner of Building 131 buckled from explosion (*left*).

Opposite page, top to bottom: The force of the explosion can be inferred from the size of the crater, the interior walls of the rooms in Building 131, and the remains of a humvee.

Most of the deaths and injuries were caused by flying glass and blunt trauma. These pictures show room interiors, with glass (*top*) and debris (*center and bottom*).

Chapter Four

The Attack

On June 25, 1996, Maj. Gen. Kurt B. Anderson, the commander of the Joint Task Force Southwest Asia (JTF-SWA), and Maj. Bennie L. Umstead II, his executive officer, took a C–21 transport from Riyadh to Dhahran Air Base. Arriving at the Khobar Towers that afternoon, they billeted for the night in a distinguished-visitors suite of Building 101, the visiting officers quarters. Their rooms were across the hall from the temporary lodgings of Brig. Gen. Terry Schwalier, the commander of the 4404th Composite Wing (Provisional). Building 101 stood southwest of Building 131, a short distance across a dirt and gravel parking lot. The next morning General Anderson was to officiate at the change of command ceremony in which Brig. Gen. Dan Dick, then the Air Combat Command inspector general, would succeed General Schwalier.[1]

The plans for this ceremony were, of course, canceled by that night's violent explosion. Witnesses later gave varying descriptions of how the Khobar Towers attack sounded, looked, and felt, depending upon exactly where they had been at 9:53 p.m. that Tuesday. Many agreed with Maj. Bennie Umstead that the explosion was not only loud, but prolonged. "It wasn't a blast like a 'boom,'" he said. "The blast lasted, it seems, like forty-five seconds.... It was a *long* noise, the loudest I ever heard. You tried to put your hands over your ears." Capt. (Dr.) R. Morris Treadway, a flight surgeon who lived in Building 127, recalled: "The shaking seemed to go on for ever." Maj. Cynthia Coles, a resident of Building 133, also emphasized the length of the explosion: "It felt like an eternity. First of all the lights went out; it went dark. I felt the wave of the blast pressure. [I felt] just surrounded by the pressure and then, instantly, the loud noise and the pressure from it, exploding again, just totally surrounding me."[2]

People heard the bomb, and felt its horrendous force, across great distances. At the time of the attack, Lt. Col. (Dr.) Douglas J. Robb, dental surgeon Lt. Col. (Dr.) Alfred B. (Bruce) Lauder, and Capt. Cinthia Y. (Cindy) Pollert were entering a carpet shop in downtown Dhahran, about three-quarters of a mile from the blast. The explosion broke the glass in the merchant's windows and brought down dust from the ceiling. "It shook and *rocked* the downtown," Dr. Robb remembered, so forcefully that he and the others at first believed the bomb was somewhere in the city itself, near them.[3] The force of the blast carried vast distances across water and desert. Its tremor was

Khobar Towers: Tragedy and Response

felt in Bahrain, twenty miles away, and Headquarters Joint Task Force Southwest Asia received phone calls indicating that distant reverberations were heard in the United Arab Emirates, more than one hundred and twenty miles away.[4]

The blast was readily visible from the military flightline at Dhahran Air Base, about five miles west of the truck-bomb. Here the maintenance team was at work on the HC–130 that had been forced to return early. SSgt. Jacques P. Bruffy, one of the engine mechanics, was facing the opposite direction from the Khobar Towers. Another airman looked over his shoulder, saw the flash in the nighttime sky to the east, and asked him: "Did you see *that*?" The ground tremor from the blast shook the maintenance shack. Within two minutes of the attack, the airmen on the flightline got the news over their radio: there had been an explosion at the Khobar Towers.

The blast occurred while MSgt. Joel Schaeffer and A1C. Ken Smith were enroute from the flightline to the compound. The other maintainers considered returning to the Khobar Towers, too—like many others that night, they wanted to help those injured in the explosion. They were instructed, however, to stay where they were and finish repairing the HC–130, and they stuck to their task.[5]

Their commander, Lt. Col. Thomas H. Shafer, praised the way the maintenance team responded to the unprecedented circumstances they faced. He pointed out that, at the time, it had to be assumed the HC–130 would be needed to carry the wounded back home. It was possible, too, that there would be more terrorist attacks: that night, no one could be certain there would be only one bombing. The maintainers, as Colonel Shafer later said, worked under combat conditions to get the 130 fixed.[6]

About four miles east of the flightline, the blast effects were vividly apparent to the airmen who were working out at the Khobar Towers gym. MSgt. Dwayne R. Berry and his exercise partner TSgt. Arthur Bisby stared at the new mirrors around the walls. Then they realized what was wrong with them: one after another, they were cracking and shattering. "They started to explode outward," Sergeant Berry said, "toward us.... The mirrors were going, one by one, boom-boom-boom." Two or three seconds passed and the lights throughout the gym flashed. Berry looked through the door into the gym's new aerobics room and saw the twenty-odd televisions all flare out, each screen flickering at the same time. The blast rocked the all-concrete building and, as he recalled, it "shook like a leaf."[7]

Capt. Russell D. Barile also was working out in the gym that Tuesday night and had reached his next-to-last set of exercises when the bomb exploded. Later he recalled feeling "the air pressure change. There was an audible hissing sound. Then the blast hit. It shook everything. Dust came down from the ceiling." Captain Barile, Sergeants Bisby, Berry, and many others ran out of the gym.[8] They found that the entire Khobar Towers complex was dark, "unbelievably dark," as Berry put it. Despite the darkness, they could see a huge, bluish cloud moving across the compound. "Then we knew," Berry said, "that it was a bomb."[9]

Several hundred yards northeast of the gym, on the sixth floor of Building 127, Lt. Cols. Thomas A. McCarthy and William Miller were waiting for a telephone call and watching *Marathon Man* in their day room, and Lt. Col. Douglas R. Cochran was doing paperwork in his bedroom when the blast struck. Like so many others, Colonel McCarthy later could recall exactly what he thought at the time of the attack. "What ran through my mind," he remembered, "was 'heat lightning,' because it [had been] a fairly clear day." Then Colonel McCarthy heard the explosion and, still sitting in his chair near the suite's picture window, immediately "saw what looked like a brown cloud, coming straight at the window. And at that point I...turned my head, and that's when the whole window blew in. Of course it happened a lot faster than that, but it seemed to happen [slowly]. The window blew in.... The glass went right by me."

The blast knocked Colonel McCarthy out of his chair toward Colonel Miller, whose leg was sliced open by a flying shard, while Colonels Cochran and McCarthy had minor cuts. None of the pilots in Building 127 suffered anything like the injuries of the airmen in Building 131, but of those in 127, Colonel Miller's wound proved the worst.[10]

Colonel Cochran crawled out of his bedroom and Colonel McCarthy heard him curse the perpetrators of the bombing. The circumstances merited the squadron commander's choice of words—and he was not the only person who used strong language that night. An airman in Building 131 who was severely injured in the attack described the first few minutes after the blast: "That was my worst nightmare. I never heard cries like that, cussing like that." And while many cursed, many—Colonel Cochran among them—also called out to their neighbors, to see if they needed help.[11]

Colonel Cochran and the officers with him began to aid one another, a phenomena that by then was taking place all across the compound. He and Colonel McCarthy put a compress on Colonel Miller's leg and got him out of their suite and into the elevator lobby at the center of the floor. Then they began checking on the other rooms. Capt. Craig E. Dye had been talking on the telephone to his wife at the moment of the blast, and the explosion immediately cut off the phones. Lori Dye, like many military wives, had had a number of overseas calls with her husband end abruptly, and she was not alarmed when the line went dead in mid-conversation. McCarthy found Captain Dye in a dazed condition and helped him into the lobby, with Miller. Dr. Mo Treadway treated Miller, and then McCarthy and another officer shouldered him down the stairwell from the sixth floor.[12] Capt. Mark E. Ladtkow had suffered some cuts that later required stiches, and his roomates took him out of the building as well.[13]

Up Eighth Street from Building 127 stood Building 131, the dormitory nearest the blast center, and by far the hardest hit. On its first floor, TSgt. George Burgess and his three suitemates were crammed together cleaning their refrigerator, when the bomb went off. The lights went out and the next thing Sergeant Burgess remembered was being on the floor. Months later, he recalled those first minutes after the attack: "It felt like I was being sand blasted.... It was like I was just in the stream [of a sand blaster]. Then it stopped and it was like, dead silence. Then you could hear water starting to run."

Khobar Towers: Tragedy and Response

Sergeant Burgess heard SrA. Michael J. Dolinar, Jr., nearby, saying that he could not see. "It was *totally* dark," Burgess emphasized. "There was no emergency lighting, or nothing. It was *dark*. It was dark and dusty. If you inhaled, it was like *dirt*." Groping in the pitch black, Burgess found SrA. Mike Dolinar's arm and could feel blood on it. Dolinar had suffered lacerations on his face and elsewhere and would be among the many airmen taken that night to the Ministry of Defense and Aviation (MODA) Hospital, on the civilian side of Dhahran Air Base, near the Dhahran International Airport.[14] When Burgess discovered his suitemate's injury in the darkness, he said to him and the others: "OK, just grab somebody's hand, we're getting out of here."[15]

The airmen found that leaving Building 131 in the immediate wake of the blast was a disorienting experience. Helping one another, they climbed over the rubble. The explosion had destroyed some of the walls, which made their trip particularly confusing. "It was weird," Sergeant Burgess said later, "because some of the walls weren't there.... They were gone.... With the walls not being there, I had no bearings.... There was nothing I could go with."

Once Sergeant Burgess found the flight of steps running down to the ground floor, he regained his orientation. His unit was nearly at the end of its tour, which meant he had been going up and down those stairs for three months. "Once I found those steps," he said later, "I knew how to get out." He *also* admitted later: "I didn't even think of the steps not being there."[16]

As the group left their dormitory, Sergeant Burgess spotted SSgt. Eric D. Ziegler, sitting on the ledge of one of the windows of his first-floor room. With the ground floor under his perch, Sergeant Ziegler sat a story and a half, or well over ten feet, above the dirt and rubble below. He and Burgess were weight lifting partners, lived down the hall from one another, and knew each other well. Burgess heard Ziegler yell down to him: "George, I'm hurt." Burgess called back up: "Okay, 'Z,' just stay there. I'll be right back."[17]

Once Sergeant Burgess and his suitemates were outside the dorm where it was lighter, they could see more of the bomb's damage. "There was glass, debris, and everything," Burgess recalled, "all over the place." In the better lighting, he also decided on their next course of action: "I could see people were starting to gather out in the parking lot, behind the building [131] that the 58th [Fighter Squadron] was staying in.... I could see people starting to gather, over there, so I took [my suitemates] out... and, hand in hand, we went out there."[18]

Sergeant Ziegler, who had called down to Sergeant Burgess, remained perched in his window. Like hundreds of others, later he could describe exactly what he had been doing and thinking at the second the bomb exploded. He experienced one of the strangest coincidences of that tragic night. Ziegler had reset his alarm clock and he was testing its "snooze" setting at precisely the moment of the explosion. In his mind, the two events fused together in a bizarre cause and effect: "I hit my snooze button and when I hit my snooze button, that's when everything blew up. It was like I'd pushed a button, and everything blew up."[19]

The Attack

The two simultaneous events disoriented Sergeant Ziegler, and so did the blast—it threw him across his bedroom. "I really didn't know what was going on," he recalled later, "except [that] I was no longer by my alarm clock, I was on the other side of the room. And I'm a big guy to move."[20]

Sergeant Ziegler worked through his disorientation and an awareness dawned: "I could see that the walls were gone and everything was gone. And I realized that it was something more than just my alarm clock going off.... Then I [thought], I don't know what's happened now, but I've got to get out of here."[21]

As Sergeant Ziegler regained awareness, he realized he couldn't see well because he had been, as he put it later, "smacked in the face" by flying debris. His right eyelid, left cheek, and left side of his nose were cut open and he had a deep puncture wound in his right palm, as well as multiple lacerations in his scalp, left arm, and right knee. Despite these injuries, Ziegler managed to crawl across his room to a window.[22]

"I thought that [window] was a doorway," Sergeant Ziegler related. "I saw a light, it was a window, and I sat up in this window." Perched more than ten feet above the ground, Ziegler could see below him groups of people who had escaped Building 131. Some of them yelled up at him, "Don't jump! Don't jump!"[23]

Sergeant Ziegler had no intention of jumping; he stayed put. The damage to the right side of his face and the dust in his eyes still prevented him from seeing much, but he heard a voice he recognized, belonging to Sergeant Burgess. "I could see lights...that was it," Ziegler recounted. "But I heard his voice. He called me 'Z.'" Ziegler yelled down for assistance, and Burgess called back the assurance he would return to help.[24]

Sergeant Burgess led his companions to the parking lot and helped Senior Airman Dolinar get seated on a curb. SrA. Steve Jerwoski, one of Burgess's suitemates, had left the group and escaped on his own. When Burgess reached the the parking lot, he realized that there were only two, not three, airmen with him. He ran back to his first-floor suite to look for Senior Airman Jerwoski, and then he went to help Sergeant Ziegler.[25]

"I went back across the hall," Sergeant Burgess related, "into Z's apartment.... There he was, sitting on his window sill there." Burgess helped Sergeant Ziegler out of the window and from the room. It was an emotional trip for the two airmen. Three of Ziegler's suitemates had been killed in the explosion, and Burgess later said: "This is where it kind of got a little tough on me. I actually had to climb over some people to get to him."[26]

Sergeant Burgess helped Sergeant Ziegler into his bedroom, where he could put on a pair of shoes. The attack had come at a nighttime hour when many dorm residents were in slippers, socks, or barefoot. The explosion had blown windows inward, and strewn glass became the most dangerous hazard left in the wake of the blast. Ziegler was one of many people who, injured or not, put shoes on as soon after the attack as they could. In Building 127, Dr. Mo Treadway and others used the contents of the large bottles that commonly sat on the tops of office water coolers to wash the glass off the feet of some of the residents of that dormitory, making it safer for them to put on their boots or shoes.[27]

Sergeant Ziegler had no water cooler at hand, but he got his shoes on, wrapped himself in a blanket, and Sergeant Burgess helped him out of the suite. They soon met SSgt. Andre L. Stanton of the 412th Operations Support Squadron, a resident of the fifth floor who had suffered a deep cut on the right side of his face and others to his nose and upper arm.[28] Capt. Russ Barile, who saw Sergeant Stanton that night, said he "looked like somebody had hit him in the head with a hammer." Capt. Michael D. Morelock, a pilot who lived on the seventh floor, helped Stanton out of the building and later the airman was taken to the MODA Hospital.[29]

By the time Sergeant Stanton met Sergeants Ziegler and Burgess, he already had received assistance from Captain Morelock and he would receive more help, too, during the hours to come. By the same token, Stanton was one of many people that night who, although badly injured themselves, helped others who needed it. He hooked Ziegler by the arm and they went out of Building 131 together. Burgess stayed in the dorm and began searching for others who had been wounded.[30]

Spending any time at all in Building 131 after the blast was dangerous, because there was no certainty that the structure would remain sound, or that there would be no more explosions. Yet Sergeant Burgess and many others returned to their dorms that night, time and again, to help their injured comrades. When, several months later, Burgess was asked how often he had gone back into Building 131, he answered: "I remember at least four times, and I know there was more."[31]

The security police rendered much good work, too, in the immediate wake of the blast. SSgt. Alfredo R. Guerrero, the first person to spot the deadly truck, had been spreading the warning along Building 131's sixth floor and was making his last stop on that level of the dorm when the bomb denotated. "I just remember hearing a large bang," he recounted soon afterward. "It went dark and I was spun around." The blast ripped Sergeant Guerrero's brick radio out of his grip and rendered his hand numb for the next two days, but the SP was able to stay on his feet.[32]

A resident who was walking near Sergeant Guerrero was knocked to the floor and some rubble landed on him. The security policeman pulled the semiconscious man to his feet and stayed with him until he began to regain his faculties. The dazed airman could stand on his own, but could not walk well. Guerrero got an arm around his waist and helped him down the stairs. By the time they reached the third or second floor, the injured man had exhausted his energy. "You can make it," Guerrero convinced him, and the two eventually made their way into the dirt and gravel parking lot southwest of the dorm where, by then, a number of people had gathered. The security policeman saw to it that the resident got into a vehicle that took him to a Dhahran hospital.[33]

A1C. Christopher Wagar had left the roof ahead of Sergeant Guerrero and SrA. Corey Grice, and had alerted the residents of the seventh, or top, floor. He later candidly acknowledged that his first thought that night had been the very human one of self preservation. "I saw my life flash before my eyes," Airman Wagar said, "and I just wanted to get out of there." Yet like so many others that night, he did his duty. Wagar raised the alarm along the seventh floor, while Guerrero worked the sixth and Senior Airman Grice the fifth. Wagar's next objective was the fourth level and he headed for the stairs. "It happened so fast," he later recalled. "Before I even got [to] the stairwell, the bomb exploded and threw me against the wall."[34]

Among the many Wagar had warned were Capts. Michael D. Morelock and Matthew Winkler, pilots of the deployed 71st Rescue Squadron. These two officers had started down the stairwell, Captain Winkler ahead of Morelock. They walked at a normal pace, as Winkler later described it, "in no rush, in no fear of my life." They had reached the landing between the seventh and sixth floors and were facing a window on that plateau when the bomb went off.[35]

"Because I was near a window," Captain Winkler recounted, "I felt the heat and I had seen the bright, orangish flash." He described the shock of the blast: "It was just *massive*. You become a rag doll. It just *hits* you." The window glass exploded into the two pilots and Captain Morelock said months later: "I remember feeling that. And that's really all I remember, until picking myself up off the floor. To this day, I don't know if I was unconscious or not."[36]

The blast hurled the two officers off of the stairwell wall behind them and threw them into a heap on the steps back up toward the seventh floor.[37] Captain Winkler, who had been nearer the landing window, had his left arm cut to the bone and suffered other severe wounds. He would be among the many patients later taken to the MODA Hospital.[38] Like a large number of the Khobar veterans, Morelock minimized his own injuries as "superficial," but he had, in fact, suffered cuts on his face, head, and neck from the flying glass. His lacerations were serious enough that later that night a pararescue jumper put him on an intravenous line and he was briefly hospitalized. Col. Thomas R. Friers, commander of the 1st Rescue Group, who saw Morelock when he returned to Florida around midnight of June 27/28, said the young pilot was "terribly beat-up looking. His face looked like he'd been in a fight with a pit bull."[39]

As Captain Morelock regained his senses, he—like Sergeant Burgess and many others that night—was impressed by the extent of the darkness. "The dust and debris was still hanging in the air," he recalled, "so you couldn't see anything. No outside light was getting in; it was very dark." Captain Winkler was injured more severely than Morelock and was less conscious than his roomate, but he, too, remembered the total darkness around them. As he put it: "You cannot believe how dark it was in that building.... You could barely see a foot or two in front of you, right after the bombing."[40]

Groping in the blackness, Captain Morelock managed to stand up. He was functioning, but still dazed, and had no sense of how little time had passed since the explosion. Morelock yelled down the stairs for help: it was only later that he realized that it was far too soon after the attack for any medical personnel to be responding.[41]

Captain Morelock then tried shouting up to the seventh floor. This time he got an answer: a call for help from Capt. Thomas F. Edman, the third resident of his suite. Morelock believed he shouldn't try to move Captain Winkler, because it was still too dark to see the extent of his injuries. He decided it would be better to return to the seventh floor and help Captain Edman and the others there. Winkler was conscious enough that he too heard Edman's calls, and he understood—and didn't feel abandoned—when Morelock told him he was going to check on their suitemate.[42]

So much debris had fallen into the stairwell that Captain Morelock could not walk up the half flight of steps. He crawled on his hands and knees and groped in front of himself, wary of encountering a sudden dropoff. Morelock and Captain Edman called back and forth to one another, while the pilot made his way slowly toward the navigator. They met near the door to their suite and Morelock led Edman back down to where Captain Winkler lay on the stairs.[43]

On the way down, Captain Edman told his suitemate he had injured his hip. Later he would be taken to King Fahd University Hospital in Dhahran, where the staff confirmed that the blast indeed had fractured his femur and damaged one of his kidneys. Among the hundreds injured by the bomb, he was one of seven who were listed as severely injured.[44] While Captain Morelock was helping Edman down the stairwell, his own head injuries were bleeding heavily. He took his shirt off and his suitemate helped him get it tied around some of his cuts.[45]

By the time the two officers made their way to where Captain Winkler was lying on the stairs, Captain Morelock's vision had improved enough that he could see how badly his suitemate was injured. He decided it would be best to leave Captain Edman with Winkler, while he returned again to look for others on the seventh floor. Morelock found that he now could see well enough to make this second trip by walking rather than crawling. Enough time had passed for some of the dust to settle, and his eyes had begun to adjust to the reduced lighting.[46]

Captain Morelock went into the suite of Lieutenant Colonel Shafer, the commander of the deployed 71st Rescue Squadron, and Capt. Christopher J. Adams, a pilot and the deployment operations officer. The visibility was far better here than in the stairwell, because the explosion had torn off the northern face of building and lights from Dhahran reached into what remained of the rooms in this part of the structure. Morelock found Captain Adams mortally wounded. The blast had struck as Lieutenant Colonel Shafer had been returning to his bedroom for a pair of shoes. When Morelock reached Shafer, the lieutenant colonel was dazed by the explosion, he was still shoeless, and his feet had been cut by glass. He later was treated at the Arabian American Oil Company Hospital. Morelock knew that any route out of the building would be covered with glass shards and other debris. The two men agreed that it would be best if the captain went alone to get medical help.[47]

Morelock took the stairs back down, stopping to reassure Edman that he would get assistance for him, Winkler, and the others still in the building. Once he was back in the interior of the dormitory, the lighting was still poor. The captain realized that if he searched every floor by himself in the darkness, this would delay getting medical help. So he stopped at each level and called in, thinking that if he heard a response, he would offer aid and if not, he would continue down the stairwell.[48]

The Attack

The captain got no replies on the sixth or fifth floors. On the fourth he encountered Sergeant Stanton. Although badly injured, Stanton by then had made his way down one flight of stairs, from his fifth-floor suite to the fourth level. Morelock made no more stops, but instead took Stanton directly out of Building 131 and got him seated at a picnic table. Although dazed and hurt, Stanton later came around enough that he was able to help Ziegler out of the dormitory.[49]

Leaving Sergeant Stanton resting at the picnic table, Captain Morelock kept his commitment to Captain Edman and the others that he would find medical help for them. The captain soon spotted MSgt. William F. Sine, a pararescue jumper of the deployed 71st Rescue Squadron. A resident of Building 131, Sergeant Sine had just walked out of his room and headed for the elevator lobby when the bomb exploded. Knocked to the floor, he suffered a severe contusion of his right calf. The blast also wrenched the sergeant's back and left his right arm greatly swollen and hanging nearly useless. Despite these injuries, Sine was helping others soon after the attack.[50]

Captain Morelock, Sergeant Sine, and SSgt. Matthew A. Wells, another PJ, went to Captain Winkler's aid. By the time they reached the landing, Captain Edman had Winkler up on his feet and had an arm around him. Sine took off his shirt and tied it into a tourniquet on the captain's dangerously cut left arm.[51] To free the PJs to help others, Morelock offered to take Winkler out of the building. Sine and Sergeant Wells agreed and headed up to see what they could do for those still on the seventh floor. Morelock, Edman, and Winkler left Building 131 together, slowly working their way down the stairwell.[52]

These three officers, like many others that night, had been alerted to the impending attack by the security police. While Airman Wagar, Sergeant Guerrero, and Senior Airman Grice had warned them and the other residents of the upper floors to evacuate Building 131, SrA. Craig J. Dick had sped to the scene in his humvee. He had parked the vehicle and was running hard toward the dormitory's rear entrance when the bomb exploded. The explosion threw him about fifty feet and knocked him unconscious.[53] The shock wave bruised one of Senior Airman Dick's eardrums and ripped away his uniform. One of his fellow SPs offered a short, honest description: it "blew his pants off."[54]

A security police patrol soon found Senior Airman Dick, and a crowd gathered around the stricken SP. The group was willing to help him, but was hesitating, uncertain how to move him safely, when Capt. Lawrence Branch, a resident of Building 131 who had escaped the attack with minor injuries, arrived on the scene. During the first minutes after the attack, Captain Branch had realized that first aid supplies would be badly needed and had gathered a large bag of sheets, pillow cases, and other pieces of cloth. He used a fitted sheet to create a make-shift litter and helped the group get Dick on to it. Volunteers then carried the SP to an ambulance that took him to the MODA Hospital.[55]

Senior Airman Dick's bruised eardrum prevented him from being put on a medical evacuation flight right away, and instead he returned to duty. Brigadier

Khobar Towers: Tragedy and Response

General Schwalier was impressed at seeing the SP at work soon after the attack and commended him on this, and on his heroics at Building 131. Airman Dick, like many, many others, modestly replied that he was only doing his job. He eventually boarded one of the medical evacuation flights to the Landstuhl Regional Medical Center, in Landstuhl, Germany, where the staff examined his bruised eardrum.[56]

Senior Airman Dick's charred vehicle continued to attract attention, for some time after the bombing. "When I saw the humvee the next day," SrA. Ronald J. Biggs, Jr., said, "it was completely burnt on the inside. The seats were [blown into] the back of it.... It was one of those things you hear about, but never see." Many who walked by the hummer mistakenly assumed Dick had been *in* it at the time of the blast. Looking at the blackened chassis and interior, they concluded that his survival had been a miracle.[57]

Chapter Five

In the Wake

The terrorist bombing of the Khobar Towers killed nineteen United States Air Force personnel. Eight of them were members of the 58th Fighter Squadron, stationed at Eglin Air Force, Florida: TSgt. Daniel B. Cafourek of Watertown, South Dakota; Sgt. Millard D. Campbell, Angelton, Texas; SrA. Earl F. Cartrette, Jr., Sellersburg, Indiana; MSgt. Kendall K. Kitson, Jr., Yukon, Oklahoma; A1C. Brent E. Marthaler, Cambridge, Minnesota; A1C. Brian W. McVeigh, Debary, Florida; A1C. Joseph E. Rimkus, Edwardsville, Illinois; and A1C. Joshua E. Woody, Corning, California.[1] Four more belonged to other units from Eglin Air Force Base: TSgt. Patrick P. Fennig, Greendale, Wisconsin, 60th Fighter Squadron; A1C. Peter J. Morgera, Stratham, New Hampshire, 33d Operations Support Squadron; TSgt. Thanh V. (Gus) Nguyen, Panama City, Florida, 33d Logistics Group; and SrA. Jeremy A. Taylor, Rosehill, Kansas, 33d Maintenance Squadron.[2]

Five of the deceased served in the 71st Rescue Squadron, stationed at Patrick Air Force Base, Florida. They were: Capt. Christopher J. Adams of Massapequa Park, New York; Capt. L. Timothy Haun, Clovis, California; MSgt. Michael G. Heiser, Palm Coast, Florida; SSgt. Kevin J. Johnson, Shreveport, Louisiana; and A1C. Justin R. Wood, Modesto, California.[3]

In addition to Eglin and Patrick, two other bases suffered a fatality. Staff Sgt. Ronald L. King from Battle Creek, Michigan, was assigned to the 55th Contracting Squadron at Offutt Air Force Base, Nebraska; and A1C. Christopher B. Lester of Pineville, West Virginia, was a member of the 88th Civil Engineering Squadron at Wright-Patterson Air Force Base, Ohio.[4]

Eighteen of the nineteen fatalities occurred in Building 131 and the other on the fourth floor of Building 133, to the west of it. The Jersey barriers on the north side of Thirty-first Street mitigated the effects of the blast against the ground level of dormitory 131. One airman was killed on this floor, but most of the fatalities took place on the three levels above it: eight on the first floor; three on the second; and three on the third. Two deaths occurred on the sixth level and one on the seventh.[5]

Lt. Col. (Dr.) Douglas J. Robb, the senior medical officer at the Khobar Towers that night, pronounced the nineteen airmen dead on the scene. He stated that the autopsies later revealed that the leading causes of death were flying glass and blunt trauma. "The severity of their injuries," Dr. Robb said, "indicated that none would

Khobar Towers: Tragedy and Response

have survived even with the best of immediate emergency medical care. The one fatality in Building 133, removed from the strongest area of the blast wave, had a large shard of glass sever his aorta—an immediately fatal injury."[6]

The bomb that killed these nineteen people also wounded hundreds of others. On July 22, the Personnel Support for Contingency Operations (PERSCO) office of the 4404th Mission Support Squadron reported to Headquarters Air Force Personnel Center (AFPC) at Randolph Air Force Base, Texas, that 327 airmen had been injured in the bombing. It categorized them as 2 very severely injured, 7 severely injured, and 318 not severely injured.[7]

In addition to the 327 reported by the PERSCO office, many others suffered less serious injuries. Dr. Robb, who was best placed to know, put the total number of patients treated at 519, of whom 317 were cared for at the Khobar Towers clinic. The other 202 were taken to hospitals in Dhahran, where 71 were admitted and 131 were treated and released.[8]

The total number of injured probably will remain unknown. In addition to the 519 patients accounted for by Dr. Robb, many other airmen refused to seek treatment and their injuries went unreported. A large number of people who were hurt that night looked around and saw scores of others who were injured much more seriously than themselves, and they refused to seek aid. Capt. (Dr.) R. Morris Treadway, Jr., a flight surgeon of the 58th Fighter Squadron, stated in this regard: "We really had to go out and *look* for people that were injured as a result of the bombing."[9]

As time passed, some of those who were less severely injured came forward. Dr. Robb said this process began the day after the bombing, when people came in "with glass in their feet, their hands, their knees, who didn't bother to come in that night" because they had been helping others who had been more seriously hurt. He saw "a pretty steady" flow of these less severely injured patients for about two days. After yet more time passed, a larger number presented themselves. Six months after the bombing, a few Dhahran veterans still were coming forward for the first time and seeking care at the base hospital at Eglin Air Force Base, Florida. By November 1997, 525 officers and airmen had received the Purple Heart for the Khobar Towers, and AFPC continued to process nominations for this medal.[10]

None of the United States Army personnel stationed at Dhahran were wounded by the bomb. The number of civilian casualties, on the other hand, was high. Nicholas Burns, a State Department spokesman who visited Dhahran soon after the attack, reported that 147 Saudis and 150 Bangladeshis were wounded. These early figures probably were too low. Air Force medical officers reported an estimated 350–400 injured civilians. "We'll never know [the number]," Dr. Robb stated, "because [the Saudis] don't talk about it like we do, but there were several hundred [Saudi and other] civilian casualties."[11]

When American medical personnel visited the Dhahran hospitals to attend to Air Force patients after the bombing, they saw a number of wounded, and some deceased, Arabs in the emergency rooms. The Ministry of Defense and Aviation Hospital alone treated 150 Saudi casualties. Secretary of State Warren Christopher

In the Wake

visited this facility on the day after the bombing and called on two injured Saudi children who had been playing near the compound when the bomb exploded.[12]

While these human losses were of paramount importance, the bomb also caused extensive physical damage all across the Khobar Towers compound. Teams formed by the wing's civil engineering squadron assessed Building 131, nearest the blast, as "destroyed." They determined that the three structures closest to this dormitory, Buildings 129, 130, and 133, were uninhabitable. In addition to these four facilities, the CE teams initially found that five others on the northern end of the compound—101, 104, 127, 128, and 132—also could not be used.[13]

Other buildings as well, all across the complex, suffered damage. Capt. Russell D. Barile, a pilot with the 71st Rescue Squadron, described a typical room in Building 103, a dormitory nearly way half across the compound from the truck bomb: "It looked like someone had taken a ... hand grenade and set if off right outside the window. The glass was all shattered. There were some mattresses turned over, things laying all over the room." It appeared, Captain Barile thought, as if someone had set off a satchel charge outside of Building 103. The destruction was so extensive that at first he believed that this dormitory, far southwest of the bomb, had been the focal point of the attack.[14]

The structure that, in fact, *had* been nearest the bomb, Building 131, suffered the greatest damage. The explosion ripped away this dormitory's entire northern face. Capt. Michael D. Morelock got a close look that night at this damage, from the interior of the building. Not long after the explosion, Captain Morelock entered the suite of Lt. Col. Thomas H. Shafer and Capt. Christopher J. Adams, which was on the seventh floor and faced north. Entering their quarters, he became aware for the first time of the extent of the dormitory's destruction. "I went into their suite," Morelock said later, "and it was when I walked into the main living room area of their suite that I realized the damage to the building.... An entire wall was gone and other walls were buckled." The northern facade of the dormitory had fallen straight down, creating a large pile of rubble. In addition to tearing off the north wall, the blast had ripped pieces of concrete from the Jersey barriers across the street and thrown them into the rooms on the dormitory's ground floor and two or three levels above it.[15]

The bomb created an enormous crater, with its center about 80 feet from the front of Building 131. TSgt. George Burgess later recalled how that night he had crawled across to the shorn edge of this dormitory and looked straight down from a height of four or five floors. He found that the crater was so large that he couldn't see all of it without moving his head. Sergeant Burgess remembered thinking at the time: "'Somebody fired a rocket at us, or a missile.' ... It was a *big* hole."[16] The crater in fact proved to be about 55 feet in diameter, as a study team from the Defense Special Weapons Agency and the Army Corps of Engineers later determined. It was 16 feet deep, relative to the original ground surface, and it displaced an estimated 28,000 cubic feet of dirt.[17]

The explosion also inflicted major structural damage to Building 133, a dormitory to the west of 131. The blast wave hit the eastern face of this structure, which stood about 400 feet from the truck, and rebounded. Across the whole complex, the explosion wrecked door frames and blasted window panes into dangerous spears of glass. In almost every case, these shards blew back into the rooms, not out, and thereby caused most of the injuries.[18]

The bomb responsible for this physical destruction and human suffering was an enormous weapon. Soon after the attack, the DSWA-ACE team estimated its yield to be the equivalent of 23,000 pounds of TNT.[19] Compared with other bombs familiar to Americans in the mid-1990s, the explosive tonnage of the Dhahran weapon was greater than either the one detonated in February 1993 at the World Trade Center in New York City or in April 1995 at the Alfred P. Murrah Building in Oklahoma City.[20]

This massive bomb left chaos in its immediate wake. MSgt. Dwayne Berry described the mayhem that he and Capt. Russ Barile found when they reached Building 131 soon after the detonation. "By the time we got there," he recounted, "there were people coming out, I mean, severely injured people; people were yelling, people were screaming, people were crying. Smoke was everywhere. Bits of clutter and debris were everywhere." Maj. Bennie L. Umstead II, who had checked into Building 101 for the night, recalled: "A lot of people were just sitting on the curbs, crying." Halfway across the compound from the bomb stood the converted garage that housed both an auditorium (the home of the Right Start briefings) and the "Khobar Konnection." In this recreation center, the explosion threw people across the room, flipped over tables, and filled the air with a smoky dust from the concrete walls. "Get out of the building," someone called out, "before the next one!" The roomful of a hundred or so people headed for the exits. On the northern end of the compound in the wake of the explosion, Lt. Col. Thomas A. McCarthy recalled, "Rumors were running amuck."[21]

The security police moved promptly to get control of the situation. SSgt. Alfredo R. Guerrero had radioed in his sighting of the truck at about 9:50 p.m. Within four minutes of his report, Lt. Col. James J. Traister, the commander of the wing's security police squadron, had initiated a 100 percent recall of the SPs on the compound that night. All security policemen at their posts called in on their brick radios and accounted for themselves. The SPs also immediately deployed a cordon around Building 120, their headquarters and armory, which was in the southeast quadrant of the compound.[22]

At 9:55 p.m., no more than two minutes after the explosion, Lieutenant Colonel Traister arrived at Building 131. He reported that there were many injured people, not only in that dormitory, but in all of the facilities on the northern half of the compound. Traister dispatched twenty-five security policemen to search and clear all of the buildings north of Thirty-third Street, the east-west avenue that bisected the complex. He also instructed these SPs to begin administering self-aid and buddy care, the Air Force's term for its first aid program.[23]

Acting on guidance that Brig. Gen. Terry Schwalier, the commander of the 4404th Composite Wing (Provisional), gave over his brick radio, the security police also quickly activated a temporary Disaster Control Group near the scene of the bombing. This was an improvised unit of security policemen who would use their own radios to manage communications in the immediate wake of the attack. Later, when time permitted choosing a site and getting hardware in place, communication specialists and other airmen would establish a Site Recovery Center, from which the wing's formal Disaster Control Group would manage the unit's return to normalcy.[24]

Even before the security police had activated their temporary DCG, they responded to a report of another attack against the compound. Shortly after the detonation,[25] airmen began seeing Saudis climbing over and under the compound's perimeter fence. These proved to be well-meaning locals, who were coming to the aid of the Americans. At the time and under the circumstances, the security police and others assumed that these would-be helpers surging toward the fence represented a wave of follow-on attackers.

At 9:57 p.m. Sergeant Guerrero got on his radio again and reported that groups of Saudis had been seen trying to enter the compound. Just four minutes had passed since the explosion that had killed nineteen people and injured hundreds of others. In the darkness and confusion, the security police quite properly assumed that terrorists were launching a follow-on attack. Twenty SPs secured the compound's perimeter, some of them coming voluntarily, and all of them moving quickly. Guerrero recounted: "You know, every SP there, as soon as they heard what was going on, immediately grabbed guns and helped out. There were people in shorts and stuff; they didn't bother to get in uniform." A survivor later recalled: "One thing that really sticks with me from that night is the sight of an airman in a T-shirt, shorts, [and] flip-flops standing guard with an M–16 at the door to the chapel."[26] The security police detained at least two of the intruders, handcuffing them to the perimeter fence.[27] Within minutes, the SPs had established a secure cordon, running along Thirty-third Street and the western, northern, and eastern boundaries of the compound.[28]

Sergeant Guerrero later described the bogus alarm: "It was chaos, because we had the local nationals climbing the fence, wanting to help, but we didn't know that, at the time.... So you could hear over the [security police] radio, 'So-and-so coming over the fence line, on this perimeter.'" Maj. Cynthia D. Coles, a nurse who was outside Building 133, recalled that there were confusing rumors of another bombing or some other attack. Dr. Mo Treadway was with a group of about fifty people near Building 127 when "someone came over... yelling and screaming that there were individuals in fatigues, with guns, climbing over the fence. Potentially, we thought we were under a ground attack, with guys crawling under the fence with guns. It was kind of a strange situation."[29]

The false alarm died down, and order began to emerge slowly in its wake. Soon after Lieutenant Colonel Traister reached Building 131, the first medical personnel began arriving on the scene. They told him that the designated casualty collection point was the Desert Rose Inn, the dining facility—the "chow hall"—that stood in the middle of the southern half of the complex. Its location carried two advantages: it was in the interior of the compound and it was just east of Building 111, the medical clinic. Significantly, these two facilities—the dining hall and the clinic—had

Khobar Towers: Tragedy and Response

medical supplies, water, tables, and other features that would prove extremely valuable during an emergency.[30]

Within minutes after the attack, officers of the Air Force Office of Special Investigations and the security police began directing people to move from the stricken northern end of the compound to the Desert Rose Inn and to help the injured reach the medical clinic. The security police quickly deployed teams, Major Umstead recalled, "on the perimeter, ushering people [to the Desert Rose Inn and the clinic]. They had guards, ushering people in—and to keep people away from the perimeter."[31]

Very shortly after 10 p.m. fire chief MSgt. Wayne Mello began using the bullhorn on his crash rescue vehicle, instructing people to go to the Desert Rose Inn and directing the firefighters of the wing's civil engineering squadron to establish a triage and patient care area there.[32] SSgt. Matthew A. Wells, a pararescue jumper who was in the gym at the time of the explosion, was among the many who responded promptly. After the casualty collection point was set up in front of the Desert Rose Inn, Sergeant Wells headed for Building 131—helping the wounded he encountered along the way and telling those who were able to walk that they should get themselves to the chow hall.[33]

By then many of the wounded were headed toward the dining hall: the false alarm of a follow-on attack had encouraged people to move quickly into the interior of the compound. Maj. Cynthia Coles described how the uncertainty of the situation motivated people to take action. "The rumor came around that they were coming again," she remembered, "and we weren't sure whether another explosion was coming, or whatever. But everyone just said, 'Run to the center of the compound,' where they had determined that if anything happened, it was the safest place, the furthest away from the perimeter." Lt. Col. (Chaplain) Dennis E. Aleson, the senior chaplain at the Khobar Towers, recalled: "We were all basically instructed to go the center of the compound, amidst all the confusion." Dr. Treadway pointed out that "a lot of people" started moving when they heard the rumor of another attack, because they had neither weapons to protect themselves nor radios to tell them what was happening.[34]

The false alarm also speeded up the task of moving the injured to the clinic. Lt. Col. Douglas R. Cochran, commander of the 58th Fighter Squadron, directly connected the two events: "We [heard] someone running, screaming at the top of their lungs, 'They're coming through the fence! They're coming through the fence!' ... We were told the triage area and casualty collection point was right outside the chow hall. So we grabbed everybody and just hustled over there." Lt. Col. Thomas McCarthy recounted: "We [had] started putting people on trucks and moving them into the interior of the compound. [The false alarm] made people put people on trucks a lot quicker and get back to the interior a lot quicker." Dr. Treadway said that during the confusion caused by the spurious alarm he and others "tried to throw a couple more people on that truck, and sent it on. Then we ran to the other side of the base, away from Building 127, and tried to figure out what was going on."[35]

In the Wake

As time passed and no second attack occurred, an attitude of calm began to develop. Within a surprisingly short period of time, a sense of order, and purpose, emerged. Chaplain Aleson recalled: "There was a momentary panic there, when somebody said there was . . . some other [threatening] activity about to happen and everybody started running in panic—but quickly calmed down." Capt. Mike Morelock was surprised how soon after the bombing order was restored: "It was amazing to me, it didn't seem to take much time at all."[36]

As the airmen turned their attention to helping one another, the sense of calm was strengthened. Major Coles vividly recalled that "the fear, and the worry about the bomb, and everything else went out the window. . . . I had my task—to do what I was trained to do—to help treat, to help take care of, the people who were injured." SSgt. Rudolph Grimm II, a dental technician, described the tenor of things at the clinic that night: "Everybody was calm. There was no screaming. People were helping other people." At a "hot wash" debriefing held on July 3, Dr. Robb looked at the other medical personnel gathered around a table with him and asked, "Was it just *me*, or was there a sense of calm that night?" To a person, the others agreed.[37]

The sense of calm that Dr. Robb identified rested on a foundation of moral and physical courage. The training the airmen had received in medical care and other areas proved helpful, but it was not the fundamental reason the recovery began as soon as it did. Training reflected a larger factor: the moral strength displayed that night by the personnel of the United States Air Force. Brigadier General Schwalier later stated: "To me, the *real* reason for the calm was the *character* of those 2,000 determined Air Force men and women . . . character that was manifested that night in the professionalism, sense of mission, selflessness, and righteous patriotism displayed."[38]

The chaplains witnessed the moral courage of the airmen, and worked to further it. Like so many others, Chaplain Aleson, the wing's senior chaplain, had been in his bedroom at the moment of the blast. And like a number of others, that night would have been his last in his quarters; the next day he would have returned to the States. The 4404th had three other chaplains, but at the time of the attack, Maj. (Chaplain) John Kovalcin, accompanied by A1C. Cynthia Bailey, was making a site visit to Seeb Air Base, Oman, and Maj. (Chaplain) Kevin Boll and SSgt. Michael O'Donnell were making one to Taif Air Base, Saudi Arabia. Only Capt. (Father) Thomas Angelo, the wing's Roman Catholic chaplain, remained with Aleson that night at the Khobar Towers. Aleson later said that, during the first minutes after the explosion, "an overwhelming feeling" settled over him. Then he quickly came to terms with the reality that "there were just two of us there. There were many, many areas of need, that we needed to be at. And only two of us to do so."[39]

Joined by his partner on his chapel readiness team, TSgt. Donnell Thompson, and by Father Angelo, Chaplain Aleson headed for the interior of the complex. The professionals of his career field, he explained, follow a piece of simple guidance: "Our number one rule is 'Go to the point of greatest need for our services as chaplains.' . . . And that was the clinic." In the area around that building, Chaplains

Khobar Towers: Tragedy and Response

Aleson and Angelo and Sergeant Thompson gave prayers, offered counseling, and—like everyone else around them—did whatever they could to aid the wounded. "We helped bear litters," Aleson recounted, "handed out bottled water. We moved among the literally hundreds of people who were on the ground outside [the clinic]."[40]

The senior officers of the 4404th Composite Wing (Provisional) responded quickly to the attack. The unit's commander, Brigadier General Schwalier, was at a desk in Building 101, the visiting officers quarters where he and his group commanders resided. One of the security measures that the wing had underway addressed the fact that all of wing's senior leaders lived in the same building. As Lieutenant Colonel Traister had stated, "If someone attacks [Building 101], we stand a good chance that we could lose our command element in one stroke." In view of this, the wing was in the process of changing the housing arrangements of its leaders. General Schwalier's successor, Brig. Gen. Daniel M. Dick, soon would arrive in Dhahran and his quarters would be in Building 107, at the center of the compound, rather than 101, near the western perimeter.[41] As the new group commanders arrived, they would take various housing, dispersed throughout the compound.[42]

In the meantime, Brigadier General Schwalier continued to use the visiting officers quarters. He already had written his end-of-tour report, and that night he was composing a letter of welcome to his successor, Brigadier General Dick, who at the moment was enroute to Saudi Arabia.[43] General Schwalier had completed three words ("Dan, Welcome to") and had begun a fourth ("Dhahran"), when the blast rocked his apartment. The force of the explosion pulled the commander's hand across his stationery, cutting short the intended "Dhahran" and rendering it "Dh—."[44] "I remember *jumping* out of my chair," Schwalier later recalled, "running a few feet behind me, to get to a window and looking out . . . and seeing a black cloud . . . rising." The explosion shattered every window in the commander's quarters and upset all the furniture. The rooms, in the words of one witness, were "absolutely trashed."[45]

Brigadier General Schwalier quickly put on his flight suit, picked up his brick radio, and checked on Col. Dale Bible. This officer, the commander of the 4409th Operations Group at Riyadh Air Base, had come to Dhahran for the change of command ceremony and was staying in the same suite as the wing commander. General Schwalier then ran across the hall to look in on Maj. Gen. Kurt B. Anderson, the commander of the Joint Task Force Southwest Asia (JTF-SWA), who also had come to Dhahran for the ceremony, and had arrived that afternoon.[46]

General Anderson's executive officer, Major Umstead, was hit by the blast wave while he was in the kitchen of their suite. The force of the explosion threw him across that room into a wall and onto the floor, and he suffered some lacerations.[47] Anderson, who had retired for the night, was cut on his arm by glass, a wound which later became infected. The JTF-SWA commander gave no thought to the injury at the time.[48]

Generals Anderson and Schwalier ran together down the stairs from their sixth-floor suites. They jogged out of Building 101 and into the large parking lot on the northern end of the compound. They then sprinted across this lot to its western end, near the softball fields, where General Schwalier's sport utility vehicle was parked.[49]

While the two senior officers were running toward Brigadier General Schwalier's SUV, the wing commander heard over his brick radio the false report, mentioned earlier, that the compound's fence had been attacked.[50] Reaching his vehicle, General Schwalier encountered the airman who served as his personal security officer. The senior officer was immediately impressed that this young NCO was ready to do his job: protect his wing commander. General Schwalier told his personal security officer that he and General Anderson would take his SUV to the bomb site, not far to the northeast. He instructed the airman to follow him, in his own vehicle. Schwalier later praised the way this young man performed his duty, not only during the trip the two generals made to Building 131, but for long afterward. The wing commander related: "I'll tell you, for the rest of that night, for the rest of the next two days, there wasn't a time—and I was in my [SUV] and I was moving a lot—there wasn't a time I didn't see him." Holding his hands closely together, the general stated: "He was never more than this far away from me."[51]

While Brigadier General Schwalier drove from the northern parking lot toward Building 131, he saw fire chief Mello, who by then was using his bull horn to direct people to the Desert Rose Inn. The wing commander questioned him and quickly learned that Lieutenant Colonel Traister was at Building 131 and that the compound's perimeter was being secured. At that point, General Schwalier later said, he became "convinced that we're already taking care" of perimeter security. His next thought was: "I need to get my chiefs together, and we need to talk about what's going on."[52]

Brigadier General Schwalier used his radio to call Col. Gary S. Boyle, the wing's support group commander and directed him to assemble the wing's battle staff "immediately." During those first minutes after the bombing, General Schwalier talked over his radio with Colonel Boyle, with Lieutenant Colonel Traister, and Colonel Bible. He also was of course in direct communication with Major General Anderson, who remained with him.[53]

At Brigadier General Schwalier's direction, the wing battle staff was to convene in the Wing Operations Center (WOC) in "Tadtown," the collection of command and operations buildings located on a section of Dhahran Air Base that was about four miles from the Khobar Towers. This area had been created as a result of the Saudi policy of keeping the key activities of their American guests grouped together in a sector away from the civilian flightlines of the Dhahran International Airport. "Tadtown" was a piece of Air Force slang—its origin was connected to the first name of then-Brig. Gen. Tad J. Oelstrom, who had commanded the 4404th Wing from May until October 1992.[54]

While General Schwalier was driving from Building 131 to the Tadtown WOC, as he later recalled, "I remember talking" to General Anderson "and saying . . . I've got to take care of the casualities—step number one. Step number two, I've got to account for my people." He continued: "And the third [step] was, I've got to assess the damage . . . . So those are the tasks that I took with me to the command post."[55]

61

Khobar Towers: Tragedy and Response

The battle staff assembled at 10:15 p.m. "The group commanders," Brigadier General Schwalier stated, "were there very quickly." The wing commander swiftly related to his subordinates the three imperative tasks he had framed in his own mind, while enroute to the meeting: take care of the casualties; account for the wing's members; and assess the damage.[56]

From the Tadtown WOC, Brigadier General Schwalier dispatched his subordinate officers on a series of assignments. Dr. Robb, the medical group commander, had not attended this battle staff meeting, because he was in downtown Dhahran at the time of the explosion. General Schwalier accordingly sent Col. Peter R. Mooy, the logistics group commander, to organize the triage area at the Desert Rose Inn. "As it turned out," Schwalier later reflected, "he was exactly the right guy to send because he was down there at the speed of light and [dealing] with the hundreds of people who were out there at the triage [area]."[57] Meanwhile, in Dhahran Dr. Robb had heard—and felt—the blast and headed for the Khobar Towers. He arrived at the medical clinic at 10:25 p.m.[58] It proved advantageous to have both Colonel Mooy and Dr. Robb on that part of the complex. The logistics officer continued to mobilize people and resources at the dining hall, allowing Dr. Robb and the other medical professionals to give their immediate attention to the hundreds of patients.[59]

Like Dr. Robb, Colonel Boyle did not attend the 10:15 meeting, for the excellent reason that he already was at Building 131. "Understandably, Gary Boyle had excused himself," Brigadier General Schwalier stated, "because he had his job as the on-scene commander and he [had] to deal with the things that were happening at the place of the explosion." Colonel Boyle had gone to Building 131 and become the on-scene commander at the bomb site. Among his many immediate responsibilities, he supervised the search of the stricken dormitory for survivors and casualties.[60]

Lieutenant Colonel Traister also did not attend the battle staff meeting—and for the same reason as Colonel Boyle. He, too, had arrived at Building 131 very soon after the bombing and already was where he was needed most: at the compound's northern perimeter, supervising the operations of the security police.[61]

As for the remaining officers at the WOC, Brigadier General Schwalier charged each with an important assignment. The wing commander sent Col. Scott Gration, his operations group commander, to the Desert Rose Inn, to oversee the accounting of the casualties and survivors. Col. Wayne L. Schultz, the vice commander of the 4404th, would remain at the WOC and supervise communications. He would help mitigate the pressure on the wing from the inevitable incoming flood of requests for information. As for outgoing communications, Colonel Schultz would ensure that they were as accurate as possible.[62]

General Schwalier also directed Maj. Kevin Greenfield, the wing's judge advocate general, to the Ministry of Defense and Aviation (MODA) Hospital to begin identifying the Air Force patients as they arrived there. Major Greenfield and his deputy, Capt. Lisa Winnecke, had been downtown with Mr. Marwan Darwish when SSgt. Alfredo R. Guerrero had called the liaison officer from the roof of Building

In the Wake

131. Dispatched by General Schwalier, Major Greenfield and Captain Winnecke went to the MODA Hospital, where they soon learned the names, ranks, and units of some of the first Khobar casualties that facility received, some of whom had been admitted, while others had been seen and released. The JAG officers talked to a number of people there and made blood donations. Greenfield and Winnecke also learned at the MODA Hospital that some Americans who initially had been taken there subsequently had been transferred to two other nearby locations:[63] the Arabian American Oil Company (ARAMCO) Hospital, just north of Dhahran Air Base; and King Fahd University Hospital, about seven blocks north of the Khobar Towers.[64] This news about the airmen at these places provided one of the earliest accountings of the Air Force inpatients and outpatients.[65]

One other assignment emerged from the 10:15 battle staff meeting. General Schwalier dispatched Colonel Bible to determine the extent of the damage to each of the compound's buildings. General Dick later praised the efforts of the operations group commander from Riyadh, and commented on his fortuitous presence at the Khobar Towers that night. General Dick noted that Bible's visit for the change of command ceremony "proved out really well. We ended up having three general officers, plus an extra colonel, at Dhahran." He then added, with emphasis: "And we had enough work for *all* of us."[66]

The three general officers General Dick referred to were General Schwalier, the wing commander; Maj. Gen. Kurt Anderson, the JTF-SWA commander; and himself, the incoming wing commander. Dick had been flying on a chartered flight from Ramstein Air Base, Germany, to Dhahran Air Base when, about 2 a.m. in the morning of the twenty-sixth, the pilot came back from the cockpit with the news that there had been a bombing in Dhahran. The aviator knew nothing further about events in Saudi Arabia, only that his company had instructed him to complete the flight.[67]

When the airplane parked on Dhahran Air Base around 5 a.m., Brigadier General Dick looked out the window. He did not see Brigadier General Schwalier, a longtime friend with whom he had exchanged several electronic mail messages that spring and early summer, as the date for the change of command had approached. The wing commander ordinarily would have been on the flightline, of course, to meet his arriving successor and give him a brief orientation tour. General Schwalier at the time was at the mortuary collection point that by then had been established at the Air Mobility Command cargo terminal on Dhahran Air Base. In his place, a protocol officer first greeted General Dick and then, within a minute, the wing commander arrived and related the tragic news to his successor.[68]

As Brigadier General Dick observed, there was pressing work for everyone. At 11:18 p.m., Major General Anderson and the other senior officers assembled in the WOC had sent a message carrying the word of the attack to a number of organizations in Riyadh. These included the theater headquarters of the United States Central Command (CENTCOM); the United States Air Force, Central Command; the headquarters of the JTF-SWA; the United States Embassy; and the United States Military Training Mission. At 11:35 Generals Anderson and Schwalier left the command post to make a firsthand survey of the bomb damage. An hour later the officers in the WOC sent a preliminary report on the bombing to a large number of Air Force headquarters and command posts across the United States.[69]

The senior officers had responded promptly at the Khobar Towers, and elsewhere the story was the same. At 9:53 p.m. that Tuesday night in Dhahran, Saudi Arabia, it was 8:53 at Ramstein Air Base, Germany, which lay two time zones to the west but, like the United States, used daylight time. A telephone call from the theater alerted Col. (Dr.) Dan L. Locker, who had been the United States Air Forces in Europe command surgeon since August 1995, and he immediately called Col. Marvin D. Meinders, Headquarters USAFE's chief for medical plans and readiness. Colonel Meinders soon joined Dr. Locker at his office, on Hoover Street to the north and east of Headquarters USAFE.[70]

From here the two officers placed phone calls to U. S. Army Col. (Dr.) Ken Farmer, the United States European Command command surgeon, and to several Air Force medical operations officers. They quickly established what aircraft and personnel were available to respond to the situation. The military services rotated the "on call" responsibility for medical emergencies like Khobar Towers, on a three-month schedule. That June the Navy had the watch and the U.S. Naval Support Activity at Naples, Italy, was its facility nearest Dhahran. Dr. Locker respected the Navy's ability to perform the mission, but he knew that at that time, as was usually the case, the Air Force's available airlift assets exceeded those of the Navy. Once he and Colonel Meinders learned what aircraft, equipment, and people each organization could get to Dhahran promptly, they concluded that the Air Force was better placed to do the job. It had three Flying Ambulance Surgical Teams, at Royal Air Force Lakenheath, the United Kingdom; Spangdahlem Air Base, Germany; and Incirlik Air Base, Turkey. The latter—about a five-hour flight from Dhahran—leaped out as the best choice. Locker called Col. Carlisle Harrison, Jr., the commander of the 39th Medical Group Hospital, at Incirlik Air Base, and alerted him that the FAST team there very likely would receive the Khobar assignment.[71]

Southwest from Dr. Locker's office, across mainbase Ramstein, the 86th Aeromedical Evacuation Squadron operated from a modest building on the flightline and, like all such units, contributed personnel to Operation Southern Watch. At any given time the relatively small squadron of 113 officers and airmen had 3 to 5 of its members serving in standard ninety-day tours in Dhahran. After the attack that night, one of these squadron members telephoned the Aeromedical Evacuation Coordination Center (AECC), which was housed on the first floor of the 86th AES building and manned around the clock. In addition to this call from the theater, at about 10:30 p.m. the Ramstein Tactical Air Control Center also notified the AECC. The duty controller there phoned Col. (Dr.) James W. Bost, who had commanded the 86th since 1994: There had been a bombing at the Khobar Towers, the caller told the commander, but details were not yet available.[72]

Dr. Bost telephoned his executive staff and asked them to report to work. They spent their next hours gathered around a table, brainstorming how the 86th would respond to the emergency. The earliest reports they had received suggested there might be as many as 400 casualties, with more than 90 of them seriously injured.[73] "We had no idea of how many [patients] would need to be moved," Dr. Bost said later, "nor when they would need to be moved. But it was our impression that with the very small aeromedical staging flight in Dhahran, . . . we were going to be needed fairly quickly." At 11:50 p.m. a call from the Tactical Airlift Control Center, at Scott Air Force Base, Illinois, confirmed the earlier report of the attack, and put the 86th on standby to make an alert launch.[74]

Col. (Chaplain) John Lundin, senior chaplain for the Kaiserslautern Military Community, which included Ramstein Air Base and the Landstuhl Regional Medical Center, recalled how the initial state of ignorance eventually dissolved. "All we knew [at first] was that it was terrible," he stated, "and that [patients] were going to be coming through here. And slowly, as time went on, it began to sort [out] as to how many people were going to actually end up here." Chaplain Lundin described the tenor of things that night: "People became very focused, and very efficient—very quickly. . . . Working together as a team, everybody becomes very helpful, as we try to figure out how to do this right, making sure that [our people] get the appropriate care."[75]

When it was 9:53 p.m. at the Khobar Towers and 8:53 p.m. at Ramstein, it was 2:53 p.m. Eastern Daylight Time at Patrick Air Force Base, on the Atlantic coast of Florida. When a Southern Watch deployment was on, the home units usually heard from Dhahran once a day, calling to have a document sent by fax to the theater or to conduct other business. It happened that at the time the bomb exploded, an airman from this Florida base was on the phone with a member of the 741st Maintenance Squadron. From there, word traveled quickly to the building of the 71st Rescue Squadron, on the west side of the Patrick flightline.[76]

That afternoon of June 25, a small party was underway at the rescue squadron. The Air Force had released the list of technical sergeants who had been selected for promotion. Among the almost 4,800 was an NCO on the staff of the 1st Rescue Group who then was working in the same building as the 71st. Col. Thomas R. Friers, the group commander, drove across the base from his office in the 45th Space Wing Headquarters to the rescue squadron's building on the flightline. After attending the promotion ceremony and congratulating the sergeant, Colonel Friers stayed for the socializing that nearly always follows such an event. During the milling around and chatting, he said later, someone asked him if he had heard about the bombing in Saudi Arabia: a gasoline truck had exploded.[77]

In a hangar across the flightline, the 741st Maintenance Squadron was recognizing one of its members with an awards ceremony. Lt. Col. Donald R. Jozayt, the commander of the 71st Rescue Squadron, attended this function, held as part of the unit's 3:30 p.m. roll call. Here he picked up the same hearsay report that Friers had gathered at the squadron building: there had been a bombing at the Khobar Towers.[78]

Lieutenant Colonel Jozayt was not entirely convinced the story was true but he returned to his office at the 71st Rescue Squadron's building and attempted to call

Khobar Towers: Tragedy and Response

the deployed unit in Dhahran. He got no answer at the operations section and tried some other numbers. Eventually he reached a staff sergeant in the command post who could offer some preliminary information, which proved accurate as far as it went. A bomb had gone off in the Khobar Towers; Building 133, the civil engineers dormitory west of 131, which billeted some members of the 71st, had been hit; the wing battle staff had convened. Colonel Jozayt asked the sergeant to call him when more was known, after the battle staff meeting.[79]

Colonel Friers had remained at the 71st's building after the promotion gathering and now the two officers waited for additional information, and tried other phone numbers. Lieutenant Colonel Jozayt finally got through to the flightline at King Abdul Aziz, where the maintainence crew was working on the HC–130 that had been forced to return early from its mission that day. The NCOs there confirmed the unfortunate news that Building 131 had been damaged, but they had little information about the personnel of the 71st Rescue Squadron. It was a senior airman, a resident of 131, who eventually called Jozayt and verified the tragic facts of the attack. This NCO had escaped the stricken dormitory and reached a telephone. Building 131 had been badly hit, he related, and some members of the 71st had been killed.[80]

Once the tragic news was confirmed, Colonel Friers quickly decided that his unit would need a central clearinghouse to cope with the information it soon would be processing. All three squadrons of the 1st Rescue Group were represented at the Khobar Towers. In addition to the C–130 crews from the 71st Rescue Squadron, pararescue jumpers from the 41st Rescue Squadron and maintenance personnel from the 741st Rescue Squadron served there. That afternoon at Patrick, there was no way to know the extent of the casualties across the three squadrons. Friers recognized that during the crisis ahead, information should be processed through a single, centralized office, and the group headquarters offered the logical location for it.[81]

The two officers left the rescue squadron's building and went to Colonel Friers's office. The group commander asked his deputy, Lt. Col. Robert H. Holloway, to call the three squadrons and begin recruiting volunteers for the crisis information center. Friers also began arranging to acquire the additional phones that doubtless would be needed in the group command section during the days ahead.[82]

Telephoning from Colonel Friers's office, Lieutenant Colonel Jozayt tried to reach Lieutenant Colonel Shafer. Unknown then to Colonel Jozayt, the deployment commander had been injured in the bombing and taken to the ARAMCO Hospital. Later that afternoon Jane Shafer, his wife, called Jozayt. She had talked to her husband over the phone and he had given her an unofficial, "close hold" accounting of the casualties of the 71st. Six members of the squadron were believed dead. Shafer himself had been released from the ARAMCO Hospital and had begun regrouping the squadron.[83]

The first communications from Dhahran came quickly to Patrick, and to Eglin Air Force Base as well. Eglin was also a Florida installation, but its location west of the Apalachicola River put it on Central Daylight Time. Here it was 1:53 p.m. when the attack occurred at the Khobar Towers.

In the Wake

Within minutes after the explosion, Col. David Hayes, the vice commander of the 33d Fighter Wing, received a call from the theater reporting that there had been a bombing in Saudi Arabia. The communication had come to Colonel Hayes because the wing commander, Col. Gary R. Dylewski, was then enroute to—as events had it—Dhahran. The 60th Fighter Squadron had been tapped to participate in a deployment to Doha, Qatar, as part of Air Expeditionary Force III and it needed some of the F–15s belonging to its sister squadron, the 58th. That afternoon Colonel Dylewski intended to take a commercial flight from Atlanta's Hartsfield International Airport to Dhahran. There he and other pilots would have picked up twelve of the 58th Fighter Squadron's jets and flown them to Doha, for the AEF III deployment. The wing commander was in the Atlanta airport when he learned of the Khobar attack; he immediately returned to Eglin.[84]

Colonel Hayes called together the wing's squadron commanders and other officers for a battle staff meeting, which convened at 3:30 p.m. in a conference room appointed with a television set. The officers turned on the TV, but left the volume down—so they could hold their discussion and at the same time wait for the Cable News Network to break the story. By the mid-1990s CNN had firmly established a reputation for rapid coverage of international events. In this case, though, the call had come to Eglin so quickly that one of the battle staff officers later could accurately claim: "We had actually beat CNN." Capt. Brenda L. Campbell, the wing's public affairs officer, recalled: "We sat and watched CNN, and they didn't have any information at all. Normally CNN is our first look at what's going on."[85]

The information that the Eglin officers had at 3:30 was sketchy. Colonel Hayes told the battle staff he had a first-hand report of a bombing in Saudi Arabia. One officer afterward recalled that the group was not "cavalier" about the possibility there had been fatalities, but suggested that their psychological defenses encouraged them to assume that the members of their own 58th Fighter Squadron had not been harmed. Information came in, as he characterized it, only "in bits and pieces," leaving the battle staff with more questions than answers. Does the bombing involve us?, the officers wondered. How bad was it? Were there injuries? Were there fatalities? The group disbanded with the understanding it would assemble again when more information was known. To meet the possibility that Eglin personnel *had* been involved in the bombing, Captain Campbell said, the officers "started gathering emergency numbers, spouses' names, spouses' numbers, so they could start contacting people" if it became necessary.[86]

By 4:15 p.m. more news had arrived, and it was not good. By that time Lt. Col. Doug Cochran had been able to call Eglin. It was definite that the attack had affected some members of the squadron, but it was not known how many. At that early juncture, thirty were unaccounted for. By 4:15, too, the wives of some of the men in Dhahran had called the battle staff officers. They had heard from their husbands and knew they had survived the bombing.[87]

At 6 p.m. the battle staff convened for the second time. By then Colonel Hayes had more information from Saudi Arabia. The explosion at the Khobar Towers had been a fairly large one. It had occurred near a dormitory where members of the 58th were housed. It was certain there had been fatalities; their extent was unknown. The assembled officers now began to discuss seriously how information about the bombing would be gathered and managed. "We then set in motion," one of them said, "plans to be able to notify families."[88]

In Washington, D.C., an officer assigned to the Air Force Operations Center, located on the mezzanine level of the Pentagon basement, had called Air Force Chief of Staff Gen. Ronald R. Fogleman at 4:16 p.m. and informed him of the bombing. General Fogleman spent the rest of the afternoon reading initial reports about the casualties and other details about what had happened in Dhahran.[89]

Chairman of the Joint Chiefs of Staff Gen. John M. Shalikashvili, accompanied by his senior communications technician Mr. Frank Angelo and others, was airborne for Panama when the news reached him. General Shalikashvili later recalled that it "was not until we landed that the full measure of the tragedy became known to us." Mr. Angelo quickly began gathering information from the National Military Command Center in the Pentagon, and from Headquarters CENTCOM in Riyadh.[90]

That afternoon Secretary of the Air Force Dr. Sheila Widnall was testifying before the House National Security Committee when she received the news. She raised her hand and told the chairman, Floyd Spence of South Carolina, that she would have to leave the hearing. Dr. Widnall said she had just been informed of an attack against Americans in Saudi Arabia "with a considerable loss of life." She stood up and left at once. Her words and actions triggered a direct response from the journalists in the committee room. Later Dr. Widnall recalled: "I just left. It was like . . . the old movie scene, where the reporters run to the phones."[91]

President Bill Clinton was in Washington that afternoon, preparing to leave for Lyon, France for a summit meeting of the Group of Seven, the world's seven most industrialized nations. The president spoke to reporters as word of the bombing came to the White House. "The explosion appears to be the work of terrorists," he stated. "And if that is the case, like all Americans, I am outraged by it . . . . Within a few hours, an FBI team will be on its way to Saudi Arabia to assist in the investigation. Our condolences and our prayers go out to the victims, families, and their friends." President Clinton closed his remarks with a commitment: "We will pursue this. America takes care of our own. Those who did it must not go unpunished."[92]

By late afternoon on the East Coast of the United States, millions of people had heard the early reports of the disaster. The bombing had occurred at night and for several hours the darkness prevented journalists from taking photographs. The situation changed after daylight returned to Saudi Arabia on June 26. After 9 a.m. that morning in Dhahran, or 2 a.m. Eastern Daylight Time, CNN began broadcasting its first videos of the bomb site. As Americans awoke that Wednesday morning and watched the news before going to work, they saw an image on their television screens that would become sickenly familiar: Building 131, with its northern face shorn off.[93]

Response

*I get goose bumps every time I tell this story [about Khobar Towers], because the people were just there, when you needed them. It was that way **all night long**, and it was that way for weeks afterward. I'm not talking about just the medics. I'm talking about **everyone**.*

Lieutenant Colonel (Dr.) Douglas J. Robb
Interim Commander, 4404th Medical Group

Chapter Six

Golden Hour

Medical professionals know that there is a limited period of opportunity to help patients who have suffered extensive injuries. Care that is given at the scene of an accident is vitally important, and research has shown that severe trauma patients who reach surgery within sixty minutes have a significantly higher survival rate than those who do not. What is done—or not done—for a person during that critical time can mean the difference between healthy recovery and permanent disability, or even between life and death. Medical professionals call this period of opportunity the "Golden Hour."[1]

Lt. Col. (Dr.) Douglas J. Robb, interim commander of the 4404th Wing's medical group and the senior doctor at the Khobar Towers on the night of the bombing, applied this phrase to the aftermath of the terrorist attack. The time between 10 p.m. and 11 p.m. on June 25, 1996, was the Golden Hour at Dhahran. During the vital sixty minutes or so after the explosion, across the entire Khobar Towers compound, some 2,000 airmen and soldiers administered medical aid to themselves and others.[2]

That night in Saudi Arabia, the Air Force's first aid program, formally referred to as "self-aid and buddy care," or SABC, more than proved its value. SABC had become increasingly important during the 1990s, as the Air Force continually deployed large numbers of airmen to forward locations where medics might not immediately be at the scene of a contingency. Airmen trained in self-aid and buddy care could help themselves and others during the critical interval of time before professional help arrived. In 1996 CMSgt David Bayliss, the manager of the medical service specialty career field and the head of the SABC program, described its extent and significance. "Every single bluesuiter," he pointed out, "except those with specialized medical training, receive self-aid and buddy care training. It's the first echelon of medical treatment before medical personnel arrive."[3]

Doubtless many airmen wondered, until the night of June 25, 1996, if their self-aid and buddy care training was just another "check-the-box" exercise. "You never know," one NCO mused, "how people are going to respond. We always train for this, that, and the other thing—but when the 'real deal' happens, how are people going to react?" Months after the attack, a medical officer acknowledged harboring doubts about how well self-aid and buddy care would work—until the night of the Dhahran bombing. Another Khobar Towers veteran conceded that during his SABC training he had often asked himself: if I ever encounter someone in the state of shock, will I recognize it? (That night near Dhahran, he got his answer: he found it was easy to perceive the condition.) This same officer drew a candid contrast between the training he had experienced and the reality he dealt with at Khobar Towers. "We . . . do exercises up the butt," he said bluntly, "and you get written up because you didn't read a card on a guy's chest that showed what his injury was." But in an actual emergency like the Khobar bombing, he concluded, when people saw real wounds, they knew what to do.[4]

Given the traumatic circumstances, it was not surprising that, in fact, there were problems in administering self-aid and buddy care. One difficulty, which had a commendable cause, was that at times so many airmen were trying to assist an injured person that they got in one another's way. Lt. Col. Thomas A. McCarthy, operations officer of the 58th Fighter Squadron, remarked that one of his "biggest challenges" that night was organizing the good Samaritans who were attempting to help one another. "People were falling over each other," he said, "trying to help." In cases where there was a surplus of caregivers, he steered the excess helpers to aid other wounded airmen or to alternate tasks.[5]

Another difficulty, which some might say also had a commendable cause, was that some airmen were reluctant to acknowledge they needed medical care. Some of the injured saw others who were more severely wounded than themselves and, selfless to a fault, they refused to accept help. Dr. Robb, Capt. (Dr.) R. Morris Treadway, and other medical professionals observed and commented on this pattern of behavior. Dr. Treadway pointed out that many of the survivors felt that their injuries were "meaningless," in relation to the death of a friend, "so they [didn't] seek care." SSgt. Rudolph Grimm II, a dental technician who aided the wounded at the medical clinic that night, recalled potential patients saying: "No, no, no, take him—he's hurt worse." A senior master sergeant, in an account he wrote in November 1997, put himself in the group described by Sergeant Grimm. With slight cuts on his legs and arms, and a deep one in his hand, he reported to the clinic: "Every couple of minutes a different medic would come over and ask me if I was OK. I told them yes and please go take care of someone with serious injuries. I got tired of this unneeded attention on myself and left the clinic area."[6] Brig. Gen. Daniel M. Dick, the inbound commander of 4404th Composite Wing (Provisional) on the night of the attack, said of the airmen like this one, "being great people, they knew that the medical system was totally overwhelmed. Not only overwhelmed that night—but in the ensuing days."[7]

There also were the small problems that always occur when stressful circumstances turn simple tasks into difficult ones. SSgt. Selena P. Husted, a law office manager who helped many people that night, vividly remembered how hard it was to get a first aid kit open. And after she did, "the gauze and stuff was sealed shut. I remember trying to get in to it, and I could not. I was ripping it open with my teeth, because I couldn't get into the stuff. It was very frustrating."[8]

Sergeant Husted, and uncounted others, overcame the small problems, and they made self-aid and buddy care one of the "success stories" of Khobar Towers. Capt.

Golden Hour

Russell D. Barile, a pilot of the 71st Rescue Squadron, detailed one specific example among the uncounted many that took place that night. Captain Barile recounted how he and SrA. Rich Dixon, a pararescue jumper, entered Building 103, a dormitory at the corner of Twelfth and Thirty-third Streets, and encountered "an individual coming down the stairwell, being helped by another one. He had a severe laceration on his right shin. Airman Dixon took off his shirt, put it on there, put direct pressure on it." Barile and Dixon then carried the man out of the dormitory.[9]

TSgt. Jefferson A. Craven, a resident of the fourth floor of Building 133 who suffered multiple wounds, stated directly that self-aid and buddy care saved his life. "If it wasn't for the four airmen that were living with me," Sergeant Craven asserted, "I wouldn't be here: that's a fact. Self-aid and buddy care got us through that [night]." Craven's account was particularly compelling in its unvarnished honesty. He said of the airmen who saved his life: "I remember fussing with them. They tried to calm me down, tell me to hang on, that the medics would be there. I said, 'Guys, you gotta wake up. You don't know how bad this is.'"[10]

Many airmen may have wondered before that night how well their SABC training would serve them, but when it counted, during the critical minutes after 9:53 p.m., they learned that it did, in spades. SSgt. Darryl A. Parker was one of the many who remembered the first aid techniques he had been taught and used them. "It was the little things," he said, "like remembering to apply direct pressure to an open wound and allowing the wound to clot as we placed bandages over the injured areas.... Being able to remember these steps, and much more, being [able] to apply the steps during a time of crisis, allowed the medical personnel to give a quick check over and move on to other more serious injuries." Sergeant Parker drew a pointed lesson from his experience at Khobar Towers: "For those of you that think you are reading the PFE [the Performance Fitness Examination Study Guide] just for testing purposes, I am here and alive to tell you that what is in that book can mean the difference between life and death." "I think those exercises *did* help," Lt. Col. (Chaplain) Dennis E. Aleson concluded. "When the bomb went off in Khobar Towers, we didn't have time to look for checklists.... But people knew what to do."[11]

Faced with a sudden disaster, the airmen administered self-aid and buddy care, improvising with whatever materials were at hand. Dr. Robb praised their resourcefulness: People arrived at the clinic with their wounds already bandaged "with towels, with T-shirts. Somebody [used] a broomstick handle for splints. Stuff they learned in self-aid and buddy care [training]."[12]

Hundreds of airmen helped each other, and although no one group could be singled out above others, many Khobar veterans praised the work of the few pararescue jumpers who were on the scene that night. These airmen, assigned to the 71st Rescue Squadron and other similar units, were skilled in two highly demanding areas: jumping from aircraft and providing medical aid as Emergency Medical Technicians. Dr. Robb pointed out that of the eight pararescue jumpers on the compound at the time, only four were left standing after the explosion. They made up for

Khobar Towers: Tragedy and Response

their numbers with their efforts. "It seemed like [the PJs] were everywhere," Dr. Treadway said.[13]

Dr. Robb recalled: "There was one guy I remember standing there, his head all bandaged up, big old pararescue pack on, with all his medical supplies. He was in shorts. There he was out on the patio [of the medical clinic], slipping an [intravenous] line in one of the casualties. I'll never forget that, as long as I live." Lt. Col. Douglas R. Cochran, commander of the 58th Fighter Squadron, referred to another dramatic episode: a PJ who had received "a pretty good cut" first sewed up his own injury, and then began giving first aid to others. Four pararescuemen received the Airman's Medal: MSgt. William F. Sine, SSgt. Matthew A. Wells, SrA. Michael D. Atkins, and SrA. Gregory E. Randall. SrA. Eric Castor received a Purple Heart; SrA. Rich Dixon and SrA. Dan Williams received Air Force Commendation Medals with the Valor device.[14]

Capt. Michael D. Morelock, a pilot of the 71st Rescue Squadron, recounted one episode that showed how *persistent* the PJs were in looking out for others. A resident of the top floor of Building 131, Captain Morelock had suffered cuts on his face, head, and neck[15] and an ambulance had taken him to the Arabian American Oil Company (ARAMCO) Hospital. A team of doctors and nurses examined the pilot, took x-rays, cleaned his wounds, and began stitching him. Morelock laughed when he recalled what happened then: "[SrA.] Mike Atkins, one of the PJs, was brought in next to me .... He was getting stitched up, too. I remember him telling the doctors exactly what *he* thought was wrong with me!"[16]

The PJs, firefighters, and security policemen used their EMT skills that night, and hundreds of other people who had no medical experience beyond their SABC training did a remarkably effective job of helping one another. This spontaneous effort by so many non-medical professionals was one of the most striking aspects of the Dhahran bombing. "I found myself working in puddles of blood to aid the injured," one NCO stated, "with no medical training at all." "Our success was not only that we had all those doctors, nurses and technicians," Dr. Robb summed up, "but that we also had 2,000 airmen and soldiers trained in first aid and buddy care."[17]

Dr. Robb identified three ways that self-aid and buddy care proved significant at the Khobar Towers. Fundamentally, it saved lives and limited injuries. SABC, he pointed out, contributed to what medical professionals "call a decrease in morbidity, because of loss of blood, or loss of function."[18]

Second, the Air Force's first aid program was a force mulitiplier. Hundreds of wounded arrived at the clinic, soon after the attack. "It doesn't take you long to get super-saturated with 200, 300 casualties," Dr. Robb stated. "We had 500 total, through the next couple of days .... I had 350 people, that night." Thanks to self-aid and buddy care, all of the initial patients at the clinic had received help of one kind or another, before they arrived there. "Those 350 people," he pointed out, "already had a bandage on them, or a dressing, or whatever they needed." He recalled that at the July 3 "hot wash" debriefing: "I looked at the other docs and said, 'Was it just *me*, or did *everybody* that came in have some form of initial first aid given to them?'

Golden Hour

And they said, 'Everyone.'" Because of self-aid and buddy care, the doctors at the clinic could give their immediate attention to the more severely injured patients, confident that in every case the others already had received some initial help. SABC, Robb concluded, "was a tremendous force multiplier.... The response couldn't have happened if we hadn't had that extra 2,000 set of eyes, hands, and ears out there, helping us out."[19]

Dr. Robb also pointed to a third, and fundamentally important, attribute of self-aid and buddy care. Instead of being traumatized, the survivors quickly focused on aiding the injured. Dr. Robb recalled that when he arrived at the clinic, "The first thing I noticed was that every casualty had two or three fellow airmen attending to them."[20]

Instead of feeling abandoned, many of the wounded were reassured because their comrades around them began helping them so promptly. Self-aid and buddy care strengthened the morale of both the injured and uninjured. By giving airmen a measure of control over events at a time of great stress, it contributed to the return of calm and order. One of the doctors at the July 3 medical debriefing remarked about how quiet the clinic had been that night. Other than the physicians and medics giving necessary directives, he recalled, you could hear a pin drop. "I think that's a tribute," Dr. Robb commented, "not only to the trust in the medical system, but to the self-aid and buddy care."[21]

While self-aid and buddy care, and other, training was not the fundamental cause of the recovery that began after the bombing, it reflected a larger point—the moral and physical courage of the airmen. As Brig. Gen. Terry Schwalier, the wing commander, later pointed out, the essential factor working that night was the high character that his personnel displayed. Hundreds of airmen demonstrated their professionalism, sense of mission, selflessness, and patriotism.[22]

These highly motivated airmen aided their comrades so thoroughly that when the injured began arriving at the medical clinic, Building 111,[23] very soon after the attack, all of them had received some initial medical help. The bomb had exploded at 9:53 p.m.[24] Within minutes, fire chief MSgt. Wayne Mello,[25] the security police, and others began directing people to the Desert Rose Inn, near the clinic.[26] The first patient arrived at Building 111 at 10:02 p.m. Dr. Treadway noticed that the initial arrivals tended to be in better condition: the less severely injured airmen walked faster, and reached the clinic sooner than those more badly wounded. The patients, he said, "rolled in and rolled in."[27] By 10:10, about thirty of the injured had gathered at the clinic and the nearby dining hall.[28]

The injured arrived at these two buildings, in the middle of the Khobar Towers compound, by a number of means. Some came alone; many were carried by other airmen—on doors that had been blown off their hinges, on ironing boards that had survived the blast, on litters improvised from whatever was at hand. Dr. Robb recalled the scene: "We saw people coming in, using blown out doors for stretchers. They were bringing people in on chairs. They were doing what is called the 'two-man buddy carry.' People always joke about it when they are doing [it in] self-aid and buddy care [training], but they were doing it—bringing them in in the two-person buddy carry."[29]

Nearly all the injured had suffered either lacerations from glass shards or blunt trauma from flying objects. An observation that Dr. Robb made about Building 131 also applied to some of the other living quarters: "The fully occupied dormitory was immediately thrown into total darkness with shards of glass, concrete, furniture, and other debris flying at high velocity. The blast occurred at a time when many occupants were in the common lounge areas of the suites. Glass patio doors in the lounge areas facing the blast produced a high volume of flying glass fragments." These dangerous shards caused the most common injury, multiple cuts from window fragments. Robb estimated that, after the most severe cases were dispatched to hospitals in Dhahran, 90 to 95 percent of the patients who remained had suffered glass wounds.[30] Blunt trauma from hurling objects accounted for the second most frequent injury. "There were a lot of contusions," Robb noted, "from people being thrown up against walls and being hit by chairs and other objects."[31]

Fortunately for the wounded, there were eighty-one medical professionals on or near the Khobar Towers that night.[32] The 4404th Medical Group's authorized manning provided for four flight surgeons. A shortfall at Patrick Air Force Base, Florida, had reduced this number to three, but the unit's interim commander, Dr. Robb, was himself a physician. So on June 25, 1996, the group did have four flight surgeons: Dr. Robb, Dr. Treadway, Maj. (Dr.) Roy Smith, and Maj. (Dr.) Steven P. Goff.[33] There were twenty-two other medical professionals—dentists, nurses, medical technicians, preventive medicine specialists, and administrative and supply personnel—assigned to the Khobar Towers clinic at the time of the attack. These officers and airmen were off duty when the terrorists struck, but responded quickly and began arriving at Building 111 just as the first patients did, soon after 10 p.m.[34]

The 4410th Aeromedical Evacuation Flight, assigned to nearby Dhahran Air Base, provided ten more medical professionals: three nurses and seven medical technicians.[35] At the hour of the explosion, a few of these med techs were off the compound; most of them, and all of the nurses, were in their dormitories. Like the medical group personnel, these professionals reacted quickly. The med techs who were away returned promptly and shortly after 10 p.m. all of them were aiding the injured, at the medical clinic and the Desert Rose Inn, and near the devastated Building 131.[36] One of the nurses immediately went to work on the Army side of the clinic, the second on the Air Force wing, and the third wherever she could best help at the moment.[37]

In addition to these personnel assigned to the 4410th Aeromedical Evacuation Flight and the 4404th Wing's medical group, there were the four PJs and twenty-eight crash rescue emergency medical technicians and firefighters of the wing's civil engineering squadron. These professionals first went to the dormitories and helped stunned and wounded residents evacuate their buildings. TSgt. George Burgess, a resident of Building 131 who helped the firefighter EMTs sweep his dormitory, recounted how they worked: "We'd look for survivors, we'd find them, we'd pull them out. . . . Every floor we went on, we'd do a sweep of the floor. . . . We went all the way to the top."[38] After the PJs and firefighters conducted these evacuation sweeps, they reported to the clinic and the Desert Rose and aided the wounded there. Their numbers brought the total of Air Force medical professionals at Khobar that night to sixty-eight.[39]

Fortunately, there were still more caregivers on the scene. The Army operated its clinic in the same facility with the Air Force, and manned it with a doctor, a physician's assistant, and eight med techs.[40] By 10:25 p.m. three allies—a British flight surgeon, a British med tech, and a French flight surgeon—had joined the effort at Building 111 and brought the total of medical professionals to eighty-one.[41]

The medical people proved equal to the challenges posed that night, and so did the available facilities. The more severely injured patients received their first treatment at the Air Force and Army medical clinic, which occupied the ground floor of a structure not far west of the Desert Rose Inn. This was Building 111, patterned along the same T shape as 131 and the other eight-story dormitories of the Khobar Towers. Its upper floors housed people who worked downstairs in the clinic and elsewhere on the compound. The crosspiece of the building's T ran north and south, parallelling Twelfth Street, and the base of the T ran east and west. The clinic was divided into Army and Air Force sections: the northern half of the crosspiece had two USAF waiting rooms and three treatment rooms; the southern half, the Army end, duplicated this pattern.[42] Airmen sometimes referred to the base of the T as the "back" of the clinic, since it was situated farthest from the front entrance, on Twelfth Street. It contained offices, an orderly room, and storage areas.[43]

The huge number of injured soon overwhelmed this small facility and the area around it.[44] During the month before the bombing, the clinic had treated an average of twenty-four patients a day. Consistent with that figure, on the day before the attack, the facility had seen twenty-five airmen. On the night of June 25, it saw hundreds. By 10:25 p.m., when Dr. Robb arrived from downtown, patients filled all six treatment rooms and two "code blues," emergency resuscitations, were taking place, one on each side of the clinic.[45] The facility soon was "overflowing," Maj. Cynthia D. Coles recalled, as "people came in, in a steady stream."[46]

The number of patients increased, and so did the severity of the cases. As Dr. Treadway pointed out, the ambulatory and less seriously injured people reached the clinic earliest. As time passed, airmen began carrying in the more severely wounded casualties. "It got to the point," Treadway explained, "that we just decided we needed to set up a triage point outside [the clinic], where we could better see people and send them to the proper area. And so we cleared most of the folks out of the clinic itself and tried to get as many ambulatory folks [as possible] to walk out, and place the injured-ambulatory in one area, and we were lining up stretchers in another area," where the medics could watch them more easily.[47]

The "triage" that Dr. Treadway mentioned comes from a French word that translates to "sorting." Medical professionals use it to mean dividing patients into categories to prioritize their care and transport. Triage is a critical process in any situation involving multiple casualties, and particularly so in cases like the Khobar Towers, with a large number of them. In emergencies like the Dhahran bombing, the caregivers must determine quickly which patients have life-threatening injuries that demand immediate attention and which can be stabilized and given more help later. By rapidly sorting the injured and prioritizing their treatment, caregivers can maximize the number of survivors.[48]

During the Golden Hour between 10 and 11 p.m., first a widespread effort of self-aid and buddy care, and then an efficient use of triage, combined together to save many lives. On the grounds outside the clinic, Dr. Robb and his fellow professionals quickly triaged hundreds of patients.[49] The caregivers rapidly separated the injured into three categories: immediate, delayed, and minimal treatment, and helped at once the "immediate" cases. Dr. Treadway recounted: "We had several medics going around giving people [intravenous lines], just hundreds of IVs. A lot of the pararescue folks that were injured were helping to put IVs in, too."[50]

Once the medical professionals had started the IV lines and given other aid to the "immediate" cases, they began a follow-on effort of "re-triage," or secondary triage. This process was required because patients, of course, do not always remain stable. An ongoing effort is necessary when there are multiple victims, and it is particularly important when there are mass casualties. The caregivers have to reassess continually the condition of the injured and update the triage. Dr. Robb summarized the process: "We triaged and stabilized, and re-triaged and re-stabilized."[51]

While the medical professionals did their life-saving work, Col. Peter R. Mooy, the wing's logistics group commander, mobilized the personnel and resources needed to support them. At the 10:15 p.m. battle staff meeting, Brigadier General Schwalier had dispatched Colonel Mooy to the Desert Rose Inn. The logistics group commander organized the support effort at the dining hall and at the clinic, which allowed Dr. Robb, the other doctors, nurses, and med techs to concentrate on patient care. Brigadier General Dick praised this arrangement: while Colonel Mooy "orchestrated the events going on at the clinic that night . . . Dr. Robb did a magnificent job" with patient care.[52]

Sergeant Grimm summarized Colonel Mooy's efforts that night: "There was a colonel on the radio, running the show. He got the lights and water there quickly." Dr. Robb vividly recalled "standing in that courtyard [of the clinic]. It hit me that there were about two hundred people out there. I thought, 'Gosh, I could use some lights around here. And I was no sooner thinking that, and there [were civil engineers] showing up, with lights.'"[53]

SSgt. Boris Rudinski, a ground equipment mechanic, was in his shop on the military flightline when he received the telephone call to bring lighting to the Khobar Towers. The bombing had knocked out almost all of the compound's street light poles, and illumination was badly needed at places like Building 131, which was being searched for casualties, and the medical clinic and Desert Rose Inn, where the injured were being treated. Sergeant Rudinski quickly transported a bank of auxiliary lights, which were carried on a four-wheeled cart, to the blast site. When

Golden Hour

he got to Building 131, he later recalled, "they were still pulling bodies out of the building. I assisted, [I] helped them with that." As for the medical clinic, the auxiliary lighting arrived there rapidly, too. "They got everything there quick," Sergeant Grimm remembered, within fifteen or twenty minutes.[54]

The episode of the lights was representative of a larger pattern that night: whenever Dr. Robb needed something, it arrived. "I remember," he said, "one of the guys saying, 'These people are going to get dehydrated. They just went through a big shock.' No sooner did I even begin to *think* about that—and there was Services [providing water] .... There were the cops with protection; there were [the Civil Engineers] with whatever we needed."[55]

There was no stronger example of the timely appearance of critically needed aid than the arrival of the ambulances that night. Dr. Robb quickly recognized that many of the injured airmen would require hospitalization. Some the patients had larger, more severe wounds than others, and some had glass that would have to be removed in emergency rooms. The medical group had its own fleet of ambulances, but it was far, far too small to cope with the casualties caused by the attack. One of these vehicles was in the repair shop that night, leaving only two available. Each had a broken air conditioning system—a common problem in that part of the world. Both ambulances were designed to carry four patients at a time—a pathetically limited capacity, given the hundreds of injured.[56] With frank honesty, Dr. Robb recalled his thinking at the time: "I remember standing there, going, 'How am I going to get all these people down to the hospitals [in downtown Dhahran] with two ambulances?' It's a hell of a lot of trips."[57]

Within minutes after the blast, an employee of the Red Crescent Society—the Saudi Red Cross—called the local Civil Defense office and asked what information was known about the explosion. At that time few hard facts were available, but the picture soon began to sharpen. At 10:15 p.m. the crew of a Red Crescent Society ambulance just north of the Khobar Towers spotted the devastation at Building 131 and called in the location of the disaster to their dispatcher, who quickly informed the Civil Defense office of the precise point of the attack. This RCS employee also immediately began dispatching the available Society ambulances—there were eight then on duty—to the scene. While the Saudis took this initiative, Brigadier General Schwalier placed a telephone call that expedited the directing of these badly needed medical vehicles to the Khobar Towers.[58]

In addition to this help, Saudi Ministry of Health and local ambulances also were soon speeding toward the compound. Driving through the gap that the bomb had created in the fence along the northern perimeter,[59] the first of these vehicles arrived at the clinic at 10:27 p.m. Others appeared on its heels, the second arriving two minutes later and the third, five. Eventually, more than twenty Saudi ambulances transported injured airmen from the Khobar clinic to hospitals in downtown Dhahran. Dr. Robb later reflected: "We'll never know [how many Saudi vehicles helped that night] .... I'm going to guess we had twenty or thirty ambulances. They just kept cycling."[60]

Khobar Towers: Tragedy and Response

In addition to the ambulances, a number of medical professionals also came to the aid of the wounded airmen. At about 11 p.m. Dr. Ronald Price and another physician from the emergency room staff of the ARAMCO Hospital arrived at the clinic. Within half an hour a Saudi Ministry of Health team of doctors reached the scene. This group was from Dammam Central Hospital, about eight miles from the Khobar Towers, and was headed by the director of that facility's emergency department.[61] The largest influx of professionals began at 12:30 a.m. on June 26, with the arrival of two surgeons and twelve nurses in four ambulances from King Fahd University Hospital, about seven blocks from the Khobar Towers. The expertise of this pair of Saudi specialists proved particularly valuable; they helped with some of the more difficult cases of removing glass and closing wounds.[62] Other local professionals also arrived after 12:30: the Saudi Rail Organization contributed a doctor and two nurses, while the King Fahd Military Medical Complex, located about twelve miles south of Khobar toward Abqaiq, and al Mana Hospital, five blocks north of the compound and near the Arabian Gulf, each sent an M.D. and an R.N.[63]

The Saudis and the Americans from the ARAMCO Hospital supplied not only physicians and ambulances, but also critically important communications support. The enormous explosion had knocked out the compound's telephone communications, and cell phone channels quickly became saturated. Under these circumstances, Saudi radio support played a vital role during the period immediately after the attack. When Dr. Price's team arrived in two ambulances at 11 p.m., they used a land mobile radio to open communications with their facility, the ARAMCO Hospital.[64]

This help complemented the extraordinary efforts of the wing's own communications squadron. Its members reached the scene by 10:45 p.m. and quickly began connecting dedicated lines directly to the Dhahran hospitals. Within two and a half hours they had a communications system in place in the Desert Rose Inn's executive dining room. This location eventually would become the Site Recovery Center, the workplace of the permanent Disaster Control Group, the successor to the temporary DCG that the security police had established soon after the attack.[65] The comm airmen also supplemented the voice communications at the dining hall with a fax machine that they brought from Building 103, a dormitory northwest of the Desert Rose. Installed in the clinic, this hardware helped deal with the high volume of patient information and other data that had to be sent and received.[66]

Communication with hospitals in Dhahran and elsewhere proved important, as did the cooperation of the Saudis. The Air Force had a memorandum of agreement with the Ministry of Defense and Aviation (MODA) Hospital, and the American airmen were confident of its help. As for the others, the night of June 25, 1996, would test their support. "In our hearts we hoped the other hospitals would respond," Dr. Robb said afterward, "but you never know."[67]

Without exception, the Dhahran hospitals did their best for the American airmen. "Everybody," Dr. Robb stated, "was welcoming our patients with open arms.... The response from the host nation hospitals was tremenduous. I don't think I could have asked for anything more." Dr. Treadway echoed Dr. Robb: "The host nation response was . . . outstanding." One of the several official investigations conducted after the bombing pointed out that, among other considerations, ambulance "transportation would have been inadequate had the Saudis not responded."[68]

At 10:30 p.m. an Air Force ambulance, one of the two available that night, made the first departure from the clinic. It carried five patients to the MODA Hospital, chosen as the primary destination because of its proximity and its MOA with the Air Force. This dispatch represented a remarkable achievement: the bomb had exploded just thirty-seven minutes earlier. The second Air Force ambulance left the clinic at 10:45.[69]

The first Saudi ambulances had reached the scene just minutes before the Air Force one made the initial departure. More and more of these host nation vehicles joined the two USAF ones, and Dr. Price directed their flow. At 11:45 he learned over his land mobile radio that the MODA Hospital was becoming overwhelmed by arrivals, and he began dispatching the ambulances to the ARAMCO and King Fahd University facilities.[70]

The ambulances used an approach that allowed them to pull up in front of the clinic, along Twelfth Street. MSgt. Dwayne R. Berry, who had been working out in the gym at the time of the attack, was among the many who helped load the vehicles. He compared the scene outside the clinic to the dispatch of "the New York City taxis at the airport. We would load an injured person inside an ambulance, and roll them in, and the next one would pull right up." The airmen tried to keep track of the patients: "We found out who that individual was and then we would pass that to a guy who was standing there. The ambulance driver would tell us, Okay, he's going to so-and-so hospital. Okay, we'd get his name, This is Senior Airman so-and-so, and he's going to [al Mana] Hospital. Okay, the ambulance is gone." The process continued: "The next [ambulance] would pull up. We bring another cart around . . . . And it went surprisingly well." By 1 a.m. of the twenty-sixth, the fleet of ambulances, two Air Force vehicles and more than twenty Saudi ones, had transported about 200 patients to hospitals in Dhahran.[71]

Recounting their rides through the city, a number of the wounded praised their Saudi drivers, while at the same time describing what was fundamentally an alarming experience. The patients found that their inability to communicate with the man at the wheel, their ignorance of their destinations, and other uncertainties raised during a night of terrorism all combined to make for a harrowing trip. Capt. Michael D. Morelock abruptly learned that his stretcher would slide back and forth, as his ambulance careened around the Dhahran street corners. "There was some confusion about where we were going," he said, "and I remember thinking that that was the scariest part of the night—that we were going to get lost, and that terrorists were going to start shooting at the ambulance." 1st. Lt. Stephanie Bronson, a civil engineer, stressed the problem of the language barrier: "I don't know how long [the trip] took, but it was an unpleasant ride, to say the least—because they didn't speak English, and we didn't speak Arabic. So we weren't sure where we were going, or if we were going to get there." Shortly after that night, U.S. Army Lt. Col. Sherry Connor, a member of the stress management team sent to Dhahran from the Landstuhl Regional Medical Center, listened to the accounts given by some of these ambulance patients. She related that they "talked about their horror of not knowing if they were in enemy hands, and where they were going—and just fear."[72]

While the ambulance rides proved a dramatic experience for some of the wounded, the preparation of the patients for transport had gone remarkably smoothly, given the circumstances. Dr. Price was impressed that the airmen at the clinic had done extremely well in that regard. An emergency room doctor, he had received training for dealing with mass casualties, and when he reached the Khobar clinic, he was frankly surprised to find an orderly scene. Dr. Robb quoted Price's words: "I was ready for mass casualties.... I showed up—and you guys had them all lined up, and IVs in them all, bleeding stopped, people had sewed up the big cuts in the clinic.... All you needed was transportation." When Dr. Price asked how all this had been accomplished, Robb replied immediately: "Training. Training paid off."[73]

One specific example was the exercise that the medical group had conducted a few days earlier, which ensured that during any emergency everyone knew the location of vital supplies. The bombing created a harsh test of reality. Dr. Robb later praised the group's performance that night. "I remember watching 'Mad Dog' [MSgt. Luis G. Madrigal, supply sergeant].... He was throwing stuff out the windows [of the clinic] onto the patio," Robb related, "because he knew where [everything] was. Everybody knew where the cots were, and everybody knew where everything was."[74]

Training paid its rewards, and by 1 a.m. of the twenty-sixth, about 200 patients had gone to nearby hospitals. Sometime around that hour, Dr. Robb assembled his doctors, nurses, and med techs. Many airmen had been hospitalized, but there remained another 150 to 200—no one knew the exact number—who still needed treatment for cuts and other injuries.[75] Dr. Robb and the others wanted, if possible, to take care of these remaining injured at the Khobar Towers, rather than further burden the local hospitals. The medical group commander asked his people directly: "Do you think we can handle these folks?"[76] Their answer was yes.

CMSgt. Paul K. Ayres, the wing's senior enlisted advisor, suggested that the dining tables of the nearby Desert Rose Inn could be used for suture stations. The chow hall, an uninspired, prefabricated building, was an unlikely setting for the heroics that followed. (One general officer quipped that there "was nothing 'executive' about its executive dining room.") Despite the building's distance from the terrorist truck, the explosion had buckled its aging walls. This damage, however, was more a commentary on the size of the bomb than on the soundness of the structure, which the civil engineers had declared safe, and the medical personnel were able to carry out Chief Ayres's idea.[77]

Dr. Treadway took the short walk northeast from the clinic to the Desert Rose Inn and began readying it for the job at hand. He later explained that an Air Force meal facility in fact offered many of the features needed by a medical one: "The chow hall was just a perfect set up. It was air conditioned. It was clean, had running water, hot and cold running water. And every table is a bed.... It worked fantastic."[78] In the Desert Rose Inn, and the clinic, the caregivers set up twenty-five to thirty suture stations.[79]

Dr. Treadway and the other flight surgeons performed their work with calm professionalism. Dr. Roy Smith had been the first physician to reach Building 131 in the wake of the blast. Later, he gave his attention to the many trauma cases that came into the clinic. ABC News named him its "Person of the Week" for the last week of June 1996.[80]

Dr. Steve Goff, a Schofield, Wisconsin, resident who had deployed to Saudi Arabia from Malmstrom Air Force Base, Montana, had declined Dr. Robb's invitation to make the dinner and shopping trip to downtown Dhahran earlier that evening. He had remained at Khobar and suffered glass lacerations in the bombing. Dr. Goff helped the patients at the clinic, undeterred by a shard in his chest.[81] Later, even while his own wound was being bandaged, he continued sewing up injured airmen. Like those around him, Goff worked tirelessly, eventually helping more than 200 patients. In view of his own injury, he was taken to King Fahd University Hospital; and on July 3, Air Force Chief of Staff Gen. Ronald R. Fogleman presented him the Airman's Medal.[82]

These flight surgeons did not work alone: nurses, med techs, EMTs, PJs, Saudi physicians, and others joined them in suturing the wounded airmen. It was training, not luck, which made this expertise available. "We teach our med techs how to sew," Dr. Robb pointed out. "That's important, in training."[83]

Fighter pilots also assisted with some of the suturing. These officers all have exceptionally healthy nervous systems and during the emergency at the Khobar Towers, they were able to hold scissors, cut sutures, dab wounds, and provide other impromptu help to the medical professionals. Dr. Robb praised their contributions: "F–15 pilots assisted the docs.... They did some good work."[84]

During the early morning hours of Wednesday, June 26, many inexperienced—but willing and capable—airmen sutured wounds. Dr. Robb recounted a single example, among a large number. He reported this exchange with one young medical technician: "Have you ever sewn before?" "Doc, my flight doc let me throw in a stitch, one time." The medical group commander then told the young tech: "You're qualified." Dr. Robb concluded the story: "I turned to Doc Treadway and I said, 'Keep an eye on him, help him out.' That's the kind of courage we saw, people stepping forward, that night."[85]

The caregivers began sewing up patients on the tables of the dining hall sometime after 1 a.m, and did not finish their work until after 5:30 on June 26.[86] About the time they were helping the last patients, Brigadier Generals Schwalier and Dick visited the Desert Rose Inn. The incoming wing commander, who had arrived at Dhahran Air Base only half an hour earlier, described the scene: "They were just finishing up stitching up folks, cleaning their wounds. I can remember we walked over and talked to one gentleman that was lying on a stretcher. He had a broken leg; the leg had been casted. It was very sad, a very *sad* event."[87]

Khobar Towers: Tragedy and Response

The airmen faced tragedies that night, but they were not left isolated from the rest of the Air Force and Defense Department. "Never at any time," Dr. Robb emphasized, "did I feel alone." Throughout the early morning hours, telephones rang with offers of help. At 3:15 a.m., after CNN had carried an early, inaccurate report that the bombing had caused multiple burn injuries, Col. (Dr.) Klaus O. Schafer, Headquarters Air Combat Command's surgeon general, called the Khobar clinic to offer a burn treatment team. At about the same time, Col. (Dr.) James Roudebush, the U.S. Central Command surgeon general, telephoned to ask if blood supplies were needed. After medical group personnel questioned the local hospitals about their holdings, it was determined that this offer, like ACC's one of a burn team, could be declined.[88]

Earlier than these calls, at 1:15 a.m., Capt. (Dr.) Ben Simmons, the U.S. Navy, Central Command surgeon general, had telephoned his service's Administrative Support Unit in Bahrain and directed it to augment the Khobar Towers clinic. The ASU dispatched ten medical personnel, and supplies. Dr. Robb chuckled when he recalled how this Navy team had to cross the King Fahd causeway from Bahrain, "with its six 'Check Point Charlies.'"[89] The unit cleared all of these security posts, and reached Building 111 at 4:50 that morning, about the time that the exhausted Khobar caregivers were beginning to sew up the last of their patients.[90]

The timely arrival of the Navy team brought welcome relief to the medical professionals who had been working since 10 p.m. the previous night. Dr. Robb put it directly: "Our kids needed a little bit of sleep." Remembering the deep fatigue of those early morning hours of the twenty-sixth, he added: "I don't know what we would have done, without [the Navy medical team] being there. We'd been up twenty-four, some of us thirty-six [hours], at *that* point, and we still had to continue twenty-four hour ops."[91]

Nor was the ASU group the only assistance enroute to the Khobar Towers. The United States Air Forces in Europe's surgeon general, Col. (Dr.) Dan L. Locker, had learned of the bombing soon after it occurred. Dr. Locker immediately had gone to his office on Ramstein Air Base, Germany, and begun coordinating the medical response from Europe with U.S. Army Col. (Dr.) Ken Farmer, his counterpart at Headquarters United States European Command, and with other officers. It soon emerged that the Flying Ambulance Surgical Team stationed at Incirlik Air Base, Turkey—a five-hour flight from Dhahran—was the unit best placed to respond to this contingency. Dr. Locker had alerted Col. Carlisle Harrison, Jr., the commander of the 39th Medical Group Hospital, at Incirlik Air Base, that this FAST team very likely would be needed at Khobar.[92]

After Dr. Locker placed this "heads up" call to Turkey, he conferred again with Headquarters EUCOM. It was firmly agreed that the FAST team at Incirlik was the strongest choice to respond to the contingency at Dhahran. At 3 a.m. at that base in Turkey, one time zone west of Khobar Towers, Lt. Col. (Dr.) Cesario F. Ferrer, Jr., activated the 39th Medical Group's FAST team. Headquarters USAFE's first message to Dr. Ferrer advised him to expect 200 injured patients, another 60 who were

Golden Hour

in critical condition or hospitalized, and 19 deceased. The FAST team had just completed its turn of three months of "on call" and was not on alert status, but within two hours Dr. Ferrer selected and activated a twenty-three member team.[93] Dr. Locker later recounted how, about two and a half hours after his second conservation with Headquarters EUCOM, he called Colonel Harrison and asked how things were going. The hospital commander replied: "We're ready to go."[94]

While Headquarters USAFE alerted the 39th Medical Group at Incirlik, events were in train elsewhere on Ramstein Air Base. At about 10:30 p.m. at Ramstein, the base's Tactical Air Control Center had notified Col. (Dr.) James W. Bost's 86th Aeromedical Evacuation Squadron of the bombing. Dr. Bost had assembled his executive staff and they developed a concept of operations for a Dhahran mission. At 11:50 p.m. the Tactical Airlift Control Center at Scott Air Force Base, Illinois, put the 86th AES on standby for an alert launch.[95]

In June 1996 the 86th AES was in its "standard mode" of providing aeromedical evacuation for Europe and southwest Asia. The squadron conducted emergency operations when necessary and also flew scheduled missions, one a week to Lajes Field, in the Azores, and one a week to Dhahran, its hub base for southwest Asia. As Dr. Bost later explained: "The scheduled missions are planned and developed missions, based on requirements at medical treatment facilities in Europe. And they are flown exactly the same each week, if there are patients to move from one facility to another."[96]

That summer the 86th AES was flying thirteen C–9 Nightingale missions a week within Europe and supplementing reserve crews on two C–141 Starlifter missions that returned to the United States each week. The squadron differed from others in that, because of its European basing, its medical air evacuation crews were trained in three aircraft. The 86th used the C–9 for its standard missions, the C–141 for ones to the United States or to other theaters, and the C–130 Hercules for tactical ones, such as to Bosnia.[97]

In addition to its routine operations, the 86th AES typically moved about twenty-two "urgent and priority" patients each month. The most efficient way to transport these airmen was to divert an aircraft already inflight, and often the squadron was able to do that. The 86th was very experienced, though, at conducting special purpose missions when it became necessary to move urgent and priority patients. The unit flew about six of these missions a month, operations of the kind required by the Dhahran bombing.[98]

When the officers of the 86th AES discussed a concept of operations during the night of June 25/26, they considered the number of aircrews they should send to Dhahran. A standard aeromedical evacuation crew had five members: two nurses and three technicians. For a mission likely to last more than about sixteen hours, the 86th augmented its aeromedical evacuation (AE) crews with an additional nurse and additional tech. The seven members then could rotate their duties while airborne, and each could gain some rest during a long flight. In this case, the executive staff knew that the flying time from Ramstein to Dhahran could be as long as ten hours, and they believed that the number of patients might be large. The group concluded that three augmented air crews would be appropriate for the Khobar mission.[99]

In addition to the three augmented crews and two flight surgeons, Dr. Bost and his staff decided to send an advanced cadre (ADVON) team, which consisted of a flight nurse, one AE technician, a duty officer, two controllers, and a Joint Medical Regulating Office flight. The guidance that the 86th AES received from Headquarters EUCOM assumed that the unit would pick up the Khobar patients and move them immediately. During their nighttime planning session, Dr. Bost and his officers concluded that it would be useful to have an ADVON team that could help manage the staging, and the flow, of patients at the Dhahran Air Base flightline. They judged correctly, as Dr. Bost related, that the medical professionals at the Khobar Towers "who would normally begin to organize and stage patients were probably already very, very involved" with giving emergency care and would welcome an ADVON team's help with management and communications.[100]

About 1 a.m. on the twenty-sixth, the officers finished this preliminary planning, left their building on the Ramstein flightline, returned to their quarters, and rested in preparation for the work ahead of them. The group reassembled later that morning and, as Dr. Bost later recalled, "we revised the C–141s that had been identified by the [Ramstein Tactical Air Control Center], the transporting aerovac crews, and we deployed [that] afternoon." The 86th AES already had built some equipment pallets for a relief mission to the Central African Republic, earlier that month, a development that saved the unit some of the time it would need to prepare for the Dhahran flight.[101]

About 2:30 p.m. on Wednesday, June 26, two aeromedical evacuation C–141s departed Ramstein for Dhahran Air Base. As planned, the first carried the 86th's ADVON team, two augmented medical crews, and two pallets of supplies and equipment. The third of the augmented air crews flew on the second of the AE Starlifters.[102]

Also traveling with the first echelon of the 86th AES was a three-member Critical Care Aeromedical Transport Team (C-CATT), of the 59th Medical Wing. When Headquarters USAFE had alerted the 39th Medical Group at Incirlik, it also put on notice this C-CATT at Ramstein. Like the FAST team in Turkey, the critical care unit in Germany began preparing to deploy in advance of its formal orders. The chain of events started as early as 10:30 p.m. at Ramstein, when the base's Tactical Air Control Center had notified the 86th AES of the Dhahran attack. Half an hour later, the Aeromedical Evacuation Coordination Center, housed in the same building as Dr. Bost's unit, alerted the C-CATT of the Khobar bombing and informed it that at least one critical care team would be dispatched within the next twenty-four hours. Maj. (Dr.) Thomas E. Grissom, an anesthesiologist, promptly mobilized a C-CATT consisting of himself, a critical care nurse, and a respiratory therapist. These three personnel flew with the 86th AES on its early afternoon flight from Ramstein.[103]

On that same C–141 with the C-CATT and medivac crews was a stress management team from the Landstuhl Regional Medical Center, about four miles south

Golden Hour

of Ramstein. Occupying about 470 acres on top of windy Kirchberg Hill, the LRMC was the largest Defense Department hospital in Europe. This facility had a long history of providing medical care during contingencies on that continent, in the Middle East, and elsewhere.[104]

The deployment of the Landstuhl stress management team was another activity that followed from Dr. Locker's telephone conversations with Headquarters EUCOM. Around 3 a.m. at Ramstein, Dr. Farmer asked the LRMC to deploy a stress debriefing team to Dhahran.[105] At the time of the Khobar attack, U.S. Army Col. (Dr.) Kevin C. Kiley was attending a conference in Heidelberg, Germany. In his absence U.S. Army Col. (Dr.) Ney M. Gore, the LRMC's deputy commander for clinical services, served as the hospital's acting commander, and he quickly began mobilizing a stress management team.[106] About 4 a.m. U.S. Army Col. (Dr.) Normund Wong, the chief of the department of pyschiatry, called U.S. Army Lt. Col. Bruce E. Crow, who had been chief of psychology since January 1995 and had led a stress management team to Riyadh after the November 1995 bombing. Colonel Wong asked Lieutenant Colonel Crow if he would be willing to lead another such group to Saudi Arabia, and Crow immediately agreed. U.S. Army Lt. Col. Sherry Conner, the chief of social work services, learned of the Dhahran attack from a phone call in the early morning hours, sometime around 3 or 4 a.m. For a while it remained uncertain whether she or another officer would serve as the team's senior social work services member. By 7:30 a.m. it was confirmed that this other professional was not available, and the assignment was hers.[107]

The Landstuhl stress management team that emerged that morning consisted of fifteen members, six officers and nine NCOs representing a broad spectrum of the hospital's professional disciplines: psychology, social work, chaplaincy, occupational therapy, nursing, and psychiatry. It was composed of Army personnel, with the single exception of TSgt. James B. Cooper, Jr., an airman who was the 86th Medical Squadron's NCO in charge of psychology services. Sergeant Cooper later emphsized how well the team worked together. "I was really proud to be a part of it," he said. "We had a really good group of people."[108]

These fifteen professionals had to begin mobilizing quickly because, among other things, they would have to secure their country clearances for Saudi Arabia. The team assembled promptly and were ready to leave Landstuhl by 8 a.m. on the twenty-sixth. "We had the vans ready to go," Lieutenant Colonel Crow said, "and it was just a matter of getting people into the vans and their bags into the vans." The LRMC stress management team was on the Ramstein flightline by about 9 a.m., and eventually boarded the first of the two C–141s carrying the 86th AES crews, supplies, and equipment. "When we got on the aircraft," Colonel Crow related, "the Ramstein-based crew, the medivac crew, was on the aircraft, so we talked to them and asked them what they knew."[109]

Dr. Locker coordinated with Dr. James Roudebush the deployment of this Landstuhl team, the C-CATT from Ramstein, and the FAST team from Incirlik. Over the phone at 3:50 a.m. in Dhahran, the CENTCOM surgeon general reviewed

Khobar Towers: Tragedy and Response

with Dr. Robb these assets and those of the 86th AES. Dr. Roudebush informed the senior physician at Khobar that the two C–141s which would carry the 86th's AE crews and ADVON team were standing ready at Ramstein. He also told Dr. Robb that there was another pair of Starlifters on the East coast of the United States, two KC–135 Stratotankers in Europe, and another two of these tankers in the eastern U.S.[110]

An intense spirit of cooperation prevailed that night. It was well evidenced in a telephone conversation that Dr. Robb remembered having with Dr. Locker, during the morning of the twenty-sixth. Their dialogue featured a series of brisk affirmatives from the Headquarters USAFE command surgeon. Locker: "Doug, what do you need?" Robb: "I could use some of *this*, a couple of . . . boxes [of suture supplies], a surgeon or two." Locker: "Check. On its way." Robb: "Combat Stress Team." Locker: "Check. Already on its way." Robb: "I could use some more med supplies." Locker: "Check. Already on its way."[111]

This concise exchange between two Air Force officers represented the professionalism that was evidenced over and over again that night. In July 1997 Dr. Robb reflected: "The people were just *there*, when you needed them. It was that way *all night long*, and it was that way for weeks afterward. I'm not talking about just the medics. I'm talking about *everyone*."[112]

The care of the wounded was an inspiring success story, but it was set against a backdrop of tragedy. Among the hundreds of patients to reach the clinic were two who were beyond help. Dr. Treadway chose the administrative area of the clinic, which could not be used to care for the wounded, as the most appropriate temporary resting place for these remains and an informal morgue was set up there at 11:55 p.m. Chaplain Dennis E. Aleson recalled that the two bodies "were put in back rooms, away from all the hustle and bustle at that point. I was called to go have moments with the bodies, which for me was having a word of prayer, praying for the individuals and their family members, who, at that . . . time, would not have a clue as to what had happened, yet."[113]

By 2:30 a.m. on June 26, mortuary services personnel knew of thirteen fatalities: the two remains at the medical clinic, and eleven others recovered at the bombing site. By 3:15 a.m., they had established a count of sixteen; by 5:30 a.m., seventeen; by mid-morning, eighteen. By mid-day on the twenty-sixth, the final number—nineteen—was certain.[114]

Chapter Seven

Accounting

The survivors of the Dhahran bombing had dealt quickly with the injuries of the wounded and respectfully with the remains of the deceased. They then turned their efforts to what Lt. Col. Douglas R. Cochran, commander of the deployed 58th Fighter Squadron, called the "next big challenge." They began accounting for the personnel of the Khobar Towers.[1]

When Brig. Gen. Terry Schwalier met with his group commanders at the Wing Operations Center, he instructed Col. Scott Gration, his operations group commander, to go to the Desert Rose Inn and oversee the accounting of the casualties and survivors. At the dining hall, Colonel Gration convened a meeting of the squadron commanders and directed them to conduct a "face to face" accounting of their personnel.[2] Many questions had to be answered, as soon as possible. Who were the survivors? Who were the injured, and where were they? At the Khobar Towers? In a Dhahran hospital? Which one? Nineteen airmen had been killed. Who were they? Who would notify their families of their death?

The terrorists struck without notice in the dead of the night, and it was not surprising that false reports sprouted in the immediate aftermath of the bombing. One officer who was at the Khobar Towers during the attack later stated that his colonel in the United States had been told there were thirty-eight confirmed dead, all of them from his unit. A first sergeant acknowledged that accounting for personnel "initially, in the chaos, was kind of hard." An officer assigned to a base that suffered casualties from the bombing said that the first report received from Dhahran had proven sadly wrong. The installation initially was told that its personnel had been on a part of the compound away from the blast, and none had been harmed.[3]

It was not remarkable that these false reports surfaced; it was remarkable that the personnel of the deployed units refuted them as quickly as they did. The squadron commanders, first sergeants, and others conducted an efficient accounting of the Khobar Towers personnel that night. Working under terrible circumstances and improvising much of the process, they got the job done. "In a couple of instances," one officer later conceded, "I think we should have been a little more careful. But overall, it was just amazing the way it worked."[4]

Two of the deployed squadrons suffered thirteen of the nineteen fatalities. The 58th Fighter Squadron lost eight personnel killed; the 71st Rescue Squadron, five.

Khobar Towers: Tragedy and Response

Because of their casualties, these two units faced the greatest difficulties in accounting for their personnel, yet they did so in timely fashion, a feat that spoke volumes about how well the airmen responded to the terrorist attack.[5]

The process posed, as Lt. Col. Doug Cochran said, a big challenge. It involved a considerable number of people. In the case of his own 58th Fighter Squadron, 259 officers and airmen had deployed to Dhahran. The personnel who lived at the Khobar Towers were serving in a provisional wing; every person did not know everyone else. It was hardly surprising that Lieutenant Colonel Cochran did not recognize on sight all 259 members of his own deployed squadron. More than 40 had come from units of the 33d Fighter Wing other than the 58th. Another complicating factor was that the members of a squadron did not necessarily live near one another. In the instance of the 58th, they were scattered among five dormitories.[6]

The attack came at about 10 p.m. at night. At that hour many people were in bed or in their sleepwear. They were not wearing uniforms or "dogtags," or carrying wallets or purses.[7] Ambulances had rushed the badly injured casualties to hospitals in downtown Dhahran. Despite the airmen's best efforts, as described by MSgt. Dwayne R. Berry, to keep track of the patients' names and destinations, the vehicles sometimes had to be dispatched without waiting for any record keeping.[8]

The trauma of the bombing, of course, further hindered the accounting. The attack left some people, as one veteran of it pointed out, in a state of "semi-shock," and they reported in good faith that they had seen individuals whom, in fact, they had not seen. Second-hand information circulated in the night. An officer in the States related: "I got a call from 'Bob,' and 'Bob' said that he saw 'Bill,' and 'Ted,' and 'Alice.'"[9]

Colonel Cochran's most pressing problem was that he had no squadron roster, and for a good reason. The immediate concern of the commanders, first sergeants, and everyone else that night, had been to evacuate the dormitories quickly. Only later did the utility of a roster come to the fore. Drawing on his own experience that night in Building 127, Cochran made the point well: "When you're picking yourself up with a whole mouthful of glass, you're not thinking about those things."[10]

The Personnel Support for Contingency Operations team maintained a computer database that would have been valuable to Colonel Cochran and the other commanders, but the PERSCO offices had been located in Building 132. This structure stood just southwest of the blast site at dormitory 131 and had been damaged by the explosion. Airmen eventually would recover the PERSCO database, but not until 4 a.m. in the morning of the twenty-sixth. The team then was able to produce a list of personnel, with their dormitory assignments and room numbers, that proved helpful to the 58th Fighter and other squadrons.[11]

While the PERSCO database was at first unavailable, the bases back in the States helped address this problem. At Colonel Cochran's home station of Eglin, for example, during the evening of June 25, Ms. Linda Brown, the director of that base's Family Support Center, and one of her staff developed a list indicating which 58th Fighter Squadron personnel were in Dhahran and which were not. She later

Accounting

described her efforts: "Colonel Cochran was trying to determine who was missing, or who they hadn't accounted for, by developing...a list of who was *there*.... We were...helping him determine who should have been there, or who wasn't there— who had been sent home early, or whatever." The same process went on at Patrick and elsewhere in the States.[12]

The 58th overcame the lack of a squadron roster and other difficulties and accounted for more than 90 percent of its personnel within an hour of the attack. There was only one way to begin: "We just sent people out," Colonel Cochran explained, "and did head counts." MSgt. Cedrick Williams, the 58th's first sergeant, went to the Desert Rose Inn, where a large number of people from various units were mingled together. He took a direct approach to identifying the members of his squadron. "I walked through the crowd," Sergeant Williams recounted, "and I was calling out '58th Fighter Squadron!' so that people in the 58th knew that they were to follow me to a certain area, so that we could...do the accountability."[13]

The 71st Rescue Squadron's early effort at accounting was similar to that of the 58th Fighter Squadron, with the added difficulty that its deployed commander, Lt. Col. Thomas H. Shafer, had been wounded in the bombing and taken to the Arabian American Oil Company Hospital. Capt. Russell D. Barile, a pilot in the 71st, had been exercising at the gym at the time of the attack and later made his way to the triage area at the Desert Rose. Here he saw Lieutenant Colonel Shafer and other members of his squadron and realized that he now was the unit's most senior uninjured officer.[14]

Captain Barile's situation with the 71st was similiar to Colonel Cochran's with the 58th. The captain knew that at 10 p.m. the rescue squadron had a maintenance crew at King Abdul Aziz Air Base, and like the 58th, its other personnel had been scattered among the gymnasium, the "Khobar Konnection," and other places across the compound. (By Lieutenant Colonel Shafer's later reckoning, at the time of the blast, ten members of the unit had been on the military flightline and twelve others in the gym or other Khobar locations.) Furthermore, the 71st was scheduled to gain some new arrivals that night. Col. Thomas R. Friers, the commander of the 1st Rescue Group back at Patrick Air Force Base, Florida, later commented on this complicating factor: "We had a couple [of people] enroute [to Dhahran] and we didn't know if they were there yet. As a matter of fact, one or two arrived about an hour after the bomb went off."[15] Barile, like Cochran, had to work without a squadron roster. The accounting, he stated, "took awhile because we didn't have a list. All the lists of personnel of the squadron were in the building [131] that blew up."[16]

In the absence of a roster, the 71st identified its survivors and casualties in much the same way as the 58th did. As Captain Barile later related: "We went basically off memory.... We spent the rest of the night trying to get a good count, trying to figure out what was going on." Like Colonel Cochran, Barile was assisted by his squadron's deployed first sergeant. In the case of the 71st, this was MSgt. Dwayne R. Berry who, like Barile, had been in the gym at the time of the blast.[17]

Khobar Towers: Tragedy and Response

Captain Barile and Sergeant Berry had some reliable starting points for their accounting. They had seen which officers and airmen had been with them in the gym, and they knew about the maintenance crew on the military flightline. Barile and Berry also could account for other squadron members—dead, wounded, and well—whom they themselves had encountered since the attack.[18]

Like Sergeant Williams of the 58th, they used a direct method to round up the personnel of their unit. As Sergeant Berry later put it, they "grabbed people" and told them to stay put "until we can get an accounting." Captain Barile got on a brick radio and called the military flightline, where there was a personnel list. Like the 58th, the 71st finished its initial accounting quite rapidly, within an hour or two of the explosion.[19]

The airmen made the accounting as quickly as they could, so that the losses could be reported without delay. Hundreds of families would agonize until the facts were confirmed. A prompt accounting was also important so that the recovery operations at Building 131 and elsewhere could be stopped as soon as possible. The blast had left the dormitories and other structures in uncertain condition and searchers could be killed or injured if walls or floors gave way. At the same time, the rescue workers wanted to be certain they had retrieved all of the injured, and all of the remains, from Building 131 and elsewhere. One officer summed up the importance of the accounting process: "We need to let people know what's going on, and I need to know whether I need to keep on digging out rubble, over there. If there's somebody who I haven't accounted for, he may be buried alive."[20]

No one had a more emotional task that night than the members of the Search and Recovery teams, who retrieved the remains from the stricken buildings and the rubble near them. Col. Gary S. Boyle, the 4404th Wing's support group commander, had arrived quickly at the bombsite and acted as the on-scene commander. The commander of the wing's services squadron and chief of the SAR teams was Maj. Robert E. (Rob) Taylor. One SAR team was organized to search damaged buildings and another the areas around them. These teams were made up of members of the services squadron familiar with mortuary affairs, assisted by firefighters from the civil engineering squadron, and by other volunteers. Later, after a mortuary collection point had been established on Dhahran Air Base, a third SAR team was assigned there.[21]

TSgt. George Burgess, a resident of Building 131, volunteered to help the SAR team that searched his dormitory. "Every time we did a floor," Sergeant Burgess recalled, "we'd come out and we'd talk to Colonel Boyle. He'd ask the condition of the floor, and if we'd found somebody." Burgess later realized that Colonel Boyle had raised these questions because he was concerned about the soundness of the structure and for the safety of the searchers.[22]

Sergeant Burgess distinguished between searching the upper levels of the dormitory, where he did not know the occupants, and his own first floor and the one above of it, where the residents had been his friends. Half a year later, his memories were vivid: "I remember doing the sweeps.... We were on the first two floors, the ground and the first floor. They were the hardest floors for me to go through, because I *knew* the people." Searching for his friends in the darkened, dust-covered rooms, the airman's emotions became so intense that he went through an out-of-body experience. "I could see myself," Burgess recalled, "bending over a body.... It was like a panoramic view. I'd actually [see myself] move around and check, to make sure I was checking [a] pulse right." He described in simple terms his extraordinary experience: "It was like there were two of me in the room. I was watching 'him' [doing] what I was doing." Even during the minutes that Burgess lived through this out-of-body experience, he recognized at some level what was happening to him, and he perservered in the job at hand. In his own words: "When I was watching myself, I thought, 'I've lost it,' but, you know, *you kept* going."[23]

After Burgess and the other SAR workers removed the bodies from Building 131, other airmen faced the equally emotional task of caring for them. Working at the bomb site, members of the mortuary services squadron began, at 11:25 p.m., the sad duty of putting eleven remains into body bags. Some Saudi Arabian soldiers told them that a local ambulance had taken at least one other deceased victim to a Dhahran hospital. Somewhat later, just before midnight, medical personnel carried two remains into the administrative rooms at the back of the clinic.[24]

At 11:30 p.m., while the SAR team members were putting the remains into body bags, the U.S. Army officer who commanded the Theater Communications Management Cell telephoned Lt. Col. Jimmy M. Quinn, commander of the 4404th Communications Squadron. Housed in the Khobar compound's Building 117, the TCMC was a United States Central Command function overseen by the 335th Signal Command, U.S. Army Forces, Central Command.[25] The Army and Air Force held joint responsibility for communications in the southwest Asian theater. The green-suited service had long experience in the region with this specialty, and cooperated closely with the blue suiters. In this case, the Army officer who commanded the TCMC called Colonel Quinn to inform him that the telephones in his facility had survived the bombing and remained in service.[26]

This was a helpful piece of information because Lieutenant Colonel Quinn needed to find a viable location for the Site Recovery Center, the facility where the permanent Disaster Control Group would operate. The wing's prebombing plans had called for putting the SRC in the civil engineering squadron's conference room, but that area proved too small to handle the communications equipment required in the wake of an attack of this magnitude. Acting on the information from the TCMC, Lieutenant Colonel Quinn and 1st. Lt. Stan S. Diamanti, one of his communications officers, set out immediately for Building 117, at the southeastern corner of the compound. The two quickly determined that a room on that structure's first floor could adequately house the SRC. By 11:45 p.m., Colonel Quinn had settled on this location in Building 117 and had begun marshaling the personnel for it. Lt. Col. Francis (Frank) W. Shealy, deputy commander of the wing's support group; Maj. Ronald D. Loyd, commander of its mission support squadron; Capt. Bob Jones, chief of the PERSCO office of the mission support squadron; and other officers helped get the SRC up and running by 11:55 p.m.[27]

Khobar Towers: Tragedy and Response

Sometime after 1 a.m. in the morning of June 26, one of the communications officers serving on the Disaster Control Group telephoned the Air Mobility Command cargo terminal, on the east side of the runways of Dhahran Air Base, and talked to Capt. Dennis V. Red about setting up a mortuary collection point. Captain Red said that an MCP could be established in the back, or northern, part of the large AMC building, which was adjacent to Dhahran's military flightline. The base's support plan provided for exactly this eventuality, because the AMC cargo terminal had many of the features a mortuary collection point needed, including a warehouse that could be cleared away promptly and a large garage. Most important, since the transports flew in fresh meat, vegetables, and other produce for the small commissary that the United States Military Training Mission operated in Dhahran, the terminal also had spacious walk-in freezers.[28]

By 1 a.m. on the twenty-sixth, before the wing's services squadron personnel had established the MCP at the AMC terminal, agencies all over the United States were flooding the telephone lines into the SRC and the Khobar Towers clinic, asking the names of patients, their status, and other questions. At least one officer who was on the compound that night was willing to acknowledge later that considerable pressure was brought to bear on the wing's personnel to identify the casualties and to "let people know what's going on." Another, from his perspective back in the States, commented that in the wake of the bombing, communication "with Dhahran at the time was not the best," because the personnel in the theater had so much to do.[29]

Around 1:40 a.m. the wing's communications squadron began preparing to move the SRC facility and its accompanying DCG personnel from Building 117 to a side room of the Desert Rose Inn, its executive dining area. Brigadier General Schwalier chose this new location because it stood closer to Building 131 than Building 117 did. Further, by the early morning hour when this decision was made, the medical caregivers had established their suture stations at the Desert Rose, making it the best place for getting immediate information about many of the Khobar patients.[30]

Communications personnel moved an initial telephone to the dining hall from Building 110, which stood just west of it. Then they laid cable, reprogrammed the switches, and by 2:45 a.m. had put fifteen phones into the new SRC site.[31] The comm airmen also brought a collection of land mobile radios, and batteries and chargers for them, to the Desert Rose Inn from Building 103, a structure on the east side of the complex that had been damaged by the attack. An Army officer who visited the SRC described it succinctly: "They had a bank of phones set up to monitor all the communications pertaining to the disaster."[32] A personnel specialist who was at the Desert Rose that morning later praised the decision to relocate the SRC, the area selected for it, and the rapid rate at which the communications squadron did its work.[33]

While the comm airmen performed their important tasks, the chaplains continued their own professional efforts. Lt. Col. (Chaplain) Dennis E. Aleson, the senior chaplain at Khobar Towers, and TSgt. Donnell Thompson, his chaplain readiness team partner, had worked through the middle of the night at the medical clinic.

Returning to their dormitory, Building 131, they came upon a group of airmen from the services squadron working in the street, placing into body bags the eleven remains that had been recovered as of that time. As Chaplain Aleson recounted, he and his partner "moved to be available to some of the people who were traumatized by that—some of those who had been searching [Building 131], the care givers, and so on." Later, the two chaplains helped the services personnel load the eleven remains into a refrigerated truck.[34]

Around 5 a.m. five airmen from the services squadron and a sixth, a volunteer from the wing's transportation squadron, drove this vehicle and two others to the Khobar Towers clinic. They removed the two remains from the back rooms of this building and respectfully placed them with the other eleven. The three vehicles then made a solemn convoy from the Khobar Towers to King Abdul Aziz and the AMC terminal, the mortuary collection point. A number of people praised the members of the services squadron for their performance during that night and the following days. Brig. Gen. Daniel M. Dick, Brigadier General Schwalier's successor, said of them: "The great services [squadron] people... had to handle all the bodies, over and over, as we tried to work the identification[s]. And there's just no way you can train for that."[35]

The chaplains worked closely with the services airmen, and they provided a valuable ministry to the people around them at the MCP. In September 1996, Lt. Col. (Chaplain) Ray Hart, Headquarters Air Combat Command's chief of chaplain readiness, spoke directly from his own experience about the role of chaplains during the aftermath of tragedies like Khobar. Chaplain Hart commented that what Chaplains Aleson and Thompson "did over there was *very comforting* to the troops. I know. I've done it." The presence of the chaplains was helpful to the services airmen and to the others who came to the AMC terminal to identify the remains of their friends. Chaplain Hart pointed out that although the mortuary services personnel were well trained, that did not remove the emotional burdens from their work. He stated: "I know more than one person has told me [they are so affected that] they can't talk about it."[36]

Beginning in the early morning hours of the twenty-sixth, survivors of the attack began arriving at the terminal to face the painful task of identifying the remains of members of their units. Chaplain Aleson described the somber proceedings: "We had representatives from those squadrons with injured members who were there with us, and we stood beside them as body bags were opened and they sought to identify co-workers.... It was difficult for all. But everyone was holding up pretty well, I have to say the people were responding to the needs of the moment, in this whole carnage, and everything around us." General Schwalier praised the courage that so many evidenced during the identifications. He mentioned in particular one airman who told him she volunteered to come to the terminal because it was the last service she could perform for one of her comrades.[37]

Among those who made the identifications was Lt. Col. Thomas A. McCarthy, the operations officer of the 58th Fighter Squadron. Lieutenant Colonel Cochran, commander of the deployed unit, had asked three of the 58th's officers to identify the squadron's deceased. Two of these were maintenance officers, and Lieutenant Colonel McCarthy served as the operations representative.[38]

Colonel McCarthy related candidly that when he arrived at the AMC terminal, he encountered "the standard...red tape there, 'You can't look at these [remains], until we get this-here [authorization].' And then there was the other side: 'Listen, we need this accountability.'" General Schwalier promptly resolved this issue: officers and airmen would be permitted to view the remains and make identifications. "They cut through the red tape," Colonel McCarthy summed up, "and that worked out, and we looked at the bodies."[39]

Officers from the services squadron provided the guidance that two pieces of direct evidence, such as dog tags or ID cards, were required to confirm an identification at the scene. The personnel of the Dover Port Mortuary at Dover Air Force Base, Delaware, held the responsibility for making the final, positive identifications. Lieutenant Colonel McCarthy recalled the guidance he received at the AMC terminal: "They basically said, 'If you're not absolutely sure, don't say anything.... We're not going to use anything you say as positive ID, we're going to use fingerprints, DNA, and dental, once they get back to Dover.'"[40]

At the time the services airmen had established the MCP, about 3 a.m. on the twenty-sixth, that facility held the eleven remains recovered from Building 131 and the two from the clinic. Colonel McCarthy and the other unit representatives viewed these thirteen bodies. "And then it was a waiting game," he recalled, "waiting for [the other remains] to come in, either from the hospitals, or from digging them up from the rubble."[41]

Earlier, while SAR teams had been putting the eleven remains from Building 131 into body bags, Saudi soldiers had told them that a local ambulance had taken at least one deceased American to a Dhahran hospital. By 3:15 a.m. this information had expanded: by then it was known that there were three remains, rather than one, at King Fahd University Hospital. This raised the fatality count from thirteen to sixteen.[42]

Around 5:30 a.m., at Building 131, services personnel located a seventeenth body. Somewhat earlier, Brigadier General Schwalier had picked up Brigadier General Dick at the Dhahran flightline, and during the time that these remains were being removed from the stricken dormitory, the two senior officers pulled up in their car and parked near the scene. General Dick later described the setting: "It was a just a *surreal* sight as I stood there and looked at the facade of the building, gone.... There was...a backhoe, there, being driven by an Arab national or a third-country national, digging in the rubble." The general, like many others, was impressed by the peaceful quality of the scene, in the wake of so great a calamity. "It seemed so—*calm*," he emphasized. "It was just like a construction site; but yet, here's this bombed out building.... They were in the process of recovering one of the fatalities out of the building at that time. But what struck me was how *controlled* everything was being accomplished, at that time."[43] A few hours after the visit by the two generals, around midmorning, services personnel located the eighteenth of the remains, also at the bomb site.[44]

The morning of June 26 was an emotional one, as survivors came to the MCP to identify their friends, and it also was a time of dramatic reunions. Lt. Col. Thomas H. Shafer, commander of the deployed 71st Rescue Squadron and a resident of the top floor of Building 131, had been injured in the attack and taken to the ARAMCO Hospital. Capt. Michael D. Morelock, a pilot of the unit who lived in a suite on the same level, had suffered glass cuts and an ambulance had carried him to the same facility.[45] Captain Morelock recalled that after the ARAMCO doctors and nurses had treated him, "That's where I met up with Colonel Shafer. He was there, too, when I came out." For about two hours that Wednesday morning, the two officers sat together, waiting for a bus that would take them back to the Khobar Towers. "That was a good point," Morelock said later, "where we could start talking about the status of the folks, and how people were doing, and what we needed to do next.... It was a good time for us to just talk, get our heads together, and just deal with what had happened."[46]

Later that morning, Lieutenant Colonel Shafer went to the AMC terminal and participated in another reunion, this one with his friend Chaplain Aleson. The minister later described the poignant meeting: "Lt. Col. Tom Shafer, who I thought may have been killed... all of a sudden he drove up, that morning in daylight, that Wednesday morning.... He was involved with me in the chapel, and he was a good friend, and I was so relieved, when he stepped out."[47]

The positive mood of this reunion soon gave way to other emotions, as the two officers turned to the task at hand. Lieutenant Colonel Shafer, like many others that morning, had come to the MCP to help identify the remains. "I stood by his side," Chaplain Aleson remembered, "as the body bags were opened and he identified some members of his unit."[48]

There were emotional episodes, throughout that day at the AMC terminal. Chaplain Aleson recalled in particular a "big, burly sergeant, six-foot plus.... I saw him go over into the far corner of the hangar and all of a sudden, he was away from us, his shoulders were heaving." This NCO himself was a father, Aleson reflected, and "as he looked at the bodies, he just started to think about the wives, and the families, of those who had been killed. And that's when it got to him."[49]

The sad process of identifying the remains of the deceased continued the rest of the twenty-sixth. Sometime during the midday,[50] two NCOs of the wing's services squadron located the nineteenth set of remains and an Army vehicle carried this last body to the AMC terminal.[51] Very early that afternoon a mortuary affairs representative reported over the telephone to Headquarters United States Air Force, Central Command (CENTAF) that nineteen Air Force personnel were confirmed dead.[52] Until 7:30 p.m. that evening, survivors continued to visit the MCP and view the remains of their comrades.[53] In eleven cases, they were able to identify positively the deceased. In the other eight they were not, and these remains later were transported to the Dover Port Mortuary as unidentified fatalities.[54]

Khobar Towers: Tragedy and Response

About 7:30 p.m., after the last visitors had tried to make identifications, the services personnel finished their tasks. They respectfully wrapped the nineteen remains, returned them to their body bags, tagged them with an evacuation number and name—if known—and placed them in transfer cases packed with ice.[55] The two chaplains, who already had provided a spiritual ministry, now contributed physical work. "That's where we began to examine the bodies," Chaplain Aleson said, and "to clean them up...and to prepare them for shipment—packing ice that would go into the transfer boxes with the bodies...preparing them for the shipment back to Dover Air Force Base." There was hard work to be done, under emotional circumstances, and the chaplains pitched in. "We were helping uncrate the transfer boxes," Aleson said. "Some of them had never been opened and we had to really work to get them open. We were just doing whatever we could do."[56]

The chaplains and services airmen completed their tasks, though they met with some difficulties. One issue was the supply of body bags: services personnel found that they had only a dozen on hand. Their Army counterparts provided three and a liner;[57] an airman had collected these at Lucky Base, the Army facility near King Abdul Aziz, and brought them to the AMC terminal shortly after 2 a.m.[58] Airmen at the medical clinic also asked the ARAMCO and the Ministry of Defense and Aviation hospitals for body bags, suggesting that these two facilities could send them in the empty ambulances they were dispatching to the compound. The MODA Hospital was able to contribute some and delivered them as asked to the clinic. After 5:15 a.m, a services airman retrieved them from there and took them to the terminal.[59] In addition to the Army and the MODA Hospital, there was a third source of help. Sometime after 3 a.m. a mortuary affairs senior NCO called all of the command posts in southwest Asia and asked them to put their available body bags on their next flights to Dhahran.[60] A French transport that left Riyadh at 7 a.m. with medical supplies, for the flight of about an hour and a half to Dhahran, complied with this request. By 12:30 p.m. this source—and others in the theater—had delivered an adequate number of body bags from their prepositioned supplies.[61] While the mortuary teams waited for these, they wrapped some of the remains in blankets.[62]

A related issue was the supply of transfer cases. Sometime after 5 a.m. on the twenty-sixth, a services NCO at Headquarters CENTAF called to ask what supplies the airmen in Dhahran needed. There were about twenty transfer cases at hand that, as it developed, would have been adequate—but there was no way of knowing so at the time. The Dhahran airmen asked for sixty and were told that, like some of the body bags, these could be flown in from assets prepositioned in the theater.[63] From this point, the story paralleled that of the body bags. The same French cargo aircraft that brought those items from Riyadh also carried a supply of transfer cases. A flatbed truck delivered them from the Dhahran Air Base flightline to the AMC terminal. Like the body bags, by 12:30 p.m. all of the transfer cases had arrived.[64]

The airmen also needed ice to pack in the transfer cases, more than they had available. As early as 9 a.m. on June 26, members of the wing's transportation squadron contracted with local sources for 1,600 pounds of it. The services personnel expedited their efforts by obtaining a broadly worded purchasing agreement.[65]

Like the medical people at the clinic, those at the AMC terminal never felt abandoned. After 11 a.m. on the twenty-sixth, a Headquarters CENTAF representative telephoned and offered a ten-member mortuary team. The Dhahran airmen at first accepted. Later the HQ called back to confirm the need and although less than a hour had passed, there had been time to reconsider. The services personnel at the MCP had processed eighteen of the nineteen remains and they could see that the headquarters team would not be needed.[66]

While the mortuary teams worked at their tasks and visitors came to the AMC terminal to try to make identifications, other Air Force members did the same at the hospitals in downtown Dhahran. At the 10:15 p.m. battle staff meeting immediately after the bombing, Brigadier General Schwalier had dispatched Maj. Kevin Greenfield, the wing's judge advocate general, and Capt. Lisa Winnecke, his deputy, to the MODA Hospital. The two officers promptly gathered information about the Air Force patients there, and also at the ARAMCO and King Fahd University hospitals.[67] Through the night, other JAG personnel joined them, establishing themselves as "points of contact," or representatives, at the MODA, King Fahd University, ARAMCO, and King Fahd Military Medical Complex hospitals, helping to identify the Air Force patients at these places and monitoring their status.[68]

At 3:20 a.m. in the morning of the twenty-sixth, Major Greenfield phoned in with a remarkably precise accounting for General Schwalier. At that hour there were thirty-four Air Force patients at MODA, two of them in the operating room. The ARAMCO hospital had seen forty-four airmen who had been injured in the bombing: it had admitted seven, and would operate on one of them later that morning. Dr. Frank Hartman had confirmed for Greenfield that the King Fahd University Hospital had admitted three Air Force patients. The King Fahd Military Medical Complex had taken two more, making a total of eighty-three patients who had been hospitalized.[69]

At 3:45 a.m. Major Greenfield and Captain Winnecke reported back to the Wing Operations Center in the "Tadtown" section of Dhahran Air Base, with a list from the Dhahran hospitals, which was "as complete . . . as possible," given the circumstances. From the WOC they went on to the Site Recovery Center, which by then was operating in the executive dining room of the Desert Rose Inn. The airmen at the SRC did not know that the JAG officers had been sent to collect information about the Air Force patients at the Dhahran hospitals and, moreover, a rumor had circulated that terrorists had bombed the mall where Greenfield and Winnecke had been shopping with Mr. Marwan Darwish and Lt. Col. Christomer Dooley. When Greenfield and Winnecke arrived at the Desert Rose, around 4:20 a.m., the blue-suiters there were not only grateful to gain the information the JAG officers brought, they were relieved to see them.[70]

During the morning hours of the twenty-sixth, more airmen became available to help, directly and indirectly, with the hospital identifications. SSgt. Selena P.

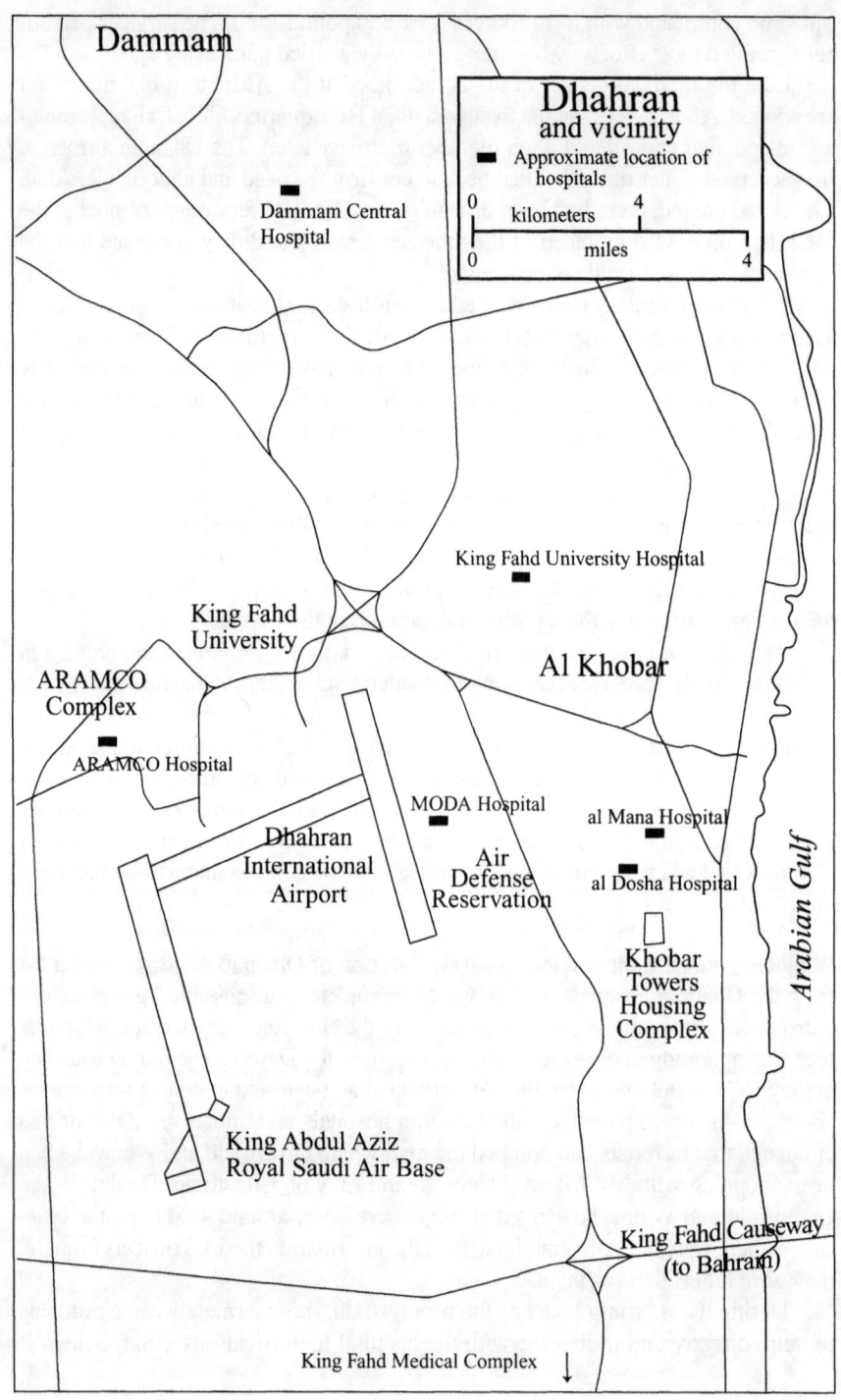

Accounting

Husted, a law office manager, was among those who contributed to the effort. Like so many others, Sergeant Husted had spent the night helping the wounded, and at about 4 a.m. that morning she lay down to get some badly needed rest. After three hours sleep, the JAG airman was roused by a telephone call directing her to report to the Site Recovery Center. By that hour, 7 a.m., a schedule was in place to keep the SRC running around the clock, with its staff working demanding shifts. An hour later on that Wednesday morning, 8 a.m., teams of medical care providers began joining the JAG representatives who were still at the downtown hospitals, working to identify the Air Force patients and to update the information about their status.[71]

While the Wednesday morning hours passed, Major Greenfield's information grew sharper. As of 8 a.m., he believed that there were about eighty-five Air Force patients in Dhahran, and he knew the identity and location of nearly all of them.[72] During the morning, Sergeant Husted carried the updated lists of names and status reports from the Site Recovery Center in the Desert Rose Inn to the WOC. At 9 a.m., when the SRC had been operating effectively from the dining hall for more than six hours, the security police deactivated their interim Disaster Control Group.[73]

During the morning, the JAG representatives at the MODA, King Fahd University, and other hospitals continued to supply information about the status of the Air Force patients in the downtown facilities, and a transition of the accounting responsibility from the legal to the medical officers began. At about 8 a.m., Lt. Col. (Dr.) Douglas J. Robb, the wing's senior physician, and other members of the wing's medical group began making patient rounds at the Dhahran hospitals. After they began this effort, late in the morning, the judge advocate general officers turned over the responsibility of the accounting for the injured to the representative of the wing's medical group on the DCG. This transfer made good sense, given that the doctors and others from the medical group would continue to visit the hospitals and determine the status of every patient.[74]

"By 10 a.m. [Wednesday] morning," Sergeant Husted later estimated, "we had the names and status of just about everybody—even if the status was pending—except for two individuals."[75] Those final identifications proved agonizingly difficult. At 4:50 p.m. that Wednesday afternoon, the care-provider team visiting the King Fahd University Hospital found a patient in the intensive care unit who had been brought there from the Khobar Towers. They immediately knew that identifying this young male airman would prove difficult. He lay in a coma, with a respirator tube down his throat. His face was lacerated, his head shaved, and his body swollen.[76]

To help with the identification, a group of officers came to King Fahd: Dr. Robb; Major Taylor, commander of the wing's services squadron; Capt. Bob Jones; and some officers from the civil engineering squadron. Dr. Robb took two Polaroid photographs of the ICU patient and brought them back to the Khobar Towers PERSCO office, acting on the possibility that someone on the compound would recognize the airman from these pictures.[77]

While these officers visited King Fahd University Hospital, half a world away, at Patrick, Eglin, and other bases across the United States, many people were wait-

Khobar Towers: Tragedy and Response

ing anxiously for information from Dhahran. The bomb had exploded at 2:53 p.m. Eastern Daylight Time on Tuesday, June 25. Col. Thomas R. Friers, commander of the 1st Rescue Group, Lt. Col. Donald R. Jozayt, commander of the 71st Rescue Squadron, and many others at Patrick had learned the tragic news from Dhahran within an hour of the attack. During the late afternoon, Colonel Friers and his deputy, Lt. Col. Robert H. Holloway, had established a crisis information center in the group's command section, located in Building 423, the headquarters of 45th Space Wing, on Patrick's Falcon Avenue.[78]

Among Colonel Friers's first concerns that Tuesday afternoon was to communicate with the group's immediate superiors at the headquarters of the 1st Fighter Wing, at Langley Air Force Base, Virginia. At the time of the Khobar attack, the wing commander, Brig. Gen. William R. Looney III, was in Azraq, Jordan, serving as the commander of Air Expeditionary Force II. Friers telephoned the wing's vice commander, Col. Felix Dupré, and gave him the unofficial information that he had about fatalities and other preliminary news from Dhahran.[79]

Another immediate concern was to develop a reliable list of all 1st Rescue Group personnel who were in Dhahran at the time of the bombing. In this regard, Colonel Friers faced some of the same difficulties as the commanders in Saudia Arabia. Drawing up a list of this kind, he commented later, was "not as easy as it sounds." It was no simple matter to account for each member of every squadron at any given time. During a typical week, two or three people from the rescue group traveled from Patrick to southwest Asia or returned home. In the case of the Khobar attack, two of the unit's members were enroute to Saudi Arabia at the time of the explosion. At first it was not known at Patrick whether they had arrived before the bombing; it turned out that they reached the theater about an hour after the attack. Friers later estimated that it took about twenty-four hours to develop an accurate list of the group personnel who had been in Dhahran at the time of the explosion.[80]

Lieutenant Colonel Holloway recruited volunteers from all three of the rescue group's squadrons to staff the crisis information center. Four airmen worked the telephones, on shifts around the clock. During the late afternoon and evening of June 25, phone calls flooded the Patrick crisis center, and they continued at a high volume through that Tuesday/Wednesday night. Colonel Holloway worked in the command section until the early morning hours of the twenty-sixth, when Colonel Friers advised him to get what sleep he could. Neither officer could know it then, but the rescue group's information center was to remain in constant operation for two and a half days.[81]

A similar scene took place at the 71st Rescue Squadron's building, on the Patrick flightline. Members of the unit worked long hours, answering telephone calls. "We acted as a switchboard," Lieutenant Colonel Jozayt said, "to patch folks [in Dhahran] in to their families at home. We tried to answer the questions of the wives and families, back here.... This continued all night."[82]

Sometime after 10 p.m. that night of the twenty-fifth, Lt. Col. Thomas H. Shafer telephoned Patrick. It was then after 5 a.m. on Wednesday, June 26, in

Accounting

Dhahran. Released from the ARAMCO Hospital, Lieutenant Colonel Shafer by that hour could give his home base a nearly complete accounting of the personnel of the deployed 71st Rescue Squadron. "Well before midnight here [at Patrick]," Colonel Friers later said, "we had a good count of exactly who was there, and an initial 'triage' report on their injuries."[83]

By the best information available at the Florida base late that Tuesday night, five members of the 71st Rescue Squadron had been killed in the bombing and nineteen others wounded. The count of five fatalities proved accurate. The figure of nineteen wounded perhaps was low, chiefly because many of the injured airmen did not come forward until after the crisis of the attack had passed.[84]

With this information available, very late that night, Brig. Gen. Robert C. Hinson, commander of the 45th Space Wing and the senior officer on Patrick, began making arrangements with the base's mortuary affairs personnel. Somewhat later, after 12:30 a.m. on the twenty-sixth, Colonel Friers called Lieutenant Colonel Jozayt at his home. The two officers discussed who would notify the two families living on or near the base of their loss. Jozayt believed that he, as the squadron commander, should take the responsibility rather than the group commander. Colonel Friers agreed and asked him to go to the base's casualty notification office.[85]

There Colonel Jozayt awaited word from Headquarters Air Force Personnel Center at Randolph Air Force Base, Texas. Although he and Colonel Friers believed they had reliable, first-hand information from Dhahran, Jozayt could not begin the notifications until he received formal confirmation from AFPC. It was after 1 a.m. Wednesday morning when he left the casualty notification office, accompanied by one of the Patrick chaplains. They drove a staff car up Florida state highway A1A along the Atlantic coast to the first household, in Cocoa Beach, and then to the second, in the south Patrick housing complex.[86] It remained for other Air Force personnel to notify the other three families. One lived in Palm Coast, roughly ninety miles north of Patrick and about a two-hour drive on either the A1A or Interstate 95. The other two households were not in Florida.[87]

West of Patrick at Eglin Air Force Base, and elsewhere, similar events took place. Eglin maintained Central Daylight Time: its clocks had read 1:53 p.m that Tuesday when the bomb exploded. Within minutes after the attack, Col. David Hayes, vice commander of the 33d Fighter Wing, had received a report of it, telephoned from the theater. With Col. Gary R. Dylewski, the wing commander, at Atlanta's Hartsfield Airport enroute to Qatar, Colonel Hayes convened the unit's squadron commanders and other officers in a battle staff meeting at 3:30 p.m. and, after more information came from Saudi Arabia, which confirmed that the wing had suffered casualties, a second one at 6 p.m.[88]

Sometime between these two battle staff meetings, Col. Lee Weitzel, commander of the 96th Air Base Wing's mission support squadron, visited the Family Support Center, located in Building 205 on Main Base Eglin. When he arrived, Linda Brown was chairing a staff meeting. "There's been a disaster at Khobar Towers," he told the group, "and we don't know what the extent of it is." Colonel

Khobar Towers: Tragedy and Response

Weitzel suggested that the Center's staff should report to the 33d Fighter Wing area of Eglin, where their help might be needed in notifying the families of what had happened. Ms. Brown and her fellow civilians locked up Building 205 and went across Eglin to the command post located in the headquarters of the 33d Fighter Wing.[89]

In terms of geography, the Family Support Center staff traveled from one part of the enormous installation to another, because Eglin Boulevard divided the 33d Fighter Wing area from Eglin Main Base. Yet in terms of military spirit, the facility was a unified whole—as the Khobar tragedy demonstrated. Colonel Dylewski, commander of the 33d, emphasized that during the aftermath of the bombing "the cooperation with main base [Eglin] was great.... Those folks from the support group, in particular, really pitched in and did everything they possibly could. *All* of the main side did." Another officer of the 33d Fighter Wing, nicknamed the "Nomads," emphasized: "There were folks who came forward and did a tremendous amount of good work for us, from the 96th Air Base side [of Eglin], who are in fact 'warriors.'" Remembering the spirit of solidarity that had prevailed during those late June days, he added with great emotion: "[They] don't wear the 'Nomad' patch, but they are Nomads in their heart."[90]

This spirit was evidenced by officers, airmen, and civilians all across Eglin that afternoon, as they communicated with the people deployed in the theater to develop a reliable accounting of personnel, and as they worked to create a process for getting information to the affected families.[91] All of the 33d's officers had been billeted in Building 127, and the survivors of the bombing had been able to account for them much more rapidly than the wing's larger and more dispersed number of enlisted personnel. Sometime before 4:15 p.m. that afternoon at Eglin, a telephone call from Colonel Cochran had confirmed that the bomb had not killed any of 33d's officers. All of the fatalities were among its airmen. "When the... *entire* enlisted corps is unaccounted for," Lt. Col. Stan Hill, the wing's battle staff director, explained, "they're *all* treated as possible fatalities"; the Eglin battle staff had to accept that "extremely difficult" working principle.[92]

The Eglin staff had to devote a yeoman effort to the accounting because, during those first hours after the attack, the members of the 58th in Dhahran faced immediately pressing problems of their own. "They were awfully busy," Colonel Dylewski stated, "trying to do their own recovery." Because of this, both uniformed personnel and civilians at Eglin contributed greatly to the effort to determine who was at Khobar, who was enroute, and who was home.[93]

During those first hours after the bombing, the battle staff officers did not yet know the status of every Eglin airman in the theater, but they felt a moral obligation to communicate with the families of the deployed personnel. "We did not have a direct responsibility," Lieutenant Colonel Hill commented, "to notify the families of the people who were deployed. But... because our number one goal in our wing is to take care of our own people,... we made a decision to call everyone whose loved one was deployed, and get information to them." He stressed an objective held at

Eglin, Patrick, and across the Air Force: "We kept the focus on the *family*.... Those [families] are what *this whole effort was about*."[94]

The battle staff officers found that the wing's emergency action cards were inadequate for the situation they faced that afternoon. These forms identified a person to notify in the event of the confirmed death of a deployed airman. The cards were fine for their intended purpose, Lieutenant Colonel Hill pointed out, but "if you just want to call and tell someone that there's been an incident, and we're trying to get information, and we'll get information to you as soon as we have it—the emergency action data card, and that system, is *not* effective."[95]

To meet their immediate need, Lieutenant Colonel Hill and some of the other battle staff members quickly prepared a script for making the initial telephone calls to the families. Another Eglin officer recalled: "They... put together a statement that they read to every person that they talked to on the phone, so that the statement wouldn't vary." Following the script, the caller identified himself, and then explained: "There was an explosion at Khobar Towers at 1355 local which caused injuries to an unknown number of people. Eglin personnel reside in this area, but there are 30 buildings and we don't know exactly which building took damage. This is all the information we have now." The script next provided several telephone numbers for the Eglin command post and advised keeping the phone lines clear, particularly those to the spouses of other deployed personnel, "so that we can contact them." The caller then reminded the family member that questions from the press could be referred to the wing's public affairs office, asked for the best telephone number to call for future communications, offered the help of the chaplains, and invited questions.[96]

When Linda Brown and her employees from the Family Support Center arrived at the 33d's command post, the battle staff officers had the telephone script ready. A few months later, she recalled what happened that late afternoon: "[We] were told that we would be calling family members to tell them—to speak from a script—telling them what was known at the time. By the time we sat down in our chairs and got ready, reluctantly, to do this, the decision was made that, no, it was inappropriate for us to be calling these families." By then the center's work day had ended and Brown sent her employees home, "to sit by the phones to wait for a civilian recall." She and another staff member remained at the command post, and worked on the list of the members of the 58th Fighter Squadron and their whereabouts, which would help Colonel Cochran with his accounting in Dhahran.[97]

Uniformed personnel, rather than civilians, made the telephone calls. "We pulled in the field grade officers," Lieutenant Colonel Hill recounted, the operations officers, the assistant operations officers, the chief master sergeants, some master sergeants, and others, and "called everyone we could get a hold of." Capt. Brenda L. Campbell, the 33d Fighter Wing's public affairs officer, recalled: "They... started calling all the spouses and all the significant [others, the] girlfriends, that people knew of, family—mother, father—if they weren't married, [or] didn't have a significant other."[98]

Khobar Towers: Tragedy and Response

Identifying and locating the people who should receive calls posed another challenge. The emergency action cards had no telephone numbers, so the battle staff officers turned to a database kept by the airmen of the 58th Fighter Squadron's orderly room. This official source was supplemented by personal information provided by fellow unit members at Eglin. Did Sergeant A have a girlfriend? Had Airman B been living with a relative other than his parents? In most cases, a fellow squadron member could answer these questions.[99]

Colonel Dylewski praised the creativity that the Eglin officers used to identify whom to call, to prepare a telephone script, and to solve other problems raised by the contingency. "There is no checklist that I know of," the wing commander said, "for a terrorist bombing on the other side of the world that kills twelve of your people." The command post personnel, as he pointed out, had "to think outside the normal battle staff 'box,' to ensure that all the proper notifications [were] done, all the right things were done for the victims' families."[100]

The use of information gathered from personnel of the 58th and from the orderly room offered an excellent example of Colonel Dylewski's point. Thanks to it, the command post telephone callers were able to talk to a great number of people. "By the time it was over," Lieutenant Colonel Hill said candidly, "we were never 100 percent successful. But we were able to reach a large volume." Having read the script, the callers also answered the questions of the spouses and others.[101]

While the Eglin officers and airmen dispensed information over their telephones, they also gained it, for by late that afternoon many of the Khobar survivors had called home from Dhahran. When some spouses heard from the Eglin command post, Captain Campbell related, they "would say immediately, 'Well, I've already talked to my husband,' 'I've already talked to my wife,' 'I've already talked to my friend.' We started gathering information [at Eglin] that way almost immediately.... Part of the way we got a lot of our initial accounting was through conversations that [spouses and others] had had directly" with their loved ones in the theater. Lieutenant Colonel Hill praised the families who, after being called by the command post, then heard from their spouse or friend in Dhahran, and immediately telephoned this news. "They would call us back, and go, 'Hey, I just heard from Bob. Bob's OK.' ... When we got a call [like that] from someone, we were able to close them out."[102]

At least one officer stated, however, that the phone calls from the survivors directly to their families posed an embarrassment to the service. "It made the Air Force look bad," he asserted. "It appeared we didn't know who was okay and who wasn't." A particular difficulty with the earliest communications from the Dhahran survivors to their homes was that they sometimes carried second and third hand information. Sometimes a husband called his wife and assured her that he was fine, and then added that he had seen airman X and officer Y, or that A had told him he had seen B. Some of these secondary and tertiary reports proved reliable, but others not. "You had to be careful with that," one officer observed, "because I know in a couple of instances we had folks who had talked to their spouse, and said, 'Oh sure, I saw so-and-so,' which actually wasn't [correct]."[103]

Lieutenant Colonel Hill emphasized that the command post treated all such second and third hand reports as hearsay. The Eglin officers never passed on to others any data they had received that way. They used only information that came from one of two sources: official channels, or "when the family called and said they had talked to their loved one."[104]

Lieutenant Colonel Hill also soon recognized that Eglin would need a single manager of the information about its Khobar personnel. While many people would serve in the command post, one person would have to take responsibility for the database. It would have to be someone who became familiar over time with "the names, the families who called in, the little things," as Colonel Hill put it. He assumed the responsibility. He explained later that he was not "trying to be indestructible," but rather, the decision "was a function of—I didn't have my normal nighttime [shift] person. [Maj. John 'Jazz'] Janazzo [the nighttime battle staff director] did it for a couple of nights, but he had another operational tasking that *he* had to go fill."[105]

As early as the night of June 25/26, Hill and the other Eglin battle staff officers knew that the nighttime shift would prove a critical time. Beginning that first afternoon of Tuesday, the twenty-fifth, telephone lines into the command post were in heavy use during the daytime. During the night the calls tapered off, giving the command post workers an opportunity to gather all their notes on the day's phone conversations and compile them into a single database.[106]

The Eglin officers also knew from the beginning, from the afternoon of the twenty-fifth, that as the bombing's fatalities became officially confirmed, their families would have to be notified as humanely and promptly as possible. In June 1996 Col. David A. Deptula, who had played a key role in planning the Gulf War's air campaign, was serving as the commander of the 33d Operations Group. Colonel Deptula prepared a list of nineteen Eglin officers, in the grades of major through colonel, who might be available for the notification duty.[107]

After Colonel Dylewski returned to Eglin, he and other officers of the 33d Fighter Wing discussed who should make the notifications. In a December 1996 interview, the wing commander identified the main factor in the determination they reached. "The appropriate decision," Colonel Dylewski said, "was that since there was... an unmanageable amount for one person to do, it wouldn't be appropriate for the wing commander to do one, and not any of the others, or two, and not any of the others.... So we decided I would do none and we would send out... teams, to do the notifications."[108]

About 6:30 p.m. in the evening of the twenty-fifth, Lt. Col. (Chaplain) Ray W. Hinsch, the chaplain of the 33d Fighter Wing, began training these teams of officers who would notify the bereaved families of their losses. Each group would consist of a chaplain, a field-grade officer, and a medical professional. Chaplain Hinch conducted a training session and concluded it with a prayer.[109]

At around 9 p.m. a phone call from Eglin's Military Personnel Flight directed Chaplain Hinsch to assemble the nineteen notification teams at the Flight's inpro-

Khobar Towers: Tragedy and Response

cessing room. About an hour and a half later, the requested time, the groups gathered at the MPF, located in Building 210 on Main Base Eglin. Earlier that night, Lt. Col. (Chaplain) Richard Parkinson at Hurlburt Field had telephoned Chaplain Hinsch and alerted him that he was sending four chaplains from that installation, just a short drive southwest of Eglin. These four professionals joined the Eglin teams at the MPF.[110]

Around 11 p.m. the Military Personnel Flight received from Dhahran the names of three Eglin personnel who had been officially confirmed as fatalities in the bombing, and by 1:30 in the morning of the twenty-sixth, two more.[111] Three of the teams set out to make the notifications. In two cases other Air Force personnel did so, because the families lived out of state.[112] The three teams completed their duty by 3:20 a.m. that Wednesday.[113] Chaplain Hinsch was informed that no more notifications would be made that morning, and he told the four Hurlburt chaplains they could return to their home installation.[114]

Chapter Eight

Wednesday: At the Khobar Towers

During the early morning hours of Wednesday, June 26, 1996, airmen remained at work on the military flightline of Dhahran Air Base. SSgt. Jacques P. Bruffy and the other maintenance crew members continued their efforts to repair the HC–130 that had returned sooner than intended, around 6:30 p.m. Tuesday evening. Working through the night, under combat conditions, they found the electrical short that had caused the fuel-correction light to flicker on and off and had brought the Combat Shadow tanker back to its base early.

They finished the repairs around 5:30 a.m. that Wednesday morning. The Saudis who lived near the Dhahran base were entitled to a period of "quiet hours," and the maintenance crew waited for 7 a.m., when they were permitted to run and test the aircraft engines. The maintainers ran a successful series of operational checks and finished their work about 8:30. Then they waited again, this time until about 10 or 10:30, when they got permission to return to the Khobar Towers. By then, Sergeant Bruffy recalled, "My uniform was getting pretty... foul."[1]

Another NCO, MSgt. Dwayne R. Berry, first sergeant of the deployed 71st Rescue Squadron, had been in the compound's gymnasium when the bomb exploded. He spent the next hours helping search for survivors, accounting for the personnel of his unit, and dispatching ambulances to the Dhahran hospitals. After these tasks, Sergeant Berry walked to the Khobar Towers Inn, the billeting office located in Building 109, just north of the medical clinic, where he met his friend Booker T. Rice, also a first sergeant.[2]

Sergeant Rice was helping the 4404th Wing's services squadron in its effort to locate additional body bags. At the time of the attack, there were only a dozen on hand at Khobar Towers, and during the early morning hours, airmen learned where there were more, in the immediate area and throughout the theater. Sergeant Rice had determined that the wing might be able to get some body bags from a facility in Oman, but at that time it was no easy task to get a line from Dhahran on the Defense Switched Network. So Rice recruited his friend Sergeant Berry to help him make telephone calls to the sultanate at the eastern end of the Arabian peninsula. Berry agreed and began some phoning, while still wearing the weight-lifters belt and exercise clothes from his gym work-out.[3]

It was a long night, too, for TSgt. George Burgess, the assistant flight chief who, with his suitemates, had been cleaning his kitchen on the first floor of Building

Khobar Towers: Tragedy and Response

131 when the blast rocked his quarters. After helping to search his dormitory and to remove the remains of the deceased, Sergeant Burgess reported to Col. Gary S. Boyle, the wing's support group commander. Colonel Boyle told him that the injured were gathering at the Desert Rose Inn and asked him if he wanted someone to take him there.

Burgess politely declined the offer. After his stressful experience at Building 131, he wanted to make the walk alone. As Burgess later put it: "I just took my roundabout way of getting back." He reported to Lt. Col. Douglas R. Cochran, the commander of his deployed squadron. Colonel Cochran asked Burgess a few questions about the state of things at Building 131, and the NCO told him what he knew from his own experiences.[4]

Lieutenant Colonel Cochran had put a priority on accounting for his squadron's personnel *before* people dispersed to quarters to get whatever sleep they could. Once that task was completed, he turned his attention to finding beds for his officers and airmen for what remained of that night, Wednesday's early morning hours. It went without saying that the airmen who had lived in Building 131 would have to move elsewhere. In the interest of safety, the security police sealed this dormitory, and the residents lost many of their belongings.[5]

Building 127, where the 58th Fighter Squadron's officers had been billeted, was one of the structures that the civil engineering assessment teams initially considered uninhabitable. Although not nearly so damaged as 131, the dormitory evidenced a crack down its center. Sleeping in those quarters was out of the question; the officers would have to spend the rest of the night elsewhere.[6]

For some people there was another reason, in addition to the physical damage to the buildings, to occupy other quarters. A number of airmen were so traumatized by the bombing that they did not want to return to their rooms. Lieutenant Colonel Cochran recognized that "some folks would not walk back into a dorm room, or a dorm building. They just felt uncomfortable with it. It brought back memories." His observation paralleled the experience of an officer who had lived on the sixth floor of Building 133, been injured in the bombing, and had escaped down the dormitory's stairwell with her suitemates. A few days later her work required her to return to the roof of the building. "That was a horrible feeling," she later recalled, "going back up those stairs that we had gone down, that night . . . taking those stairs, to the top." Perhaps inevitably, Building 131 in particular became the subject of rumors of odd goings-on. One airman asserted: "I know the cops really hated to go in that building."[7]

The members of the 58th Fighter Squadron, 71st Rescue Squadron, and other units went about the business of finding alternative housing for the night. With many of dormitory rooms unusable, Lieutenant Colonel Cochran's officers and airmen looked elsewhere. "By three in the morning," he recounted, "we had found enough units that didn't have that much damage, so that they could take in folks. The British squadron had a lot of room left over, some extra beds." Sergeant Burgess recalled: "We all ended up going over to the British barracks . . . . We stayed in the

Wednesday: At the Khobar Towers

British building, and even [there] their windows were blown out." Despite this damage, though, their ally's dormitory provided a place where the airmen could take showers and try to sleep.[8] In all, the British took in about a hundred American airmen for the remainder of the night. The French, too, offered some of their rooms. As late as the morning of Friday, the twenty-eighth, fourteen airmen remained housed in the French dormitory.[9]

Before the members of the 58th Fighter Squadron dispersed to the British dormitory and elsewhere for a few hours rest, Lieutenant Colonel Cochran gave them a short talk. He told them to reassemble later that same Wednesday morning, at 9 a.m., at their old, stricken quarters. There at Building 127, he said, they would be given the "game plan" as to what the unit would do next. Lt. Col. Thomas McCarthy, the squadron's operations officer, praised Cochran's leadership that night. "He carried everything on his shoulders," Colonel McCarthy stated. "He did not rest until everything was done and taken care of, to the expense of his own health."[10]

Lt. Col. Thomas H. Shafer performed the same role for the 71st Rescue Squadron. Released from the Arabian American Oil Company (ARAMCO) Hospital that Wednesday morning,[11] he began regrouping his officers and airmen.[12] Col. Thomas R. Friers, commander of the 1st Rescue Group, later spoke highly of Colonel Shafer's performance in the wake of the bombing.[13]

For Lieutenant Colonel Shafer, and everyone else, it proved a short night. Many officers and airmen had no chance whatever to rest. The experience of Lt. Col. (Chaplain) Dennis E. Aleson, senior chaplain, and TSgt. Donnell Thompson, his readiness team partner, was typical of scores of others. A communication from Headquarters Air Combat Command's chaplains' office that Wednesday evening reported: "[Chaplain] Aleson and TSgt Thompson haven't had sleep in 37 hours, but the adrenalin is flowing . . . . [Chaplain Aleson] will call with an update after he gets some rest." The entire 4404th Wing, as its incoming commander, Brig. Gen. Daniel M. Dick, later pointed out, got virtually no sleep "for two solid days. Everybody was just running on adrenalin."[14]

Some people had the chance to lie down and rest during the early morning hours of that Wednesday, but discounted the opportunity as worthless. A senior master sergeant who was treated at King Fahd University Hospital the night of the twenty-fifth/twenty-sixth later recalled: "I was sewed up and returned to base around 0500 [Wednesday, June 26]. I was too keyed up to sleep. I went up to my room, washed off the dried blood stains, put on my uniform and went to work." Still others tried to restore their exhausted minds and bodies, with poor results. One airman stated flatly: "None of us had a restful sleep that morning."[15]

At 9 a.m. Wednesday, as planned, the members of the 58th Fighter Squadron reassembled at Building 127.[16] Here they learned the "game plan," as Colonel Cochran had called it, for the next two days. First, the officers and airmen would move from the Khobar compound to the military flightline, within the well-secured Dhahran Air Base. Since the squadron already had been scheduled to leave soon, everyone had begun packing before the night's attack. People would go back into Building 127, retrieve their bags, and move to the hangar area. At that hour, no one could be entirely certain of the structural safety of the dormitory. After turning off the building's electricity and water, the civil engineers permitted the members of the 58th to reenter it, under the guidance that the airmen file back into one room at a time and gather their personal items quickly.[17]

Lieutenant Colonel Cochran later said of the move to the flightline: "I felt more secure. I knew that I had everybody inside a guarded area." "The flightline area was more secure" than the compound, one airman contended. "Nobody's going to get to the resources." Another recalled: "The next night [Wednesday/Thursday, June 26/27] we stayed with our aircraft. I felt a *little* more secure."[18]

The second part of the game plan involved preparing to return to the United States. "Airlift was being shuffled around," Colonel Cochran stated. The plan, as the deployed squadron commander explained it that Wednesday morning, and later, "was to fly the main body, most squadron members, out the next morning [Thursday, June 27].... After the main body flew out, we were going to fly the jets out." The timing turned out to be "amazing," as Lieutenant Colonel McCarthy pointed out: the bombing did not change the squadron's departure date.[19]

While the 58th Fighter Squadron moved to the flightline, the 71st Rescue Squadron billeted in the Khobar Towers Inn, in the interior of the compound, near the clinic.[20] SSgt. John McCarthy remembered that he and other NCOs moved into the suites there, sometime between 3 and 5 a.m. that Wednesday morning, and tried to get what sleep they could. When they awoke, their first sight was of Master Sergeant Berry, their first sergeant, along with two other NCOs, "running around and getting us a set of clothes, and some toiletries, and some answers." Sergeant McCarthy said of that Wednesday, the twenty-sixth: "We all tried to make sense of the bombing and relax the best we could."[21]

Over on the military flightline, the new quarters of the 58th Fighter Squadron took on the informal character of a campground. Lieutenant Colonel McCarthy referred to it in exactly those terms: "We set up a camp over by our hangar, by where our jets were." The airmen adjusted quickly to the makeshift arrangement. One NCO described the mood as "somber," and recalled that people cooperated well. When someone didn't have enough clothes, Colonel Cochran noticed, they traded around for them.[22] The airmen slept on cots and took showers in portable facilities. When some of the wounded began returning from the Dhahran hospitals that Wednesday morning, bunks were set up for them and for the more severely injured who eventually would have to be flown out of the base.[23]

Many of the amenities on the flightline, and on the compound, were provided by the two large American communities in Dhahran. The Arabian American Oil Company's area lay just off the northwest edge of Dhahran Air Base, and McDonnell Douglas occupied a compound jutting out into the Arabian Gulf, a little more than eight miles north of the Khobar Towers. During their longtime presence in Saudi Arabia, these two organizations had gained the goodwill of the host government, and they also enjoyed close relations with the American military personnel stationed in the country. "In Dhahran," one airman reflected, "you're separated from your family, so you bond with the people there."[24]

When tragedy struck, the Americans in these Dhahran communities responded. Lt. Col. (Dr.) Douglas J. Robb, the interim commander of the 4404th Medical Group, recalled: "Within one or two days of the bombing, every single day we got get-well cards, food, cookies, clothing from . . . the ARAMCO compound . . . . There were more pairs of Levis, shirts, toothpaste, and toothbrushes than you could shake a stick at." The ARAMCO and McDonnell Douglas communities, Master Sergeant Berry remembered, "brought us tons and tons of clothes—T-shirts, underwear, socks, jeans, shoes, belts. Once the word got to the first sergeants, all our guys went over and they gave us the first run at things."[25] Bruce Hamel, a native of San Antonio, Texas, who lived in one of these communities, was impressed with how much these corporate families wanted to help the airmen. He spoke for many of his neighbors: "We want to say thank you for being here. This is our home—a home that wouldn't be here if you weren't here." In addition to the thank-you gifts, Americans who lived near Khobar Towers also volunteered for the clean-up effort that continued for weeks after the attack.[26]

The gifts from the Americans in Dhahran were heartfelt in their simplicity. One family of four on the ARAMCO compound, in a gesture typical of many others, sent a batch of cookies and a note: "To the US Air Men & Women: We are thinking about all of you at this sad time . . . . We thank you for your work here." The schoolchildren of the American compounds sent some of the most touching gifts. One girl's hand-drawn card carried this message: "Hi. I'm Kathryn, I bet I know how you feal about loosing a friend because my friend Marshell moovd and here's a picture of how I felt." Dr. Robb commented about some of the artwork that he and others received from the neighboring children: "You know, you get these cards from the kids—first, second, third, fourth graders. When you think about it, it's scary for the kids: bombs going off in their town." He went on to observe that a "two-way healing process" took place: "One for us. And two, it was kind of a catharsis for the children, to express their feelings."[27]

Like the Americans at ARAMCO and McDonnell Douglas, the French and British were quick to help the Khobar airmen. These allies provided housing immediately, the night of the bombing, and the next day they began contributing to the clean-up that was to continue through the summer. Beginning that first Wednesday, British and French crews set to work with brooms, shovels, and cleaning equipment.[28]

The allies also helped the wing's support group to reoccupy fairly quickly Building 132, which housed the Personnel Support for Contingency Operations offices. The 4404th particularly needed the use of its PERSCO records and facilities, to account for personnel, to deal with the other administrative work created by the bombing, and to arrange for many of the airmen to return to the United States. This part of the Khobar Towers' recovery had begun soon after the blast, when Maj.

Khobar Towers: Tragedy and Response

Ronald D. Loyd, commander of the mission support squadron, had gone back into Building 132 to make certain that none of his office workers had been trapped there. Later, about 4 a.m. on the morning of the twenty-sixth, PERSCO recovered its database, critically valuable under the circumstances. Capt. Bob Jones, chief of the office, and other team members reentered their devastated work area and found the computers and data that were so important in accounting for the wing's personnel. After clearing the broken glass and debris away from the hardware, they carried it to Captain Jones's quarters, in suite 5-2 of Building 109, the Khobar Towers Inn. Working from this temporary location, the PERSCO team completed the task of accounting for the Khobar Towers personnel.[29]

As Lieutenant Colonel Shafer noted, the PERSCO team was able to regain its Building 132 offices remarkably soon. The French workcrews continued to help the wing's support group, and on the afternoon of Thursday, June 27, they finished picking up many of the glass shards that had made the workspace hazardous. Volunteers from the support group and the PERSCO team cleaned the damaged offices in Building 132, covered the blown-out windows with plastic, and ensured that every room had a functioning air conditioner.[30]

By the twenty-seventh, the PERSCO team again was operating in its old offices. The physical activity expended during the move proved theraputic and the prompt return to a familiar setting boosted morale. Although surrounded by plastic windows and other reminders of the bombing, the team members were more comfortable in Building 132 than they had been in their temporary quarters, and they could focus better on the issues ahead of them. With the accounting for personnel completed, their next tasks included doing the administrative work needed to support the imminent return to the United States of a large number of airmen and, during the days ahead, finding replacements for those who had been killed in the bombing, taken from the theater by medical evacuation, or wounded so badly they could not perform their jobs properly.[31]

The PERSCO team, support group, and other airmen received valuable help from the British and French and from the Saudis. The host nation had a history of reasonably good relations with the United States, predating the Gulf War. The Saudi medical staffs, Dr. Robb noted, remembered helping the Americans during and after Operation Desert Storm. In the case of the Khobar Towers, Robb expressed gratitude for the support he received, "not only from the Americans [in Dhahran], but from the host nation. Stuff I'll never forget, as long as I live."[32]

The airmen also were helped by the third-country nationals or "TCNs," as the Americans usually called them. The Saudis, like many other Middle Easterners, often hired workers from Bangladesh, India, Pakistan, the Philippines, and other Asian nations to cook, clean, maintain facilities, keep the grounds, and do other work. A number of Air Force members praised these TCNs for their generous willingness to be helpful. Right after the bombing, a false alarm of a second attack was raised—in part because so many Saudis and other nationals had tried to enter the compound to aid the Americans. SSgt. John C. Orlando said of the TCNs: "They

Wednesday: At the Khobar Towers

were bringing water around.... They cooked food for us.... They were very helpful. People will *surprise* you with their compassion." MSgt. Cedric Williams, the first sergeant of the 58th Fighter Squadron, recalled: "The TCNs working in the dining hall ... were probably as shocked [by the bombing] as we were. They made sure everybody got food."[33]

The meals were a welcome feature on that Wednesday, particularly to the wounded airmen who already had begun to return to the Khobar Towers. By Dr. Robb's accounting, the ambulances had taken 202 airmen to hospitals in Dhahran after the bombing. These facilities admitted 71 patients, and treated and released the other 131, who began coming back to the compound during the morning of the twenty-sixth.[34]

Nearly all, if not all, of these ex-patients returned to Khobar Towers on buses. The experience of 1st. Lt. Stephanie Bronson, a civil engineer, was typical of many. A Saudi ambulance had carried her and a few others to the ARAMCO facility, just northwest of King Abdul Aziz Air Base. An American doctor on the staff removed the glass shards from the lieutenant's feet and did some stitching for her and the others with her. She and her group spent the early morning hours of Wednesday in the hospital lobby, exchanging stories with other Air Force veterans of the bombing. The ARAMCO staff made some phones available and the airmen called, or tried to call, their families. Eventually a bus returned them to the Desert Rose Inn. They arrived sometime after 7 or 8 a.m, late enough that the dining hall no longer was being used for suturing patients.[35]

A1C. Richard J. Lavallee, Jr., was another of the many ARAMCO patients who returned to the Khobar Towers by bus that morning. Using crutches because his right leg had been injured, Airman Lavallee rested in a hospital waiting room until transportation arrived. He recounted: "At about 0430, a bus came to take us back to Khobar Towers. I got off the bus and had to ask around where our unit was staying. They were staying in the Khobar Towers Inn (billeting); I got to my room at about 0500." Lieutenant Colonel Shafer and Capt. Michael D. Morelock were also among the many who returned to the compound by bus.[36]

While these "walking wounded" returned to Khobar on their own steam, the Air Force patients who remained hospitalized received a high quality of treatment. Dr. Robb credited the Saudi doctors and staff members for giving the airmen "compassionate and skillful care." When flight surgeons and other Air Force medical professionals visited the Dhahran hospitals during the morning and early afternoon of the twenty-sixth, they came away impressed that their hosts had attended to both the mental and physical health of the USAF patients. The Saudis had grouped together the Americans, protected them with security guards, given them magazines published in English, and provided them with telephones to make calls without charge. Army Col. (Dr.) Edward B. Freyfogle was the chief of the Surgery Department of the Landstuhl Regional Medical Center and became thoroughly familiar with the Khobar Towers patients later, after they arrived in Germany. He commended the Dhahran staffs for the "excellent job" they had done in "triaging and stabilizing" their Air Force patients. His praise reflected on both the Saudi medical professionals and the USAF's aeromedical evacuation system: "When we saw the patients, we were very... pleased at how well they had been cared for."[37]

Many of the airmen who had been patients at the ARAMCO Hospital spoke favorably of that particular facility. SSgt. Eric D. Ziegler, the Building 131 resident who had tested his alarm clock at the instant of the explosion, spoke well of the treatment that he had received on the hospital's cardiac care unit. He described ARAMCO: "It's like a modern, stateside hospital. They had *everything*, and they were ready" to care for a larger number of injured airmen than they in fact received. Sergeant Ziegler was particularly impressed that one of the nurses used her own credit card to call his wife in Florida and let her know how he was doing. Capt. Mike Morelock praised the ARAMCO personnel: "People were just really friendly and helpful." Like Ziegler, Lieutenant Bronson described the facility as "a nice, big, clean hospital," and recalled that the staff made telephones available for calls to loved ones in the States.[38]

Although the local professionals had provided high-quality treatment, American medical, and other, officers wanted the hospitalized airmen moved to the Landstuhl Regional Medical Center, near Ramstein Air Base, Germany, as soon as possible. The patients were receiving very good physical care, but their morale would be stronger in a more familiar setting. U.S. Army Col. (Dr.) Ney Gore, the LRMC's acting commander, praised the Saudis for doing a "magnificent job," yet at the same time stressed that the patients would be happy to transfer to an American facility. An Air Force nurse commented: "The medical care [in Dhahran] is very good; however, there is always a big push to get our troops back home, and get them into our own system." Although the airmen received first-rate care, at least a few were unnerved by their foreign setting. In contrast to the experiences reported by many at the ARAMCO Hospital, at least one Air Force patient at King Fahd University Hospital told an interviewer that she spent the night of June 25/26 "terrified... because she didn't speak to anyone who spoke English, until the next morning."[39]

The effort to move the hospitalized airmen from Dhahran to Landstuhl began at about 8 a.m. that Wednesday morning, when Dr. Robb and other members of the wing's medical group started making the rounds of the Dhahran hospitals, visiting the Khobar patients, evaluating their condition, and determining which of them should be transported to the military flightline on Dhahran Air Base and then medevaced to Germany. As the medical professionals undertook this effort, they also assumed the responsibility of accounting for the injured, a task initially given to the JAG officers.[40]

Dr. Robb was keenly aware that accounting for the patients in Dhahran and ensuring their continued care would prove challenging. He based his expectations on hard experience: he had arrived at Ramstein Air Base the morning after the August 28, 1988, air show disaster, which had resulted in about 500 total casualties. Robb later said he had learned from that tragedy that: "The medical response is one

Wednesday: At the Khobar Towers

thing, but the aftermath is another." On that Wednesday in 1996, he drew on his *flu-tag* experience: "The next morning [June 26] I got the folks to 'go door to door.' And I said, 'You need to call every single hospital.'" Telephoning every facility ruled out the possibility any airmen would go unaccounted.[41]

While Dr. Robb and the other care providers made their rounds during the late morning and early afternoon, the number of hospitalized patients continued to decline, as airmen were discharged and returned to the Khobar Towers. At 8 a.m., about the time Robb and the others set out, the Mohammed al Dosha Hospital, a private facility located about three blocks north of the Air Force compound, released four airmen, who were picked up by an independent duty medical technician from the United States Military Training Mission (USMTM). At 2:10 p.m. al Mana Hospital discharged one patient and, forty-five minutes later, ARAMCO four more.[42]

The rounds made by the Air Force care providers established definite information about the numbers, locations, and status of the patients in the Dhahran facilities. As of 5:30 p.m., sixty-five airmen remained hospitalized. The great majority were at three locations: the Ministry of Defense and Aviation (MODA) Hospital, thirty-five patients (thirty-three in stable condition, two seriously injured); King Fahd University Hospital, eighteen (fourteen stable, three seriously injured, one very seriously injured); and ARAMCO, eight (seven stable, one very seriously injured). Three stable airmen remained at Mohammed al Dosha Hospital, and another in the same condition at al Mana.[43]

In the case of one of the King Fahd University patients, uncertainty remained. At about 4:50 p.m., the care provider team visiting that hospital had discovered an airman in intensive care, who had been brought there from the Khobar Towers. It was obvious at first sight that identification would be difficult. The young man lay in a coma, on a respirator; his head had been shaven, and his body was swollen. Dr. Robb photographed him with a Polaroid camera and took two prints back to the compound, hoping they would help someone recognize this ICU patient.[44]

At 7:30 p.m. that evening, two members of the wing's civil engineering squadron who had studied the Polaroids identified the patient as belonging to their unit. They believed he was A1C. Christopher B. Lester, a recent arrival in Dhahran from Wright-Patterson Air Force Base, Ohio.[45] By that hour, wing personnel had identified positively eleven of the nineteen remains at the Air Mobility Command's terminal, leaving eight unidentified. These eight deceased were sent to the Dover Port Mortuary, Dover Air Force Base, Delaware, as unidentified remains. At the same time, the PERSCO office categorized eight, exactly the same number, airmen as being on "duty status, [but their] whereabouts unknown," or "DUSTWUN."[46]

Following the identification made by the two CE squadron members, the PERSCO office reported Airman Lester's status to Headquarters Air Force Personnel Center (AFPC) at Randolph Air Force Base, Texas, as "very severely injured." When this report was made, one of the Khobar personnel officers urged the AFPC to be cautious about it. Doubtless others at the time agreed with this advice.[47]

Khobar Towers: Tragedy and Response

The most compelling reason for caution was that many wing personnel believed that Airman Lester looked very much like SrA. Paul A. Blais, who on the evening of the twenty-sixth remained among the missing. There was strong potential for a case of mistaken identity. Veterans of the bombing later pointed out that the two young men had similar facial shape and features, hair color, and small mustaches that were trimmed identically.[48] Brig. Gen. Daniel M. Dick, who had come to Dhahran to serve as the wing's next commander, studied the ID cards of the two airmen and the Polaroids taken in the ICU room, and concluded there was "no way in the world" he could distinguish one young man from the other. The general declared: "These guys could have been twin brothers."[49] The identification also was hindered by the fact that the ICU patient at King Fahd University Hospital was heavily bandaged, on a ventilator, and badly swollen, which made it difficult to get finger or foot prints. To compound the problem still further, Airman Lester had been at the Khobar Towers only a week, which reduced the number of wing personnel who knew him well.[50]

It was a time of wrenching uncertainty for the families of Airmen Blais and Lester. In North Carolina, Curtis Taylor, a retired Air Force master sergeant and Blais's stepfather, found himself on an emotional pendulum. At first he refused to believe that the young man he had raised from age five was dead. "I said, No, absolutely, he's alive," Mr. Taylor later stated. "They'll find him." Then he slowly began to resign himself to the news. There were eight unidentified remains, and eight DUSTWUNs. The numbers added up, Taylor said. And yet again, he could not give up. "There was still a little something," Taylor believed, "that said he is alive." Maria Taylor, Blais's mother, also had conflicting thoughts. She hoped her son would come home, but she knew "it was a horrible blast. In my heart, I knew Paul was dead somewhere. Not many people can survive something like that." Across the United States many people anxiously followed the news: in Orlando, Florida, Paul Blais, the airman's natural father; in Pineville, West Virginia, Lester's family; and elsewhere, other relatives and friends.[51]

Officers of the wing's mortuary services squadron explained to those around them that two sources of evidence were necessary to identify any remains: dog tags, fingerprints, or certain recognition by someone who knew the deceased.[52] *Official* identification of remains could be done only by the Dover Port Mortuary,[53] and the status of any Air Force member could be announced officially only by Headquarters AFPC's Casualty Center, at Randolph Air Force Base.[54] The reality of the matter, however, was that the officers and airmen at the Khobar Towers were under pressure to expedite the identifications. Spouses, parents, and other family members were telephoning the home bases of their Air Force relatives, the AFPC, and elsewhere, and these offices in turn were calling Dhahran. One airman at the Khobar Towers acknowledged "getting pressure from Randolph," because the Casualty Center was receiving telephone calls asking: "Is my son alive? Is my daughter alive?"[55] Speaking specifically of the Blais-Lester identification, one airman recalled: "Generals and high-level people were calling, wanting to know what was happen-

Wednesday: At the Khobar Towers

ing." Addressing a closely related issue, one officer acknowledged: "There was tremenduous pressure—quite honestly, too much pressure—to get the guys out, to get the fatalities back home."[56]

At 10:35 that Wednesday night, an officer from the office of the surgeon general at Headquarters U.S. Central Command telephoned the 4404th Medical Group and asked the unit to verify the status of every Khobar patient by categories that detailed each airman's condition. The caller also asked for Airman Lester's home phone number and Social Security number. The medical group confirmed this information with the PERSCO office, and provided it as asked.[57] This was where the Blais-Lester case stood, as of midnight of June 26/27.

The Air Force eventually would take criticism on this issue of identifying its personnel. The *New York Times*, for example, reported on the Blais-Lester case on July 1, and noted pointedly: "The confusion was not sorted out until Friday evening, more than three days after the blast."[58]

In addition to the Blais-Lester case, the airmen in Dhahran dealt with many other issues on June 26. While the care providers had made their rounds that morning, the 4410th Aeromedical Evacuation Flight had taken the first steps in the aeromedical evacuation of the Dhahran patients. This provisional unit, manned like other Southern Watch units on a temporary-duty basis, included three nurses and seven medical technicians. The 4410th, as one officer outside the flight pointed out, had been "*extremely* involved in the initial response to the bombing." Its members had suffered injuries themselves, and had helped suture and otherwise care for patients at the medical clinic.[59]

Now the 4410th took on another responsibility. Since there were no Aeromedical Staging Facilities or Mobile Aeromedical Staging Facilities in Saudi Arabia, the unit took the first step toward establishing one. Around 10 a.m. the 4410th secured the use of a C–12 hangar that stood next to its own building on the military flightline and belonged to the Greater USMTM Transportation Service, and so carried the earthy acronymn of "GUTS." Later, with the arrival that Wednesday night of personnel from the 86th Aeromedical Evacuation Squadron, this building would be developed as the ASF and holding area for the Khobar patients who would be medevaced to Europe. The GUTS hangar would provide, as one nurse explained, a secure area where the medical personnel stored their patient records, medical supplies, and communications equipment. The ASF also was the place, the same officer summed up, "where we planned to collect, triage, tag, label, . . . rank [the patients] in terms of on-loading and off-loading. So that's where we would maintain our operation, for the next couple of days."[60]

Having secured the GUTS hangar for the ASF, members of the 4410th joined those of the medical group at the Site Recovery Center at the clinic. That midafternoon these officers began making the preliminary arrangements for two AE missions that would leave Dhahran the next day, Thursday, the twenty-seventh. Maj. Cynthia Coles, a registered nurse in the 4410th, recounted that her unit "set up shop in the clinic, along with the medical group. We were working medevac issues, while

Khobar Towers: Tragedy and Response

[Dr. Robb's medical teams] were out at the facilities, trying to get information and feed it back to us. As soon as they got their data—names, types of injuries—they handed it back to us."[61]

While the members of the wing's medical group, the 4410th, and others in Dhahran extended themselves that Wednesday morning, the first forty of what eventually would become a much larger Federal Bureau of Investigation team arrived in Dhahran. President Bill Clinton, in his first remarks to reporters about the attack, on Tuesday afternoon at the White House, had announced that within hours a group of FBI agents would be enroute to Saudi Arabia to assist in the investigation of the terrorist action.[62] The first members of this team reached the bomb site the next morning. Mr. Marwan Darwish, the wing's liaison officer with the Saudis, secured their country clearances and made other arrangements for their stay. The Air Force Office of Special Investigations provided the initial quarters for the FBI team.[63]

As the first FBI agents reached the scene that morning, the wing's judge advocate general personnel were taking on a new task. In the immediate wake of the bombing their primary job, like everyone's, had been to care for the wounded. Later Maj. Kevin Greenfield, the 4404th's JAG, and others had gone to the Dhahran hospitals and had begun the process of accounting for personnel. During the morning of the twenty-sixth, they turned over that responsibility to the wing's medical group and took up another issue: property claims.

While human losses, of course, held paramount importance, material ones also needed attention. The Khobar Towers airmen had lost tens of thousands of dollars worth of personal items, destroyed in their dormitory rooms by the bombing or sealed off from them in its aftermath. As one NCO observed, "there would be hundreds of people who didn't have [anything], not even a toothbrush." Donations from ARAMCO, McDonnell Douglas, and others provied some immediate relief, but the JAG would have to address the fundamental problem that the wing had suffered a large loss in personal property.[64]

Processing property claims posed a considerable job, and the legal airmen had to tackle it quickly. Around 11 a.m. that Wednesday, Brig. Gen. Terry J. Schwalier, the wing commander, asked Major Greenfield to present a briefing at the command's 1 p.m. staff meeting that would describe the JAG's plan and procedures for dealing with the property claims. For his part, the commander made the commitment that, in the words of one of the legal officers, "he would get us whatever we needed."[65]

While continuing to man their seat on the Disaster Control Group, the JAG airmen took on several tasks at the same time. First, they had to find a place to do their claims work. The JAG offices, like the PERSCO ones, had been located in Building 132 and, also like them, had been destroyed. Capt. Lisa Winnecke, the wing's deputy JAG, searched the compound and determined that the best alternative was the "Ark," the Khobar Towers chapel, located in Building 13 in the southwest corner of the compound.[66]

Working space posed one issue; having enough personnel was another. Maj. Brian G. Koza of the 4409th Operations Group's JAG office telephoned from

Wednesday: At the Khobar Towers

Riyadh and offered some assistance. The Khobar Towers airmen accepted his offer, and by 11 a.m. they knew that TSgt. Rita E. Adams, a paralegal aide, would be on the next flight to Dhahran.[67]

In addition to space and manning, the legal airmen needed equipment. Early in the afternoon they went through their old office in Building 132, looking for items that could be salvaged. At first they pieced together enough hardware to assemble two computers, but one of the pair later gave out. "We were able to scrape together a computer," SSgt. Selena P. Husted related, "but we didn't have a typewriter." She praised a Saudi contracting official who later supplied them with one. In an era of high-speed electronic processors, this nineteenth century invention still held considerable value. Until the airmen got a typewriter, they had to fill out the claims vouchers by hand. This was extremely slow work, particularly, as Sergeant Husted pointed out, "when you're talking about paying fifty claims a day."[68]

The legal airmen accomplished a great deal that Wednesday afternoon. Major Greenfield, accompanied by Sergeant Husted, briefed the JAG's claims plan to Generals Schwalier and Dick and other senior officers at the 1 p.m. staff meeting. About an hour later, Major Greenfield and Sergeant Adams, who had arrived as expected, began videotaping the damaged dormitory rooms. Through the middle of the afternoon, Lt. Col. Christomer Dooley sat in for the JAG on the DCG, while Captain Winnecke rested so she could report at 6:30 p.m. to relieve him for the night shift. At the same time Major Greenfield and the other available JAG personnel moved equipment from their old office and set up the new one in the Ark.[69]

By the middle of the afternoon, the JAG airmen were confident enough about starting the claims process that they announced their hours of operation. The wing's public affairs office quickly distributed a flyer that publicized the new location and advised airmen that they could file their property claims from 8 a.m. to 8 p.m., beginning the following day. An article on the front page of the next issue of the wing's newsletter, published Friday, the twenty-eighth, reinforced this publicity.[70]

Wednesday evening the legal and finance officers discussed the best way to pay out the property claims. It was decided that JAG office would make available an emergency advance of up to $50 to airmen who needed toiletries and clothing. The operating principle was that "since members had suffered an obvious loss, they should be compensated right away." The legal personnel eventually processed 161 claims related to the bombing, totaling about $69,000.[71]

At 2:15 p.m., while the JAG airmen were removing whatever equipment they could salvage from their bombed-out office, Brigadier General Schwalier learned that within a matter of hours his unit would be hosting Secretary of State Warren Christopher. President Clinton had considered making a trip to the Khobar Towers, but decided that the arrangements required for a visit by the commander in chief might interfere with the investigation of the bombing. In his place he sent Secretary Christopher, who was then in Egypt and would fly to Dhahran that evening.[72]

Acting on this short notice, the wing quickly began preparing for the secretary's arrival. Army Col. James R. Ward, commander of Army Forces Central Command-

Khobar Towers: Tragedy and Response

Saudi Arabia, made the arrangements for the visit with the American Embassy in Riyadh. As for the necessary preparations at Dhahran Air Base and the Khobar Towers, General Schwalier later commended the work done by the wing's protocol officer, 1st. Lt. Dawn Harrington. She and many other airmen had to accomplish a number of tasks, quickly. Communications personnel, for example, had to rapidly install ten telephones and three international, direct-dial phone lines for the journalists who would cover the secretary's trip.[73]

Around 6 p.m. Brigadier General Schwalier and Maj. Gen. Kurt B. Anderson, the commander of the Joint Task Force Southwest Asia, went to the military flightline to meet Secretary Christopher's aircraft. While waiting in a private room set aside for distinguished visitors, the two generals conferred with Saudi Foreign Minister Prince Saud Faisal, Interior Minister Prince Ibn Abdul Aziz Nayef, and the American chargé d'affaires for Saudi Arabia, Mr. Ted Katouf. The secretary of state's airplane arrived a little after 6 p.m., and soon after he debarked, he made a few remarks to the press, emphasizing that the Dhahran bombing would not "deter the United States from carrying out in any way" its mission in the region.[74]

Secretary Christopher talked briefly with his American and Saudi greeters in the distinguished-visitors lounge. Joined also by Prince Bandar bin Sultan, the Saudi ambassador to the United States, and other Saudi officials, the secretary completed a rapid itinerary. He went first to Building 131 and saw the damage done at the immediate scene of the bombing. Walking with Princes Faisal and Bandar near the dormitory, the secretary vowed that investigators would find the perpetrators of what he called a "dastardly act of cowardice."[75]

Around 7:30 p.m. Secretary Christopher visited the MODA Hospital, where he saw both American and Saudi patients who had been injured by the bomb. He called on a young Saudi boy and girl who had been playing in al Khobar Park when the truck exploded[76] and also on two airmen who then were in the MODA Hospital's intensive care unit.[77] On one of the regular-care wards, while Secretary Christopher and Prince Bandar were at the bedside of TSgt. Harold R. Jautakis, from the 33d Operations Support Squadron at Eglin Air Force Base, the NCO entreated the senior American diplomat: "If you can catch the people who did this, you really should punish them bad." Prince Bandar promised Sergeant Jautakis that punishment would be meted out unquestionably: "It will be swift, harsh justice."[78]

From the MODA Hospital, Mr. Christopher returned to Dhahran Air Base's distinguished-visitors lounge, where he conducted a press conference. It was evident that the secretary had been moved by what he had seen and heard on his brief tour. His voice broke at times as he condemned what had been a "direct attack on the United States and on our friends and allies," and he promised that the terrorists would be found and brought to justice, "however long it takes." The secretary praised the heroism of the airmen who had faced the attack. He recounted to the journalists how SSgt. Alfredo R. Guerrero had spotted the truck and then, rather than flee, had raised the alarm. "Many are alive today," Mr. Christopher concluded, "because of his heroism." The secretary of state returned to his plane and left at about 9:30 p.m.[79]

Wednesday: At the Khobar Towers

Secretary Christopher left Dhahran with a favorable impression of the care that the injured had received, and more help was on the way to them. A stream of medical professionals arrived at the Khobar Towers during late Wednesday afternoon and into the night. The first of these to arrive was the 39th Medical Group Flying Ambulance Surgical Team. Lt. Col. (Dr.) Cesario F. Ferrer, Jr., had activated this FAST team at Incirlik Air Base, Turkey, at 3 a.m. local time, one time zone west of the Khobar Towers. Within two hours, twenty-three medical professionals, selected by Dr. Ferrer, were ready to leave for Dhahran. "When the call came in," he said later, "we didn't have to ask anybody twice—we even had some people disappointed they couldn't come with us."[80] By 7 a.m. a "mobility line" confirmed that each member of the FAST team had the legal identification and other documents, such as records of up-to-date immunizations and DNA testing, needed to leave Turkey. Medical, intelligence, legal, and finance officers all briefed the deploying officers and airmen. The 39th Medical Group's pharmacist reviewed the travel and personnel medications of the individual members and checked the medication roster of the team to verify that it was current and complete. By 11:30 that Wednesday morning, airmen of the 39th Wing had loaded the FAST team's four pallets of gear and medical supplies on a C-141, and the twenty-three members had boarded the Starlifter. Within minutes, the transport left Incirlik for Dhahran.[81]

Once airborne for Saudi Arabia, the FAST team divided into three components. Maj. (Dr.) Daniel DeCook, a general surgeon, served as chief of a surgical team that consisted of himself; Maj. (Dr.) Stephen Garner, an orthopedic surgeon; Maj. (Dr.) Sylvia Cayetano, an anesthetist; and an operating room staff. A medical team included Capt. Belinda Haines, a medical nurse, who served as its chief; Capt. (Dr.) Timothy Tuel, a family physician; Dr. Ferrer, himself a flight surgeon and the FAST team's commander, who backed up Dr. Tuel; five nurses; and a number of technicians. The support team was made up of SSgt. Diego Cevallos, a logistic technician; SSgt. Ray LeGrand, an administrative tech; and three other techs. MSgt. Troy R. Hoopes acted as the FAST team's NCO in charge.[82]

The FAST team landed at Dhahran Air Base at 4:35 p.m. and, not long after 5, reported to Dr. Robb at the medical clinic.[83] He quickly outlined the help he needed, beginning that evening and continuing for the next several days. First, the FAST team could contribute the staff that would be required to keep the clinic running on a twenty-four-hour schedule. The U.S. Navy's Administrative Support Unit in Bahrain had dispatched a ten-member medical team that had made a timely arrival at Khobar, reaching the clinic just before 5 a.m. that morning. These ASU professionals had spelled their exhausted Air Force colleagues, who had been sewing patients and otherwise working, straight through the night. The Navy team had rendered valuable help during some crucial hours, but had to start on its return trip to Bahrain, shortly after the FAST team landed at King Abdul Aziz. With the ASU team's departure, Dr. Ferrer's group was needed to keep the clinic running around the clock.[84]

The FAST team promptly integrated its members with those of the clinic's medical and administrative staffs.[85] "Really," Dr. Robb candidly acknowledged,

Khobar Towers: Tragedy and Response

"the FAST team took over our clinic." At 7 p.m. that Wednesday evening, one of his main objectives was met, when the Khobar Towers clinic began operating on a twenty-four basis. The crisis of the bombing's immediate aftermath had passed, but many airmen still needed follow-up care. For days after the bombing, the clinic continued to see seventy to eighty patients every twenty-four hours. Dr. Daniel DeCook, chief of the Incirlik surgical team, commented: "After the initial surge of casualties, they would have been hard pressed to deal with the smaller injuries. We did what we could do best for them." Patients who had been treated the night of the attack returned to the clinic to have their wounds examined or re-dressed, their stitches removed, or to receive other follow-on care. The FAST team, and the others who continued to work at Building 111 during those late June days, spent most of their time, as Dr. Ferrer put it, "caring for the walking wounded," as opposed to treating the more severely injured, who remained in the Dhahran hospitals.[86]

In addition to staffing the clinic, Dr. Robb's second major request of the FAST team was that its physicians help with making the rounds of those patients still in the city. He and others had been doing that since that morning, and the FAST professionals now could augment their effort. The Incirlik personnel would contribute their medical opinions as to which patients could be evacuated by air and would help assess what support they would need. Later that same night of the twenty-sixth, Dr. Ferrer would attend the initial planning meeting for the aeromedical evacuation.[87]

Dr. Robb saw other tasks for the Incirlik professionals. Beside making rounds at the Dhahran hospitals and working at the clinic, they could help set up and staff the ASF that was being established in the GUTS hangar on the Dhahran flightline. The FAST team also would contribute some administrative support in tracking patient information and would provide some spot manning, beyond the shifts at the clinic.[88]

In addition to the FAST team, other important medical help also reached Dhahran Air Base that Wednesday night, with the arrival at 10:10 p.m. of personnel and equipment of the 86th Aeromedical Evacuation Squadron, commanded by Col. (Dr.) James W. Bost, and accompanied by a three-member Critical Care Aeromedical Transport Team (C-CATT), commanded by Maj. (Dr.) Thomas E. Grissom, from the 59th Medical Wing. About 2:30 p.m. that afternoon at Ramstein, two aeromedical evacuation C–141s had left Germany carrying the first echelon of the 86th AES: two flight surgeons, three augmented (seven-member) AE crews, a six-member advanced cadre (ADVON) team, and two pallets of supplies and equipment. Dr. Grissom's accompanying C-CATT consisted of himself, an anesthesiologist; Capt. Van Billingsley, a critical care nurse; and TSgt. Terrance Pinkston, a respiratory therapist. The 86th AES and C-CATT had been able to respond rapidly because, as Dr. Bost later put it, "Our crews have been trained that things often happen quickly."[89]

These units arrived at Dhahran Air Base shortly after 10 p.m. local time, and immediately began contributing to the recovery that was underway at the Khobar Towers. Through the middle of the night of June 25/26 at Ramstein, Dr. Bost and his officers had brainstormed a concept of operations for their deployment to Dhahran.

Wednesday: At the Khobar Towers

They had anticipated that the 4410th Aeromedical Evacuation Flight would select the C–12 GUTS hangar, adjacent to its own building, to use as an ASF. "As we were sitting there thinking about it," Dr. Bost recalled, "the Aeromedical Evacuation Flight sits there right on the ramp, right next to a large hangar that was used for U.S. aircraft. And so we started deciding that, if we could get the aircraft moved out of that hangar, we could simply change that into a staging operation." The officers of the 86th also knew that the 4410th—just three nurses and seven medical technicians—would welcome the help of the AE unit. During their planning session at Ramstein, Bost and his staff made the sound assumption that the "people [of the 4410th] who would normally begin to organize and stage patients were probably already very, very involved, and did not have the capability to do it."[90]

Lt. Col. Jacqueline E. Murdoch, chief nurse of the 86th AES and a member of its ADVON team, recounted the unit's nighttime arrival, about twenty-four hours after the bombing. "We hooked up with [the 4410th]," she said, "as we always do when we fly our routine missions into Dhahran. We got a feel for what needed to be done."[91]

After the ADVON team consulted with the 4410th, they attended a meeting with Dr. Robb and members of his medical group, personnel of the 4410th, and Dr. Ferrer, the chief of the FAST team. The officers of the 86th AES learned from this session that they should prepare the ASF at the GUTS hangar for thirty ambulatory patients and fifteen litters. For the benefit of the new arrivals, Dr. Robb reviewed the status of the airmen in the Dhahran hospitals, who had been visited during the rounds made that day. Major Coles of the 4410th summarized the meeting: the medical team "and the aerovac people got together, and we went over patient by patient and decided whether [each] needed to be aerovaced out."[92]

During the hours and days ahead, the personnel of 86th AES and Dr. Grissom's three-member C-CATT team helped their Dhahran comrades in multiple ways. Perhaps their most obvious contribution was material: the medical crews brought intravenous fluids, litters, stanchions, blankets, and other essential AE equipment. The 86th also brought important administrative help. As Lieutenant Colonel Murdoch explained, the medevac of the Khobar patients required considerable planning and management. A process had to be put in place for collecting "all these injured personnel, staging them, doing our paperwork, our manifesting—because even in a disaster situation, we always need to maintain good records, good accounting of who's on our airplanes, social security numbers, and so forth.... We needed to process people through, we needed to give each one a summary medical record, to tell us what we needed to do in flight."[93]

The 86th's ADVON team provided this support. Sending this management cell to Dhahran, Dr. Bost commented later, "turned out to be a good decision." The ADVON team proved helpful in collecting patients, preparing them for flight, and unloading them. "It was *key*," Dr. Bost concluded, "to making the operation go."[94]

Dr. Bost emphasized the same point in an after-action report he wrote the next month. "An aeromedical evacuation response to the Khobar Towers bombing," he pointed out, "was generated in a very short period of time.... Deployment of an

Khobar Towers: Tragedy and Response

ADVON Team with patient management capability was critical to flight line staging and mission organization." Dr. Grissom reported: "The C-CATT responded in a timely fashion with the 86 AES for the terrorist bombing of the Khobar Towers."[95]

The medical professionals in Dhahran consistently praised the support they received from the 86th AES and the C-CATT and FAST teams. Capt. (Dr.) R. Morris Treadway, Jr., flight surgeon of the 58th Fighter Squadron, commended the aeromedevac units for their quick arrival. Dr. Robb said of the C-CATT and FAST teams: "I don't know what we would have done, without them being there."[96]

In addition to this aid, another group arrived on the same Starlifter that brought the 86th AES and C-CATT teams: the stress management team from the Landstuhl Regional Medical Center. During the early morning hours of the twenty-sixth in Germany, Army Lt. Col. Bruce E. Crow, the LRMC's Chief of Psychology, had organized a group that represented a spectrum of the hospital's disciplines, including psychology, social work, chaplaincy, occupational therapy, nursing, and pyschiatry. Landstuhl was an Army facility, and all but one of this stress management team's fifteen members were "green suiters." The Air Force member was TSgt. James B. Cooper, Jr., the 86th Medical Squadron's NCO in charge of psychology services.[97]

This group got off their C–141 at Dhahran Air Base shortly after 10 p.m. and, like both the 86th and the C-CATT, had reached Dhahran almost exactly twenty-four hours after the terrorist attack. It was a timely arrival. A professional concensus holds that stress debriefing teams are most effective when they can intervene within eight to seventy-two hours of the event. Sergeant Cooper said of Landstuhl group's arrival within twenty-four hours: "That was on the money. We saw that as a very good thing, that we could get there so quickly after the bombing."[98]

Lieutenant Colonel Crow telephoned back to Landstuhl's operations center and reported the team's safe arrival. The group waited a short time for a bus that would carry them on the ten-minute ride from the military flightline to the Khobar Towers. Sergeant Cooper recalled: "Initially, when we got on the ground there, we had to wait a little bit.... Some people met us and briefed us as to what was going on, what had occurred." From these earliest encounters with Air Force personnel that night, the LRMC team learned that the bomb had killed and injured military personnel, and not any family members, a piece of basic information that was very helpful in planning the stress debriefings.[99]

The bus took Lieutenant Colonel Crow's group to the Khobar Inn where, twenty-four hours after the attack, the billeting office continued its efforts to find rooms for the many dormitory residents displaced by the bombing. "It was still very chaotic," one of the Landstuhl officers recalled. "There were a lot of people trying to get rooms." With the billeting office doubling and tripling airmen into rooms, the LRMC group felt fortunate to get lodgings, on the fourth and fifth floors of the Khobar Inn.[100] Entering the rooms, one officer was abruptly confronted with the destruction that had *caused* the team's visit: "And I don't think it truly *hit* me until I walked into my suite" and saw that "the windows had been blown out. The glass, most of it, had been cleaned up, but the curtains were torn."[101]

Wednesday: At the Khobar Towers

After settling into their rooms about 11 p.m., a few members of the stress management team walked the short distance east from the Khobar Inn to the Desert Rose, for a late-night meal. Most turned in for the night, knowing, as Sergeant Cooper put it, "the next day would be very busy."[102] Lieutenant Colonel Crow, the officer in charge, wanted to meet some of the Khobar personnel that night and get a leg up on the work ahead. He, Sergeant Cooper, and Army Lt. Col. Barry Minsky, the Landstuhl team's chaplain, went over to the medical clinic, just to the south of the Khobar Inn, and met with Dr. Robb and MSgt. Patrick R. Stark, the medical group's first sergeant. The doctor gave the Landstuhl group a helpful introductory briefing, and the discussion then turned to where they could conduct their sessions. Since the clinic, Building 111, was one of the eight-story Khobar "towers," it offered enough space to suit this purpose. The medical group made available to the Landstuhl team their conference room, a nurse's office, and two day rooms.[103]

After meeting with Dr. Robb at the clinic, Lieutenant Colonel Crow and Chaplain Minsky made the short trip to Building 13, the location of the Ark.[104] Here at the compound's chapel they learned that Khobar's religious professionals already had arranged for any airman to receive counseling, at any hour around the clock. When the terrorists had struck, roughly twenty-four hours earlier, there had been only two chaplains on the compound: Chaplain Aleson, the wing's senior chaplain, and Capt. (Father) Thomas Angelo, its Roman Catholic one. The military's religious community responded quickly to the attack. An Air Force chaplain on a site visit in Oman returned to Khobar; two Navy chaplains reported from Bahrain; two more Air Force chaplains came from Riyadh;[105] and a Royal Air Force chaplain, visiting British troops in the area, also joined the group. By the middle of Wednesday morning, less than twelve hours after the bombing, Chaplain Aleson summed up, "we had eight chaplains, and additional support." With these professionals on the scene, the Khobar airmen could receive religious counseling twenty-four hours a day. "The chapel itself," Chaplain Aleson pointed out, "was not heavily damaged, and became a round-the-clock operation."[106]

After Colonel Crow learned that the chaplains were so well staffed for counseling, he next wanted to meet with the medical representative and other members of the Disaster Control Group. While Chaplain Minsky went back to the Khobar Inn and joined those who had turned in for the night, Crow and Sergeant Cooper[107] headed for the Site Recovery Center, which by then had been operating in the executive dining room of the Desert Rose Inn for almost twenty-four hours. The NCO, the only blue-suited member of the Landstuhl team, later reflected that Colonel Crow wanted him along "basically because I 'speak Air Force.'"[108]

At the Desert Rose, Colonel Crow and Sergeant Cooper first "grabbed a quick bite to eat in the dining facility" and then visited the SRC. They introduced themselves to the Disaster Control Group and talked with them, a conversation that was important, as Cooper later explained, in helping the stress management team to learn quickly how the wing operated and where its units were located. The Landstuhl group wanted to find out when the 4404th held its important meetings, so

Khobar Towers: Tragedy and Response

that its own sessions could be scheduled around them, and it wanted recommendations about which personnel should be debriefed first.[109]

While Colonel Crow was talking with Capt. Cindy Pollert, the medical group's representative on the DCG, one of the more fortuitous events in the recovery at the Khobar Towers took place. The three ranking officers then on the compound—Generals Anderson, Schwalier, and Dick—walked into the room together. It was a striking turn of luck for the Landstuhl team; they would lose no time searching for Khobar's senior leaders. Colonel Crow took his opportunity: "I introduced myself to General Schwalier, told him who we were . . . told him that the team was ready to go, and asked him what guidance he could give us."

General Schwalier walked Colonel Crow over to a map of the compound that had been pinned up on the wall of the executive dining room. The wing commander pointed out to the stress team chief the buildings that had been hardest hit by the bombing, and identified the 58th Fighter Squadron, the 71st Rescue Squadron, and the other units that had occupied them. The personnel in those dormitories, General Schwalier told Colonel Crow, concerned him the most. He advised the debriefing team to give its highest priority among them to the fighter squadron, because it was scheduled to return to Eglin that next day, Thursday, the twenty-seventh, at 10 a.m. Crow later recalled his immediate thought: "Oh my goodness, how are we going to touch base with these folks?"

In light of General Schwalier's information and priorities, Colonel Crow decided he would send part of his team to the King Abdul Aziz flightline early the next morning. Crow reported later in writing the guidance that he had given at the time: "Time and circumstances permitting, the team will conduct an appropriate level of debriefing prior to the squadron's departure." At the least, they would be able to meet with the unit's commander and flight surgeon.

The chance meeting with General Schwalier and the other senior officers at the SRC proved invaluable to the Landstuhl team. If not for this lucky encounter, Colonel Crow would have gone to bed with much less information about the units that most needed his team's attention. Above all, he would have remained ignorant of the imminent departure of the 58th Fighter Squadron.[110]

Colonel Crow and Sergeant Cooper had done more than a good day and night's work. After the meeting with the generals, they left the Desert Rose, returned to the Khobar Inn, and turned in for what remained of the night.[111]

Across the Khobar Towers compound some were joining them in getting badly needed rest, while others were heading for the military flightline, where a moving ceremony would take place during the early morning hours. For most airmen, that June 26 had been a tiring day. For a number of them, like MSgt. Kevin Smith, it had been "pretty much a clean-up-where-you-live day." For some, the memories of that Wednesday blurred as the pace of events accelerated. "That day seemed to go pretty quickly," Capt. Michael D. Morelock recalled, "just because there was so much going on at that point."[112] For all of them, one thing was certain. By the end of June 26, 1996, at Khobar Towers, a remarkable recovery had begun.

Chapter Nine

Wednesday: Elsewhere

When the bomb exploded in Dhahran, Army Col. (Dr.) Kevin C. Kiley, commander of the Landstuhl Regional Medical Center and U.S. Army Europe Regional Medical Command, was attending a conference in Heidelberg, Germany. In his absence, Army Col. (Dr.) Ney M. Gore, the LRMC's deputy commander for clinical services, was the acting commander of the hospital and the ERMC.[1] Sometime shortly before 3 a.m. on Wednesday, June 26, 1996, Dr. Gore received a telephone call from Headquarters U.S. Army Europe's Crisis Action Team (USAREUR CAT). There had been a bombing in the Khobar Towers, Saudi Arabia. Hundreds had been injured; the exact numbers of wounded and killed were unknown. The details were sketchy, but it was certain that a large percentage of the casualties were Americans.[2]

It happened that Dr. Kiley also had been away from Landstuhl seven months earlier, at the time of the Riyadh bombing. Reflecting on the two episodes later, Dr. Gore recalled that he had been new to his assignment at the time of the earlier attack and acknowledged that he had felt pressed by his responsibilities. Then he added that by the time of the June 1996 Dhahran bombing, he knew the Landstuhl hospital and its people and he felt better about his situation.

Dr. Gore had much to do, and quickly, beginning at that 3 a.m. hour. He knew that Landstuhl had some time to get ready for the arrival of any patients from Dhahran, but how much time was unknown. Dr. Gore began a long round of telephone calling.[3]

Among his first calls was one to Army Col. (Dr.) Edward B. Freyfogle, chief of the LRMC's surgery department. Dr. Gore passed on the initial information that he had: the number of casualties was unknown, but presumed to be many. Dr. Freyfogle in turn began notifying the members of the surgery department. He also took another measure, at that early hour. Dr. Freyfogle spoke fluent German and, in addition to being chief of surgery, he also served as liaison to the medical facilities in the area, including the Bundeswehrzentralkrankenhaus (military central hospital), located in Koblenz, and the University of Hamburg Hospital. The American surgeon described the former as Germany's "Walter Reed, Wilford Hall, and Bethesda, all rolled into one." Dr. Freyfogle took the step of calling these German hospitals and putting them on standby to help. Although events proved their assistance unnecessary, he later said with confidence: "I'm absolutely positive they would have supported us, lock, stock, and barrel."[4]

Like Dr. Freyfogle, Dr. Gore also telephoned some of the area hospitals. Landstuhl could readily make available 180 beds, and another 40 without great difficulty. During those earliest hours, however, the number of Dhahran casualties remained unknown, and the hospital's acting commander knew that his facility might need help. Dr. Gore spent a good bit of the time before 4 a.m. placing calls to German hospitals and planning for that contingency. The Heidelberg and Würzburg University hospitals agreed to provide additional beds, if needed.[5]

Dr. Gore arrived at a preliminary plan if the LRMC received a large number of severely injured airmen: aeromedical evacuation aircraft would bring the casualties from Dhahran to Ramstein. From there the 86th Aeromedical Staging Flight, the only ASF in Europe, a ten-member unit commanded by Lt. Col. Dawn M. Oerichbauer, would transport the patients the four miles south to Landstuhl. Clearly the LRMC would be the best place, at least at first, for those patients who needed the most care. After Landstuhl had admitted all of the critical-care airmen it could readily receive, its staff would triage the others. The more severely injured of them would be transferred to Heidelberg, about fifty miles away, and the less so to Würzburg, more than twice as far.[6]

In addition to making these calls, Dr. Gore also moved to ensure that there would be rapid, well-coordinated communication among the LRMC and other organizations. Soon after 3 a.m., he alerted the hospital's plans, operations, and training division to establish an emergency operations center. As Army Maj. Gary Newman, the chief of the PO&T division, was able to report later, the "activation of the EOC went smoothly." This hospital emergency command center soon was in communication with the USAREUR CAT, the Headquarters United States European Command CAT, Headquarters United States Air Forces in Europe, and many other organizations that already were coordinating medical help for the wounded airmen at the Khobar Towers.[7]

Also among Dr. Gore's early morning calls was one that began the mobilization of a stress management team. In response, Army Lt. Col. Bruce E. Crow quickly had organized a fifteen-member unit that represented many of the hospital's disciplines. These professionals were ready to leave Landstuhl by 8 a.m., were on the Ramstein flightline around 9, and, along with the 86th Aeromedical Evacuation Squadron and Critical Care Aeromedical Transport Team, left at about 2:30 p.m. The Landstuhl stress management team would reach Dhahran that night, roughly twenty-four hours after the bombing.[8]

In addition to this telephoning, Dr. Gore also was soon in communication with the hospital's department of nursing. Army Col. Carolyn Bulliner, its deputy commander, learned about the bombing by a phone call from the nursing supervisor on duty at the time, and shortly afterward, she discussed the news with Dr. Gore, who happened to be her neighbor. Within an hour of hearing about the attack, around 4 a.m., Colonel Bulliner reported to the hospital, as did Dr. Gore. During these hours

Wednesday: Elsewhere

before Wednesday's dawn, she said later, "We were trying to find out the magnitude of the issue, and how soon we would need to start reacting."

A person unfamiliar with the workings of the enormous Landstuhl facility might assume that Colonel Bulliner's obvious course was to begin calling her staff and directing them to report to the hospital, but in fact, this was not the case. The stress management team, which needed to secure country clearances and make other arrangements, had to be mobilized quickly, but this was not the situation with the nursing department. In this instance, it was better to take a longer view. "I knew if we had many casualties," Colonel Bulliner later explained, the necessary manning "would stress the staff—if not over a day, at least over many, several days." So an early recall of a large number of nurses would have been a mistake. It wasn't until about 6:30 a.m. that Colonel Bulliner "let the staff know what had happened, because by that time we were pretty well aware" that no patients would be arriving at Landstuhl until at least much later in the day.[9]

About an hour and a half earlier, around 5 a.m., Army Sergeant Mike Ertell had telephoned Ms. Marie Shaw, chief of the LRMC's public affairs office, and told her the news from Khobar Towers. The two of them represented the office's entire staff, and they quickly agreed they would report early that workday. Ms. Shaw had been working at Landstuhl since the early 1980s, and she realized from her long experience that patients would be coming to the LRMC—and so would members of the international press.[10]

Once at work that morning, Marie Shaw set up a press center in the hospital's managed care division, which had the necessary telephone lines and computers that her own modest office lacked. She also knew that she and Sergeant Ertell alone wouldn't be able to cope with the large number of journalists who soon would begin arriving at Landstuhl. Ms. Shaw called the public affairs offices of Headquarters U.S. European Command and U.S. Commander in Chief, European Command, both at Stuttgart (Vaihingen, Germany), discussed the situation, and asked for assistance. These organizations realized that they, too, would be stressed for manning if any of the Dhahran patients were brought to Europe. Headquarters USCINCEUR's public affairs office agreed to detail one person to the LRMC. Vaihingen was only about seventy-five miles to the southeast, and this officer reported to Landstuhl that afternoon. In addition to getting this help, Ms. Shaw also quickly arranged to have enough press badges and escorts ready, when the media representatives began arriving.[11]

The press center began taking calls that morning, but Ms. Shaw could not yet confirm for the inquiring journalists that any of the Dhahran airmen would be transported to Landstuhl. She instead directed their attention to a blood drive that the hospital's department of pathology and area laboratory services began preparing that morning. Landstuhl had been providing plasma for the Army's forces in Bosnia and recently they had been asked for more. In view of this request and the arrival of an unknown number of Khobar Towers patients, the blood drive's goal, as Army Maj. Michael Daines, chief of the pathology department, stated, was 100 units. It eventually collected 140.[12]

Khobar Towers: Tragedy and Response

By the time the pathology staff was setting up this blood drive in the hospital's Heaton auditorium, representatives of at least five international news organizations—the Associated Press, National Broadcasting Company, Columbia Broadcasting System, Air Force News, and one British newspaper—already had arrived at Landstuhl. Dr. Kiley returned from Heidelberg that morning and conducted a press conference, held also in the Heaton auditorium. Although Ms. Shaw still could not give these reporters information about the numbers and arrival times of the Khobar patients, she did give them the opportunity to cover the preparations for the blood drive, interview Dr. Kiley and others, and do some filming.[13]

Marie Shaw had the best possible reason for not telling the journalists how many patients were coming: the hospital staff did not yet know. Dr. Freyfogle later recalled the tenor of things that morning: "Of course, we were clamoring for news, to separate the facts from the rumor. And we'd get driblets, here and there." "In any situation like this," Lieutenant Colonel Oerichbauer reflected, "there is a hurry-up-and-wait, hurry-up-and-wait, until you get the definitive answer in."[14]

One thing was certain that Wednesday morning: given that the flight time from Dhahran to Ramstein was about six hours, no patients could reach Landstuhl soon.[15] The LRMC staff was guaranteed a fixed amount of planning time, and made excellent use of it. Dr. Freyfogle later reflected that every event involving mass casualties can be categorized into one of two groups. There are imminent ones, like the Ramstein air show disaster, in which the number and types of injuries are unknown, and no time available for planning. And there are distant ones, like the Khobar Towers bombing, in which the number and condition of the injured may be uncertain at first, but are known by the time the patients are transported to Landstuhl. These cases allow time for planning and preparing. The LRMC staff used wisely the hours before the airmen arrived. "We spent most of the day [Wednesday the twenty-sixth] planning," one of the hospital's senior officers said later. "We had the *time* to make some smart decisions, as opposed to having to [make the] 'knee-jerk-reaction' kind of decisions that are not always the best."[16]

One specific example of this came that morning, when Dr. Kiley, Colonel Bulliner, and other staff members discussed how the arrival of the Khobar patients might affect the nursing department's staffing and the hospital's ongoing operations. If the LRMC had to care for a large number of airmen for two days or longer, the facility might have to curtail some of its services. The officers considered this issue, and decided that the salient point was that there was no evidence yet that the number would be extraordinarily high. "Since we already had surgeries scheduled—patients planning to have their surgery," Colonel Bulliner related, "[we decided] that we would go ahead and do the surgeries. [We would] pretty much keep operations as normal during the day as we could."[17]

At noon Dr. Kiley convened an all-hospital staff meeting in the LRMC's conference room. Dr. Gore gave a detailed briefing, using the information he had, as he later said, to dampen any anxieties that might have developed.[18] The senior staff members gave reports that confirmed that Landstuhl at that hour already stood well prepared to receive a large number of Khobar patients. Colonel Bulliner described her department's plans for housing a hundred airmen and discussed the numbers of available beds, on four of the hospital's wards. The LRMC could accept twenty, perhaps as many as thirty, intensive-care patients, without any augmentation. In addition, the United States Army Medical Materiel Center, Europe, in Pirmasens, fewer than fifteen miles south of Landstuhl, held in storage five modules that could increase the hospital's critical-care capacity. The USAMMCE could send these bed packages to the LRMC and they could be set up that day, well before any Dhahran flights would land at Ramstein.[19]

At this same meeting, Major Daines reported on the blood drive and Col. (Dr.) Frederick A. Steckel, chief of radiology, detailed his department's preparations. Lt. Col. Theodore S. Nam of the department of pyschiatry announced that a family support center, staffed by chaplains, Red Cross workers, the hospital's social work services professionals, and others, would open the next morning. Marie Shaw described the news media's high interest in Landstuhl's preparations for the Dhahran airmen, and her creation of a press center. Other attendees gave equally detailed, and confident, reports. This all-staff meeting was followed by a conference among Dr. Kiley and the chiefs of his medical departments. This session, too, carried a positive tone.[20]

The afternoon provided other instances of the Landstuhl staff using its preparation time to good advantage. Colonel Bulliner related one example: the decision to put all of the Khobar patients on a single ward. She emphasized that she "left the planning of how we were going to manage the patients" to her senior staff, "who were very, very competent. They had dealt with these kinds of issues before." They weighed the merits of having the airmen all on one ward, or on two or more. That afternoon the exact number of patients remained unknown, but it was certain that one ward would accomodate them. The senior nurses, Colonel Bulliner recounted, "came back to me and said, 'You know, it will probably be better if we put all the patients on [Ward] 14, rather than trying to put them on a couple different wards, to move all the existing patients off that ward and just have that for Saudi patients.' That worked just beautifully.... That was the staff's idea."[21]

In the nursing department, and elsewhere in the hospital, personnel leaves were curtailed: not canceled, but curtailed. The Landstuhl Regional Medical Center stood ready to receive the Khobar patients. "Then," Marie Shaw stated, "we had the long wait."[22]

Across the Atlantic Ocean from Landstuhl, at Patrick Air Force Base, Florida, the 71st Rescue Squadron was continuing to cope with the aftermath of the bombing. The unit's executive officer, Capt. Stephanie Shaw, reported to work that Wednesday morning and found that telephones were "ringing everywhere.... It took...about a week before the phones finally stopped ringing."[23]

Calls also continued to ring into the crisis information center that Col. Thomas R. Friers had established at the headquarters of the 1st Rescue Group, in Patrick's Building 423, across the base from the 71st's building on the flightline. The volume of communications remained so high that representatives from the group's three squadrons continued to man the center for two and a half days. Most of the calls were incoming—from family members asking about their relatives who were serving Southern Watch assignments in Dhahran. Colonel Friers later reflected, "And of course, the hardest part: we continued to get calls from [the families of] some of those that I was pretty sure were deceased, but I couldn't say anything, yet."[24]

The difficult task of notifying the families of their losses had begun during the earliest hours of the twenty-sixth. During the daytime of that Wednesday, another notification remained to be made. As Lt. Col. Donald R. Jozayt, commander of the 71st Rescue Squadron, later recounted, someone would have to make the drive north and west from Patrick to Orlando, the home of Paul Blais, the natural father of SrA. Paul A. Blais. "We were to tell the father," Lieutenant Colonel Jozayt said, "he's missing, but presumed dead."[25]

Colonel Friers well knew that Lieutenant Colonel Jozayt had been awake into the early hours, performing the stressful task of notifying two of the bereaved families of their loss. Rather than arouse the squadron commander, the group commander telephoned instead the 71st Rescue Squadron. A major and a sergeant from the unit made the drive to Orlando. Mr. Blais was himself a veteran and he interpreted the arrival of an Air Force officer and NCO at his home to mean that his son was dead. No, they told him, there was some hope.[26]

That Wednesday afternoon, Colonel Friers and Lieutenant Colonel Jozayt met with Lt. Col. (Father) Phillip D. Nguyen, the 1st Rescue Group's chaplain. The three officers discussed their initial ideas for a memorial service for the Patrick airmen who had been killed in Dhahran. They envisioned a brief, small, and private ceremony, which would be held perhaps as early as Friday, the twenty-eighth.[27]

Not long after this preliminary meeting, events began moving in a different direction. Early that evening, a member of the headquarters staff of the 1st Fighter Wing, at Langley Air Force Base, Virginia, telephoned Colonel Friers with a "heads up." President Bill Clinton, then at the summit meeting of the Group of Seven in Lyon, France, might attend the Patrick Air Force Base memorial service for the Dhahran airmen. The caller emphasized that this was no more than a "heads up," and that the information was to be kept "close hold."

Colonel Friers left his office only somewhat later than usual in the evening of the twenty-sixth. Lt. Col. Robert H. Holloway, his deputy, had run the crisis information center until the early morning hours of that Wednesday, then had gone home to get what sleep he could, and now reported to relieve the group commander. When Colonel Friers arrived at his house that night and turned on his television's CNN channel, he heard the newscaster announce that President Clinton would be attending the Patrick ceremony.[28]

At Eglin Air Force Base, the tempo and tenor of events was much the same as at Patrick. The 33d Fighter Wing's battle staff had first met at 3:30 p.m the previous day and eventually would devote seven meetings to the Khobar Towers recovery. Between these meetings, it worked continuously on accounting for Eglin's person-

Wednesday: Elsewhere

nel, notifying the bereaved families, and many other issues. On Wednesday, June 26, the battle staff remained manned by more than twenty officers and airmen, as it would the next day as well. As the process of accounting for Eglin's personnel reduced the number of airmen categorized as "duty status, whereabouts unknown," Lt. Col. Stan Hill, the wing's battle staff director, himself took responsibility for these cases.[29]

During one of the earliest battle staff meetings, it had been decided that a project officer should be assigned to each one of the bereaved families, and by Wednesday, Lieutenant Colonel Hill was also able to begin working closely with these points of contact.[30] Col. Gary R. Dylewski, commander of the 33d Fighter Wing, regarded the creation of these POCs "one of the best decisions we made.... At every battle staff meeting, we could get an update [from the family project officers] on what [every] family's situation was." The POCs knew immediately if their particular family needed airline tickets, billeting, money, meals, counseling, transportation, or other assistance. These project officers, Colonel Dylewski emphasized, "did an unbelievable amount of work around the clock, and they spent a lot of money out of their own pocket, when they couldn't get the money that was available, immediately.... There are a thousand stories out there, that we'll never know, about the families getting taken care of by these folks." The wing initially agreed to assign one airman per family and then came to realize, as Linda Brown, the director of the base's Family Support Center, said, that "this was a twenty-four-hour job." Eventually, two or three POCs worked with each family."[31]

Linda Brown contributed great energy to one of Eglin's most important recovery efforts, the "People Place." "The People Place," Lieutenant Colonel Hill explained, "was a concept from the 96th Mission Support Squadron commander," Col. Lee Weitzel. Organized by Ms. Brown and her Family Support Center staff, this operation made available, on a twenty-four-hour basis and in a single building, many services that Eglin families would need during the days following the Khobar tragedy: information and referral assistance, crisis counseling, child care, a spouse-to-spouse program of volunteer "supporters," Red Cross resources, line badge and identification card replacement, travel vouchers, chaplain support, and several others. When Linda Brown had attended the battle staff meeting on Thursday evening, she had been asked to set up this collection of valuable services, gathered into a single location, convenient to the families they would help.[32]

Colonel Dylewski credited Linda Brown with the idea of establishing the People Place in the 33d Fighter Wing's Field Training Detachment building, rather than asking the unit's family members to make the long trip to the Family Support Center on Eglin Main Base.[33] The FTD facility, Building 1363, proved an excellent location for this operation. It stood not far south of the taxiways of the 33d Fighter Wing, and just west of the unit's headquarters, on Nomad Way.[34]

The FTD building was a training facility, and its classrooms were well suited to the immediate need. Its administrative offices had desks, telephones, photocopiers, and fax machines. Had Linda Brown been forced to set up the People Place in a vacant building, it would have become necessary to locate and install all of this office equipment, at a loss of hours or even days to Eglin's families—at the very time when they most needed help. In addition to this advantage in hardware, the FTD building offered an even more important benefit, its own professional workers. "The resident staff of the Training Detachment (Building 1363 which became the People Place)," Linda Brown wrote in her after-action report, "was outstanding. On Saturday and Sunday, they left admin offices open so we could use phones, desks, fax, and xerox. They arranged for [signs that would direct] visitors to the People Place."[35]

After a noon meeting of the Family Support Center's staff and others, the People Place opened at 2 p.m. on Wednesday, the twenty-sixth. The FTD staff and 33d Fighter Wing personnel blanketed the enormous base with signs that gave directions to the building.[36] Colorful flyers publicized the People Place and listed many of its multiple services. In a personnel message welcoming the returning Nomads, Colonel Dylewski alerted them to the assistance that was available at the FTD building: "No one has all the answers on how we will rebuild the damage done by the terrorists' cowardly act. But as aid in the first step in the long and painful healing process, Team Eglin has pulled together an extensive group of mental health and family support experts who will work *24 hours* a day for as long as it takes to help get everyone through the difficult days ahead."[37]

Staffed by the Family Support Center director herself and only fourteen others, the People Place met Colonel Dylewski's commitment of round-the-clock operations. Linda Brown later stated: "We thought we could handle it, but the People Place was running twenty-four hours [a day], and we spread ourselves thin."[38] In addition to being small, the staff was divided: it worked from two locations. After the People Place opened on the twenty-sixth, some of its operations moved into the hangar of the 58th Fighter Squadron, a short distance north of the FTD building and on the taxiways.[39] From these two places, this diverse, enormously valuable service continued to support Eglin's families into July.[40]

"The People Place and the battle staff," Colonel Dylewski later reflected, "were the centers of activity around here." Pointing to the People Place's counseling and other activities, he stated that it "rendered invaluable service." Lieutenant Colonel Hill praised the variety of services it offered, emphasizing that "the Red Cross, hospital, and the crisis action intervention teams from the hospital...all kinds of support from the community was focused in the People Place." In her after action report, Linda Brown summed up: "The People Place provided an oasis of comfort, physically located exactly where it should have been—in the [33d Fighter Wing] work area. The People Place represented the whole base to the 33 FW and the 33 FW to the rest of the base and civilian community." About six months after the tragedy, Ms. Brown commented: "I was greatly comforted that the 33d battle staff *always* remained focused on the families of the victims."[41] She emphasized the same point in her after action report: "The 33 FW and People Place focus never was diverted from the families and 33 FW personnel."[42]

Wednesday: Elsewhere

In the conclusion of Ms. Brown's report, she reflected on the inestimable worth of the People Place. "The money spent and the hours worked," she wrote, "were appropriate; the victim-families have been tragically impacted, but they have no doubt Eglin and the surrounding civilian communities care. Though never envisioned by the various base disaster support plans, the People Place proved invaluable as an information outlet for the outpouring of public sympathy and concern, and for centralized services and support."[43]

While Linda Brown and many others worked during that Wednesday afternoon to get the People Place up and running, Capt. Brenda Campbell, the 33d Fighter Wing's public affairs officer, had spent long hours preparing to work with journalists during the days ahead. As soon as the news had arrived on Tuesday afternoon, she was certain there would be an "astronomical" press interest in the Khobar Towers bombing. Immediately after the first reports from Dhahran, Captain Campbell's small office quickly began receiving assistance from Main Base Eglin because, as she later said, "they have a lot of resources that we needed"—manning and other help. The public affairs office of the Air Force Development Test Center, for example, issued a press release on Tuesday evening, and promptly sent a copy to the 33d Fighter Wing. In addition to such help from Main Base Eglin, Captain Campbell also was gratified that she "immediately had people calling... from Hurlburt asking me if I needed help." This neighboring installation reinforced the 33d Fighter Wing with PA officers who were experienced, Campbell said, with "the magnitude of what we were going to face."[44]

Not far behind these reinforcements, members of the international press began arriving at Eglin during Wednesday's early morning hours. "Before you knew it," Captain Campbell recalled, "we had people on our doorstep. I mean it was within hours." The journalists remained at Eglin in large numbers from that Wednesday through Monday, the first of July.

Captain Campbell and the other public affairs specialists gave their first attention to helping Maj. Gen. Stewart E. Cranston, the AFDTC commander, and Colonel Dylewski prepare for a press conference, which they would hold at 9 a.m. on the twenty-sixth. "We worked all night," Campbell related, "to get questions ready, to get answers ready." Early that morning, the PA officers briefed General Cranston and Colonel Dylewski, in advance of their press conference.[45]

The 9 a.m. session with the journalists went well. "This is obviously an extemely difficult time for all involved," General Cranston told the reporters. "We are, of course, mobilizing all of our resources to provide what comfort we can to the families that have suffered a loss."[46]

A common theme ran through these experiences at Eglin, Patrick, Landstuhl, and elsewhere throughout the Air Force. In the aftermath of the tragedy, people readily did whatever their circumstances required. Landstuhl's Dr. Freyfogle stated: "If I've learned anything from mass-casualty experiences, it is that 100 percent of the people will do anything they are told to do, under those circumstances. That, you can absolutely count on." Patrick's Colonel Friers expressed great confidence and

Khobar Towers: Tragedy and Response

pride in the people both "over there, and back here." Eglin's Colonel Dylewski emphasized that on his base, the response "wasn't like a normal staff action, that would take days to get something done.... People realized that it needed to be done now, because people needed it, and people were hurting."[47] And so it was on Wednesday, June 26, 1996, everywhere in the United States Air Force.

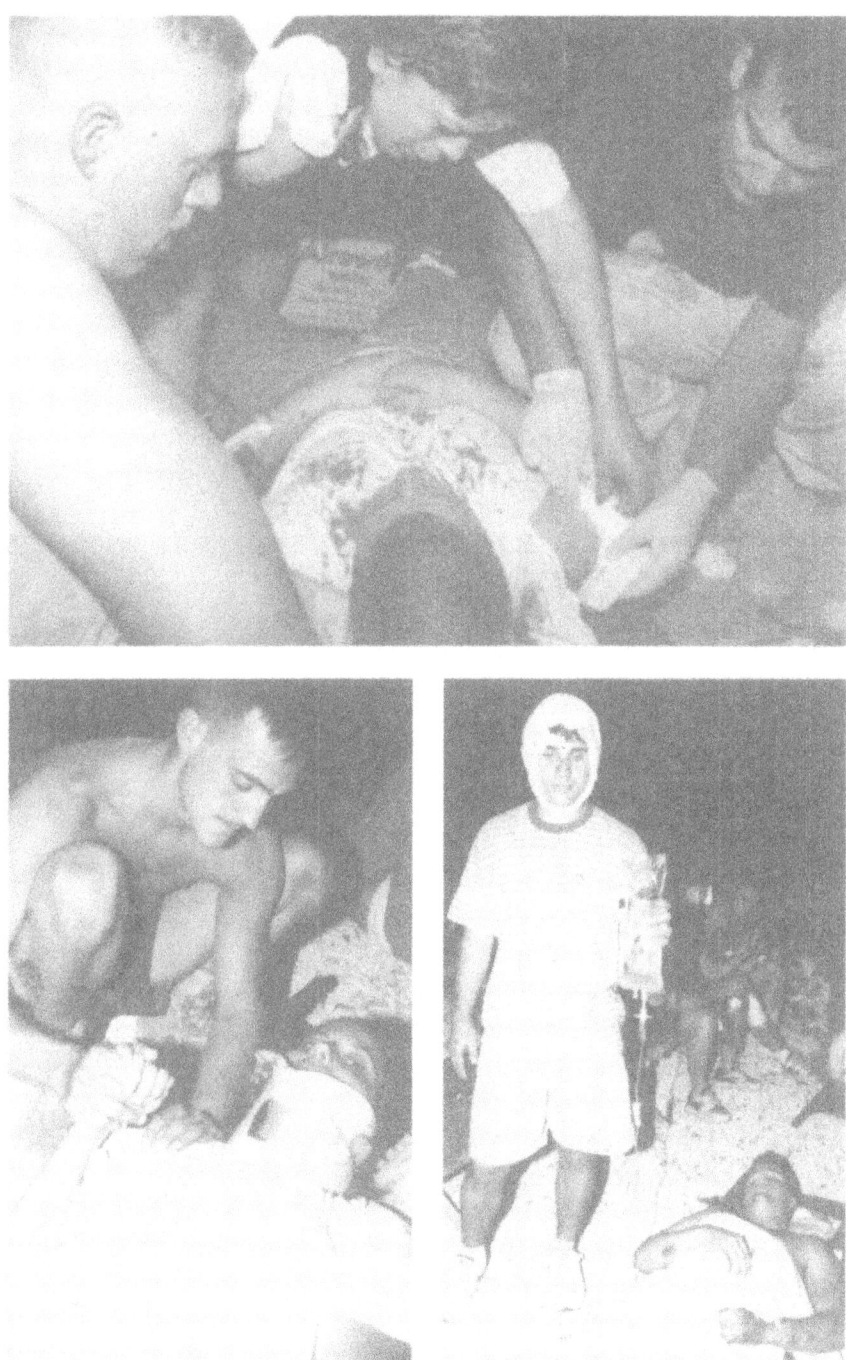

Help for the wounded in the parking lot behind Building 131, with more the severely injured receiving help from those with lesser injuries.

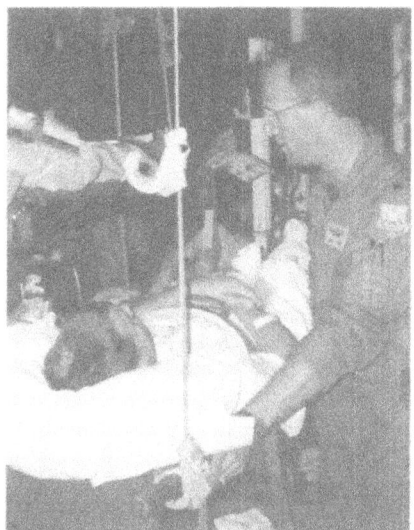 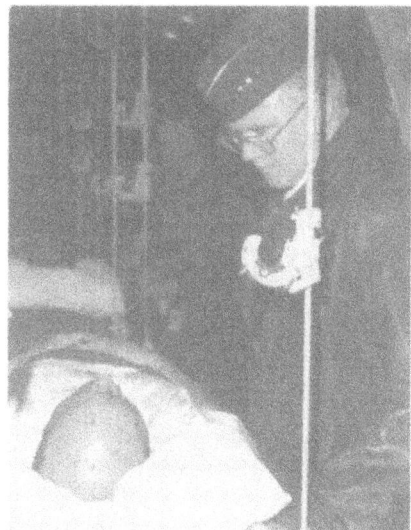

Lt. Col. (Dr.) Douglas Robb with patients aboard the medical evacuation aircraft (*top left*), Gen. Michael Ryan, commander, U.S. Air Forces in Europe, with patients on the aircraft in Germany (*top right*), and Landstuhl Regional Medical Center (*above*).

Opposite page: Lt. Col. (Chaplain) Dennis Aleson speaks at the departure ceremony (*top*), a casket is loaded into a C-5 (*center*), and all 19 caskets aboard the aircraft (*bottom*).

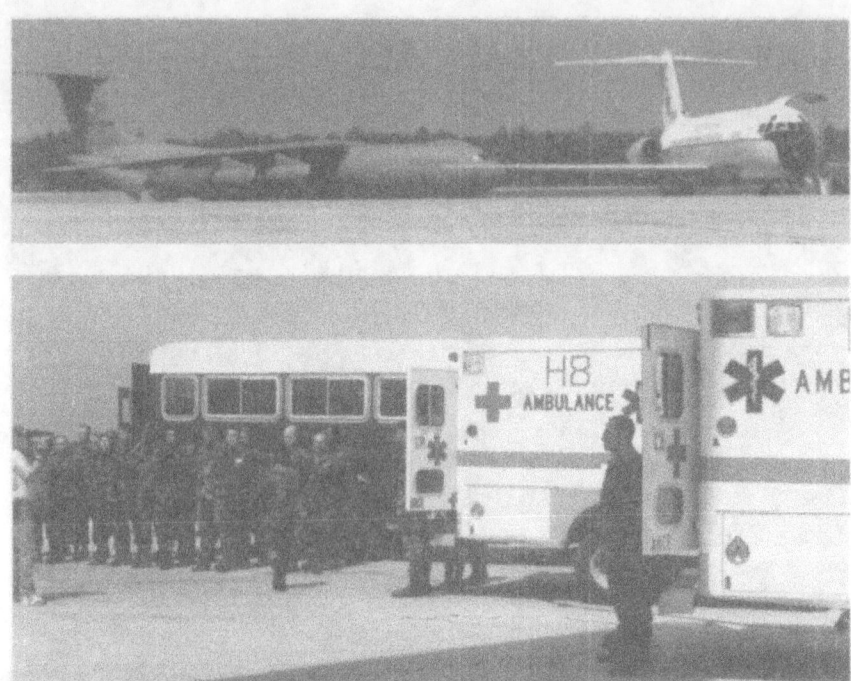

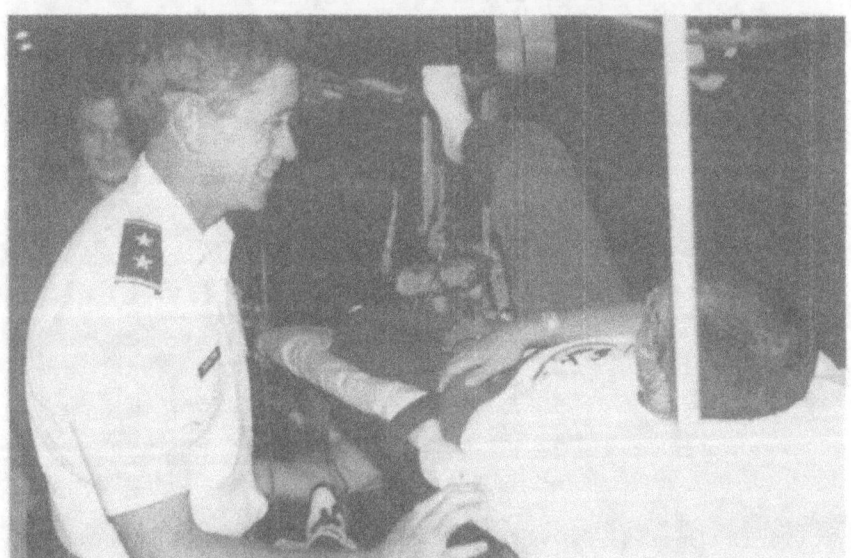

A C–141 and a C–9 on the Eglin runway (*top*). Ambulances waiting for patients (*center*) at Eglin. Maj. Gen. Stewart Cranston, AFDTC commander, and Capt. (Dr.) Morris Treadway (behind General Cranston) visit patients aboard the medevac aircraft (*bottom*).

Opposite page: Patients are assisted off and carried off the medevac aircraft.

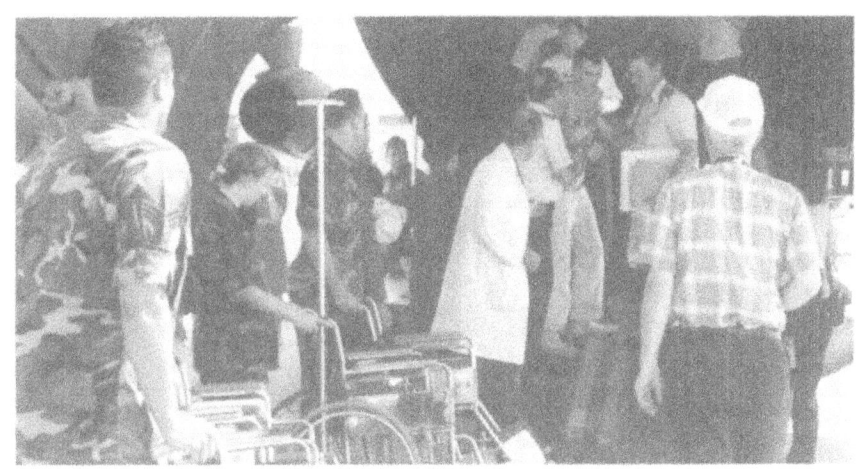

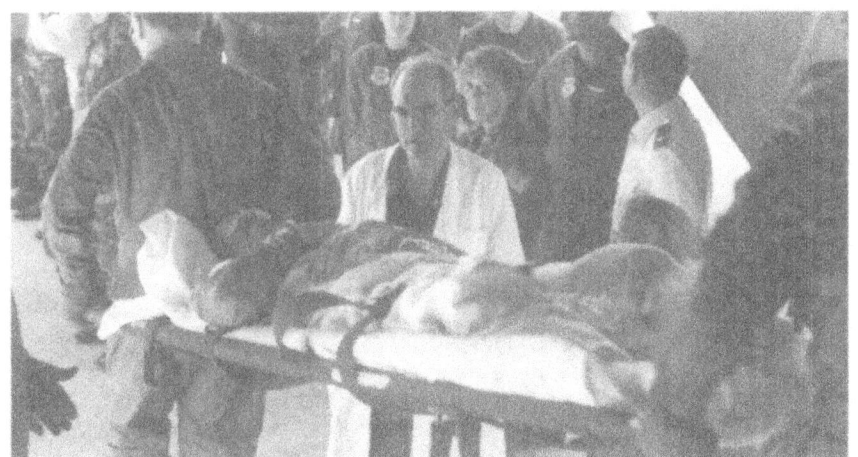

At Eglin, Khobar veterans speak with members of the press (*top*); Col. Gary Dylewski, 33d Fighter Wing commander, Maj. Gen. Stewart Cranston, and President Bill Clinton talk at the foot of the stairs to President Clinton's aircraft (*above*); and F–15s fly a missing man formation (*left*).

Opposite page: During the Eglin memorial ceremony, an enormous flag hangs in King Hangar (*top*), injured airmen at the front of the audience (*center*), and Colonel Dylewski and President Clinton speak at the ceremony (*bottom*).

An overall view of the Patrick AFB Khobar memorial during the dedication ceremony (*top*), the Patrick memorial with engraved portraits of the five airmen from Patrick killed in the attack (*above*), and a flyover of an HC–130 during the ceremony (*left*).

Opposite page: The Khobar memorial at Eglin AFB (*top*). A row of memorials in front of the Enlisted Heritage Hall on Gunther Annex, Maxwell AFB, Alabama (*center*), with a close view of the Khobar memorial (*bottom left*). The Khobar memorial at Prince Sultan Air Base, Saudi Arabia (*bottom right*).

Secretary of the Air Force Sheila Widnall and Lt. Col. Douglas R. Cochran, commander of the 58th Fighter Squadron (*top*). Capt. (Dr.) R. Morris Treadway (*above*). Col. Thomas R. Friers, commander of the 1st Rescue Group (*right*).

Opposite page: Brig. Gen. Terryl J. Schwalier and Maj. Gen. Kurt B. Anderson, commander of Joint Task Force Southwest Asia at a press conference (*top*). Gen. Ronald R. Fogleman presents Maj. (Dr.) Steven P. Goff an Airman's Medal (*center*). Secretary of Defense William J. Perry speaks to reporters in front of Building 131 (*bottom*).

Acting Secretary of the Air Force F. Whitten Peters speaks at the dedication of the Patrick AFB memorial (*top*). Secretary of Defense William S. Cohen and Chairman of the Joint Chiefs of Staff Gen. John M. Shalikashvili announce at a press conference that Brig. Gen. Terryl J. Schwalier will not be promoted to major general (*center*). Maj. Gen. Daniel M. Dick (*left*), as a brigadier general, succeeded Gen. Schwalier as 4404th Wing commander.

Chapter Ten

Three Departures from Dhahran

Col. Scott Gration, commander of the 4404th Composite Wing's operations group; Lt. Col. (Chaplain) Dennis E. Aleson, the wing's senior chaplain; and CMSgt. Paul K. Ayres, the unit's senior enlisted adviser, planned the memorial service and departure ceremony for the deceased airmen of the Khobar Towers. This memorable event took place during the middle of the night of Wednesday/Thursday, June 26/27, 1996. The ceremony was conducted in a floodlit area around the nose of a C–5A Galaxy on the military flightline of Dhahran Air Base. This transport aircraft, tail number 60022, had been in Dhahran when the terrorist bomb exploded. Following the ceremony, it would carry the remains of the nineteen airmen back to the United States, to the Dover Port Mortuary at Dover Air Force Base, Delaware.[1]

After midnight, a group of well over one thousand Air Force personnel began assemblying in a sharply deployed squadron formation. Many others from the United States Military Training Mission (USMTM) also came to pay their respects. One Saudi national was present: Colonel Abdullah al-Qahtani, who was the Royal Saudi Air Force security wing commander for King Abdul Aziz and the director of the Joint Forces Support Unit for the Eastern Province, a role that made him the liaison officer to the American and other foreign military personnel in Dhahran.[2]

The United States flag, and two others, stood in the floodlit area. By June 1996 the 71st Rescue Squadron had served in Operation Southern Watch more than two years, so long that the unit kept one stand of its colors in Dhahran. The third flag was that of the 4404th Composite Wing (Provisional). A podium with a microphone wired to a series of speakers also stood in place.[3]

The ceremony began less than twenty-eight hours after the bombing. A few minutes before 1:15 a.m., two operators directed a flightline tractor into the area in front of the C–5A. Behind this vehicle rolled four pallet trailers, each carrying four flag-draped transfer cases, followed by a fifth carrying three of them. Earlier that night, mortuary services personnel and volunteers had loaded these caskets onto the trailers and had secured in place each of the flags,[4] and members of the 71st Rescue Squadron had placed their unit's patch on the five transfer cases of their comrades.[5] Now, around 1:15, the operators positioned the train of pallet trailers near the nose of the great transport aircraft. At the suggestion of Maj. Gen. Kurt B. Anderson, com-

Khobar Towers: Tragedy and Response

mander of the Joint Task Force Southwest Asia, public affairs personnel taped the ceremony, which was telecast by American news agencies during the following days.[6]

Chaplain Aleson came to the podium and spoke briefly, reading verses of scripture he had selected, and Chief Master Sergeant Ayres also delivered a few short remarks. It was about 1:20 a.m. when Brig. Gen. Terry Schwalier stepped forward, addressed the group, and led it in a long, final salute of their comrades.[7]

Then the first of nineteen parties, each made up of six pall bearers, approached the lead trailer and the first of the nineteen flag-draped caskets.[8] The units that had been stricken by the bombing contributed volunteers to these groups, and Maj. Robert E. (Rob) Taylor, the wing's services squadron commander, had instructed them in the procedures for the ceremony. One party after another reverently took one of the nineteen transfer cases from its flightline vehicle and slowly carried it up the ramp into the C–5A. At about 1:40 a.m., the last pall bearer group brought the final case into the transport.[9]

Chaplain Aleson later recalled a poignant episode that occurred during the memorial service. While the ceremony was taking place, he related, "around the nose of the C–5A, on the tarmac . . . in [the] darkness, . . . a couple of hundred yards away was . . . the weekly rotator that had landed. And the people [of the 27th Fighter Squadron, from Langley Air Force Base, Virginia] were just getting off that; they were later than normal." Chaplain Aleson was struck by the timing of their debarking: "So this is the scene that was greeting them, as the newcomers into the AOR, the area of responsibility, arrived. You can imagine what was going through their minds."[10]

General Schwalier recalled the same episode. "As they taxied in," he said, "they saw the wing in formation by the C–5, knowing what had taken place, knowing what was going on. It made an impression on the arriving airmen," as well as those participating in the service. After the departure ceremony, the wing commander made a point of meeting this incoming rotator and addressing its passengers.[11]

General Schwalier characterized the ceremony as extremely emotional and very well done.[12] General Anderson also spoke highly of the way in which the memorial service was conducted. Lt. Col. Thomas H. Shafer, commander of the deployed 71st Rescue Squadron, pointed out that, although by the time this ceremony was held only a few members of his unit remained in Dhahran, the event was very meaningful for those who *were* still there. He also believed that this service helped the maintenance airmen who had been on the military flightline at the time of the bombing feel connected to what had happened at the Khobar Towers. One young airman from another unit doubtless spoke for many of his comrades: "We needed to say goodbye in our own way, and heal . . . . They are your fellow servicemen; they deserve that respect."[13]

An officer from the 58th Fighter Squadron and one from the 71st Rescue Squadron served as escorts for the flight to the Dover Port Mortuary. The second of these representatives was one of the rescue squadron's pilots, Capt. Michael D. Morelock. Minutes before the bombing, a security policeman had warned him and his roomate, Capt. Matthew Winkler, to leave their room on the top floor of Building 131. Both had been wounded in the blast, Captain Winkler the more seriously of the

Three Departures from Dhahran

two. Captain Morelock had taken a wild ambulance ride to the Arabian American Oil Company Hospital, had been treated there, and returned to the Khobar Towers by bus with Lieutenant Colonel Shafer the morning of the twenty-sixth.[14]

Captain Morelock later recounted that, during that Wednesday afternoon, he was asked to perform the escort assignment by a lieutenant colonel or colonel unknown to him. He recognized the honor of performing this duty and readily accepted it, but he was troubled by some of his immediate circumstances: he was still wearing the scrubs of the ARAMCO Hospital and needed a flightsuit or a desert camouflage uniform. "I didn't have any [travel] orders," he later recalled. "I had an ID card, because I had gone back [into my bedroom] for that. So it was just me and an ID card."[15]

A medical technician loaned Captain Morelock his flightsuit. The pilot found that it was a size too small, but was happy to have it. As for his lack of travel orders, Morelock related: "I was concerned about what was going to happen when I arrived. They said don't worry about it, you'll be taken care of when you get out there."[16]

The ceremony planners originally had hoped that the remains of the deceased would depart Saudi Arabia at midnight of the twenty-sixth and twenty-seventh. Members of the unit's operations group had been in communication with Air Mobility Command, working to locate an aircraft and pilot to accomodate that departure time. AMC officers identified a KC–10A Extender, which performed as both a transport and tanker, but it developed that the pilot who was bringing this airplane to King Abdul Aziz was not qualified to perform air refueling, required by any flight from Dhahran to Dover Air Force Base. The Air Mobility Command planners then looked for a pilot who could fly the C–5A that was at hand. They found one at al Dhafra Air Base, the United Arab Emirates, and dispatched a C–141 Starlifter to bring him to Dhahran. Adopting this alternative postponed the departure from midnight until about 3 a.m. June 27.[17]

"Once we lifted off," Captain Morelock said, "I slept. That was the first time I had slept, the whole time [since the bombing].... Once I got on the airplane, it caught up with me."[18]

The C–5A climbed into the early morning sky over Saudi Arabia. The aircraft would refuel once during its nonstop flight to the United States; its estimated time of arrival at Dover Air Force Base was 11:15 a.m. Eastern Daylight Time.[19] The remains of the nineteen deceased airmen had left Dhahran.

During the evening of that same Thursday, June 27, the wounded airmen also began leaving Saudi Arabia. At 7:30 that morning, Lt. Col. (Dr.) Douglas J. Robb, interim commander of the wing's medical group, met with representatives of the 4410th Aeromedical Evacuation Flight; the 39th Medical Group Flying Ambulance Surgical Team (FAST team), which had arrived from Incirlik Air Base, Turkey, at about 4:30 p.m. the previous afternoon; the 86th Aeromedical Evacuation Squadron, which had come from Ramstein Air Base, Germany, shortly after 10 p.m. the night before; and the Landstuhl Regional Medical Center stress management team, which had arrived on the same C–141 as the 86th AES.[20]

During this meeting on Thursday morning, these care providers reviewed how the patients would be discharged from the Dhahran hospitals and how the FAST team and others would transport them to the Aeromedical Staging Facility that had been established in the Greater USMTM Transportation Service ("GUTS") hangar on the Dhahran Air Base flightline. The great majority of the hospitalized airmen were at three facilities: the Ministry of Defense and Aviation (MODA) Hospital, King Fahd University Hospital, and the ARAMCO Hospital. One of the 4404th Medical Group's ambulances, a fleet of MODA ambulances, and one of the hospital's minibuses would transport the patients from that facility to the ASF. Two medical group ambulances and a King Fahd University ambulance bus would bring the airmen from that hospital to the flightline. In the case of ARAMCO, its own vehicles would fill the role. A General Motors Suburban belonging to the medical group was assigned to a fourth hospital, Mohammed al Dosha.[21]

Following this meeting, around 8 a.m., the medical care providers made the rounds of the Dhahran hospitals and began preparing for the discharge of some of the patients and for their medical evacuation.[22] The medical group's information that morning was that sixty-six airmen remained at these local facilities.[23] Five of these patients were in seriously injured condition, and two were very seriously injured.[24] Subtracting these seven, there were fifty-nine airmen who were candidates for aeromedical evacuation. The care providers selected, as one Air Force doctor stated, a mixture of lesser injured ambulatory patients and a few of the "moderately injured" for the first flight from Dhahran (of an eventual four flights).[25] One NCO later recalled how he learned that he would soon be leaving Saudi Arabia. That Thursday morning, two senior officers came into his room at King Fahd University Hospital and chatted with him. "They were going to pull us [patients] back to the main hangar," he related, for flights to the Landstuhl Regional Medical Center.[26]

Six members of the Landstuhl stress management team accompanied the medical professionals when they made these rounds, two of them (an officer and an enlisted member) going to each of the three hospitals that held nearly all the remaining patients. Army Lt. Col. Bruce E. Crow, the officer in charge of the group, described how its members interacted with the airmen who were about to be discharged. They asked informal questions, he said, such as "'What do you need?' 'Does your family know you're here? '. . . From the more psychological point of view [they asked], 'How are you doing?' and just addressed whatever needs they could."[27] Army Lt. Col. Sherry Connor, another member of the Landstuhl team, commented along the same lines. They went to the hospitals, she reflected, "to provide some crisis intervention and get a better understanding of what was going on, to help assess the patients."[28]

Lieutenant Colonel Connor accompanied Dr. Doug Robb and others to the King Fahd University Hospital. The medical group commander, she recalled months later, "amazed me. He hadn't had any sleep for two days, but he was still going, and still

Three Departures from Dhahran

sharp." Colonel Connor remembered in particular that, after meeting with a hospital director, Dr. Robb fielded questions from journalists of the Cable News Network. "I was sitting next to him when they interviewed him," she related, "and I was just amazed at how well he did, with what little sleep" he had been able to get.[29]

The medical professionals and debriefers set out for the hospitals around 8 a.m. By then the members of the 4410th AEF, of the advanced cadre of the 86th AES, of the FAST team, and those of the stress management team who had not gone to the three Dhahran facilities had assembled at the ASF hangar. There they made the final arrangements for receiving the airmen from the hospitals. The caregivers' plans for ordering food offered a good example of their thorough preparations. This was no time for a shortage of meals, and they arranged to have enough of them for sixty people delivered to the GUTS hangar. These five dozen servings represented one more than the total number of patients to be medevaced eventually—and far more than were needed immediately for the patients who would depart on the first two flights.[30]

It was also around 8 a.m. that four members of the stress management team met with Lt. Col. Douglas R. Cochran, commander of the 58th Fighter Squadron, and some of the unit's medical personnel.[31] Alerted by General Schwalier that the Dhahran veterans of the squadron would be departing that Thursday, Lieutenant Colonel Crow had sent this quartet from their Khobar Towers billeting to the military flightline, half an hour earlier.[32] The Landstuhl group already knew, from General Schwalier's discussion with their team chief, that they would not have much time to interact with the officers and airmen of the 58th before the unit's personnel returned to Florida. After they arrived at the AMC terminal, they saw that it was not an appropriate setting for their stress management debriefings. Given the rough setting and the limited time, they recommended to Colonel Cochran that the 58th receive formal debriefings after it returned to its home base. A member of the stress management team telephoned the Eglin base psychiatrist and advised him of the circumstances.[33]

With the preparations at the ASF complete, at 9 a.m. the Air Force care providers notified the doctors at the MODA Hospital, and later at the other facilities, that the patients who had been identified for the first aeromedivac flight should be ready by 11:30 that morning. Earlier, when the Americans had begun discussing with the Saudis the discharge and evacuation of the Dhahran patients, the host-nation physicians were impressed that the Air Force caregivers would be able to move the injured airmen so soon. The aeromedical evacuation capabilities of the United States, or American "care in the air," had advanced to a point beyond the assumptions of the local doctors. The Saudis, Dr. Robb later reflected, "probably found it hard to believe we had aircraft with capabilities for advanced cardiac life support, suction, ventilators, all the cardiac equipment you would need, and the critical care nurses. And ... the physicians you've been working with are the ones that are going to back" to Landstuhl with the patients.[34]

Dr. Robb understood the initial reaction of the Saudi physicians and he had invited them to tour the aeromedical evacuation C–141s that would transport the airmen to Europe. "They were amazed," he found, "at the capabilities we had." Like Dr.

155

Khobar Towers: Tragedy and Response

Robb, Col. (Dr.) Dan L. Locker, the United States Air Forces in Europe's surgeon general, noted that the Saudis were impressed with the USAF's medical capabilities, particularly the level of care that could be given to airborne patients. Dr. Locker described the intellectual exchange that took place between the medical professionals of the two nations: the Saudis learned about the advanced medevac facilities and procedures of the United States Air Force, while the Americans gained from the Dhahran doctors detailed information about the status of the patients.[35]

In addition to the Saudis' lack of experience with the capabilities of American "care in the air," the strong professional "investment" in the airmen they had aided shaped their first reaction to the prompt discharge of the Air Force patients. They had provided the Americans, as Dr. Robb was prompt to say, compassionate and skillful care. Then, much sooner than the Saudi physicians expected, they were told that these patients would be leaving their hospitals. "Remember," Dr. Robb pointed out, "these weren't 4404th Medical Group patients. These were MODA's patients; ARAMCO patients; [King Fahd] University Hospital's patients."[36]

Recognizing the professional investment that the Saudis had in the injured airmen, Dr. Robb first invited the Dhahran care givers to tour the medevac C–141s, and later asked them also to help load the patients onto these aircraft. The local professionals expressed their appreciation at being given this opportunity to participate in the medical evacuation. "It brought closure to them," Dr. Robb observed, "because they had become part" of the successful response to a terrible tragedy.[37]

At about 12:30 p.m. that Thursday, the FAST team began bringing the first patients to the ASF.[38] The Landstuhl team members who had gone to the hospitals that morning remained there, and they and other care givers also helped transport the airmen to the flightline. Once there, they remained at the GUTS hangar, interacting with the patients while they waited to board their C–141 and making themselves available to the medical professionals, as well. "We talked to [the airmen]," Colonel Connor recalled, "who were coming around and waiting. We just basically tried to be there to listen, to be supportive."[39]

When the C–141 made its return flight to Germany, carrying the patients to Ramstein Air Base, the aircraft would not be able to fly at as high an altitude as it had while inbound to Saudi Arabia. The flightline crews accordingly loaded additional fuel onto the Starlifter. At the same time, the physicians at the ASF assessed the patients as they arrived from the three principal Dhahran hospitals and Mohammed al Dosha, and determined which would travel on the first medevac flight and which on the second.[40]

Around 4:30 p.m., the FAST team and other care givers began loading the first patients. Twenty-two airmen boarded the medevac C–141, ten of them ambulatory, twelve on litters.[41] Brigadier General Schwalier later described the scene, as the patients passed through a "gauntlet" of about five hundred well-wishers. "I remember being so impressed," the wing commander stated, "as each nurse would team up with a casualty, and one at a time they'd come down the gauntlet.... They had a process that they were following that was pretty impressive."[42]

Three Departures from Dhahran

An augmented (seven-member) aeromedical evacuation crew of the 86th AES would man this C–141, tail number 40629, during its return trip to Ramstein.⁴³ At 5:35 p.m. this initial AE flight from Dhahran, mission AMRF44015179, launched from the King Abdul Aziz flightline. Dr. Robb used a defense switched network phone line to place a direct call to Army Col. (Dr.) Ney M. Gore, the acting commander of the Landstuhl hospital, alerting him that the first of the Khobar patients now were airborne for Germany.⁴⁴

Twenty-one patients, twelve of them ambulatory and nine on litters, boarded the second AE C–141, tail number 60137, mission AMRF44013179. The after-action report of the 86th AES related in precise, military prose: "The first flight left at 1735L [local time] and the second at 1942L. All casualties were enplaned without incident."⁴⁵

The 86th AES had brought three augmented crews to Dhahran. One had manned the first medevac flight, and another took responsibility for the second. The third crew, as one of its members summed up, "would stay behind and manage the follow-on collection of patients for subsequent missions."⁴⁶ No airman on either of the first two AE flights required critical care, and the three-member Critical Care Aeromedical Transport Team that had flown in with the 86th AES also could remain in Dhahran. This C-CATT team would stand available for a third or later AE flight.⁴⁷

The FAST team stayed as well, and would continue to staff the Khobar Towers clinic for another four days. "We got our money's worth out of the FAST team," observed Capt. Michael Weems of the 4410th AEF. "They were a huge help because the people here were exhausted."⁴⁸

Shortly after 7:40 p.m., the second of the AE C–141s climbed away from the runway on what the Saudis called King Abdul Aziz Air Base. The first two medevac aircraft and their patients had left Dhahran.

The 58th Fighter Squadron's farewell to Dhahran became a story of frustration. The F–15 unit was scheduled to leave Dhahran Air Base at 10:30 a.m. in the morning of Thursday, the twenty-seventh.⁴⁹ A commercial charter, a Lockheed L–1011 TriStar,⁵⁰ would carry the squadron's main body, about 150 personnel, back to Eglin Air Force Base, Florida.⁵¹ This civilian transport had arrived during the memorial service on the flightline, bringing to Dhahran the members of the 27th Fighter Squadron from Langley Air Force Base, Virginia, who were rotating in behind the 58th. Now it would return the "Nomads" to Eglin.⁵²

Lieutenant Colonel Cochran, the deployed squadron's commander, and five other fighter pilots would fly the unit's F–15s from Dhahran to their Florida home. Five of these Eagles were "C" models; one was a "D."⁵³ After the aircraft and the main body left, twenty-two maintenance personnel would remain in Dhahran.⁵⁴

The senior officer of the departing main body was Lt. Col. Thomas McCarthy, the operations officer of the 58th Fighter Squadron, who had been in Lieutenant

Khobar Towers: Tragedy and Response

Colonel Cochran's suite at the time of the bombing and who had gone to the mortuary to help identify the remains of the deceased. That Thursday morning, after the squadron had spent more than a day in its "encampment" on the Dhahran military flightline, the departing members began packing up. A fleet of trucks carried them and their baggage to the AMC terminal.[55]

The squadron members settled themselves into the seats of the L–1011. The civilian captain of the commercial airplane, who was well familiar with the religious prohibition of alcohol in Saudi Arabia, came on the intercom and announced that he would buy drinks for all of the airmen, as soon as they were over Egypt. "There was a loud, thunderous cheer," Lieutenant Colonel McCarthy remembered, "as we took off." Exhausted by the events of the preceding day and night, nearly all of the 150 or so passengers soon fell asleep. Among them was TSgt. George Burgess, the young airman who had helped search Building 131 in the wake of the explosion. "I remember we took off, and I said, 'Thank you!,'" he recalled. "I was relieved, as soon as I felt the wheels go up. I thought, 'OK,' and I fell asleep." A few minutes later, TSgt. Mike Goff noticed that the plane leveled off sooner than he expected.[56]

After the L–1011 had been airborne for about half an hour, Colonel McCarthy related, the stewardess and captain approached and told him, "they've got a problem, they're going to have to turn around." There was trouble with one of the airliner's slats, a difficulty that explained Sergeant Goff's observation: the plane could not climb above 10,000 feet. Colonel McCarthy continued the story, in present tense: "We turn around and land back at Dhahran. Everybody gives this big cheer because they think we're at Shannon, Ireland, or, at the least, in Cairo, and I had to tell them, 'No, we're back in Dhahran.'" Sergeant Burgess, among the many who had fallen asleep, remained slumbering until a stewardess woke him and told him they were landing. He remembered vividly how his mood swung from elation to depression: "I said, '*All right!*' And she said, 'We're back. We had to go back.' I said, 'Oh, no.'"[57]

While the 58th Fighter Squadron's main body made its short, disappointing flight, Lieutenant Colonel Cochran remained a busy officer. He knew that as of that Thursday morning, at least ten members of the unit remained hospitalized in Dhahran. He and Capt. (Dr.) R. Morris Treadway, Jr., a flight surgeon, set out to check on these patients. When they returned to King Abdul Aziz, they learned the bad news: the L–1011 had a "blown flap" and had been forced to return. There were, as Dr. Treadway readily saw, "a lot of unhappy faces." Brigadier General Schwalier met with these Khobar veterans after their unfortunate return, and characterized their mood candidly: "I remember talking to the very emotional and angry and still shell-shocked Air Force professionals [of the 58th Fighter Squadron]—I would describe them in that way."[58]

At 2:30 p.m. that afternoon, Col. Dale Bible, the commander of the 4409th Operations Group who had come to Dhahran for the wing's change of command ceremony and stayed on to help in the wake of the attack, received some bad news about the L–1011. The airliner was "hard broke": its slat problem could not be readily fixed. Even had it been repairable, no mechanic who was qualified to work on this

Three Departures from Dhahran

commercial plane was available in Saudi Arabia at the time. Fixing the TriStar was not an option; a substitute aircraft would have to be found.[59]

From AMC's perspective, several factors came to bear on this problem. The command's airlift planners were responsible for maintaining the efficiency of all transport scheduling, around the globe. C–5s that ordinarily could have been sent to Dhahran to pick up the stranded airmen were flying other missions at the time.[60]

The airmen of the 58th Fighter Squadron, and others on the scene in Dhahran, had a different perspective. "Our sense," Brigadier General Schwalier said, "was that the AMC bureaucracy would not bend to the needs of the field commander, in that situation." The Eglin airmen had difficulty accepting the contention that there were missions with a higher priority than their return home. When it became known that two C–141s would substitute for the L–1011, Lieutenant Colonel McCarthy was told that these transports had no comfort pallets. He said flatly: "Believe me, nobody cares about comfort pallets, at this point."[61]

General Schwalier focused his attention that afternoon on the answer rather than the question. "I didn't care what the problem was with the airplane," he said later, "what I cared about was getting those people home." He asked the Wing Operations Center to tell the AMC schedulers: "We need to get these people home. I don't care if it's an alert aircraft; get a live aircraft here." The wing officers found that AMC was "unbending." General Schwalier related what happened next: "So [Brig. Gen.] Dan Dick [the incoming commander of the 4404th Composite Wing] got involved. [He] spent the rest of the afternoon—taking much too much time, making phone calls to the [airlift controllers]—talking at the general officer level."[62]

There was evidence that, in addition to the generals in the theater, officers even more senior in rank actively intervened to arrange the transportation for the stranded airmen of the 58th Fighter Squadron. One officer who was in Dhahran that day later stated: "I guess [Air Force Chief of Staff] General [Ronald R.] Fogleman, along with the generals in southwest Asia *made some C–141s available to us* .... The leadership of the Air Force ... did some good work."[63]

The generals and the AMC planners identified two C–141s that would substitute for the broken commercial airliner. After an afternoon and evening of frustrating delay, eighty members of the 58th Fighter Squadron boarded one of these Starlifters, with the call sign Reach 60140, and sixty-eight others went on the other, call sign Reach 50269. The first of these transports left Dhahran at 7:08 p.m. that Thursday night, the second about twenty minutes later. The two C–141s made a stopover at Rota Naval Station, Spain, where they were well received. Lieutenant Colonel McCarthy commented: "They took care of us *great*. They opened up the dining hall, fed us meals, and got us back on the airplane."[64]

As Colonel Cochran intended, the squadron's F–15s left Dhahran after the main body. Three of the fighters, using call signs Cube 34, 35, and 36, arrived on Moron Air Base, Spain, on Friday, June 28, at 2:49 p.m. The other three, Cube 31 through 33, landed there about two hours later. At 9 p.m. that night, the six fighters together launched from the Spanish base for the flight over the Atlantic to Eglin.[65]

Khobar Towers: Tragedy and Response

The 71st Rescue Squadron left Saudi Arabia without the frustration encountered by the 58th Fighter Squadron. The HC–130 unit had begun its departure earlier than the F–15 one had. By the time of the flightline memorial service, as Lieutenant Colonel Shafer later pointed out, many members of the rescue squadron already had left Dhahran Air Base. The unit's situation was not typical. Its personnel usually served sixty-day rotation tours, rather than the standard ninety,[66] and the squadron itself had been assigned to Dhahran for more than two years. A special operations group was scheduled to assume its mission,[67] and the members of the 71st had to "swap out" quickly with the arriving personnel. Because this rescue squadron had served on Southern Watch so long without being relieved by another unit and because its people did not serve the standard-length tour, it had no experience with making a unit-to-unit transition. Nonetheless, as Colonel Shafer stated, the circumstances dictated that the best course was to send home as many people as promptly as possible.[68]

The bombing had indisputably affected the unit. Five members of the 71st Rescue Squadron had been killed and a number of others wounded. Capt. Russell D. Barile, the pilot who had become the unit's senior officer when Lieutenant Colonel Shafer was hospitalized, was the only aircraft commander who remained uninjured. No radio operator had survived the attack; a copilot would have to fill the role. Colonel Shafer himself was the only remaining navigator, and he had been injured. Just two of the squadron's loadmasters, and only one flight engineer, remained uninjured.[69]

On Thursday, June 27, the 71st Rescue Squadron began planning for the departure of its few remaining members. Its deployed first sergeant, MSgt. Dwayne Berry, scheduled the unit's debriefing sessions with the stress management team that had arrived the previous night from Landstuhl. When he had finished this task, Lieutenant Colonel Shafer advised him: "Dwayne, we're going to get people out of here." The deployed squadron commander asked the first sergeant to consult with the Travel Management Office, and begin making the arrangements for nineteen of the unit's members to leave Dhahran on that night's rotator flight back to the United States. Colonel Shafer identified the people who would leave with that group, and the word of the departure plans moved quickly through the 71st. During the twenty-seventh, Captain Barile later recalled, "They told us, 'Hey, everyone's going home.'"[70]

Captain Barile's information proved accurate: everyone in the rescue squadron *was* going home, in groups. After the first nineteen left on the twenty- seventh, other members of the 71st soon followed them. Some would return to Patrick Air Force Base on the afternoon of Friday, the twenty-eighth, others on the following evening. A few squadron members remained in Dhahran a while longer, for the unit still had a fair amount of administrative and other tasks to finish. Captain Barile himself and Master Sergeant Berry, whose work with the first sergeants council kept him busy, were among those who stayed in the theater a few more days. The last sizeable group, twelve members of the unit, departed on July 1.[71] The Khobar veterans of the 71st Rescue Squadron and of the 58th Fighter Squadron had left Dhahran.

Chapter Eleven

Honoring and Remembering

At 10:45 a.m. on Thursday, June 27, 1996, about a half hour ahead of its estimated time of arrival, the C–5A Galaxy carrying the remains of the nineteen airmen landed at the Dover Port Mortuary at Dover Air Force Base, Delaware.[1] At 12:15 p.m., an arrival service, closed to all journalists except those who represented Air Force News, was conducted on the Dover flightline. Air Force Chief of Staff Gen. Ronald R. Fogleman, Secretary of the Air Force Dr. Sheila Widnall, Chairman of the Joint Chiefs of Staff Gen. John Shalikashvili, the families of the deceased, and about seven hundred Dover personnel met the C–5A. Instead of delivering a eulogy, General Fogleman in silence pinned a Purple Heart on, and then saluted, each of the nineteen flag-draped caskets. From Dover Air Force Base, the remains of the deceased airmen were transported to funeral homes selected by their families.[2]

Personnel at the Dover Port Mortuary positively identified eighteen of the nineteen remains. Only one name remained on the list of unidentified airmen, SrA. Paul A. Blais.[3] However, the doctors and other personnel at the Dover mortuary studied the forsenics of the nineteenth set of remains and determined that they did not match the medical records of Airman Blais.[4]

After this development, Air Force personnel in Dhahran believed it most likely that the patient who remained in the intensive care unit of King Fahd University Hospital was Senior Airman Blais, and the remains at Dover were those of A1C. Christopher B. Lester. Beginning in the earliest morning hours of Saturday, June 29, at Khobar Towers, and throughout that day, medical and other personnel made continuous efforts to identify positively the ICU patient. Acquaintances of both men visited the intensive care ward to try to make an identification. Medical personnel took blood samples. (It turned out that both airmen had type "A+," yet another similarity between them.) They also did footprinting, dental mapping, and fingerprinting.[5]

At 5 p.m. Lt. Col. (Dr.) Douglas J. Robb, the interim commander of the 4404th Wing's medical group, accompanied by dental surgeon Lt. Col. (Dr.) Bruce Lauder and dental technician SSgt. Rudolph Grimm II, arrived at the King Fahd hospital. Dr. Lauder and Sergeant Grimm took x-rays of the patient's teeth. At 6:15 the first of their films were processed, and confirmed the patient's identification. His tooth number thirty-two had been extracted: the identical condition appeared in the dental

Khobar Towers: Tragedy and Response

records of SrA. Paul Blais.[6] In the meantime, Dover personnel had matched the medical records of A1C. Christopher Lester with the last set of remains at the mortuary. Air Force officials formally expressed regret for "all hardship and pain caused to both families" by the unfortunate delay in making these identifications.[7]

Well before the Blais-Lester case had been resolved, at 12:25 a.m. on Friday, June 28, the first of the aeromedical evacuation C–141s, tail number 40629, had arrived at Ramstein Air Base, Germany. It was met at the flightline by personnel of the 86th Aeromedical Staging Flight, commanded by Lt. Col. Dawn M. Oerichbauer, and by four buses that transported the Khobar Towers patients the four miles south to the Landstuhl Regional Medical Center.[8]

There were poignant scenes during this trip through the early morning darkness. At the front of one of the buses, an Army nurse stood near the litter of an airman whose eyes were covered with patches and reassured him during the ride to the hospital. "I remember one of the eye patients," she recalled, nine months later. "I held his hand, the whole way back, and explained to him where we were going, and that he was okay."[9]

The second AE C–141, tail number 60137, reached Ramstein at 1:45 a.m. Capt. Matthew Winkler, who had been wounded while evacuating Building 131, praised the Landstuhl staff for the reception they gave the arriving patients. When the buses rolled up Kirchberg Hill, passed through Gate 2, and stopped in front of the huge hospital, its personnel "were ready to go—ready to help us," he related. Captain Winkler continued: "We pulled up in buses, there were rows and rows of wheel chairs, and rows and rows of people with stretchers, ready to carry people that couldn't walk."[10]

One distracting incident occurred during the otherwise smooth arrival. An unattended briefcase, discovered near the hospital entrance, understandably stirred the emotions of those nearby. It was soon established, however, that this small piece of luggage posed no threat: a press team had unintentionally abandoned it.[11]

The forty-three patients were promptly admitted to the LRMC, each with a doctor assigned to them. One nurse remembered the quiet tension that prevailed before the airmen came onto her floor. Then, "when the first wheelchairs arrived on the ward," she recalled, "there was an aura of 'Here come our heroes.'"[12]

Across the Atlantic Ocean, June 27 had been a busy day at Patrick Air Force Base, Florida. Col. Thomas R. Friers, the commander of the 1st Rescue Group—and others—learned that their installation's memorial service for the Khobar airmen would be held on Sunday, the thirtieth. The details of the ceremony began to take shape on the twenty-seventh, as officials at the White House and officers at Headquarters USAF provided more information to the local planners at Patrick.[13]

That Thursday afternoon the base staff held a meeting to plan for the memorial service. Brig. Gen. Robert C. Hinson, the commander of the 45th Space Wing and Patrick's senior officer, was on leave to attend his son's wedding, so Col. Patrick J. Carr, the 45th's vice commander, chaired the session. He advised Colonel Friers that he would take care of the base support for the memorial service, so that Friers could continue to look after the people of the 71st Rescue Squadron and others of the rescue group. Colonel Carr "really *did*" take care of the base, Friers later emphasized. He also stressed that "the base and the community bent over backwards. It was *unbelievable*."[14]

During the evening of the twenty-seventh, Patrick's Wellness Center sponsored a dinner and a seminar to help the base begin its healing process. A psychiatrist, a pyschologist, and base chapel and Red Cross personnel participated in this evening program. They "did a super job," Colonel Friers concluded, for the "71st Squadron family" and for others on the base.[15]

On the following day, Friday, June 28, Colonel Friers and Lt. Col. Donald R. Jozayt, commander of the 71st Rescue Squadron, held a midmorning news conference, which the local television and radio stations carried "live." Colonel Friers gave the press an overview briefing, describing the role that Patrick's 71st Rescue Squadron played in Dhahran, the number of people it typically had stationed there, and what was then known about the situation. Lieutenant Colonel Jozayt answered a number of questions from the reporters. The officers were able to announce that Patrick's first returning airmen would arrive that afternoon.[16]

Roughly four hundred miles to the northwest, at Eglin Air Force Base, the twenty-seventh was an equally busy day. The 33d Fighter Wing's day-to-day flying operations were canceled, allowing personnel to concentrate on the Khobar recovery. The unit's commander, Col. Gary R. Dylewski, later reflected: "It was a busy time, but not unmanageable—thanks to the great help we got from everybody at Eglin."[17]

Twenty or more people continued on duty in the Eglin battle staff, around the clock. The base remained tightly focused on helping its families. When any specific issue arose, Lt. Col. Stan Hill, the battle staff's director, explained, "Team Eglin" addressed it by answering what was always the fundamental question: "What is right for these families?"[18]

Eglin's personnel kept up with their work, and they met a stern pace to do it. "We were answering 2,000 phone calls a day," Capt. Brenda Campbell, the 33d Fighter Wing's public affairs officer, stated. "We had a stack, three inches thick, of news queries." Captain Campbell praised the help she received from other agencies. In the immediate wake of the bombing, public affairs officers—*experienced* public affairs officers—had come to her assistance from the Air Force Development Test Center on Main Base Eglin and from nearby Hurlburt Field. Over the following days, others arrived—from Tyndall Air Force Base, Florida; Wright-Patterson Air Force Base, Ohio; and Langley Air Force Base, Virginia. Eventually, twenty-five PA officers mobilized at the modest office of the 33d Fighter Wing.[19]

Back in Dhahran, a third of the way around the world, there was no stronger evidence of the continuing recovery than the 4404th Composite Wing's remarkably prompt return to flying its missions. On Thursday, June 27, the C–130s of the rescue squadron returned to the air; and the following afternoon, the F–16s were back on their Operation Southern Watch patrols. Normal flight operations resumed on the twenty-ninth. Dr. Robb expressed admiration for the air and flightline crews: "It was almost like we didn't miss a beat. We started flying missions as soon as we could."[20]

Khobar Towers: Tragedy and Response

The airmen knew that their deceased comrades would want them to resume the Southern Watch mission as quickly as possible. Getting Air Force planes back into the sky was one way of paying tribute to the airmen who had given their lives. Another was the formal memorial service that the 4404th Composite Wing held at 10:30 a.m. on Friday, June 28.[21]

The wing planned and organized this service within just twenty-four hours. Lt. Col. (Chaplain) Dennis E. Aleson, the senior chaplain in Dhahran at the time of the bombing, pointed out: "We had a lot of people doing a lot of different things to make this happen. And it happened with class." He then offered a reminder about the condition of the wing's personnel on that Thursday and Friday: "We're talking about people who at this stage were operating on almost nothing but adrenaline."[22]

Chaplain Aleson's description applied to himself as well as hundreds of others. Like so many around him, from the time of the explosion just before 10 p.m. on Tuesday, he had continued to function on very little sleep. Late Thursday night, he had "hit a wall" and been forced to take a few hours nap. By 4 a.m. Friday, he was rested enough that he could begin working on the opening statement and meditation that he would give during the memorial service later that morning. Aleson's work was disrupted when, because of a false bomb threat, the security police cleared his building. Finally he outlined his meditation on three small pieces of paper. He later recalled thinking at that time: "OK, Lord, it's up to You. This is going to happen."[23]

Others also worked hard that morning of the twenty-eighth to prepare for the ceremony. Airmen of the services squadron turned the Air Mobility Command passenger terminal into an appropriate setting for a memorial service. They hung white cloth backdrops and brought in nineteen flower arrangements, one for each of the deceased. Personnel from the communications squadron set up a sound system. Chairs were brought in from another terminal, enough to seat more than 400 people. An order of service, titled "Honoring and Remembering," was prepared.[24]

Unlike the memorial service held during the early morning hours of Wednesday, which had been closed to the press, this one was opened to the news media. The Cable News Network and other national networks televised parts of the ceremony. "There were TV cameras all over the place," Chaplain Aleson remarked.[25]

The service began at 10:30 a.m., with Chaplain Aleson giving a short statement of purpose. Maj. (Chaplain) John Kovalcin delivered the opening prayer. It closed with: "Give us more courage to persevere in our mission. And Almighty Father, embrace us to ease our pain—wipe away our fears and mend our hearts—in Your name, Lord, we pray."[26] The congregation of several hundred people sang the hymn "Faith of Our Fathers," and Father Kovalcin then read Psalm 90 and Psalm 23.[27]

Three senior officers—Brig. Gen. Terry Schwalier, the wing commander; Col. Scott Gration, commander of the wing's operations group; and Lt. Col. Thomas H. Shafer, commander of the deployed 71st Rescue Squadron—then offered some personal reflections. "This memorial service is not about nineteen anonymous people," Lieutenant Colonel Shafer stated. "These were my friends. Captain [Christopher J.] Adams was also my room mate." The blast had struck as Colonel Shafer had been returning to his bedroom for a pair of shoes. His feet had been cut, and he had been left dazed and surrounded by broken glass and other debris. Someone had found a pair of boots for him: they were the ones that had belonged to Capt. Chris Adams. In his remarks during the memorial service, Colonel Shafer said of these boots: "I still am wearing them. I can't take them off. I don't really want to."[28]

Chaplain Aleson later reflected on Colonel Shafer's presentation: "No one had the attention of the people more than he did.... It was very emotional." Chaplain Aleson also pointed to a remarkable coincidence that occurred in the order of service. He had chosen the poetic lines of Isaiah 40:31 to fill what would have been a blank space on the lower righthand side of the program. Colonel Shafer, without consulting him, had selected exactly the same Scripture for the text of his own remarks: "Those who hope in the Lord will renew their strength. They will soar on wings like eagles; they will run and not grow weary, they will walk and not be faint."[29]

Following the personal reflections, Chaplain Aleson gave a meditation and the congregation sang "Lord, Guard and Guide the Men Who Fly." This hymn ended with the lines: "Aloft in solitudes of space, Uphold them with Your saving grace. O God, protect all those who fly, And all who work and serve nearby." Capt. (Father) Thomas Angelo offered the closing prayer.[30]

This memorial service formed an important part of the healing process that was just beginning in Dhahran. Brigadier General Schwalier praised those who had contributed to it and commented that it was "done superbly." U.S. Army Gen. J. H. Binford Peay III, commander of United States Central Command, and Maj. Gen. Kurt B. Anderson, commander of Joint Task Force Southwest Asia, also spoke highly of the service. Chaplain Aleson commented on its value to the airmen in Saudi Arabia: it "helped us turn beyond our present moment to the future."[31]

In Germany, on the Friday of the memorial service in Dhahran, the wounded airmen of the 4404th spent the day in their beds at Landstuhl Regional Medical Center. They received excellent care, delivered by a one-to-one physician-to-airman ratio. "We decided fairly early on," Army Col. (Dr.) Edward B. Freyfogle recalled, "that every patient would have an attending doctor," and added that the number of patients made that policy possible. "The attending doctor would be in charge of that patient, to include lining up every single consultation, until some other service or doctor had agreed to accept that patient, under his or her personal service." The airmen commented favorably on the care they received at Landstuhl.[32] Capt. Matt Winkler praised the LRMC staff's "excellent, excellent job.... They did a super job." For SSgt. Eric D. Ziegler, who had been testing his alarm clock when the blast struck Building 131, the highlights of his LRMC stay were simply the chance to rest and to take a shower—his first since the twenty-fifth of June.[33]

Nearly all of the airmen who had arrived at Landstuhl during the early hours of Friday, the twenty-eighth, left the hospital for the United States on the morning of the next day, Saturday, the twenty-ninth.[34] The hospital originally planned to discharge the Khobar airmen on Sunday, June 30, but this was advanced a day, primarily to allow the patients who were well enough to make a trans-Atlantic flight to return to

Khobar Towers: Tragedy and Response

the States for the memorial services that would be held that weekend.[35] "We got them evaluated," Dr. Freyfogle summed up, "and then, all of a sudden, they were out of here." The patients' charts had be photocopied and much other administrative work done—quickly—to meet the new discharge date. But the impetus for an early return home became compelling, once it was known that President Bill Clinton would be attending the memorial services. "The president wanted you home," Captain Winkler said. "Everybody wanted you home."[36]

On the afternoon of June 28, as Colonel Friers had announced at that morning's press conference, Patrick greeted its initial returnees. The first airmen of the 71st Rescue Squadron to leave Dhahran were the nineteen who had departed on the twenty-seventh. A "rotator" from the theater brought this group, largely maintenance personnel, into Atlanta's Hartsfield International Airport. Colonel Friers praised the cooperation from the locals there: "Everybody bent over backward for us."[37]

Colonel Friers felt strongly that the Khobar veterans should return to their home base on an HC–130 Combat Shadow, the aircraft they flew for their country. "It was really neat to put them on [their] own unit airplane," he said, "and let them land on the runway they had departed from." An airman who returned with a later group that also was met by an HC–130 and by personnel of the 71st Rescue Squadron was pleased to see the familiar aircraft, and the familiar faces. "That was very nice," he commented. "That was touching, to me."[38]

The HC–130 carried these Air Force members back to their Florida home station that Friday afternoon, where a very large and enthusiastic crowd awaited them. Base personnel had learned from airmen in the theater the names of the passengers on this first returning aircraft, on the one following it, and, a day later, on a C–9 Nightingale that would transport the wounded Patrick airmen from Landstuhl. A thorough telephone and door-to-door effort informed the families of the Khobar veterans of the identities of these passengers and the arrival times of the three aircraft. In addition, as Lt. Col. Donald R. Jozayt, the commander of the 71st Rescue Squadron, pointed out, "everybody who was at work" that Friday "came out to meet the airplanes. It was pretty uplifting."[39]

It was a sunny Friday afternoon on Florida's "Space Coast" when the HC–130 taxied up to the waiting crowd at Patrick. The second aircraft followed it closely, and an enormous gathering of people cheered the two aircraft. The members of the crowd, most of them women and children, wore colorful summer clothing and waved small American flags as the planes taxied in.[40]

A jubilant welcoming met the returning airmen, who soon were off the aircraft and hugging and kissing their families. Colonel Friers recalled the scene on Patrick's ramp: "the people out there with flags, it was great." A young airman said later, with considerable feeling, that he was impressed by the large size of the crowd and the outpouring of emotion: "It put a tear in my eye. I didn't expect that. News people, everything like that. I didn't expect *that* much."[41]

David Wittman, Bob Grover, and other reporters from Brevard County's Channel 2 News, and other local journalists covered the return of the Patrick airmen.

Honoring and Remembering

Among the early returnees, Capt. Ben Walsh spoke to the press soon after leaving the HC–130. First Lt. Stephanie Bronson, a civil engineer, was an officer from Patrick who, when these first two aircraft arrived at her home base, was still in Dhahran. She had been treated for the glass cuts in her feet at the Arabian American Oil Company (ARAMCO) Hospital and the staff there had made a telephone available to her, but she had not been able to reach her husband, Donald Bronson. As of that afternoon, Friday, the twenty-eighth, while other families were being reunited on the Patrick flightline, her spouse still had not heard from her. Donald Bronson gave television reporters an interview from the couple's quarters in South Patrick's housing, which a local station ran under the trailing title "Waiting for Word." Lieutenant Bronson eventually got through to her husband on a phone line, continued her work with the 45th Civil Engineering Squadron that helped the recovery at the Khobar Towers, and left Saudi Arabia for the United States on September 19.[42]

The press continued to report on events at Patrick, and a second happy arrival occurred on the following evening, when another group of the 71st Rescue Squadron returned to Patrick. This time a rotator from the theater flew to Philadelphia International Airport. Once again, the local cooperation was strong: when the military aircraft approached, the airfield manager immediately gave it permission to land. Again, as in Atlanta, the Khobar veterans went directly onto an HC–130, which took them to their homecoming at Patrick.[43]

On that Saturday evening, the C–9 carrying the patients from Landstuhl arrived at Patrick at about the same time as the Combat Shadow. Among these returnees, who deplaned wearing "Ramstein Air Base" T-shirts, was stretcher-borne Capt. Thomas F. Edman, a resident of the seventh floor of Building 131 who had been severely wounded and treated at King Fahd University Hospital.[44] A child held a sign declaring "Welcome Home Matt," when Capt. Matthew Winkler, Captain Edman's suitemate, left the C–9. His wife, Kim Winkler, gave an interview to local reporters, as did MSgt. William F. Sine, one of the pararescue jumpers who had done such good work in the wake of the bombing.[45]

Lt. Col. Thomas H. Shafer, commander of the deployed 71st Rescue Squadron, and another eleven members of the unit returned to the States a few days after their comrades. They left Dhahran on July 1, and spent twenty-four hours in Frankfort, Germany. On July 3, a Delta Airlines flight brought them into Atlanta's Hartsfield International Airport where, like the others, they were met by an HC–130 that carried them to their home base. These arrivals were joyous occasions, but there remained the inescapable fact that five of the airmen, as one officer of the 71st poignantly stated, returned to Dover rather than Patrick.[46]

The same was, of course, equally true at Eglin. The Khobar veterans returned there primarily in three groups: the main body of the 58th Fighter Squadron, the officers who flew the squadron's F–15s back to the base, and the wounded who returned on a medevac aircraft. Just as at Patrick, a joyous homecoming awaited the main body of the squadron when it reached Eglin at about 1 p.m. on Friday, the twenty-eighth. A large crowd dressed in comfortable summer attire stood along the runway

Khobar Towers: Tragedy and Response

in the 33d Fighter Wing's area of the base. Many of the women and children carried American flags and a few held clumps of red, white, and blue balloons. When two C–5s taxied up, a young child asked, "Where's he going to stop?" A mother answered: "Right here. Right here, honey, right here in front." The two huge transports rolled to a stop. The crowd members raised their national flags high, and the engines of the big planes stirred the air and set these hand-held banners fluttering.[47]

The crowd rivetted its attention on the aircraft that parked to their right. Its door opened and a man in a desert battle dress uniform came down the short exit ladder. He was followed immediately by another, and another, and another, each ducking his head down under the door and making the brief steps down to the tarmac. A reception line awaited the deplaning airmen. Among its members were Maj. Gen. Stewart E. Cranston, commander of the Air Force Development Test Center; Col. Gary R. Dylewski, commander of the 33d Fighter Wing; and Col. David A. Deptula, commander of the 33d Operations Group. These officers gave each of the arriving airmen a quick salute, a long handshake, and sometimes a friendly slap on the shoulder.[48]

The crowd of friends, children, and wives, some carrying flowers with yellow ribbons, rolled forward to greet the returnees. "It's good to be back!," a young airman called into a nearby video camera. A scene of hugging, kissing, and crying followed and then several of the Dhahran veterans began to walk off the flightline, carrying their infant children.[49]

"I was glad to touch down, *I'll tell* you," said TSgt. George Burgess, who had helped search Building 131 in the wake of the bombing. An officer offered his perspective on the reception: "We made it back to a *real good* welcome.... Everybody's concern was with two things: the families, and the concern with the people who were *not with them*, either because they were deceased or injured." Capt. (Dr.) R. Morris Treadway, a flight surgeon who had resided in Building 127, was a little surprised by the size of the turnout at Eglin and by the amount of press attention. "We don't realize how big a deal something like this is," he reflected. "We get caught up in doing our jobs.... Here we were, at the center of world events."[50]

Anticipating that the press would take an intense interest in the returning airmen, public affairs officers had designated an area near the edge of the flightline where the Khobar veterans who wanted to meet with the journalists could do so. At the same time, those who wanted to be reunited with their families, avoid the media representatives, and go to the privacy of their homes were equally able to do so. No doubt many of the returning airmen agreed with one of their comrades who praised this arrangement. "It was good," he said, "the way they had it set up. It wasn't like the media could come out and greet you, which I was thankful for.... If you wanted to talk to the media, you could. The rest of [the returnees could] just funnel off."[51]

The first airman who entered the press area was met with the obvious request: "Tell us what happened." As he began to reply to this question, a second of the Eglin returnees, SSgt. John C. Orlando, took up a position a bit further down the flightline and also started talking to the journalists. Sergeant Orlando said, among other things, that while he was happy to see his wife and son, he felt grief for the families whose

Honoring and Remembering

loved ones were not returning. Soon a third airman, and then others, joined in the discussion with the press. Capt. Brenda Campbell, the 33d Fighter Wing's public affairs officer, later expressed pride in the Dhahran veterans who met with the journalists. "There were a couple [of them]," she said, "who were just brilliant. I mean, young guys standing up there telling it like it was. They were just fantastic."[52]

There was another dramatic return to Eglin, when, at 1:55 p.m. on Saturday, June 29, six F–15s (five "C" models and one "D") appeared in the summer sky over the northern Florida base. The fighters had left Dhahran the previous day and flew to their home station by way of Moron Air Base, Spain. Two of the six Eagles flew off to the side, and as the main body of four neared the Eglin flightline, one aircraft pulled off to create a "Missing Man" formation. Lt. Col. Douglas R. Cochran, commander of the deployed 58th Fighter Squadron, taxied his fighter into the parking space farthest to the left of the awaiting crowd. He was greeted first by his wife, who wore a "broken wings" pin on her shirt, and two children, and then by Major General Cranston and Col. David Hayes, the vice commander of the 33d Fighter Wing. The other five pilots parked and soon were out of their jets as well.[53]

Not long after these six F–15s had returned home, a medevac C–141, tail number 60137, arrived behind them. Near where this aircraft taxied in, General Cranston, his wife Peggy Cranston, and Colonel Dylewski formed a reception line to greet Secretary of the Air Force Dr. Sheila Widnall and Air Force Chief of Staff Gen. Ronald R. Fogleman and their spouses, Mr. William S. Widnall and Mrs. Fogleman, always addressed as Miss Jane Fogleman. Ambulances and medical buses stood nearby, as the C–141 rolled to a stop. Generals Fogleman and Cranston boarded the aircraft and spoke to the patients on their bunks, welcoming them home.[54]

The ambulatory wounded exited the C–141, wearing T-shirts they had received at Landstuhl: white ones, with the Air Force emblem in black at their center, "Ramstein" above this symbol and "Germany" below. As at Patrick, the crowd waited patiently and then a joyous scene followed. SrA. Michael J. Dolinar, Jr., who had left Building 131 with TSgt. George Burgess and had been treated at the Ministry of Defense and Aviation Hospital, was carried from the aircraft on a litter; six of his friends crowded around him. An anxious young woman climbed into an ambulance that carried a wounded airman, her boyfriend. The C–141's crewmembers said that the patients had been both "solemn" and "cheery" during the flight home.[55]

After greeting the returning wounded, General Fogleman, Secretary Widnall, and their spouses also visited the "People Place," which was not far from the 33d Fighter Wing's taxi-line. This center already had helped start the healing process at Eglin, and it would continue to support the grieving base during the days ahead. Linda Brown, its manager, later praised the dignitaries for their time spent at the People Place, in a few heartfelt words: "That was valuable."[56]

At 11 a.m. on the following morning, Sunday, June 30, a memorial service was held in Eglin's Hangar 130, commonly known as King Hangar. It stood north of the Eglin Parkway, a main avenue divided to run one way in each direction. King Hangar was located on the base's flightline between the shopette and Building 1.[57]

Khobar Towers: Tragedy and Response

Large as King Hangar was, that Sunday morning a congregation of about 4,500 overflowed its capacity. An enormous American flag hung from an overhead crane, usually used to lift aircraft parts.[58] Twelve wreaths, one for each of the deceased airmen from Eglin, stood in front of the congregation. Eleven survivors of the bombing were in the front row. Some had walked to the ceremony, some had come in wheelchairs, and some had been wheeled in on hospital beds.[59] Members of the families of the deceased also sat in the front row.[60]

General Cranston escorted President Bill Clinton to his seat.[61] The chief executive's visit to Eglin had been well planned, and a number of officers praised the advance work done by the White House. One complimented in particular the professionalism of the president's staff, another that of the White House press corps.[62]

The Eglin memorial service began with Col. (Chaplain) LaVerne L. Schueller, who would later survive the September 11, 2001, terrorist attack on the Pentagon, giving the welcoming remarks. Lt. Col. (Chaplain) Ray W. Hinsch, who had headed Eglin's family-notification teams, delivered the invocation. The congregation sang two verses of "America the Beautiful," and Chaplain Hinsch read Psalm 91. Mrs. Kathryn Rash sang "On Eagle's Wings," and Chaplain Schueller read from the Gospel of John.[63]

Then Colonel Dylewski came to the podium. He began his remarks by reminding the congregation that "Freedom involves risk. As proud members of the 33d Fighter Wing, we bear the burden of that risk each time we set foot on foreign soil or launch missions into the dark of night." The deaths of the Eglin airmen, Colonel Dylewski stated, "may cause us to ask many questions, but of one thing I am certain: If they could speak to us today, they would tell us to press on. And press on, we will."[64]

Following Colonel Dylewski's remarks, President Clinton walked up the blue-carpeted steps to the podium. He wore a dark suit, white shirt, and a black tie with a muted white pattern. After acknowledging the many civilian and military dignitaries present, the president turned to the heart of his remarks: "To those brave servicemen who were injured, we thank God for your presence here today. To the families of the twelve men who we honor today who died in the service of our nation, these men represented the best of America, and they gave America their best."[65]

"There is a passage in Isaiah," President Clinton reminded the congregation, "in which God wonders, 'Whom shall I send, and who will go for us?' Isaiah answers: 'Here am I, Lord. Send me.'" The president continued: "These men we honor today said to America, 'Send me.'"

Near the close of his remarks, President Clinton listed the names of the twelve deceased airmen from Eglin. Referring to the nickname of the 33d Fighter Wing, the commander in chief said: "Our Nomads have ceased their wandering. They have come home."[66]

Chaplain Schueller gave the benediction, and after the postlude, pilots of the 59th Fighter Squadron flew over King Hangar in a "Missing Man" formation. Reflecting on the memorial service months later, Colonel Dylewski said that it had

Honoring and Remembering

been "done right for the families" and also praised the dignified conduct of the journalists who covered the ceremony.[67]

As President Clinton left King Hangar, he spoke with each of the families in the front row and hugged the young son of TSgt. Thanh V. (Gus) Nguyen.[68] He also shook hands with each of the wounded airmen. President Clinton's "coming out here," one officer commented, "that was a class act." A1C. Cielito Valencia, a resident of Building 131 who had been severely injured, greatly appreciated the president's visit, although, he ruefully reflected, he wished he had met him under other circumstances.[69]

A motorcade of a dozen or more vehicles took the chief executive from King Hangar to Air Force One. President Clinton shook hands with General Cranston and Colonel Dylewski, talked with them briefly, then mounted the airplane's stairs. He saluted the farewell party and entered the presidential aircraft. Air Force One taxied off and launched for Patrick, flying into a blue sky dotted with a few small clouds.[70]

President Clinton was scheduled to reach Patrick at 1:20 p.m.; he arrived somewhat earlier than that. Brig. Gen. Robert C. Hinson, the commander of the 45th Space Wing who had been on leave to attend his son's wedding, drove through the night to reach the base that Sunday morning. Colonel Friers helped him prepare for the president's arrival and the memorial service by briefing him about the recent events at Patrick. When President Clinton deplaned from Air Force One, he quickly got into a staff car with General Hinson and his wife, Karen Hinson. The chief executive traveled from base operations on the flightline to the base chapel (Building 439), named the Seaside Chapel because it stood on the eastern edge of Patrick and was not far west of the Atlantic Ocean, just across Florida state highway 1A1.[71]

President Clinton met with the families of the deceased airmen from Patrick in the annex of the Seaside Chapel. This facility had been chosen because its individual rooms allowed for the privacy of the bereaved relatives. Lt. Col. Donald R. Jozayt, commander of the 71st Rescue Squadron, escorted President Clinton from room to room. "It was quite obvious" to Lieutenant Colonel Jozayt, Colonel Friers commented several months later, "that the president was quite *moved* by the whole thing."

While President Clinton met with the families, Florida Governor Lawton M. Chiles, Jr., Gen. John Shalikashvili, and other dignitaries traveled to the base conference center (Building 401), where they met a large group of Patrick's Khobar veterans. "A lot of them," Colonel Friers noted, "were badly beat-up, cut up, banged up. Some of them were on crutches, or in wheel chairs." From here, the dignitaries went to the base theater (Building 431), next to the Seaside Chapel, where the memorial service began at 2:50 p.m.[72]

A large national flag filled the wall behind the theater stage and formed a backdrop to the speaker's podium, chaplain's chair, altar, and choir. Seven wreaths stood between the stage and the congregation: one for each of the five Patrick airmen, and for SSgt. Ronald L. King, who had deployed from Offutt Air Force Base, Nebraska, and for A1C. Christopher B. Lester, from Wright-Patterson Air Force Base, Ohio.[73] A short flight of stairs ran from the theater floor to the stage.[74]

Khobar Towers: Tragedy and Response

There were about 750 seats in the theater, and additional chairs supplemented them. People also stood at the back of the room and around the sides. The congregation totaled about 1,000. The original intention had been to limit attendance to members of the 1st Rescue Group. After it was learned that the president would participate in the ceremony, the guest list was expanded to include visiting dignitaries, local civic leaders, and a few airmen who until recently had been members of the rescue group.[75] Two television cameras in the theater made it possible for many others on Patrick to watch the ceremony and also provided a video "feed" to the Cable News Network and other outlets.[76]

The Patrick Chapel Choir, composed of nineteen women, nine men, and an organist, sang a prelude. Colonel Friers escorted President Clinton to his seat, and Lt. Col. (Father) Phillip D. Nguyen, chaplain of the 1st Rescue Group, offered an opening prayer. The base chapel choir and congregation sang "Lord, Guard and Guide the Men Who Fly," a hymn that also had been sung at the Dhahran memorial service, and Capt. Mahender Dudani read from the Scriptures.[77]

Colonel Friers walked to the speaker's podium, pausing at the base of the stage stairs to acknowledge the seven wreaths. During his remarks, he verbally—and physically—saluted the deceased airmen and spoke with gratitude for the support that Patrick had received from the community around it, and the nation. "The outpouring of love has been absolutely overwhelming, and we thank all of America for that."[78]

President Clinton followed Colonel Friers at the podium. He made much the same remarks as he had at Eglin, tailored somewhat to this second audience. "While the modern world brings to all of us many new opportunities," the chief executive pointed out, "it also leaves us more open to the forces of intolerance and destruction, and especially to terrorism." Speaking of the nineteen airmen who were killed in the bombing, President Clinton said: "They were taken before their time, felled by the hands of hatred in an act whose savagery is matched only by its cowardice."[79]

One officer who was present later recalled that the President's words were "well received.... He was clearly moved, no doubt of it. I think it was really great that he came."[80]

Maj. Gen. (Chaplain) William J. Dendinger, the Air Force chaplain, pronounced a benediction, Mr. Stewart Trushkowsky bugled "Taps," and the chapel choir and congregation sang "When Peace Like a River." Colonel Friers escorted the president from the theater, introducing him to each of the wounded airmen, who were seated in the front row. "The president stopped," Colonel Friers later recalled, and chatted with some of the wounded "and then we went outside.... His car was waiting."[81]

President Clinton had made an unhurried departure from Eglin, and did the same from Patrick. "He stayed," Colonel Friers continued, "shaking my hand and for a minute or so, and just chatted." A limosine took the president to the flightline, where he shook hands with many in the crowd, talked with people, and posed for a photograph with one couple. He stood talking with General and Mrs. Hinson for some time, before climbing the stairs into Air Force One. President Clinton gave a final wave to the crowd, and then stepped through the aircraft door.[82]

Honoring and Remembering

The president's visit to Patrick represented only one aspect of the enormous national, and local, support for the base in the aftermath of the tragedy in Saudi Arabia. A sign in front of the First Baptist Church in Cocoa Beach was typical of many marques seen along the Space Coast, throughout the summer of 1996: "P.A.F.B.: We Support You; We're Praying For You." Local businesses offered various forms of help. With family members of the deceased arriving to attend the memorial service, hotels offered free or discounted rooms, rental agencies loaned cars without charge, and other retailers volunteered their goods or services.[83]

Colonel Friers said of the local community: "This place—absolutely unbelievable, the support we got from this place." Another Patrick officer noted candidly that in the past he had often taken telephone calls from residents complaining about the noise from the air base. Following the bombing, the content of these communications abruptly changed: We were "getting calls all the time, people wanting to do something. [It was] pretty overwhelming." An airman who had been deployed to Dhahran during the tragedy praised his neighbors. "They were very, very much concerned," he related. "They really pitched in with my family while I was gone."[84]

In addition, organizations and individuals, most of them neighbors of Patrick—but also others from around the world—sent financial contributions to the families of the deceased airmen. The 1st Rescue Group headquarters established the "Patrick Pantry Organization" and ensured that these donations were properly distributed. Colonel Friers said of these contributions: "You couldn't have asked for better support. It was unbelievable."[85]

In a July 1 letter published four days later in the *Missileer*, the Patrick base newspaper, Colonel Friers expressed heartfelt thanks for this outpouring of community support. "Nothing can ever prepare you," he stated, "for the shock, grief, and utter disbelief that comes with a tragedy like we experienced last week." He noted that "total despair can quickly take over," but "that was not the case here at Patrick AFB for one simple reason—the 45th Space Wing, the entire Patrick AFB family, and the surrounding communities pulled us through." Colonel Friers closed by pointing out that the "healing has begun and we are back at work sending our [rescue] people in harm's way [so] that others may live. We will never forget our comrades who gave the ultimate sacrifice nor the caring, giving people of the Space Coast and Patrick AFB."[86]

The support of the community surrounding Eglin was equally heartening. Colonel Dylewski was unstinting in his praise of the response from people on—and around—the base. "The efforts put forth," he reflected, a half year after the tragedy, "by the organizations on this base and by individuals on this base, and outside, in the local community, were just incredible. Everybody did whatever was necessary, *gave* whatever was necessary—time, money, energy, concern." He summed up: "Anything we needed and asked for, somebody stepped up and provided it."[87]

Lt. Col. Stan Hill, director of the 33d Fighter Wing's battle staff, asserted: "The local community was just absolutely marvelous. We got absolutely tremendous support from the people along this coast." Lt. Col. Thomas A. McCarthy, the deployed

Khobar Towers: Tragedy and Response

58th Fighter Squadron's operations officer, agreed: "I thought that both the base community and the civilian community around here *were outstanding*, as were a lot of the American people. We're *still* [in December 1996] getting letters from people, expressing their condolences, their pride."[88]

On Wednesday, July 3, three days after the memorial services at Eglin and Patrick, Gen. Ronald Fogleman visited the Khobar Towers. The Air Force chief of staff later explained the timing of his trip: "I waited for about a week until after all the high-profile people had gone through Dhahran and then went to Saudi Arabia myself." (Secretary of State Warren Christopher had visited Dhahran on June 26, and Secretary of Defense William J. Perry was there three days later.) General Fogleman arrived early in the morning of July 3 and was met by Brigadier General Schwalier. The wing commander escorted the chief of staff to his quarters, a suite in the middle of the United States Military Training Mission compound on Dhahran Air Base.[89]

At General Fogleman's quarters, Brigadier General Schwalier briefed him on the events before and after the bombing. This meeting presented these two senior officers with their first opportunity for a one-on-one talk. After General Schwalier gave his briefing, he said to General Fogleman that he recognized that the bombing would have an impact on the Air Force and that, at the appropriate time, he would offer his resignation. In a December 1997 interview, the chief of staff recalled this meeting with General Schwalier, the wing commander's suggestion that he resign, and his reply to that offer. "I sat down with [Brigadier General Schwalier]," General Fogleman recounted, "listened to what he had to say—to include his offering to retire to remove any kind of a target for people to attack both the institution and individuals. I told him at that time that I did not want him to retire but to get the facts out." In this same interview, General Fogleman quoted his own remarks to General Schwalier at the time: "This is an important issue having to do with whether we support our troops in the field when we send them out there, and if you have screwed up, you can expect to be held accountable. If you haven't, then I will support you."[90]

After this candid exchange, the two generals visited the Ministry of Defense and Aviation Hospital, King Fahd University Hospital, ARAMCO, and other Dhahran hospitals that had cared for the wounded airmen, and in appreciation, General Fogleman presented their staffs with plaques.[91] At each of these facilities, the chief of staff offered his thanks, and at one of them, he received a particularly noteworthy reply. After General Fogleman expressed his heartfelt gratitude to one senior Saudi health administrator, the official answered that it was a solemn medical duty to treat all patients, that medicine knows no cultural boundaries.[92]

The two generals returned to the Khobar Towers to tour the bomb site in front of Building 131, and then walked to the medical clinic, Building 111. Brigadier Schwalier later offered the opinion that General Fogleman "was a wonderful influence, that day." The chief of staff stopped to talk with every group of people he encountered. "You could see... on their faces—there were smiles," General Schwalier noted, that the airmen appreciated General Fogleman's conversations with them.[93]

Honoring and Remembering

One particularly memorable episode highlighted the chief of staff's visit to the clinic. When General Fogleman and his group arrived at this facility, a week after the attack, it remained busy. Many airmen who had received stitches on the night of the bombing were having their sutures removed and the clinic staff was hard at work.

SrA. Andrea Richards, a medical technician of the deployed 79th Fighter Squadron, was completely focused on her business when General Fogleman entered the clinic about 10:45 that Wednesday morning. He engaged several of the medical personnel in conversation, as he did everywhere he went that morning. The clinic staff chatted with him while they went about their work: with one salient exception. Airman Richards was so absorbed in helping a patient that she remained oblivious to the fact that the Air Force's senior general was at her elbow. When the chief of staff tried to draw her into a conversation, the young airman gave perfunctory answers and remained intent on her job. Brigadier General Schwalier recalled the young NCO's demeanor: "She didn't care if it's the president . . . *who* it is, she's got a job to do."

Soon everyone in the clinic was closely watching the interaction between General Fogleman and Airman Richards, and doubtless wondering how the four-star general would react to her casual-at-best attention to his comments. The chief of staff was not angered by the airman's apparent disinterest, but instead was impressed with her intense dedication. General Fogleman, after receiving only brief answers to a series of questions, finally asked Senior Airman Richards what she was going to do when she returned to the States. She replied that she had to study for her airman promotion test: she was up for staff sergeant.

"It was beautiful, the next few moments," Brigadier General Schwalier later recalled. General Fogleman "looked over to his exec, his ops officer at the time, and said, 'Gee, can't we take care of that?'" The aide realized immediately that the chief of staff was suggesting that this single-minded airman should receive a stripes-for-exceptional-performers promotion, commonly known by its acronymn—a STEP promotion. The executive officer answered, "Sir, I think that is within your authority." General Fogleman told Senior Airman Richards: "Young lady, we're going to take care of that, right now. You are a staff sergeant."

At that moment everyone in the clinic began clapping. Suddenly it all dawned on the young NCO—that it was the Air Force chief of staff who had been speaking to her, that she had received a STEP promotion, and that her new grade and pay rate would take effect immediately. To the amusement of every observer, Staff Sergeant Richards indulged in a celebratory dance. "It was a *great moment*," Brigadier General Schwalier said. "It was just wonderful."[94]

After this high-note event, General Fogleman finished his morning with a walk to the "Ark," the Khobar Towers chapel, which was located in Building 13, in the southwest corner of the compound. This building was the workcenter of the wing's religious professionals and also, since the afternoon of Wednesday, June 26, of the judge advocate general personnel who were processing the property-loss claims of the Dhahran airmen. General Fogleman encouraged the chaplains and lawyers, and thanked them for their efforts.

Khobar Towers: Tragedy and Response

The chief of staff then walked from the Ark back into the center of the compound, for lunch at the Desert Rose Inn. While passing the clinic, General Fogleman and his escorts saw the very recently promoted Staff Sergeant Richards, talking to two other airmen of that rank. She was showing them her new stripes and—for the first of many times during her life—she was telling the story of how she had received them.[95]

Just after the noon hour, an impressive ceremony followed the midday meal at the Desert Rose. Using a hand-held microphone, General Fogleman addressed a large group of airmen who sat around the rectangular dining tables that, just the week before, had served as operating tables. The chief of staff gave a compelling twelve-minute speech on the significance of the oath taken by every member of the United States Air Force. It was, as Brigadier General Schwalier later reflected, "an emotional moment for all concerned."[96]

General Fogleman then presented four Airman's Medals, to Maj. (Dr.) Steven P. Goff, SSgt. Alfredo R. Guerrero, SrA. Corey P. Grice, and A1C. Christopher T. Wagar. Dr. Goff, a week earlier in this same Khobar Towers dining hall, had rendered aid to others, undeterred by a glass shard in his own chest. While his own wound was being bandaged, he continuing sewing up patients. Staff Sergeant Guerrero had spotted the truck-bomb and radioed other security policemen about it. Along with Guerrero, Airman First Class Wagar and Senior Airman Grice had alerted the residents of the top floors of Building 131 to evacuate their dormitory, minutes before the bomb exploded. The three SPs also had assisted the wounded in the wake of the blast. These four men received a firm, "well-done" handshake from General Fogleman, and a long sustained round of applause from their comrades.[97]

The audience at the Desert Rose Inn was made up of airmen who, like Dr. Goff and the three security policemen, served in support functions. Brigadier General Schwalier wanted General Fogleman to visit also with some of the wing's "operators," so from the dining hall the group drove to Dhahran Air Base. There the chief of staff addressed a group of flightline personnel in a drive-through hangar that housed some of the fighters that flew Southern Watch missions, and he commended the aircrews for renewing their operations so promptly after the terrorist attack.[98]

Major General Anderson later met General Fogleman at the base's Air Mobility Command ramp, and leaving at about 2 p.m., the two officers flew to Riyadh. Brigadier General Schwalier later commented that it was evident that the chief of staff had been through an emotional day. About two weeks after the visit, General Fogleman himself wrote: "When I visited the [4404th Wing on] July 3, I was extremely impressed with the professional manner in which every person was handling the aftermath of this attack on our people.... It is an honor to be associated with the outstanding men and women in today's Air Force."[99]

Chapter Twelve

After the Attack

President Bill Clinton first spoke to the press about the Khobar Towers bombing at the White House on the afternoon of Tuesday, June 25, 1996. He told reporters that within a few hours a Federal Bureau of Investigation team would be on its way to Dhahran to help investigate the terrorist attack. The next morning, the first forty of what eventually would become a much larger FBI team arrived on the compound. With the Air Force Office of Special Investigations providing their original quarters, these professionals soon were at work, gathering, preserving, and studying the evidence left in the wake of the attack.[1] One of the FBI agents joined the Air Force personnel who staffed the Site Recovery Center just after 10 a.m. on June 27, and about half an hour later, the FBI team set up a command post of its own in the Furniture Management Office, the underground garage that had been converted to a storage facility, just west of the stricken Building 131.[2]

The Air Force supported the FBI effort in a number of ways. First, it joined the White House in providing aircraft to fly the investigating agents to Saudi Arabia and back to the United States as needed. Second, large numbers of airmen selflessly volunteered time from their off-duty hours to help the FBI team sift through the rubble at the bomb site and in the dormitories, looking for forensic evidence. Brig. Gen. Terry Schwalier, the commander of the 4404th Composite Wing (Provisional), praised the hundreds of members of his unit who contributed to this effort, while at the same time they continued to pull their required shifts. Third, the airmen provided other forms of aid. For example, when the FBI had difficulty getting supplies through the Saudi Arabian customs offices quickly, wing members donated more than 200 uniforms and other provisions to the agents.[3]

Perhaps the Air Force's most unusual contribution to the FBI's effort involved the "boom box" portable radios that airmen during the 1990s commonly carried with them on deployments. The terrorist bomb had destroyed a large number of these popular items, along with other pieces of personal property, in the Khobar Towers dormitories. During the days after the attack, airmen brought many of these "trashed" (as one staff sergeant aptly described them) boom boxes to the wing judge advocate general's office. Their owners offered these radios, and other items of substantial value that obviously had been ruined, as evidence that they were entitled to an advance payment on their claims of personal property losses. The JAG personnel examined the boom boxes, quickly confirmed that they were damaged beyond repair, and piled

177

Khobar Towers: Tragedy and Response

them in a corner. A trash dumpster would have been the next stop for these radios, but one of the FBI agents pointed out that the magnets in their speakers could be used to sift through the sand and rubble, and locate metal objects. As one airman concluded the story of boom box magnets: "They made nifty little tools, and all the volunteers got one."[4]

In addition to the FBI investigation, Congress conducted several hearings about the bombing and published two reports on it within about two and a half months. The first of the these, an August 14, 1996, staff report of the House National Security Committee, chaired by Floyd Spence of South Carolina, suggested that the Dhahran attack represented an intelligence failure. (Coincidently, Secretary of the Air Force Dr. Sheila Widnall had been testifying to this same committee, when the bombing took place.) This House panel report's primary observation was that the "unpreparedness of U.S. forces stationed in Saudi Arabia for the magnitude of the terrorist bomb in Dhahran raises significant questions about the adequacy of the intelligence support. While intelligence information was provided, it was not of either the quality nor the quantity necessary to alert commanders to the magnitude of the terrorist threat they faced." Moreover, this committee report developed the theme that the Air Force's ability to protect its forces in Saudi Arabia was hindered by the service's acting on the pretense that Operation Southern Watch was only a temporary mission, despite the fact that it had been conducting it for four years and it was unlikely that Iraq would begin complying with the United Nations resolutions any time soon. "The Department of Defense needs to review other ongoing operations," the committee concluded, "to ensure that U.S. force protection needs and U.S. security interests are not being compromised by the limitations inherent in running quasi-permanent operations under the politcally acceptable rubric of 'temporary' operations."[5]

On the other hand, the House National Security Committee report did not fault the actions of individuals stationed in Dhahran or elsewhere in the region. It, in fact, praised the commanders in the theater for their aggressive and proactive security efforts after the November 1995 Riyadh bombing. It singled out for favorable comment Lt. Col. James J. Traister, the commander of the 4404th Composite Wing's security police squadron.[6]

The second Congressional report, published about a month later, arrived at a polar-opposite conclusion. The work of the Senate Select Committee on Intelligence, chaired by Senator Arlen Specter of Pennsylvania, it focused on the question of whether or not the Dhahran bombing represented an intelligence failure. This Senate committee took no interest in the contention of its House colleagues that the pretense of Southern Watch being a temporary mission had hindered the protection of Air Force personnel in Saudi Arabia. The Senate committee instead riveted its attention on the issue of the alleged intelligence failure and concluded emphatically that there had not been one. "The totality of the threat information available to the Department of Defense," it asserted, "as well as the posture of the Intelligence Community at the time of the Khobar Towers bombing makes clear that an intelligence failure, either in collection, dissemination or analysis, did not occur. Military commanders in the

After the Attack

region and in Washington received highly relevant threat information for a year and a half prior to the Khobar Towers bombing."[7]

While these Congressional reports were being prepared, another investigation was underway, one that eventually would overshadow them. Three days after the Dhahran bombing, Secretary of Defense William J. Perry directed a task force to make "an assessment of [the] facts and circumstances surrounding [the Khobar Towers] attack and of the security of U.S. forces in the U.S. Central Command Area of Responsibility."[8] To head this effort, Secretary Perry selected Gen. (U.S. Army retired) Wayne A. Downing, who had just retired on May 1 as the commander in chief of the U.S. Special Operations Command. During the Gulf War he had commanded the Joint Special Operations Command. His nearly thirty-four years of active duty also included two combat tours during the Vietnam War and service in Operation Just Cause, the Panama contingency of December 1989.[9]

Secretary Perry asked General Downing's task force to begin its assessment "as soon as possible" so that the secretary could "advise the president and the Congress of the conclusions reached at the earliest possible opportunity." The panel was to report within forty-five days (roughly, in mid-August) or to notify Secretary Perry if it needed more time.[10] This initial charter stated that General Downing was not to "conduct an investigation to fix fault or find wrongdoing; however, evidence of possible negligence or wrongful misconduct by U.S. personnel should be forwarded to USCENTCOM for disposition." On July 10, Secretary Perry amended this original charter, directing the panel to identify those officials who were responsible for actions needed to improve, or upgrade, the protection of the forces in southwest Asia. Two days later, on the twelfth, he stated in a letter to two Senators that the Downing commission would determine personal responsibility for the Khobar Towers attack and whether there had been a breach of duty. The task force began its work by reviewing previous reports and documents about force protection in southwest Asia and then started interviewing service personnel who were involved with security issues at Dhahran and elsewhere in the theater.[11]

While General Downing's commission started its investigation, the 4404th Wing's change of command ceremony, postponed from Wednesday, June 26, by the bombing the preceding night, was held on Monday, July 15. The extension of Brigadier General Schwalier's tour was determined on the night of the attack, during one of his earliest telephone conversations with Lt. Gen. Carl E. Franklin, commander of U.S. Central Command Air Forces. General Schwalier later recalled this exchange with General Franklin: "'Terry, we'd like you to stay.' And I said, 'Sir, that's exactly what I expect.' . . . That was the communication."[12]

By the time of General Fogleman's July 3 visit to Dhahran, it had been determined that the proposed change of command ceremony would be held on the fifteenth, and it was then that General Schwalier first learned of the new date. General Schwalier also recalled this communication: "When the chief came over, he said, 'I've talked to [Brig. Gen. Daniel] Dick; we want you to stay until the fifteenth. I've talked to the Chairman [of the Joint Chiefs of Staff] about that.'"[13]

Khobar Towers: Tragedy and Response

Maj. Gen. Kurt B. Anderson, commander of the Joint Task Force Southwest Asia, presided over the occasion, as Brigader General Schwalier relinquished command to Brigadier General Dick. The departing wing commander later characterized the ceremony as very well done and praised General Anderson's conduct of it. Brigadier General Dick also commended the professionalism that the JTF-SWA commander and others brought to the event.[14]

General Dick came to the Dhahran assignment from Langley Air Force Base, Virginia, where he had been Headquarters Air Combat Command's inspector general. He then had more than 3,300 flying hours in F–4 Phantoms and F–16 Fighting Falcons and had been an instructor pilot in both of these fighters. General Dick had commanded the 33d Tactical Fighter Squadron at Shaw Air Force Base, South Carolina, and the 388th Fighter Wing at Hill Air Force Base, Utah.[15]

It was an interesting sidebar to the Khobar Towers story that Generals Dick and Schwalier were longtime friends. During October 1984 through February 1985, they had been members of the same F–16 class at the 58th Tactical Training Wing's school on MacDill Air Force Base, Florida. Schwalier was then a lieutenant colonel; Dick a major. The two young officers checked out on the fighter with a class of fewer than twenty officers, roomed near each other in the same dormitory, and played golf together. They accordingly got to know each other quite well, and remained in communication during their subsequent careers.[16]

Following the change of wing command from General Schwalier to General Dick on July 15, the former commander remained in Dhahran several more days. On the nineteenth he met with General Downing and his task force. General Schwalier then returned to the U.S. and began his next assignment, in the Pentagon. He became the chief of a directorate within Headquarters USAF's Deputy Chief of Staff for Air and Space Operations.[17]

Like their wing commander, the airmen veterans of the Khobar Towers bombing promptly returned to their duties in the States. Journalists found it remarkable that nearly all of them, including the wounded, soon were back at work in the assignments they had held before deploying to Saudi Arabia. Among the hundreds of these men and women, TSgt. Donald Herlacher returned to his maintenance duties with the 71st Rescue Squadron at its home station on Patrick Air Force Base, Florida, along with the other maintainers who had worked on the HC–130 that had been forced to come back to base earlier than planned on the night of the bombing. MSgt. Dwayne R. Berry, who had been exercising in the gym at the time of the explosion, also was back at work on Patrick in early July. Lt. Col. Douglas R. Cochran, Lt. Col. Thomas A. McCarthy, and the other officers of the 58th Fighter Squadron who had been in the command suite of Building 127 on the night of the attack soon resumed their duties on Eglin Air Force Base, Florida. TSgt. George Burgess, SSgt. Eric D. Ziegler, and many other airmen who had been billeted in Building 131 also were able to return to their assignments at Eglin and elsewhere. In October 1996, an interviewer asked Sergeant Ziegler about how he and others around him had survived the attack in relatively good shape. "We all got pretty lucky, I guess," he commented. "I still have aches and pains in my left hip, my palm is not completely healed and I don't have full range of motion in [my] fingers, but I'm back at work." SSgt. Alfredo Guerrero who, with A1C. Christopher Wagar, had first spotted the truck-bomb, attracted for a time the attention of the national press. By late August, he too was serving again with his home unit, the 95th Security Police Squadron on Edwards Air Force Base, California.[18]

On July 10, 1996, Lt. Col. (Dr.) Douglas J. Robb, Jr., the interim commander of the 4404th Wing's medical group, relinquished command of this unit to Colonel Rolando R. Santa Ana. Dr. Robb returned to Moody Air Force Base, Georgia, where he commanded the 347th Aerospace Medicine Squadron. He might have agreed with the contention that good fortune was an element in the prompt return of so many Air Force members, including the wounded, to their duties in the States. But Robb emphasized two practical points: the immediate "buddy care" that the airmen gave one another that night and the excellent medical treatment that they received from Saudi and American medical professionals, then and later.[19]

While many veterans of the bombing resumed their duties at their home stations, senior Department of Defense officials considered an important "force relocation" for Saudi Arabia. On July 4, Secretary of Defense Perry told a group of reporters: "We had under consideration before the [Khobar Towers] bombing—and will intensify that consideration—moving some of the forces out of Riyadh. It's an urban area, and it's the hardest area to try to gain protection for." About two weeks later, Secretary Perry announced that as many as 4,000 American military personnel stationed in Riyadh, Dhahran, and perhaps other Saudi cities would move into more remote sites in the desert.[20]

The Khobar airmen were destined for Prince Sultan Air Base, located in the sands about seventy miles south-southeast of Riyadh. The Saudis had begun developing this facility, named for Prince Sultan bin Abdul Aziz, the kingdom's second deputy premier, Minister of Defense and Aviation, and inspector general, shortly before the Gulf War. During that conflict, the Americans knew it as al Kharj Air Base, an installation with the name of the province in which it was located, and of a small town about fifteen miles away.[21] Ironically, the 4404th Wing's direct predessor unit had been stationed there during the summer of 1991.[22]

When U.S. Air Force personnel first deployed there during Operation Desert Shield, construction had been underway for only about a year and the airmen found little in the way of facilities. Lt. Gen. Charles A. Horner had remarked that "Al Kharj ... started out as a runway/parking apron—and nothing else—surrounded by sand."[23] The earliest American arrivals found that the tallest fixture on the base was a one-foot taxi light.[24] USAF engineering teams soon transformed al Kharj into a viable installation, which the Americans affectionately nick-named "Al's Garage," or "Camelot,"[25] and during the Gulf War it served as an important fighter and C–130 base. After that conflict it was largely abandoned, but later the Saudis began a construction program, erecting several buildings that would support their air defense and other operations. They were many years from completing their construction program,

Khobar Towers: Tragedy and Response

however, when the American airmen began moving there from Dhahran during the late summer of 1996.[26]

A new chapter in the history of Prince Sultan Air Base began early in the morning of August 2, when Lieutenant General Franklin, who was visiting Saudi Arabia at the time, telephoned Brigadier General Dick. The CENTAF commander asked the new wing commander to come to Riyadh for a conference that night. Accompanied by most of his group commanders, General Dick flew on a KC–135 Stratotanker to the Saudi capital and met with General Franklin in the JTF-SWA conference room. At this nighttime session, General Dick later related, the CENTAF commander briefed him and his subordinates that they "were going to move two bases [Riyadh and Dhahran] and . . . were going to do it in forty-five days." Some of the Americans serving in Riyadh would move to the Eskan Village compound, about a dozen miles from the capital. Other Air Force personnel at Riyadh, and all of those at the Khobar Towers, would go to Prince Sultan Air Base, roughly seventy miles.[27]

General Dick related that after his August 2 meeting with General Franklin, he and his officers "stayed in Riyadh for several days to hold the initial meetings with the Royal Saudi Air Force." These discussions took a few days because, he explained, it was a feature of Saudi culture that even though Prince Sultan and Secretary Perry had agreed the Americans would move to Prince Sultan Air Base, "that doesn't necessarily mean that everybody agrees with that." Once the meetings began, General Dick observed that many of the senior RSAF officers "weren't real fired up over it, this whole idea. Because the Saudis were building Prince Sultan, obviously, for *their* use."[28]

The Saudis were favorably impressed, however, with how rapidly the United States Air Force began accomplishing the daunting task of moving two bases within a month and a half. On August 5, U.S. Army Maj. Gen. Norman Williams (Headquarters U.S. Central Command's J–4) and General Dick, accompanied by about twenty other American officers, visited Prince Sultan Air Base for the first time. Late during the previous day, the Saudis had given the USAF permission to land five C–5 Galaxies on the base. Early on the fifth, the first of these enormous transports arrived and General Dick and his group came in later that morning on a Saudi C–130. "When we landed [at Prince Sultan]," the wing commander related, "we stepped out on the ramp and the Saudis went, 'Oh, one of your C–5s is already here.'"

What the Saudis did not know was that the Americans were rapidly generating more of these huge cargo planes. On August 5, the Arab hosts treated Major General Williams and his party graciously, giving them a thorough tour of Prince Sultan, an informative round of briefings, and an excellent meal. The visit ended in the afternoon and, as the Americans were preparing to reboard the Saudi C–130, one of the RSAF generals noticed that there now were two Galaxies parked on the ramp. "Oh," he said to his guests, "I see there that another one of your C–5s is here." General Williams was able to smile at him and reply, "No, that's the fourth and fifth C–5, the other ones have already come and off-loaded today while we have been in briefings." General Dick said of this episode: "At that moment, I felt tremendous pride in what

After the Attack

the United States Air Force could do. The Saudis couldn't believe how fast we could move."[29]

The move from Khobar Towers to Prince Sultan, designated "Operation Desert Focus," had to be completed within forty-five days, and it immediately encountered difficulties. Although the Saudi construction program had erected many buildings, the base lacked electricity, water, and sewage systems. "We literally started out," General Dick recalled, "kind of sitting in the dirt," eating Meals Ready to Eat, the cold rations that all military members called by their acronym, "MREs."[30]

The base also lacked an aircraft control system. When the first C–5s arrived, General Dick explained, an aircraft controller "had to go out on the runway... to make sure there were no camels or wild dogs on it. When the C–5 showed up, it flew over the base, [the controller] got them on the radio and said, 'It looks like the runway's clear, so you can land if you want.'"

In addition to aircraft control, other communication systems were poor or nonexistent. "When I got [to Prince Sultan]," General Dick related, "the phone book was one page . . . because there were only about twenty phones in the entire wing . . . . The phones didn't work half the time." Nor could the base's radios be relied on, because there were no transmitter towers to amplify their signals.[31]

These deficiences were overcome by the hard work, day and night, of Colonel Suzanne M. (Sue) Waylett's 823d Rapid Engineer Deployable Heavy Operational Repair Squadron Engineer—much better known by its acronym "RED HORSE"—from Hurlburt Field, Florida; of Colonel Peter Mooy's logistics group of the 4404th Wing; and of many others. General Dick summarized at the time the achievements of the RED HORSE engineers at Prince Sultan Air Base: "They literally built this entire place. This is a phoenix that has risen out of the desert." The move from Dhahran represented the new wing commander's first extensive experience with the "loggies" and he was impressed that these specialists "know how to contract and move equipment, move vehicles, move stuff. I've got a tremendous respect for the logistics community." General Dick added: "I just had never worked with them before. They are truly magnificent."[32]

The move from Riyadh to Prince Sultan involved a shorter distance than from Dhahran to the same place, and less materiél, and so it was completed ahead of the transfer from the Khobar Towers. "Basically, Riyadh went first," General Dick recounted, "Dhahran went second . . . . The big airplanes [tankers and airborne warning and control system aircraft based at Riyadh] could carry a lot of their own stuff down [to Prince Sultan]. Riyadh was only about sixty miles from [Prince Sultan]. That was the easy piece."[33]

Despite all the problems, the move from Dhahran to Prince Sultan was more than worth the effort—it was necessary. A month before the undertaking, Secretary Perry contended: "We cannot deal with [terrorist] attacks adequately just by moving fences and just by putting more Mylar on glass. We have to make some fundamental, drastic changes in the way we configure and deploy our forces." In a February 5, 1997, interview, General Dick pointed out: "We were stuck in an urban environment

Khobar Towers: Tragedy and Response

in both Dhahran and Riyadh. We needed to get out of that urban environment. Coming here into the middle of no place, at Prince Sultan, was exactly the right thing to do." Addressing the same point almost exactly a year later, he emphasized that the new station "was safe" and that the move had been "the right thing to do."[34]

The Khobar Towers complex that the Air Force vacated remained as it had been before the bombing, with one exception. In the autumn of 1997, a little more than a year after the Americans departed, the Saudis razed Building 131, the most badly damaged structure on the compound. A group of Saudi military police and other officials watched as a demolition team exploded a set of charges that brought down the dormitory.[35]

For the airmen who left the Khobar Towers for Prince Sultan, the greatest challenge of their move could not have been foreseen and, unfortunately, came in the middle of it. At this particularly inopportune time for the Americans, Saddam Hussein declared both the northern and southern "no fly" zones null and void and on August 30, 1996, Iraqi armored columns overran the Kurdish city of Irbil. This turn of events forced the 4404th Wing to prepare for combat. The Iraqi dictator's aggression, General Dick remembered with dismay, "threw such a wrench into the system for us. Now, I not only had to continue moving, but I had to prepare and conduct combat operations against Iraq."[36]

On September 2, several crews made up of third country nationals were at work on Dhahran Air Base, pulling down trailers, packing materials, and otherwise making ready for the move to Prince Sultan. While they labored, Saddam's aggression led to an abrupt directive to the 4404th Wing: prepare to attack Iraq's air defense system. In the midst of an enormous move, the airmen responded quickly. At sunset, wing personnel escorted the TCNs off Dhahran Air Base, and then threw themselves into the new job at hand. They worked through the night of September 2/3, a humid, miserable run of hours during which the temperature never dropped below 92 degrees Fahrenheit. By 3 a.m. on the third, the wing's maintenance crews had a "package" of fighters ready. "God love those great maintenance guys," General Dick declared, "we loaded up all of the airplanes, we had all of the missions planned."

While the maintainers were hard at work, Chairman of the Joint Chiefs of Staff Gen. John M. Shalikashvili conferred through the night with Saudi Arabia's King Fahd bin Abdul Aziz. The monarch decided not to let the United States use bases within his kingdom for attacks against Iraq. The 4404th Wing's air crews woke up on September 3 to learn this disappointing news.

The unit had readied for combat—without showing its hand. "As the sun came up the next morning," General Dick related, "when the TCNs came back to continue working on the trailers to move them and continue packing up, everything looked exactly like it did when they went home the night before. There was absolutely no tip off to anybody of the tremendous activity that took place that night."[37]

Denied the use of Saudi bases, President Clinton directed cruise and Tomahawk missile attacks against Iraq and extended the southern no-fly zone over that country from 32 to 33 north latitude, a line just south of Baghdad. On September 3 and 4,

After the Attack

B–52s of the 2d Bomb Wing, based at Barksdale Air Force Base, Louisiana, launched cruise missiles, and U.S. Navy warships in the Arabian Gulf fired Tomahawks against air-defense targets in southern Iraq.[38]

Despite Saddam's aggression, the move continued. On September 13, the Iraqis fired SA–6s at three of the 4404th Wing's F–16s. The date happened to be a Friday and yet on that supposedly unlucky day, every one of Saddam's weapons missed. Around 10 p.m. on that night, with the deadline to complete the move just four days away, the Iraqi dictator's truculance introduced another complication. At that hour Lieutenant General Franklin told Brigadier General Dick that, since King Fahd had denied the Americans the use of Saudi bases, the wing commander should move to Shaikh Isa, Bahrain, half of his squadron of F–16CJs and his entire squadron of F–16CGs, which were arriving from Misawa Air Base, Japan, and have these fighters ready for combat by the next morning. "So we had to set up operations," General Dick later explained, "and establish another air base right in the middle of the move. Again, remember, I'm conducting combat operations against Iraq."

A lone tragedy marred the wing's dramatic accomplishment. In late September, after the formal period of the move had passed, A1C. Roberto D'Amato fell from a two-and-a-half-ton truck loaded with baggage. Airman D'Amato, a security policeman who had just arrived from Dhahran on a C–130, suffered fatal injuries.

At 3:36 p.m. on September 17, the last of the wing's F–16s left Dhahran for Prince Sultan. The launch of this fighter meant that the move was completed within its forty-five day limit—to the day. General Dick summarized the experience: "Between the terrorists, the time line, Saddam, bases in other countries, it was a heck of a forty-five days."[39]

Overcoming the many obstacles that General Dick had summarized, the wing had moved more than 78 aircraft, over 4,000 USAF personnel (230 British and 170 French military members also left Khobar for Prince Sultan), and about 25,000 tons of equipment—all within the demanding deadline of forty-five days.[40] Secretary Perry called it "a logistics miracle." "The things we did," General Dick stated, "were absolutely amazing. I just can't tell you how proud I was of the men and women in the Air Force, and the 4404th."[41]

On August 30, in the midst of the move from Dhahran to Prince Sultan, Secretary of Defense Perry forwarded the report of General Downing's task force to Secretary of the Air Force Dr. Sheila E. Widnall and Air Force Chief of Staff General Ronald R. Fogleman. "I ask that you consider and, as you deem appropriate, take action," the secretary wrote in a cover letter, "concerning issues raised in the report regarding how the Air Force organizes, trains and equips to support forces deployed to a unified command. I have made no determination as to any individual actions or omissions, subjects on which I defer to your judgment and disposition."[42]

Acting on this guidance from Secretary Perry, on September 4 Secretary Widnall and General Fogleman directed Lt. Gen. James F. Record, the Twelfth Air Force commander, "to consider and to make recommendations on issues raised in General Downing's report regarding"—they then followed Secretary Perry's word-

Khobar Towers: Tragedy and Response

ing—"how the Air Force organizes, trains and equips to support forces deployed" to U.S. Central Command. "This is a critical task," the secretary and chief of staff stated. "You are to identify the Air Force resources you require in support of it, and they will promptly be made available to you."

In addition to this tasking, Secretary Widnall and General Fogleman also gave Lieutenant General Record's task force a legal authority that General Downing's had not held. They designated him, as the commander of the Twelfth Air Force, "the disciplinary review authority and General Court-Martial Convening Authority regarding any actions or omissions by Air Force personnel, associated with the bombing of the Khobar Towers in Dhahran, Saudi Arabia, on June 25, 1996 . . . . Appropriate disposition regarding any individual, whether consisting of no action, administrative action, nonjudicial punishment, court-martial, or otherwise, is entirely within your discretion as commander, Twelfth Air Force, under applicable directives."

The secretary and the chief of staff asked General Record to submit a written report within ninety days, although in mid-September Dr. Widnall told reporters that the general would be given more time if he requested it. She also commented that she did not think the Khobar Towers bombing resulted from "cultural" or organizational problems in the Air Force. Secretary Widnall contended that the terrorist attack suggested just the opposite: it was a rare event that stood in sharp contrast to the usual, safe day-to-day operation of the Air Force.[43]

General Record was well experienced in how the Air Force supported the unified commands, as his own Twelfth Air Force, which he had commanded since June 1995, contributed the USAF component of U.S. Southern Command. He was also a veteran of the Vietnam War (with more than 600 combat missions), and had served as the deputy commander of Joint Task Force Middle East, the vice commander of Twelfth Air Force, and the commander of JTF-SWA. These, and several other assignments, made him highly qualified to head a task force on the Dhahran bombing.[44]

The panel, consisting of ten colonels and one lieutenant colonel from a cross-section of career fields, had been working about two weeks when, on September 16, Deputy Secretary of Defense John P. White released the findings of the Downing task force. Addressing its original task, to assess security in U.S. Central Command's area of responsibility, the report found that force protection "practices were inconsistent in Saudi Arabia and the Arabian Gulf region." The Downing Report's fifth finding stated: "Because of the lack of published standards (*Finding* 1), inadequate command structure (*Finding* 3), and existing command relationships (*Finding* 4), standards and practices for force protection vary widely. In the absence of definitive guidance, site commanders approach force protection based on general guidance from their service commmands and/or their own knowledge and experience and that of their staff."[45]

The Downing Report also addressed the issue later added to its charter, to determine the officials responsible for the attack. Some of the panel's findings directed responsibility in a general way—impersonally and broadly. It contended, for example, that the chain of command had not provided adequate guidance about security to Brigadier General Schwalier and the other commanders in the theater. The Downing

After the Attack

Report's first finding stated: "There are no published DoD physical security standards for force protection of fixed facilites."[46] It also concluded that the commanders had not been supported with adequate funds. Finding 2 reported: "Force protection requirements had not been given high priority for funding."[47]

In addition to these general findings, the Downing Report directed specific attention to the commander of the 4404th Composite Wing. Its Finding 20, doubtless its most controversial one, stated: "The commander, 4404th Wing (Provisional) did not adequately protect his forces from a terrorist attack." Brigadier General Schwalier was the only person whom the Downing Report singled out as bearing some responsibility for the failure to protect the forces.[48]

Among the many points addressed by the Downing task force, some of which remain classified, one of the most debated was the fact that the northern perimeter fence stood not far from the dormitories at that end of the compound. This proximity had allowed the terrorists to bring the bomb close to Building 131. The Downing Report stated: "During his tour of duty, Brigadier General Schwalier never raised to his superiors force protection matters that were beyond his capability to correct. Nor did he raise the issue of expanding the perimeter or security outside of the fence with his Saudi counterparts in the Eastern Province." Press accounts published in July 1996 also highlighted the subject of moving the northern perimeter fence.[49]

Another controversy followed from the fact that the windows of Khobar's dormitories and other buildings had not been treated with Mylar, an inert plastic. Some commentators argued that this covering or one similar would have reduced the flying glass shards that had caused most of the casualties. The Downing Report stated: "In the 4404th Wing (Provisional) budget, items such as Mylar, a shatter resistant window film coating, and surveillance systems for the fence line were deferred until budgets in later years, despite the fact that funds for requested items, even unfunded requirements, had never been denied by U.S. Air Forces Central Command or U.S. Air Combat Command."[50]

The Downing Report also directed attention to the inadquate alarm systems of the American compound, still another issue that would remain controversial. "The warning systems in the U.S.-occupied portion of Khobar Towers were limited to Giant Voice," it stated, "a system designed during Operation Desert Storm to alert people of Scud missile attacks, and manual warnings, like knocking on doors . . . . Although Giant Voice provided an audible siren and voice capability, the system had limited application." The task force also reported: "Procedures to test the evacuation system and the emergency warning system at Khobar Towers were never exercised. The Giant Voice procedures were elaborate, unwieldy, and did not work."[51]

The report also pointed to the lack of evacuation practices, another disputed issue that became influential over time. The report contended: "The 4404th Wing (Provisional) and subordinate groups and squadrons did not practice evacuation procedures. There was an evacuation of two buildings for a suspected bomb package in May 1996 that served to replace a planned rehearsal of evacuation procedures. One planned exercise was apparently canceled because of Saudi sensitivities."[52]

Khobar Towers: Tragedy and Response

Following the release of the Downing Report, the Department of the Air Force issued an official statement on that study. "The Downing Report," it noted, "will provide U.S. Central Command and the Air Force additional proposals to consider in some very specific areas to include clarifying command relationships, responsibilities and authority, and improving the integration of command guidance." The statement concluded by directing attention to the work underway by General Record's group. "The Secretary of the Air Force and the Chief of Staff," it related, "have directed Lt. Gen. James F. Record to consider and make recommendations on issues raised in the Downing report regarding how the Air Force organizes, trains and equips support forces deployed to U.S. Central Command. His focus will be on the matter of force protection."[53]

Two days after the release of the Downing Report, on the morning of September 18, Secretary Perry testified about the Dhahran bombing to the House National Security Committee, and that afternoon to the Senate Armed Services Committee. One military journalist reported that the secretary of defense addressed the Congressmen with "his voice choking back emotion" and that he "disarmed most of his congressional critics by a forthright acceptance of responsibility for the bombing." Secretary Perry told the House committee: "I will not participate in the game of passing the buck. I will not seek to delegate responsibility for this tragedy on any of my military commanders." "They have served our country with enormous distinction and considerable sacrifice," he continued, "and they deserve our gratitude, not our blame. To the extent that this tragedy resulted from a failure of leadership, that responsibility is mine, and mine alone."[54]

On October 31, about a month and a half after Secretary Perry's testimony, General Record reported to General Fogleman and Secretary Widnall, and on December 11, the results of his work became public. His study group made thirteen recommendations to improve the protection of forces assigned to Central Command and elsewhere. These included designating a general officer-led Air Staff organization to oversee force protection, developing Air Force Instructions to supplement Defense Department guidance on force protection, and developing formal statements of requirements for surveillance systems for installation security.[55]

The Record Report addressed a number of controversial points that had been discussed in the Downing Report and in the press. On the issue of the northern perimeter fence, it pointed out that "Neither the July 1995 nor the January 1996 AFOSI [Air Force Office of Special Investigations] Vulnerability Assessment contained a recommendation to extend the perimeter or enhance stand-off distances." The Record Report contended that the northern perimeter distance was adequate, in view of the size of a bomb likely to be used against the compound and went further to state: "The RSO [Regional Security Officer, in the U.S. Embassy in Riyadh] indicated that [his office] would not have questioned an 80-foot stand-off distance even if the known threat had included a 1,000 pound bomb.... Additionally, the U.S. Consul General in Dhahran stated that 'the thought of a 20,000 or even 5,000 pound bomb driving up was pretty inconceivable.'"[56]

After the Attack

As for installing Mylar, the report noted that "Brigadier General Schwalier programmed for [a] four million dollar [Mylar] project in the Wing's Five-Year Facilities Improvement Plan. Brigadier General Schwalier made this decision to defer immediate installation after discussions with his Support Group and Civil Engineering Squadron commanders, and considering a variety of factors, including the then-known threat, the effects of other security enhancements which had been or were being implemented to mitigate risks, the cost and complexity of the project, the absence of DoD [Department of Defense] or Air Force requirements for the installation of Mylar, the fact that Saudi approval would have been necessary, and other competing priorities."[57]

The Record Report addressed the Downing task force's findings concerning the absence of an alarm system. "The Downing Report was critical of the lack of a fire alarm system," it stated, "suggesting that the Wing might have been more successful in evacuating the building if it could have relied on a fire alarm system rather than the floor-by-floor notification system that was used. The Civil Engineering Squadron commander at Khobar Towers at the time of the bombing, Lt. Col. Robbin Schellhous, explained that the installation of a fire alarm system (in addition to the smoke detectors already there) was not a high priority because the buildings were constructed out of concrete." The Record Report added: "There are no DoD standards for warning systems, and the Saudi construction standards for Khobar Towers did not require a fire alarm system."[58]

On the subject of building evacuations, the Record team reported: "While some Wing personnel interviewed by the Downing Task Force stated that they were not aware of any building evacuations prior to the June 25th bombing, a review of the 4404th Security Police Squadron Desk Blotters reveals at least eight buildings were actually evacuated at Khobar Towers because Wing personnel discovered suspicious packages. In fact, Building 131, the building in front of which the bomb exploded, was evacuated [on] May 9, 1996 because of a reported suspicious package, which turned out to be a tool box." The report continued: "The buildings were evacuated in five minutes or less, an interval which the Support Group commander and the Wing Fire Chief, who were in charge of the evacuation scenes, considered to be as fast as possible. The testimony suggesting no evacuations may be attributable to the fact that Wing personnel worked in shifts around-the-clock."[59]

General Record had been given disciplinary-review authority and court martial-convening authority. On December 20, 1996, he reported: "I have considered everyone in the military chain of command with Force Protection responsibilities associated with the Khobar Towers incident. I have not discovered any evidence that causes me to believe anyone in that chain of command, or elsewhere, committed any offense punishable under the [Uniform Code of Military Justice] or failed to meet Air Force standards."[60]

Three days later Secretary Widnall and General Fogleman reported to Secretary Perry and Deputy Secretary of Defense White on the Record Report. They forwarded to these senior officials General Record's recommendations about force protection in Central Command's area of responsibility and elsewhere. Secretary Widnall and General Fogleman also reviewed the Record group's finding that no service member had been derelict in the performance of his duty and that no court-martial action was warranted. They concluded: "We support Lt Gen Record's conclusion and believe that no further action is required."[61]

About a month later, on January 29, 1997, Deputy Secretary White replied to Secretary Widnall. He noted that "the Air Force will be conducting a further review of those issues, focusing on several matters that were not fully considered by Lieutenant General Record," and stated: "My review of the Record report leads me to conclude that such further examination is a prudent course of action and I commend you for it." Mr. White agreed with Secretary Widnall's, and General Fogleman's, conclusion "that no action under the Uniform Code of Military Justice is called for against any member in the chain of command." While expressing this agreement, he also stated that the Air Force's "further review" would give "further consideration to the propriety of administrative action," as opposed to action under the UCMJ.

Deputy Secretary White pointed to a number of specific issues that he believed deserved further study, beyond the work of the Record group. He stated, for example, that the first part of its report "lacks sufficient explanation of the rationale upon which certain recommendations are offered. Among these are recommendations that relate to command and control of [intelligence from human sources] service personnel, 'expanding' the rules of engagement in countries where there is no status of forces agreement, and Lieutenant General Record's conclusion that there is no need for organized intelligence assets at the wing level."

Mr. White listed some other specific issues meriting further investigation. "First," he noted, "I recommend a stronger effort to assess communications deficiencies at the time of the bombing." Second, he suggested "a more thorough development of the facts" about the planning and practicing for evacuations that the 4404th Wing had done before the attack. "Third," he listed, "the facts concerning training, equipping and manning the guard force warrant greater examination." Mr. White also suggested further study of the procedures for transporting personnel and moving convoys, a subject addressed by the Downing Report, but not included in General Record's charter. "Finally," he concluded, "notwithstanding that extensive and commendable efforts were made to protect the Khobar Towers complex from a penetration attack, additional factual investigation of the adequacy of efforts to protect against the very type of attack that ultimately occurred is necessary."

While suggesting to Secretary Widnall that another study group be commissioned to pursue these issues, Secretary White set no deadline for its work. "The wisdom of your decision to continue the examination into the outstanding issues highlighted by the Downing and Record reports," he stated, "must be matched by a degree of thoroughness that will only be achievable if sufficient time and effort are dedicated to this review.... I encourage you to take as much time as you believe necessary to carry out this additional assessment."[62]

After the Attack

About a week later, on February 5, 1997, Secretary Widnall and General Fogleman asked Air Force Inspector General Lt. Gen. Richard T. Swope and Air Force Judge Advocate General Maj. Gen. Bryan G. Hawley to examine the issues that Mr. White had suggested deserved further study. Secretary Widnall and General Fogleman also gave Generals Swope and Hawley a second task. While they and Mr. White agreed with General Record's finding that no court-martial action was warranted, they told the generals: "The first matter to be addressed is whether the actions or omissions of any Air Force member merit administrative sanctions."[63]

Lieutenant General Swope and Major General Hawley were highly qualified to head such an investigation. General Swope had been the weapons officer of the 555th Tactical Fighter Squadron at Udorn Royal Thai Air Base, Thailand, during the Vietnam War; the inspector general at Headquarters Pacific Air Forces, 1989–1990; commander of the Thirteenth Air Force, 1994–1996; and Air Force inspector general since April 1996. General Hawley had long experience in Air Force legal assignments, as a staff judge advocate at base, numbered air force, and major command legal offices. He had held that position at Ninth Air Force and USCENTAF, 1988–1990; at Headquarters Military Airlift Command (and chief counsel, U.S. Transportation Command), 1990–1991; at Headquarters Air Combat Command, 1994–1996; and at Headquarters USAF since February 1996.[64]

These two senior officers were supported by an investigative team of twelve members, nine appointed by Lieutenant General Swope on February 6 and three others by Major General Hawley eleven days later. Headed by a team chief and a legal advisor from the Air Force IG office, this group included experts in the areas of security, human-source intelligence, fire and disaster preparedness, counterintelligence and anti-terrorism, and intelligence, as well as additional legal advisors.[65] Consistent with Mr. White's suggestion, Secretary Widnall and General Fogleman assigned no deadline to their study.[66]

The Swope-Hawley Report was completed in April 1997, although not published until months later.[67] It concluded that the commanders of the 4404th Wing "and all those in the force protection chain of command" were "vigorous and diligent and fully engaged in providing the full range of security for the Khobar Towers compound. No administrative sanctions are warranted."[68]

The Swope-Hawley Report addressed the several specific issues that Mr. White had listed. It also discussed a number of the particular points that had been widely debated during the months after the bombing, including the proximity of the northern fence to the dormitories at that end of the compound. The Swope-Hawley Report noted the efforts of Air Force personnel to get this boundary moved further north, away from the housing area, and stated there were "indications that suggested that the Saudis would never agree to move the perimeter." The report quoted the consul general in Dhahran as saying "Now for them [the wing] to have extended the perimeter, I think it would have required moving of heaven and earth."[69]

As for the issue of window coverings, the Swope-Hawley Report found that Brigadier General Schwalier had concluded "that the threat was not high enough to warrant its immediate installation. Specific information concerning Mylar that he had available was that its utility was uncertain, installation required special skills and estimates were approximately $50 a square meter." The report also pointed out that "the standoff distances for the postulated threat achieved by the fence-barrier combination plus the additional distance provided by added Saudi security at the northern perimeter were thought to be adequate to prevent a major problem. Though he deferred immediate installation, the wing commander included Mylar in his long range plan to ensure his successors would not lose sight of a potential option for risk reduction should it be necessary."[70]

The Swope-Hawley team examined the issue of the Khobar Towers alarm system and reported that the "decision not to install a fire alarm system was based on the construction of the facilities and the opinions of numerous fire chiefs and headquarters fire protection specialists that such a system was not required. Based on these inputs, the wing commander, support group commander and civil engineering squadron commander deferred the planned upgrade, programming the $250K cost for a fire alarm system into the wing's first Five-Year Facilities Improvement Plan." The study team did not believe it could state positively that the use of a bomb-threat alarm, as opposed to a fire alarm, would have reduced significantly the number of casualties. "While the activation of an automated system (not fire) for the building would most likely have had more people moving toward exits," the Swope-Hawley Report stated, "the short time between recognition of the threat and the explosion makes any meaningful estimates of survivability unlikely."[71]

As for building evacuation exercises, the Swope-Hawley Report found that the wing had no formal program to practice them. However, like the Record Report, it emphasized that the airmen had evacuated some of the facilities on the compound several times during the months before the bombing, when suspicious packages had been reported. Based on evidence from security police blotters and airmen interviews, the Swope-Hawley team charted fourteen such evacuations that took place between November 14, 1995, and June 14, 1996.[72]

When the results of the Swope-Hawley investigation eventually were published, two Air Force reports were on record supporting General Schwalier's actions. These two documents, however, proved less influential with the press and public opinion than the findings of the Downing task force and of some of the Congressional investigators, which had received earlier publicity. In March 1997, well before the release of the Swope-Hawley Report, the *Air Force Times* reported that "the Downing commission finding that 'the commander of the 4404th Wing (Provisional) did not adequately protect his forces from a terrorist attack' has prompted questions from Congress and the public about why no disciplinary actions have been taken."[73]

While criticism of the wing commander mounted, General Fogleman put his own views on the record. As controversy grew during the late summer of 1996, he emphasized the difficulty of recognizing small pieces of significant information within mountains of intelligence, and counseled against second-guessing the commanders in the field. "You can go back with that 20-20 hindsight," General Fogleman stated that September, "and see all this stray voltage and say, 'Well, everybody knew that.' Well, everybody *didn't* know that."[74]

As the investigations continued, the chief of staff became concerned that action against General Schwalier would have a chilling effect on other local commanders. "There are many commanders sitting out there in the field waiting to see what happens in this case," he told the Senate Armed Services Committee on February 25, 1997. "If they, despite their absolute best efforts, are targeted by somebody in an act of war, and somebody is killed and, no matter what they have done, this town, this city, this climate cries for their scalp, I hate to think what this will do to the force."[75] General Fogleman also pointed out to the committee that, by the time of the bombing, General Schwalier had implemented thirty of thirty-six recommendations to improve the security of the Khobar Towers that the AFOSI had made in its Vulnerability Assessments, a fact noted in the Record Report.[76]

During the investigations, and after his retirement, General Fogleman stated that those who had called for punishing the Dhahran wing commander had not seen all the facts. In a December 1997 interview with military historian Richard H. Kohn, he asserted: "I watched people in Washington make statements on the basis of no factual knowledge whatsover."[77]

On July 28, 1997, General Fogleman announced that he would retire before September 1, a year before his four-year term as chief of staff expired. He became the first Air Force chief of staff to cut short his tour voluntarily. General Fogleman stated he was retiring early in part because he believed that one or more Air Force officers would be unfairly held responsible for the terrorist attack in Dhahran.[78]

Press reports connected General Fogleman's announcement to "a decision due this week" by Secretary of Defense William S. Cohen, who had succeeded Secretary Perry on January 24, 1997,[79] "on whether to sanction Air Force officers for leaving" the Khobar Towers complex "vulnerable to the June 1996 explosion." In his statement on Monday, July 28, General Fogleman said: "I reached my decision this weekend after much deliberation, and it is my intent that this announcement defuse the perceived confrontation between myself and Secretary Cohen over the Khobar Towers terrorist bombing last year."

Although press reports emphasized the connection between the Air Force chief of staff's early retirement and Secretary Cohen's impending announcement about Brigadier General Schwalier's promotion, General Fogleman's decision had a larger context. While the chief of staff said on July 28 that he intended to defuse the perceived confrontation between the secretary of defense and himself, he also stated: "My values and sense of loyalty to our soldiers, sailors, Marines and especially our airmen led me to the conclusion that I may be out of step with the times and some of the thinking of the establishment. This puts me in an awkward position." General Fogleman emphasized an issue larger than General Schwalier's promotion as he continued: "If I were to continue to serve as Chief of Staff of the Air Force and speak out, I could be seen as a divisive force and not a team player. I do not want the Air Force to suffer for my judgment and my convictions."[80]

Khobar Towers: Tragedy and Response

Professor Kohn, in an introduction to his interview with the retired Air Force chief of staff, published in December 1997, pointed out that "General Fogleman's decision to leave was neither a resignation nor an act of protest; it was a retirement. Had he resigned in protest, he would have waited until the Secretary of Defense announced his decision in the Schwalier case and explained publicly and unambiguously that the request for retirement was the product of disagreements over specific decisions and policies." "Instead," Kohn noted, "General Fogleman chose to leave quietly."[81]

In his final remarks during his interview with Professor Kohn, the chief of staff did not speak narrowly about the Dhahran bombing, but rather in much broader terms. "In my heart, on the personal level and on the professional level," General Fogleman stated, "I concluded that my continued service was not in the best interest of the Air Force, in Washington where I was serving, given my beliefs, and considering the advice I was offering to our national leadership."[82]

The Senate had confirmed Brigadier General Schwalier's promotion to major general before the Khobar Towers bombing. It was to become effective on January 1, 1997, but the Air Force announced that action on it would be delayed, "pending the resolution of an inquiry into the circumstances surrounding the June 25, 1996, terrorist bombing of Khobar Towers in Saudi Arabia."[83]

On July 31, 1997, three days after General Fogleman's early retirement, Defense Secretary Cohen, accompanied by Chairman of the Joint Chiefs of Staff Gen. John M. Shalikashvili, presented his report, "Personal Accountability for Force Protection at Khobar Towers," at a Pentagon briefing and press conference. Addressing the assembled journalists that day, Secretary Cohen stated: "I found that Brig. Gen. Terryl Schwalier, the wing commander at the time, did not adequately assess the implications of a possible attack on the perimeter of the Khobar complex. As a result, he did not develop an effective plan for responding to a perimeter attack. Based on this finding, I have concluded that it would not be appropriate to promote Brigadier General Schwalier to the rank of major general."[84]

In Secretary Cohen's July 31 press conference, he discussed two specific issues that his report also developed. "As my report explains," the secretary stated, "there were several security deficiencies, but two of them stood out. First, Khobar Towers had no effective alarm system to warn of an impending terrorist attack. Second, the evacuation plans for the residents in Khobar Towers were inadequate, and the command had not developed, tested, and trained personnel to use evacuation plans."[85]

On the same day that Secretary Cohen presented his report, General Schwalier issued a statement announcing that he had requested retirement. He cited three things that constantly had been "at the forefront" of his thoughts before, and after, Secretary Cohen announced his decision. "First," General Schwalier said, "my overriding emotion is one of sadness for the victims and their families. Our airmen did—and continue to—carry out the duties our government sends them to do in faraway places. These duties and places involve risk. We, as Americans, must be proud of them and support them." He continued: "Second, my strong desire is that the cowards respon-

After the Attack

sible for this tragedy—the terrorists—be captured and punished. Third, my intense hope is that commanders in the field will not be unduly criticized every time something bad happens." General Schwalier went into retirement, and the question of his promotion remained an issue for many years.[86]

In the aftermath of the Khobar Towers bombing, Americans remained frustrated that the perpetrators were not captured and punished. From the outset of the investigation, United States officials were disappointed with the cooperation they received from Saudi Arabia. Soon after the attack it became evident that the enormous differences between the criminal justice systems of the two countries, combined with the Saudi view that the Khobar Towers bombing was an internal matter of their kingdom, would prove frustrating to American investigators.[87]

An incident that took place the morning after the explosion exemplified how the two nations, within a matter of hours after the bombing, already were responding very differently to it. The Saudi government regarded the terrorist strike as an embarrassment and wanted the visible evidence of it destroyed as soon as possible. Accordingly, when Brigadier Generals Schwalier and Dick arrived at Building 131 around 5:30 a.m. on June 26, a Saudi or third-country national was bulldozing the site. The United States government, in contrast, believed the scene of the attack should be preserved, because it contained evidence critically important in determining who was responsible for the attack. It took the intervention of the wing commander and other senior officials to stop the bulldozing.[88]

Episodes like this one convinced many Americans, from the earliest days of the investigation, that they would have difficulty getting full cooperation with the Saudis. U.S. officials found that although the local authorities collaborated closely with the FBI team in the forensic study of the bomb fragments on the compound, they were not cooperative in regard to the suspects they held in the case.[89] Very soon after the bombing, the Saudi government began detaining a number of their own nationals, who were virtually all, if not all, radical dissident Shiite Muslims.[90] FBI director Louis J. Freeh traveled to Saudi Arabia twice within seven days in July 1996, to ask law enforcement officials there to observe U.S. legal standards in the investigation and to gain access for American investigators to the suspects being held. He was not successful in either effort.[91] In late January 1997, Mr. Freeh and Attorney General Janet Reno complained publicly that Saudi officials were not sharing the results of their investigation of the bombing.[92]

In the face of these frustrations, there seemed to be a break in the Khobar Towers case during the spring of 1997. On March 18 in an Ottawa suburb, the Royal Canadian Mounted Police arrested on an immigration charge Hani Abdel Rahim al-Sayegh, a Saudi national who was a Shiite Muslim dissident.[93] Canadian investigators concluded that the Dhahran bombing was the work of a militant group of Shiite Saudi Arabians, with links to Hezbollah, the pro-Iranian organization based in Lebanon. They identified two conspirators in the Khobar Towers plot: Ahmed

Khobar Towers: Tragedy and Response

Ibrahim Ahmad al-Mughassil, whom they characterized as its "mastermind," and Jaafar Chueikhat, who was arrested by Syrian agents soon after the attack and was found dead in his prison cell in Syria under suspicious circumstances.[94] Canadian officials alleged that Mr. Sayegh drove the white Chevrolet Caprice used as a getaway car by the bombers and the Canadians sought a deportation order for him in one of their federal courts.[95] In May that court ruled that Sayegh could be deported, and the following month, Canadian immigration officials and Mounties brought him to Washington, D.C.[96]

At first, FBI and other Justice Department officials hoped that Sayegh would provide valuable information about the Khobar Towers bombing. They intended to arraign him on charges of conspiring to kill American nationals in a case unrelated to the Dhahran attack. In exchange for a reduced sentence on these charges, Sayegh was to tell what he knew about the Khobar bombing and perhaps shed light on the question of whether the attack had been planned solely by Saudi dissidents or whether the Iranian government also had been involved.[97]

This arrangement came unravelled in early July, when the suspect denied having any information about the terrorist act in Dhahran and contended that he had been in Iran at the time. Sayegh's attorney stated that his client had misled his own lawyers as well as FBI agents about the extent of his knowledge of "individuals and practices" related to terrorism inside Saudi Arabia, suggesting that he did so with the hope of being deported from Canada to the United States, rather than to Saudi Arabia. In a D.C. federal court on July 30, Sayegh pleaded not guilty to the conspiracy charges, which unhinged his agreement with the American authorities.[98] Lacking the evidence necessary to bring the suspect to trial, Justice Department officials dropped the charges against Sayegh that autumn and later extradited him to Saudi Arabia.[99]

Mr. Freeh publicly held the Saudis responsible for the collapse of the Sayegh case, stating that they had failed to provide evidence against the suspect that could be used in a U.S. court. The American government was frustrated by this particular episode and, more fundamentally, by the lack of Saudi cooperation in the investigation. Moreover, the two nations arrived at different assessments of the responsibility for the bombing. Based on evidence the Canadians had gathered in the Sayegh case and on information from other sources, U.S. officials suspected that the Khobar Towers attack had been perpetrated by Saudi Shiite extremists, supported by Iran's radical Islamic government.[100] Saudi Arabia took another point of view. On May 22, 1998, Interior Minister Prince Ibn Abdul Aziz Nayef, who controlled his country's police force, stated that the bombing was solely the work of Saudi dissidents and flatly denied any Iranian or other foreign involvement.[101]

As U.S. officials became increasingly frustrated with the Saudis over the investigation, the Americans wound down their efforts in Dhahran. Although the Justice and Defense Departments vowed that they would not close the Khobar Towers case, the FBI withdrew virtualy all of its investigators from Saudi Arabia. By June 1998 only one agent, who served as a legal attaché and liaison to the Saudis, remained in Dhahran.[102]

After the Attack

Three years later, however, the Khobar Towers case took a heartening turn. On June 21, 2001, a federal grand jury in Alexandria, Virginia delivered a forty-six-count indictment against thirteen Saudis and one Lebanese national, charging them with carrying out the Dhahran bombing. The prosecutors secured this legal document just days before the five-year statute of limitations would have expired on its charges of attempted murder and conspiracy.[103]

The June 21 indictment did not include any Iranian nationals, nor did it directly accuse Iran of legal responsibility for the Khobar Towers attack. In a press conference held the same day, however, Attorney General John Ashcroft, who had assumed that post on February 1, forcefully addressed this subject. He blamed unnamed Iranian officials for the bombing, stating that they had "inspired, supported, and supervised" the fourteen men named in the indictment, all of whom, he pointed out, were members of Hezbollah.[104]

The June 2001 indictments again raised hopes of a break in the case. "I am very confident that they will be brought to justice," Mr. Freeh said of those who had been indicted, "and hopefully in the United States, some of them, at some point." Air Force Chief of Staff Gen. Michael E. Ryan, stated: "These indictments send the message to all terrorists that they will be hunted down and will pay for their crimes."[105] President George W. Bush, who had taken office in January 2001, reasserted the commitment to pursue the case, made by President Clinton five years earlier. At the time of the indictments, President Bush told the families of the Khobar Towers victims: "Your government will not forget your loss, and will continue working, based on the evidence, to make sure that justice is done."[106]

The optimism raised by the indictments soon dissipated. According to Saudi Interior Minister Prince Nayef, eleven of the fourteen suspects named in the document already were being held in jails in his country. The United States had no extradition treaty with Saudi Arabia. In an interview that Prince Nayef gave soon after the indictments, he made it clear that extraditing the eleven suspects was not a negotiable issue. "The trials must take place before Saudi judicial authorities," he asserted, "and our position on this question will not change. No other entity has the right to try or investigate any crimes occurring on Saudi lands."[107]

Mr. Kenneth Katzman, a Middle East analyst with the Congressional Research Service, offered a reason for Saudi Arabia's position on the investigation. "If the Saudis give these people to us," he suggested, "they're going to obviously be afraid that the FBI will develop stronger evidence that the Iranians were involved. That would just completely throw them off track with Iran.... The foreign policy drove how this thing was going to come out."[108]

Many years after the Khobar Towers bombing, the case remained unresolved. With the passing of time, it became less likely that the eleven prisoners held by the Saudis would be brought to justice in an American court, and less likely that any of the other three suspects would be arrested. In December 2006, federal trial judge Royce C. Lambeth ruled that Iran bore significant responsibility for the Dhahran bombing and its government should pay damages to surviving family members of

Khobar Towers: Tragedy and Response

airmen killed in the attack. There was considerable uncertainty, however, that the fifty-five relatives who participated in this lawsuit would ever obtain any of the damages awarded them.[109] Uncertainties like this, controversies, and frustration continued to surround the Dhahran terrorist attack.

Nonetheless, a few firm conclusions can be drawn about the Khobar Towers tragedy. First, the bombing had a larger context, which emerged in the horrendous events that took place about five years later in New York City, Washington, D.C., and southern Pennsylvania. After September 11, 2001, it became possible to view the attack at the Khobar Towers, like those at the World Trade Center in February 1993, Riyadh in November 1995, the American embassies in Kenya and Tanzania in August 1998, the *USS Cole* in October 2000, and others, as precursors to the despicable assaults on the World Trade Center and the Pentagon that led President George W. Bush to declare war on terrorists around the world.[110] American officials believed that the Dhahran bombing had been perpetrated by Saudi dissidents, supported by Iran, rather than the al Qaeda network and the Taliban government of Afghanistan, who were responsible for the September 11 attacks.[111] Nonetheless, the tragedy in Dhahran in 1996 prefigured the ones in New York and Washington five years later.

Second, Americans can be proud of their airmen who were on duty at the Khobar Towers on the night of June 25, 1996. These men and women were keenly aware that they served in a dangerous part of the world and yet they were quietly determined to perform their mission, without fanfare. Captain Matthew Winkler, a pilot of the 71st Rescue Squadron who was wounded in the bombing, offered a point of view shared by many others in his situation. "We knew we were in a hot spot," he stated. And then he added, without a hint of emotion: "It comes with the territory. It comes with our job."[112]

Third, the caregivers in Dhahran and elsewhere held a common attitude about helping the airmen who had been wounded by the bombing. Although they of course regretted that the tragedy had taken place, they welcomed the opportunity to use their professional skills to aid their comrades. Like Captain Winkler, SSgt. MaryAnna Schuchman of the Landstuhl Regional Medical Center also spoke for many of her fellow professionals. "I'm just really glad that I was able to help," she stated, "when the time came."[113]

Finally, one of the most heartening aspects of the Khobar Towers tragedy was that the airmen received superb professional care. An exchange between one caregiver and one patient at Landstuhl no doubt represented the gratitude expressed by hundreds of other Khobar Towers veterans. Captain Lydia E. Vasquez, a medical-surgical nurse at the LRMC, recalled asking one of her patients, "What can I do to make things easier for you?" The airman replied: "You're doing it already. I'm so grateful to be here."[114]

Epilogue

The conduct of Iraqi leader Saddam Hussein brought about Operation Southern Watch and other military operations to enforce a series of United Nations resolutions. In mid-September 2002, roughly a year after al Qaeda's terrorist attacks on the United States, President George W. Bush called on the United Nations to confront the Baghdad dictator, who had been defying the UN for more than a decade. The chief executive stated that the United States, with or without the support of the United Nations, would act if Saddam failed to comply with the UN resolutions that called on him to end his programs of weapons of mass destruction. On the evening of March 17, 2003, President Bush issued an ultimatum that Saddam and his sons must leave Iraq within forty-eight hours.[1]

Saddam ignored this warning, and the United States launched a military action, Operation Iraqi Freedom, with American and British ground forces moving from northern Kuwait into Iraq. Air operations soon followed, and American units began entering Baghdad on April 5. Saddam went into hiding, but soldiers of the 4th Infantry Division captured him in December 2003.[2]

It took only about three weeks to seize Baghdad and remove Saddam from power. Operation Southern Watch contributed a great deal to this success. The twelve years of sorties that had enforced the southern and northern no-fly zones had given the Air Force valuable information about Iraq's military behavior; and before Operation Iraqi Freedom began, the American airmen increased their Northern and Southern Watch strikes, helping to reduce the air defenses that Saddam could employ against them. In addition, Prince Sultan Air Base was the site of the Combined Air Operations Center that directed air operations during the Baghdad campaign and during Operation Enduring Freedom's strikes against al Qaeda and the Taliban in Afghanistan. At the height of these operations, Prince Sultan Air Base provided a home to about two hundred coalition aircraft.[3]

In these and other ways, Operations Northern and Southern Watch contributed to Operation Iraqi Freedom. But at the same time, the coalition's success in ending Saddam's regime meant that the flights to enforce the no-fly zones were no longer needed. Operation Southern Watch, which had brought the American airmen to the Khobar Towers, ended when Operation Iraqi Freedom began.[4]

With the end of Saddam's regime, the Air Force also began to leave Prince Sultan Air Base. The CAOC went into "mothball" status and the USAF aircraft left during the spring and summer of 2003. During an August 21 ceremony that inactivated the 363d Air Expeditionary Wing, its commander spoke poignantly of the

Khobar Towers: Tragedy and Response

short, but significant, history of the Air Force presence at Prince Sultan. "We came here under difficult circumstances following the Khobar Towers bombing," Col. James Moschgat reflected. "The mission thrived and prospered here, and I believe our legacy will live on."[5]

Operation Southern Watch came to an end. The dictator it contained during the 1990s had been defeated and captured. But the mission that the United States Air Force once served in Dhahran, Saudi Arabia—and the nineteen airmen who gave their lives for it—were not forgotten.

On June 25, 1999, the third anniversary of the bombing, Acting Secretary of the Air Force F. Whitten Peters dedicated a Khobar Towers exhibit in the Enlisted Heritage Hall on the Gunther Annex of Maxwell Air Force Base, Alabama. It features a dramatic backdrop, an enlarged photograph of Building 131 after the terrorist attack. In front of this compelling image are three manequins in the uniforms worn by three of the airmen who were killed in the bombing: A1C. Justin R. Wood, SSgt. Kevin J. Johnson, and MSgt. Michael G. Heiser. The exhibit also displays artifacts that were recovered after the explosion, and an Air Force News videotape relates the story of the bombing and its aftermath.[6]

This visual presentation includes coverage of another Khobar Towers memorial, one that was dedicated at Prince Sultan Air Base about a year after the attack. One Air Force writer said of this monument: "Many airmen deployed to Prince Sultan Air Base often would visit a place on [that] base that held the reason for why they were there. That place was the Khobar Towers Memorial." In June 2003, as the Air Force was departing Prince Sultan, a ceremony was held at this monument and it was then moved to the Air Force Museum, at Wright-Patterson Air Force Base, Ohio. The memorial's inscription reads: "Their sacrifice shall blaze as a flame in our hearts."[7]

Leaving the Enlisted Heritage Hall video program with its coverage of the Prince Sultan/Wright-Patterson memorial, a visitor sees twelve monuments in front of the building. Among them is one, sponsored by the Michael G. Heiser Foundation, of a sword mounted on a stone base. Its front is inscribed: "Khobar Towers Dhahran, Saudi Arabia June 25, 1996." Two of its other faces list, by base, the casualties of the terrorist attack. The fourth side reads: "The sword of retribution and vigilance for our 19 lost warriors so others may live."

Located appropriately near this memorial is one to another casualty of terrorism, SMSgt. Sherry Olds, a graduate of the Senior Noncommissioned Officer Academy who was killed in the bombing of the U.S. Embassy in Kenya, two years after the Khobar Towers attack. It is also fitting that Gunter's monument to the Dhahran casualties stands near one to Operation Iraqi Freedom, which ended the reign of Saddam Hussein. The actions of this Iraqi dictator had necessitated Operation Southern Watch and brought the American airmen to the Khobar Towers.[8]

A year after the official opening of the Gunther exhibit, on the fourth anniversary of the bombing, a beautiful memorial was dedicated at Patrick Air Force Base. A striking monument of nine panels in rose granite, it stands at the southern end of

Epilogue

the installation's ceremonial area, just north of Thor Street and the 45th Mission Support Group Headquarters, Building 425. The other three sides of this park-like setting are bordered by Falcon Avenue on the west, Edward H. White Street on the north, and Titan Road on the east. A large flagpole flying Old Glory is the most prominent feature of the ceremonial area. Its perimeter is decorated by a colorful display of the flags of the fifty states and by the palm trees often found in this part of Florida. Not far northeast of the ceremonial area stands Building 439, the Seaside Chapel where, on Sunday, June 30, 1996, President Bill Clinton met with the families of the deceased airmen from Patrick. Just south of this chapel is Building 431, the base theater where, on the same day, the memorial service was held.[9]

The curved design of Patrick's Khobar Towers memorial draws the viewer's eye to its center. On its central panels are the portraits and names of the five airmen from Patrick who gave their lives in Dhahran: Capt. Christopher J. Adams, Capt. L. Timothy Haun, MSgt. Michael G. Heiser, SSgt. Kevin J. Johnson, and A1C. Justin R. Wood. Below these names appear those of the other fourteen Air Force casualties.[10]

Another beautiful Khobar Towers memorial, this one of gray granite, stands on Eglin Air Force Base, Florida. Appropriately, it is just across Nomad Way from Building 1312, the home of the 58th and 60th Fighter Squadrons (eight of Eglin's casualties were members of the 58th and one was a member of the 60th), and not far from Building 1315, the headquarters of the 33d Fighter Wing. A walkway lined by four granite benches, two on either side, leads the visitor from Nomad Way into a small plaza with the memorial, four more benches, and poles that fly the flags of the United States and of the 33d Fighter Wing. An encircling stand of oaks and pines, common on Eglin, buffer the area from the nearby parking lots and roadways.

Running across the top of the memorial are the poignant words President Clinton spoke at the Sunday, June 30, service: "Our Nomads have ceased their wandering." Below this quotation are twelve panels, one for each of Eglin's casualties: SrA. Jeremy A. Taylor, TSgt. Daniel B. Cafourek, A1C. Brian W. McVeigh, TSgt. Patrick P. Fennig, A1C. Brent E. Marthaler, SrA. Earl F. Cartrette, Jr., Sgt. Millard D. "Soup" Campbell, TSgt. Thanh V. (Gus) Nguyen, A1C. Joseph E. Rimkus, A1C. Joshua E. Woody, A1C. Peter J. Morgera, and MSgt. Kendall K. Kitson, Jr. Each panel has its airman's portrait, name, his city and state of enlistment, unit, career field, and an epitaph.

In front of this gray granite memorial and centered between the plaza's two flagpoles is a distinctive monument, with a flaming sword like the one on the emblem of the 33d Fighter Wing. Its inscription reads: "This monument is dedicated to the brave warriors who were killed by a terrorist bomb at Khobar Towers, Saudi Arabia, on June 25, 1996. They made the ultimate sacrifice as guardians of this grateful nation. We shall never forget them." The base of this monument stands above a pool, which is encircled by seven granite markers. Here the visitor can read the names of the Dhahran casualties who were from bases other than Eglin: the five from Patrick; A1C. Christopher Lester, Wright-Patterson Air Force Base, Ohio; and SSgt. Ronald L. King, Offutt Air Force Base, Nebraska.[11]

Khobar Towers: Tragedy and Response

At night the area is floodlit, and during the day mockingbirds call from the nearby oaks and pines. The visitor also hears another sound, for the Khobar Towers memorial is not far from Eglin's flightline. Overhead there is a prolonged, growling rumble that turns back into itself. A fighter climbs into the sky, and the United States Air Force continues to perform its mission.

Appendix: Biographical Sketches

The twelve biographical sketches below are based on information compiled by the 33d Fighter Wing's Office of Public Affairs, Eglin Air Force Base, Florida. The ranks and names are given as in the text.

Technical Sergeant Daniel B. Cafourek
—Home of record: Watertown, South Dakota.
—33d Fighter Wing Maintenance Professional of the Year, 1995.
—Considered by most as the "Resident Mechanic of the F–15."
—From a close friend: The consumate professional, indisputably recognized as the squadron's finest crew chief. He carried out his duties with quiet resolve and dedication to detail. The first certified technician in the wing.
—Personally, Dan had one of the largest hearts and strongest commitments to friendships. His stoic demeanor was shed when carousing with friends, when his fun-loving and utterly hysterical persona shone through. He loved his wife, friends, fast cars, tuning up his '93 Mustang, and rock and roll.

Sergeant Millard D. Campbell
—Home of record: Angelton, Texas.
—Nicknames: "Dee" and "Soup."
—Noncommissioned Officer, Daily Flight Operations.
—Dee accepted his duties without question, and carried them out with resounding quality and expertise. He effectively transitioned into his current position prior to deploying to Saudi. The job requires the technical knowledge to make quick and precise decisions. He not only performed brilliantly at that position but also at operations scheduling.
—Dee was quiet and mild mannered. He was the right hand of all supervisors. He made sure all operations specialists assigned to him were well taken care of. He always made sure all the younger airmen had somewhere to go during the holidays.
—Dee loved baseball and was drafted out of high school to play professionally, but he declined that opportunity and took a scholarship to attend college. After meeting his loving wife Marie (his equal in personality and character), he joined the Air Force. He played squadron softball and, of course, led the team in hits, home runs, and runs batted in. Dee is a class act who will be missed by all.

Senior Airman Earl F. Cartrette, Jr.
—Home of record: Sellersburg, Indiana.
—Nicknames: "JR" and "Spoon-man."
—A practical joker who kept times in Saudi light-hearted.

Khobar Towers: Tragedy and Response

—Drew a clown character on the squadron bulletin board to convey light-hearted messages.
—A crew chief by trade, he was assigned to the Support Section.
—He enjoyed auto racing and spent time rebuilding a Chevy Nova. His father had owned this car and then sold it before he passed away in 1992. JR bought it back and was rebuilding it as a tribute to him.

Technical Sergeant Patrick P. Fennig
—Home of record: Greendale, Wisconsin.
—Flightline Expeditor.
—Pat was well traveled, having served in seven assignments during sixteen years of service.
—He excelled as a Flightline Expeditor because he was able to juggle the many demands of daily flying while taking care of the young men and women on the flightline. He was loved and respected by his subordinates because of his devotion to them. Pat was selfless; he was the first to volunteer for any deployment. During 1993–1996 he deployed in support of Operation Uphold Democracy and Operation Southern Watch three times.
—Pat loved the Air Force, traveling, shooting, scuba diving, and spear fishing. He liked the finer things in life: gourmet food, good wine, good scotch, and he wouldn't hesitate to pay $50 for a good, hand-rolled cigar.
—Pat lived life to the fullest and seized every minute!

Master Sergeant Kendall Kitson
—Home of record: Yukon, Oklahoma; born in Virginia.
—Nickname: "K.K."
—Had a down-to-earth sense of humor.
—Remembered for his straightforward sayings, such as: "Let me look into my crystal ball and see what I can find to support the mission."
—Always kept his cool as production superintendent, even when the jets were not cooperating.
—Enjoyed boating and fishing and volleyball with the troops in Saudi.

Airman First Class Brent E. Marthaler
—Home of record: Cambridge, Minnesota.
—Was nominated the 58th Fighter Squadron's "Airman of the Quarter."
—Winner of the Top Performer of the Month for TAMS Flight in January 1996.
—Crew chief of the squadron commander's jet, always observed putting in an "extra effort" to keep his jet flying.
—Great attitude: polite; instrumental in keeping spirits high.
—At shift change, Brent would enthusiastically yell to his comrades: "Good morning, mid shift."
—Devoted time teaching Sunday School class to children at the Eglin Base Chapel.

Biographical Sketches

Airman First Class Brian W. McVeigh
—Home of record: Debary, Florida.
—Crew chief.
—Had a very quiet personality.
—Enjoyed weight lifting: one pilot recalled, "Brian would crush your hand when you shook hands with him at the jet."
—He was a big fan of auto racing.

Airman First Class Peter J. Morgera
—Born in Massachusetts.
—Came to Eglin Air Force Base from the 53d Fighter Squadron, Spangdahlem, Germany.
—Assistant Dedicated Crew Chief: earned an Air Force Achievement Medal for maintaining his aircraft at a 90.2 percent fully mission-capable rate, well above the 84 percent standard for the Air Force in Europe.
—Deployed to Incirlik, Turkey, in support of Operation Provide Comfort.
—Assigned to the 33d Operations Support Squadron in January 1996 as an end of runway technician.
—Volunteered to go to Saudi so he could upgrade to five level the right way, "By crewing jets."
—Pete was a reliable and hard-working professional.
—He enjoyed playing darts, shooting pool, and going to the beach.
—He was a very caring individual—never without a smile.

Technical Sergeant Than V. Nguyen
—Born in Saigon, South Vietnam.
—Nickname: "Gus." When he arrived in the U.S., he and his brother had the same first name; he was baptized in the Roman Catholic Church and given the name Augustino.
—Gold Flag Combat Oriented Repair Initiative Manager.
—Directly responsible for his wing being recognized as having the most productive Gold Flag program in Air Combat Command.
—A key contributor to a Gold Flag grand total savings of $4.613 million in fiscal years 1994 and 1995 and in the first quarter of fiscal year 1996.
—Vietnamese linguist protocol volunteer for Eglin Air Force Base.
—Volunteered many hours in the community helping victims of Hurricane Opal.

Airman First Class Joseph E. Rimkus
—Home of record: Madison, Illinois.
—Nickname: "Dinky."
—Weapons Load Crew.
—Very respectful, well mannered—he always wore a necktie when visiting his grandmother because she liked seeing him in one.
—Always volunteered for additional duties and never complained.

Khobar Towers: Tragedy and Response

—Enjoyed playing basketball.
—Was a "closet barber": while in Saudi, enjoyed cutting his friends hair.

Senior Airman Jeremy A. Taylor
—Born in Kansas.
—Assigned to the 33d Maintenance Squadron as a jet engine mechanic.
—Son of a career military father, a retired Chief.
—Played soccer in high school, became an avid beach volleyball player at Eglin.
—During 1993–1996, coached childrens' soccer teams on Eglin; during 1995, coached womens' softball.
—An outgoing personality who enjoyed cookouts with his fellow mechanics.
—Very close to his family: talked to them on the phone every Sunday.

Airman First Class Joshua E. Woody
—Home of record: Corning, California.
—Weapons Load Crew.
—A selfless worker with an outgoing personality. He was upbeat, spirited, and always had a smile on his face.
—He was an accomplished high school wrestler.
—Recently married, he was looking forward to returning home to his new spouse.

The five biographical sketches below appeared in the 45th Space Wing *Missileer*, 1:1 (July 5, 1996), 1, 8, and 9:

Captain Christopher J. Adams was called "Chris" by his friends. He had two loves in his life: his best friend and fiancee Air Force Capt. Karen Oullette and their new 32-foot cabin cruiser "Diamond Ring." He named his boat for his girl because after their upcoming wedding, Chris and Karen were going to sail "Diamond Ring" to the Bahamas for the honeymoon that will never be . . . . Most of their friends received the wedding invitations a few days before the blast.

According to friends, Captain Adams knew he and Karen were getting married five years ago. It was the last thing on their "Five Year Plan." They were right on schedule, too, according to his friend and fellow squadron member Capt. Jed Hudson. The five years were up in October, time to settle down and start a family.

"Chris would drop everything in a second to help someone else," said fellow pilot Capt. Ted Ferguson, who also was Captain Adams' roommate. The two captains met when they were stationed at Pope Air Force Base, North Carolina, in 1990, assigned to the 41st Tactical Airlfift Squadron.

The captain's peers said his concern was always his people. "That was his job as an officer. When he had a decision to make as an aircraft commander, his concern was always his crew—what was best for his crew," said Capt. George Kochis, pilot. "And everyone's input was important, from the junior airman up."

Biographical Sketches

Captain Ferguson agrees. "Chris would do anything for the good of the squadron and the good of its people. One year at Christmas, Chris volunteered to take a Saudi rotation for a married guy so he could spend the holiday with his family."

Captain Adams also volunteered for and participated in airlift operations during Operation Desert Calm and was selected to fly a sensitive mission filming the oil fires of Kuwait during Desert Storm. He later deployed to support Provide Promise, the humanitarian airlift to Bosnia, and flew 16 missions under combat conditions.

Captains Hudson and Adams were with Chris the day before he shipped out to Saudi. They took Diamond Ring for a voyage on the Indian River, and promptly ran her aground. . . . Captain Hudson said they spent a good part of the night trying to get the boat free so he could dock it and catch his flight the next day.

The loadmasters affectionately referred to **Airman First Class Justin R. Wood** as "Junior," because he was the youngest member of the squadron. They even gave him his own aircraft . . . the eight-foot C–130 model mounted in front of the 71st. It was meant to be a joke—to raze the young loadmaster, who squadron members described as "successfully guillible" as the new guy.

Junior joined the 71st on January 5, 1995. He was the first active duty loadmaster to go from civilian to fully qualified loadmaster, a job normally reserved for experienced personnel. He was on his second deployment to Saudi Arabia and just two weeks shy of his 21st birthday—which he would have celebrated July 16—when he died. But during his short life, he managed to fly 34 combat support missions, and his actions contributed to the squadron being credited with 10 lives saved.

Squadron members describe Airman Woods as the person who kept everyone laughing with his Jim Carey "Ace Ventura" impressions.

He was always "on" according to MSgt. Julien Johnson. "He was just like a puppy is. The energy he gave off to the rest of the squadron was uplifting," said Sergeant Johnson, a fellow loadmaster. "There wasn't a down side to Justin. He was full of energy. He could put a smile on anyone's face."

That's the hard part for his buddies in Dormitory Building 506, said Senior Airman Robert Carceiri, who was Airman Woods' fellow loadmaster and dorm neighbor.

"We are like a family. He was always making everyone laugh. He was the happiest person I knew," Airman Carceiri said.

"You couldn't walk by him without cracking a smile," said Sergeant Johnson. "The only time I ever saw him down was when he fell in love with Pocahantas at Disney World."

"Yeah," said Airman Carceiri. "He did everything he could to get her attention . . . but she just brushed him off."

But that was Junior being Junior, according to Sergeant Johnson. "He was always moving, doing something. Once, when we were in Nevada, we went to Las Vegas and he won $90 in a nickel slot machine. When they came to give him the money they found out he wasn't 21 and he was asked to leave the premises and told to not come back."

Khobar Towers: Tragedy and Response

That was cool with Junior, because he took that 90 bucks and bought rollerblades. He spent the rest of his time off rollerblading everywhere.

"That's just the way he was," said Sergeant Johnson. "He was an entertainer. I still can't believe he's gone."

Anyone who didn't really know **Captain Leland Timothy "Tim" Haun**, would describe him as a quiet person. But he was very well rounded, according to his peers, who described him as a jokester, artist, comedian, ferocious reader of books, but first and foremost a family man. He earned a Bachelor's Degree in Industrial Arts from Fresno State University in July 1989 and joined the Air Force that same month as a navigator.

His first duty assignment was to the 41st Electronic Combat Squadron at Davis-Monthan Air Force Base, Arizona, where he made quite a name for himself during a training exercise, according to MSgt. Julien Johnson, a loadmaster with the 71st.

"On the HC–130 we do a lot of radar jamming," Sergeant Johnson said. "During this particular exercise, they were going in with the ground forces, and their objective was to knock out the communication with the ground battlefield. Instead of hitting the battlefield, Captain Haun cut the comm with the chow hall and the battle line. Nobody got called for breakfast or lunch, so the war games came to a standstill because nobody had eaten anything. The next day they got debriefed and were told that certain frequencies couldn't be jammed anymore because people had gone 18 hours without eating."

He was known for those same types of antics at the 71st.

Captain Haun joined the rescue squadron in June 1994. He was credited with saving a life when he participated in a rescue off a ship, 1,600 miles off the coast of Florida.

The captain distinguished himself in Dhahran, too, according to his friend and coworker Captain Kochis.

"He played volleyball in college and was very good at it, but he wouldn't play in Saudi with us. . . . I guess we weren't good enough for Tim," he joked.

The other thing was the volume of mail Captain Haun received in Saudi. "He always had mail coming in from his family. Constantly. And he always sent letters to them, too," Captain Kochis said. "He would get at least two letters a day from home!"

"How can I explain to you how great this guy was?" said Captain Jenson. "I mean, I know how I feel, but I can't describe it. There really aren't any words. But that's what he was—great."

Master Sergeant Michael G. Heiser joined the 71st Rescue Squadron in December 1995 as an airborne communications system operator and C-Flight superintendent. He hadn't been at the squadron long before he went away to the HC–130 Combat Rescue School at Kirtland Air Force Base, New Mexico, which is a must for all members of the squadron who participate in rescue operations. He graduated from Kirtland and had only been back in the squadron a few months before he was sent to Dhahran to put to practice what he spent months learning.

Biographical Sketches

Sergeant Heiser was new, but he made a good first impression on his flight commander, Capt. Ben Walsh: "When I called him in and told him he was going to be the new flight supervisor, Sergeant Heiser expressed concern to me that he was too new to do a good job. I told him I knew he could do the job or I wouldn't have selected him. He was that conscientious."

Like Captain Adams, Sergeant Heiser was in the process of settling down in a new house with his fiancee, Nancy, when he was killed.

Staff Sergeant Kevin J. Johnson was referred to simply as "K.J." None of his fellow engineers remember why or how he got his nickname, but his friend TSgt. Bruce Soto said K.J. really enjoyed the moniker.

But his real passion was flying.

According to coworker TSgt. Dave Lovell, K.J. was always flying. Since becoming a C–130 flight engineer in 1983, he amassed a total of 5,600 flying hours in a C–130 aircraft, 87 of those hours in combat and 280 in combat flight support. A lot of those hours were spent away from his three children and his wife.

"His wife Shryl wants it known that he loved to fly, and he enjoyed the life [of a flyer]," said Sergeant Soto, fighting back tears as he talked about the guy he's known since 1984, when they were both assigned to the 62d Tactical Airlift Squadron at Little Rock Air Force Base, Arkansas. "His devotion to duty was paramount. He never hesitated to volunteer for a mission. He was always 100 percent committed and always available when we needed him."

K.J.'s devotion to duty had also paid off in a way he will never know. His peers never got a chance to tell K.J. that right after he left for Saudi, they had recommended him for upgrade to flight evaluator—the highest level of proficiency a flight engineer can attain.

In addition to his flying, K.J. worked in supply as an additional duty. TSgt. Charles "Stretch" Meador, a loadmaster who worked with Sergeant Johnson in supply, said he could always hear K.J. coming, because the sergeant insisted on carrying his keyring in the bottom pocket of his flightsuit.

"He couldn't sneak up on you. You could hear him a mile away," Sergeant Meador said. "I used to hear him down the hall and yell out, 'Hey, K.J.,' and he wondered how I always knew it was him."

In addition to being devoted to both his family and the military, Sergeant Johnson was dedicated to the Lord. He was a faithful member of the Holy Name of Jesus parish in Indiatlantic, which held a memorial service for its brother on June 28.

His Christian beliefs helped through another tragedy in 1985, when a C–130 from his unit crashed at Fort Hood, said Sergeant Soto. K.J. was there to help the families of those who died, just as others are gathered around his family now in their time of grief. . . . K.J. would have wanted it that way.

This biographical sketch of **Staff Sergeant Ronald L. King** appeared in a booklet published on the occasion of the 55th Wing's 1999 Birthday Ball:

Khobar Towers: Tragedy and Response

Looking for a way out of Battle Creek, Michigan, and to see the world, Ronald L. King enlisted in the Air Force on September 17, 1976. The next 20 years were filled with exactly what he yearned for—excitement, travel, and education. In 1985, after nine successful years as a reprograhics technician, he cross-trained into the contracting career field. In 1986, he moved to Nellis Air Force Base, Nevada, and specialized as a supply buyer and small purchase administrator. In January 1989, he volunteered for assignment to Dhahran, Saudi Arabia, where he negotiated a $100,000 contract for training aids for the Royal Saudi Infantry Corps—the first of its kind. Returning to the states in January 1990, he was assigned to the 55th Contracting Squadron, Offutt Air Force Base, Nebraska. Serving as a purchasing agent in the commodities flight, King became an expert in computer purchases. During Operation Desert Shield, he often put in extra hours to ensure emergency computer purchases were made. In three weeks, King purchased 1,181 items, exceeding the standard by 470 percent! In December 1992, King moved to Ankara Air Base, Turkey, in support of Operation Provide Comfort, a humanitarian relief effort in northern Iraq. During the next 10 months, he was responsible for the administration of the Turkish Base Maintenance Contract, where he identified 55 unauthorized contract modifications totaling over $46 million in unrecorded costs. He also discovered an undetermined amount of relief aid not reaching the Kurdish refugees, tracked down the vendors, and reestablished required delivery dates. Having applied for retirement in 1996, he volunteered to postpone his plans and accept a final temporary assignment to the 4404th Wing (Provisional) at King Abdul Aziz Air Base, Dhahran. Much of his time was spent purchasing materials and supplies for the fitness center renovation. Just days short of returning home to his family, he was killed in the truck bomb explosion at the Khobar Towers. King's love of country, pursuit of excellence, and outstanding professionalism reflect great credit on himself, his family, his squadron, and the Air Force. He was posthumously awarded the Meritorious Service Medal and the Purple Heart for outstanding service to his country.

This biography of **Airman First Class Christopher B. Lester** appeared in the order of service at his memorial service at Wright-Patterson Air Force Base, Ohio, on July 1, 1996:

Airman First Class Christopher B. Lester was a Power Production Specialist for the 88th Civil Engineer Squadron. Airman Lester was born in Wyoming County, West Virginia, on February 15, 1977. He graduated from Pineville High School in 1995.

Airman Lester entered basic military training on July 19, 1995. He graduated from Basic Power Production Specialist School at Sheppard Air Force Base, Texas. On November 26, 1995, he was assigned to the 88th Civil Engineer Group, Wright-Patterson Air Force Base, Ohio.

Airman Lester took charge of maintenance on 35 mobile generators immediately upon arrival at Wright-Patterson. He also was being trained to maintain aircraft arresting barriers. He was a top-notch airman, dedicated to learning the most he could in his career.

Biographical Sketches

Airman Lester was awarded the basic Civil Engineer Badge on November 7, 1995. His military decorations include the Purple Heart, Air Force Outstanding Unit Award, National Defense Service Medal, and the Air Force Training Ribbon.

Airman Lester enjoyed softball, basketball, weightlifting, as well as riding motorcycles with members of his shop. He volunteered his time to support squadron fund raisers, such as working at King's Island.

Airman Lester volunteered for this contingency tour in Saudi Arabia and was looking forward to the challenge. It was his first deployment.

On Tuesday, June 25, 1996, Airman Christopher Lester, in the company of 18 fellow airmen, was translated from the Church militant to the Church triumphant. His body will await the resurrection in his home town of Pineville, West Virginia.

He is survived by his mother, Judy; father, Cecil; sister, Jessica; brother, Cecil, Jr.; his fiancee, Andrea Brooks; together with a great number of family and friends, and a nation that is deeply grateful unto God for one who has served faithful unto death.

Notes

Chapter One

1. "Daily Aircraft Discrepancies," 25 Jun 96, 2359 zulu time, in History of the 4404th Wing (Provisional), 1 May–31 Jul 96, 12 vols., vol. 7, supporting document II–D56; interview with SSgt. Jacques P. Bruffy, C–130 engine mechanic, 71st Rescue Squadron, Patrick AFB, Fla., 5 Feb 97; "MX 25 Jun [Daytime]," an undated note written by Lt. Col. Thomas H. Shafer, commander, deployed 71st Rescue Squadron; "71st Rescue Squadron History," web page of the 71st Rescue Squadron, 24 Aug 98. The History of the 4404th Wing (Prov.) for 1 May–31 Jul 96 hereafter is cited as 4404th Wing History, with a volume number and, for volume one (the narrative volume), a page number. For volumes two through twelve (the volumes of supporting documents) a supporting document number is given and, in the cases where that document has page numbers, a page number. This official unit history is classified secret-no foreign-warning notice: intelligence; all of the material used from it, throughout this work, is unclassified. Among the 4404th Wing History's supporting documents is the wing's after action report on the Khobar Towers bombing: "Khobar Towers' Terrorist Bombing 25 Jun 96: After Action Report," Sep 96. 4404th Wing History, vol. 8, supporting document VI–1. This document is for official use only and could not be used directly in a published work. It nonetheless was helpful in confirming many details found in other, open sources. The front section quotation is from an interview of Col. Gary R. Dylewski, Commander, 33d Fighter Wing, by SSgt. Yancy Mailes, Historian, 33d Fighter Wing, Eglin AFB, Fla., 18 Dec 96. Col. Dylewski was promoted to brigadier general on 1 Aug 99 and to major general on 1 Jan 02 (USAF biography of Maj. Gen. Gary R. Dylewski, Jun 02). The "Tragedy" section quotation is from a memorandum from the Air Force Office of Special Investigations Operating Location Central Command to the deputy commander in chief, US Central Command, 25 Jun 96.

2. Bruffy interview; Shafer, "MX 25 Jun [Nighttime]."

3. Interview with Capt. Matthew Winkler, pilot, 71st Rescue Squadron, Patrick AFB, Fla., 5 Feb 97.

4. Bruffy interview; SSgt. John McCarthy's account of the Khobar Towers attack, undated, late Jun or early Jul 96; A1C. Richard J. Lavallee, Jr.,'s account of the Khobar Towers attack, undated, late Jun or early Jul 96.

5. Winkler interview; undated map of the Khobar Towers, provided by the Air Force Manpower and Personnel Center to the Air Force Chief of Staff's operations group. A number of maps were used to prepare this work. This one was referred to more often than the others and is cited hereafter as the "Air Force Khobar Towers map." A modified copy of it appears on page 11 in chapter one. Among the several other maps used, another particularly helpful one was the undated "ARCENT-SA Building Evacuation Plan: Khobar Towers, Dhahran, Saudi Arabia." Lt. Col. Sherry Conner, DSW, USA, chief, social work services, U.S. Army Europe Regional Medical Command and Landstuhl Regional Medical Center (LRMC), Landstuhl, Germany provided a copy of this map. It is cited hereafter as the "Army Khobar Towers map" to distinguish it from the more frequently referenced "Air Force Khobar Towers map."

6. Interview with MSgt. Dwayne R. Berry, A-forms administrator and deployed first sergeant, 71st Rescue Squadron, Patrick AFB, Fla., 5 Feb 97; author's interview of Brig. Gen. Daniel M. (Dan) Dick, Commander, 4404th Composite Wing (Prov.), Langley AFB, Va., 4 Feb 98. Brig. Gen. Dick was promoted to major general on 1 Aug 98 and retired on 1 Jul 03 (USAF biography of Maj. Gen. Daniel M. Dick, Jul 03).

7. Interview with SSgt. Eric D. Ziegler, crew chief, 58th Fighter Squadron, Eglin AFB, Fla., 4 Dec 96; interview of TSgt. George Burgess,

Notes to pages 6–10

assistant flight chief, 58th Fighter Squadron, by SSgt. Yancy Mailes, historian, 33d Fighter Wing, and the author, Eglin AFB, Fla., 5 Dec 96; interview of A1C. Cielito Valencia, supply technician, 58th Fighter Squadron, by SSgt. Yancy Mailes, historian, 33d Fighter Wing, Eglin AFB, Fla., 11 Feb 97.

8. Berry interview. The 71st Rescue Squadron moved from Patrick AFB, Fla., to Moody AFB, Ga., in May 97 ("71st Rescue Squadron History").

9. Berry interview.

10. Air Force Khobar Towers map; interview with Lt. Col. Thomas A. McCarthy, operations officer, 58th Fighter Squadron, Eglin AFB, Fla., 4 Dec 96; interview with Capt. (Dr.) R. Morris Treadway, Jr., flight surgeon, 58th Fighter Squadron, Eglin AFB, Fla., 5 Dec 96.

11. Interview of Col. Douglas R. Cochran, Commander, 58th Fighter Squadron, by SSgt. Yancy Mailes, historian, 33d Fighter Wing, Eglin AFB, Fla., 20 Dec 96; McCarthy interview. A fourth officer, assistant operations officer Maj. Steve Moore, also lived in the suite, but already had returned to Eglin AFB with the unit's advanced cadre (McCarthy interview). On the pattern of three suites per floor, twenty-four per dormitory, see Air Force News Service (AFNS), SSgt. Joel Langton, 45th Space Wing public affairs, "Officer recalls Khobar Towers tragedy," 27 Jun 2000, and "Typical Building/ Suite Floor Plan," chapter one, page 8, copy provided by Lt. Col. (Dr.) Douglas J. Robb, Commander, 347th Aerospace Medical Squadron.

12. Burgess interview; McCarthy interview.

13. McCarthy interview; Cochran interview.

14. McCarthy interview.

15. Burgess interview.

16. Ibid.; John Lancaster, "Bombing Increases U.S. Troops' Sense of Isolation in Saudi Arabia," *Washington Post*, 29 Jun 96, A–22.

17. Ziegler interview.

18. Ibid.

19. Ibid.; biography of TSgt. Patrick P. Fennig, prepared by Capt. Brenda Campbell, 33d Fighter Wing public affairs office, undated.

20. Ziegler interview.

21. Interview with SSgt. Alfredo R. Guerrero, security policeman, 95th SP Squadron, California City, California, 9 Nov 96; Capt. Leah Bryant, "Tested by terror: Command cop becomes hero when he puts job above self," *Leading Edge* 38:8 (Aug 96), 5; Steven Watkins, "'They didn't hesitate,'" *Air Force Times* 56:49 (8 Jul 96), 13; Lt. Gen. Richard T. Swope, Inspector General, and Maj. Gen. Bryan G. Hawley, Judge Advocate General, "Report of Investigation: Khobar Towers Bombing, Dhahran, Saudi Arabia," Apr 97, 3 vols., 1:36 (hereafter cited as Swope-Hawley Report). After the Khobar Towers bombing, the Air Force redesignated its security police, or SPs, as security forces.

22. Guerrero interview; interview with SSgt. Selena P. Husted, law officer manager, 45th Space Wing, Patrick AFB, Fla., 6 Feb 97; interview with Lt. Col. (Chaplain) Dennis E. Aleson, senior chaplain, 4404th Composite Wing (Prov.), Nellis AFB, Nev., 7 Nov 96.

23. Guerrero interview.

24. Ibid; Watkins, "They didn't hesitate," 13.

25. Guerrero interview; Bryant, "Tested by terror," 5.

26. Guerrero interview; "Khobar Tower Chronology of Events," SP squadron entry for 25 Jun 96, 2150, in a chronology compiled by SrA. Ronald J. Biggs, Jr., historian, 4404th Composite Wing (Prov.), 8 Aug 96. SrA. Biggs integrated several chronologies which had been prepared by subordinate units of the 4404th Wing and made them available in this one valuable source (hereafter cited as "Khobar Chronology"). These chronologies also appear in the 4404th Wing's after action report on the bombing.

27. Air Force Khobar Towers map; Bruce W. Nelan, "Gulf Shock Waves," *Time* 148 (8 Jul 96), 21. Pictures taken by Capt. Robert L. (Bob) Jones of the 99th Mission Support Squadron, Nellis AFB, Nev., and other amateur and professional photographers were helpful in describing the features of the area. "Jersey" or "New Jersey" barriers, heavy concrete obstacles similar to the ones first used to control traffic on the New Jersey Turnpike in the 1950s.

28. Executive Summary of "Report of Khobar Towers Bomb Damage Survey," prepared by the Defense Special Weapons Agency and the Army Corps of Engineers, Jul 96, 3 (hereafter cited as Bomb Damage Survey Executive Summary); Air Force Khobar Towers map. The "Climatological Data" chart in the 4404th Wing History, vol. 1, 124, shows that the weather on

25 Jun 96 was unremarkable. The photographs taken by Capt. Jones again were helpful in writing this paragraph.

29. Schwalier conversation notes, 23 Feb 99; Watkins, "They didn't hesitate," 13; wing Operations Center Log of Events, entry for 25 Jun 96, 2200, in 4404th Wing History, vol. 10, supporting document VI–11; Nelan, "Gulf Shock Waves," 21; interview with SrA. Ronald J. Biggs, Jr., Historian, 4404th Composite Wing (Prov.), Nellis AFB, Nev., 8 Nov 96; "The Khobar Towers Bombing Incident," Staff Report of the House National Security Committee, 14 Aug 96, 2 (hereafter cited as HNSC Report). The reference to "31st Street" in the last of these sources is confusing because the street jogged twice and the section of it that was south of al Khobar Park was entirely within the Khobar Towers compound. The report apparently means that the two vehicles were on Thirty-first Street *west* of the park and used that route to enter its parking lot. An undated commercial map, the Eng. Zaki M.A. Farsi map of the "Eastern Region: Dammam-Al Khubar-Dhahran-Qatif" (hereafter cited as the Eastern Region map), proved extremely helpful in establishing the street patterns of al Khobar. The author conducted a tape-recorded oral history interview with Brig. Gen. Terry Schwalier (USAF, ret.) on 23 and 24 Feb 99, cited many times elsewhere throughout these notes, and also took notes on their conversations during those two days. The notes on these conversations and the interview are cited by date, either 23 or 24 Feb 99.

30. Biggs, "Khobar Chronology," entry for SP squadron, 2150, 25 Jun 96; Schwalier conversation notes, 23 Feb 99; Nelan, "Gulf Shock Waves," 21; Bomb Damage Survey Executive Summary, 4. Some press accounts had the Caprice following the truck, rather than preceding it (David B. Ottaway and Brian Duffy, "Iranian Aide Linked To Bombing Suspect," *Washington Post*, 13 Apr 97, A–8). Gen. Schwalier, who, as commander of the 4404th Composite Wing (Prov.), had as much information about the attack as any American, stated that the Caprice entered the lot ahead of the truck. SrA. Biggs, who worked with the Federal Bureau of Investigation team that investigated the bombing immediately afterward, said the same (Schwalier conversation notes, 23 Feb 99; Biggs interview; see also the wing Operations Center Log of Events, entry for 25 Jun 96, 2200). One official report, the HNSC Report, 2, first mentions the car as following the truck. But four sentences later in the report's narrative, without explanation, it refers to the truck as being "positioned behind the car." Presumably the order of the two vehicles is reversed in the first mention; once this assumption is made, the account flows logically. Beyond this slip, the HNSC Report is a valuable source on the movements of the car and truck. Other official reports speak about both vehicles, but say nothing about the order of their approach. After the attack, many sources referred to the bomb-vehicle as a sewage truck (Schwalier conversation notes, 23 Feb 99; Dick interview with author; Rebecca Grant, "Khobar Towers," *Air Force Magazine* 81:6 (Jun 98), 47). The FBI investigators concluded that the explosives in the truck were covered with sewage (Bomb Damage Survey Executive Summary, 4). SSgt. Guerrero and the other airmen of course had no idea of the tanker's contents that night.

31. Schwalier conversation notes, 23 Feb 99; HNSC Report, 2; Biggs interview.

32. Guerrero interview; Schwalier conversation notes, 23 Feb 99; HNSC Report, 2. In Mar 97, while Canadian officials sought a deportation order from their own country for Hani Abdel Rahim al-Sayegh, a suspect in the bombing, it was alleged that Mr. Sayegh drove a "signal car" on the night of 25 Jun 96. In this version, Mr. Sayegh pulled a vehicle into the parking lot north of the Khobar Towers complex, and a second car and a tanker followed him. Sayegh flashed his lights, signalling the other two vehicles to enter the parking lot (Anthony DePalma, "Canada Links Pro-Iranian Group To Saudi Attack at U.S. Barracks," *New York Times*, 28 Mar 97, A–6).

33. HNSC Report, 2; Guerrero interview. To illustrate that tanker trucks were common in the area, on 24 Feb 99, Gen. Schwalier showed the author a photograph of one being searched by security policemen and their dogs, at the main gate of the Khobar Towers.

34. Guerrero interview.

35. Ibid.; Nelan, "Gulf Shock Waves," 21.

36. Guerrero spotted the truck at about 10:50 p.m.; the explosion took place at 10:53. Biggs, "Khobar Chronology," SP squadron entries for

Notes to pages 12–15

25 Jun 96, 2150 and 2153; "Khobar Towers Bombing: Medical Response: Force Protection Lessons Learned," an undated briefing prepared by Lt. Col. (Dr.) Douglas J. Robb, Commander, 347th Aerospace Medicine Squadron, for Air Force Chief of Staff Gen. Ronald R. Fogleman. The wing Operations Center Log of Events, entry for 25 Jun 96, 2200, gives an estimated time for the explosion and puts the time between Guererro's sighting and the blast at three to four minutes.

37. Guerrero interview; Bradley Graham, "Bomb Won't Deter U.S. in Gulf, Officials Say," *Washington Post*, 27 Jun 96, A–1; Swope-Hawley Report, 1:75; Biggs, "Khobar Chronology," SP squadron entry for 25 Jun 96, 2151; Biggs interview; 4404th Security Police Squadron Commander's End of Tour Report, 14 Mar–26 Jun 96, in 4404th Wing History, vol. 8, supporting document VI–7 (hereafter cited as SP Commander EOTR).

38. Husted interview; SSgt. Selena P. Zuhoski [nee Husted], 45th Space Wing's judge advocate's office, to Dr. Perry D. Jamieson, Air Force History Support Office (AFHSO), 30 Oct 98 and Nov 98; US Military Training Mission staff telephone directory, 1 Jul 97; Swope-Hawley Report, 1:75; Biggs, "Khobar Chronology," judge advocate entry for 25 Jun 96, 2240.

39. Biggs, "Khobar Chronology," SP squadron entry for 25 Jun 96, 2151; Swope-Hawley Report, 1:75.

40. Swope-Hawley Report, 1:75; Biggs interview. The Saudis designated this organization the Royal Saudi Land Force Military Police. They commonly were called the "Red Berets" or, even less formally, the "Red Hats," referring to color and style of their uniform caps (Swope-Hawley Report, 1:44).

41. Guerrero interview; Graham, "Bomb Won't Deter U.S.," A–1.

42. Guerrero interview; Schwalier conversation notes, 23 Feb 99. See also Biggs interview and a document written by SrA. Craig J. Dick. The "humvee" or "hummer" derived its nicknames from HMMWV, the acronym for its full designation: High Mobility Mulitpurpose Wheeled Vehicle. It gained a popular reputation during the Gulf War akin to that of the jeep during World War II. By the early twenty-first century, its commercial version had become a high-priced status vehicle.

43. Guerrero interview; Watkins, "They didn't hesitate," 13; MSgt. Louis Arana-Barradas, TSgt. Ray Johnson, and SSgt. Carl Norman, "Southern Watch Continues Despite Bombing," *Airman* XL:8 (Aug 96), 18.

44. Watkins, "They didn't hesitate," 13; Guerrero interview.

45. Winkler interview; "25 Jun 96: Mike Morelock," an undated account written by Capt. Michael D. Morelock; interview with Capt. Michael D. Morelock, pilot, 71st Rescue Squadron, Patrick AFB, Fla., 4 Feb 97.

46. Winkler interview.

47. Watkins, "They didn't hesitate," 13.

48. Winkler interview; Morelock interview; "25 Jun 96: Mike Morelock."

49. Morelock interview; Winkler interview; interview with Col. Thomas Friers, Commander, 1st Rescue Group, Patrick AFB, Fla., 4 Feb 97.

50. Aleson interview. Chaplain Aleson, a close friend of Lt. Col. Shafer, talked to him the morning after the attack. Their meeting at that time is discussed in chapter seven.

51. Morelock interview; Winkler interview.

52. Notes taken during a telephone conversation with Lt. Col. Thomas H. Shafer, deployed commander, 71st Rescue Squadron, 20 Feb 97; Winkler interview; McCarthy interview.

53. Guerrero interview; Biggs, "Khobar Chronology," SP squadron entry for 25 Jun 96, 2153; Robb, "Medical Response."

Chapter Two

1. Secretary of Defense William J. Perry, Report to the President on the Protection of U.S. Forces Deployed Abroad, 15 Sep 96, 2; Eliot A. Cohen, director, *Gulf War Air Power Survey*, 5 vols. (Washington, D.C., 1993), III: part 2 (Support), 8; First Lt. Ken Hoffman, "USMTM: A History of Training," *Southern Watch* 6:17 (23 Apr 97), 5. For a valuable overview of the background of diplomatic and military events in Southwest Asia before 1990, see Richard G. Davis, "Roots of Conflict: A Military Perspective on the Middle East and the Persian Gulf Crisis," a monograph published by the Center for Air Force History in 1993.

2. The strength of the Iraqi units in Kuwait is from the unclassified version of the Department of Defense's *Final Report to Congress: Conduct of the Persian Gulf War* (Washington, D.C., 1992), 4. On King Fahd's decision to accept American forces into his territory, see what is to date the best diplomatic history of the Gulf War: Lawrence Freedman and Efraim Karsh, *The Gulf Conflict 1990–1991: Diplomacy and War in the New World Order* (Princeton, N.J., 1993), 86–89 and 92–93.

3. A good starting point in the literature on the Gulf War is Rick Atkinson, *Crusade: The Untold Story of the Persian Gulf War* (Boston and New York, 1993). The reader then can turn to the memoirs of two senior leaders: Colin L. Powell with Joseph E. Persico, *My American Journey* (New York, 1995) and H. Norman Schwarzkopf with Peter Petre, *It Doesn't Take a Hero* (New York, et al., 1992). Tom Clancy with Gen. Fred Franks, Jr. (USA, ret.), *Into the Storm: A Study in Command* (New York, 1997), a combination of biography and memoir, recounts the 1991 Gulf War ground campaign from the perspective of one of the corps commanders. Michael R. Gordon and Bernard E. Trainor, *The Generals' War: The Inside Story of the Conflict in the Gulf* (Boston, et al., 1995) represents the first significant revisionist work about the conflict. There is a sizeable literature on the Gulf War air campaign. Readers who are daunted by the lengthy five volumes of the unclassified *Gulf War Air Power Survey* can read Thomas A. Keaney and Eliot A. Cohen, *Gulf War Air Power Survey Summary Report* (Washington, D.C., 1993). Richard P. Hallion, *Storm over Iraq: Air Power and the Gulf War* (Washington and London, 1992) argues the thesis, as its first page "boldly" declares, that "air power won the Gulf war." Tom Clancy with Gen. Chuck Horner (USAF, ret.), *Every Man a Tiger* (New York, 1999), uses the same format as Clancy's work with Gen. Franks and recounts the air campaign from the viewpoint of its commander. The numbers of Air Force personnel assigned to the theater can be found in the *Gulf War Air Power Survey*, 5: part 1 (Statistical Compendium), 124.

4. Schwarzkopf, *It Doesn't Take a Hero*, 481–91; Resolution 687 (1991), adopted by the Security Council at its 2981st meeting, on 3 Apr 1991. UNSCR 687 also called for a UN observer unit to monitor a demilitarized zone which would be established along the Iraqi-Kuwaiti border, extending ten kilometers into Iraq and five into Kuwait. This DMZ would have created a "trip wire" against a future repetition of Saddam Hussein's aggression to the south. Gen. Schwarzkopf opposed the idea, the State Department withdrew its support for it, and this provision of UNSCR 687 went unenforced (Resolution 687 (1991) and Atkinson, *Crusade*, 490–91).

5. Patrick E. Tyler, "Baghdad Formally Agrees to 'Unjust' U.N. Conditions For Permanent Cease Fire," *New York Times*, 7 Apr 91, A–1.

6. Atkinson, *Crusade*, 488 and 489; Freedman and Karsh, *The Gulf Conflict*, 410–11, 420.

7. Atkinson, *Crusade*, 489; Freedman and Karsh, *The Gulf Conflict*, 419–20. The terms of the temporary cease-fire at Safwan permitted the Iraqis to make helicopter flights, in view of the air campaign's damage to their roads and bridges. Saddam exploited this provision to use his gunships against the Shi'ites (Atkinson, *Crusade*, 489; Freedman and Karsh, *The Gulf Conflict*, 407, 420).

8. Resolution 688 (1991), adopted by the Security Council at its 2982d meeting on 5 Apr 91; Paul Lewis, "U.N. Votes to Condemn Handling of Iraqi Rebels," *New York Times*, 6 Apr 91, A–5; Atkinson, *Crusade*, 490.

9. Clifford Krauss, "U.S. Will Airdrop Food And Clothes To Kurds In Iraq," *New York Times*, 6 Apr 91, A–1; Clyde Haberman, "6 U.S. Planes Begin Airlifting Relief To Kurds In Iraq," *New York Times*, 8 Apr 91, A–1; William T. Y'Blood, "From the Desert to the Mountains," in Bernard Nalty, ed., *Winged Shield, Winged Sword: A History of the United States Air Force*, 2 vols. (Washington, D.C., 1997), 2:486. See also Robert H. Scales, Jr., and the Desert Storm Study Project, *The U.S. Army in the Gulf War: Certain Victory* (Washington, D.C., 1994), 341–53.

10. Elaine Sciolino, "U.S. Warns Against Attack By Iraq on Kurdish Refugees," *New York Times*, 11 Apr 91, A–10; Scales, *Certain Victory*, 351–52.

11. Andrew Rosenthal, "Bush Accuses Iraq of Breaking Truce in Fighting Rebels," *New York Times*, 14 Mar 91, A–1; Thomas L. Friedman, "Decision Not to Help Iraqi Rebels Puts U.S. in an Awkward Position," *New York Times*, 4 Apr

91, A–1.

12. Patrick E. Tyler, "Elusive Victories in Iraq," *New York Times*, 25 Jul 92, A–1; Atkinson, *Crusade*, 498; Michael R. Gordon, "British, French and U.S. Agree To Hit Iraqi Aircraft in the South," *New York Times*, 19 Aug 92, A–1.

13. John Lancaster, "Allies Declare 'No-Fly Zone' in Iraq," *Washington Post*, 27 Aug 92, A1; Gordon, "British, French and U.S. Agree."

14. Resolution 949 (1994), adopted by the Security Council at its 3488th meeting, on 15 Oct 94; Perry, Report to the President, 3.

15. Col. M. Perini, HQ Air Combat Command/PA2, to the Directors of the HQ Air Combat Command Staff, 26 Jun 96; MSgt. David Masko, "Coalition partners ready to move to Prince Sultan," *Southern Watch* 5:34 (4 Sep 96), 3; HQ US Central Command biography of Gen. J.H. Binford Peay III, Oct 94; USAF biographies of Gen. John P. Jumper, Sep 05; Lt. Gen. Carl E. Franklin, May 98; and Maj. Gen. Kurt B. Anderson, Jun 96. Lt. Gen. Jumper was promoted to general in Nov 97 and became Air Force Chief of Staff in Sep 01.

16. 4404th Wing History, vol. 1, 1; Y'Blood, "From the Desert to the Mountains," 487; Schwalier interview, 23 Feb 99.

17. Schwalier interview, 23 Feb 99; USAF biography of Brig. Gen. Terryl J. Schwalier, Feb 96; Grant, "Khobar Towers," 42. The Arabic name of the Eastern Province appears on a map in Richard M. Swain, *"Lucky War": Third Army in Desert Storm* (Fort Leavenworth, Kans., 1997), 5. Grant, "Khobar Towers," 42, notes that Gen. Schwalier was the wing's twelfth commander and narrowly speaking this is correct. If the TAC lineage, which began with Col. Robert Hinds as the unit's first commander, is taken into account, Gen. Schwalier was the wing's thirteenth commander (Gen. Schwalier's comments on "Khobar Towers: Tragedy and Response" manuscript, 21 Oct 04).

18. 4404th Wing History, vol. 1, 3–5 and 95–99. The names of the wing's key personnel also appear in the entries of Biggs, "Khobar Chronology," and were discussed with Gen. Schwalier in a conversation on 23 Feb 99. Commenting on the "Khobar Towers" manuscript in Oct 04, Gen. Schwalier noted that Col. Schultz had been a member of the *Colorado* Air National Guard. Col. Scott Gration was promoted to brigadier general on 1 Oct 99 and to major general on 1 Apr 03 (USAF biography of Brig. Gen. Jonathan S. Gration, Feb 05). In Jun 96 the medical group commander's position was in transition from a three-months assignment to a one-year one. There was a gap between the tours of Lt. Col. (Dr.) Robert N. Bertoldo, the last group commander to serve three months, and Col. (Dr.) Rolando R. Santa Ana, the first to serve a year. It was filled by Dr. Robb (4404th Wing History, vol. 1, 3–5, 95–99; interview with Lt. Col. Douglas J. Robb, Commander, 347th Aerospace Medical Squadron, Moody AFB, Ga., 6 Jun 97; "Change of Command Ceremony: 440th Medical Group (Prov.), King Abdul Aziz Air Base, Kingdom of Saudi Arabia," 10 Jul 96). Dr. Robb was promoted to colonel on 30 May 2000 and to brigadier general on 1 June 2007 (USAF biography of Brig. Gen. (Dr.) Douglas J. Robb, July 07).

19. Y'Blood, "From the Desert to the Mountains," 487; Schwalier interview, 23 Feb 99.

20. Y'Blood, "From the Desert to the Mountains," 487; Schwalier interview, 23 Feb 99; 4404th Wing, wing Operations Center, Air Tasking Order chart for 25 Jun 96, in 4404th Wing History, vol. 7, supporting document II–D56.

21. Gen. Wayne A. Downing (USA, ret.), "Force Protection Assessment of USCENTCOM AOR and Khobar Towers: Report of the Downing Assessment Task Force," 30 Aug 96, 14 (hereafter cited as Downing Report). The wing was operating from eleven locations in four countries at the time Gen. Schwalier reported. Schwalier interview, 23 Feb 99. The deployment of air expeditionary forces to the region expanded these numbers at times to as many as twelve sites in five countries (Grant, "Khobar Towers," 42).

22. Statement by Gen. J.H. Binford Peay, Commander in Chief, U.S. Central Command, Central Command news release, 27 Jul 96; Philip Shenon, "G.I.'s in Saudi Arabia on Alert as Plan for Attack Is Reported," *New York Times*, 12 Jul 96, A8; 4404th Wing History, vol. 1, 93.

23. Perry, Report to the President, 5; Col. M. Perini to the Directors of the HQ Air Combat Command Staff, 26 Jun 96.

24. Friers interview; notes taken during a telephone conversation with Capt. Robert L. Jones,

Personnel Support for Contingency Operations (PERSCO) officer, 99th Mission Support Squadron, Nellis AFB, Nev., 20 Jun 97.

25. Col. M. Perini to the Directors of the HQ Air Combat Command Staff, 26 Jun 96; Jones conversation notes, 7 Nov 96.

26. Swope-Hawley Report, 1:63.

27. LRMC Stress Management Team's After Action Report, 20 Aug 96, 1.

28. Guerrero interview; Jones conversation notes, 20 Jun 97.

29. Interview with Lt. Col. Donald Jozayt, Commander, 71st Rescue Squadron, Patrick AFB, Fla., 4 Feb 97.

30. Grant, "Khobar Towers," 42; Downing Report, 14; LRMC Stress Management Team's After Action Report, 20 Aug 96, 1; Dick interview with author.

31. Jones conversation notes, 20 Jun 97.

32. Commenting on a draft of this work in Oct 04, Gen. Schwalier pointed out that the 58th Fighter Squadron was the wing's primary air-to-air unit, but not its only one. The 4404th's F–16s also flew air-to-air missions.

33. 33d Fighter Wing's public affairs biography of Lt. Col. Douglas R. Cochran, May 95; Cochran interview.

34. Ziegler interview; McCarthy interview.

35. John Lancaster, "Few See Saudi Stability Threatened by Militants," *Washington Post*, 27 Jun 96, 24; Perry, Report to the President, 2; Patrick Pexton, "Desert Moves," *Air Force Times* 57:4 (26 Aug 96), 3.

36. Schwalier interview, 23 Feb 99.

37. Notes taken during telephone conversations with Saeed Al Ahmed, Islamic Section, and Alice Umbarac, Press Section, Royal Embassy of Saudi Arabia, 10 Jul 97; Peter Mansfield, *The Arabs* (London, et al., 1985), 206, 348.

38. "The Remarkable Transformation of the Dammam–Dhahran–Al-Khobar Triangle," webpage of the Royal Embassy of Saudi Arabia, 29 Jun 98; Mansfield, *The Arabs*, 348; Umbarac conversation notes, 10 Jul 97.

39. Downing Report, 47; Bradley Graham, "Perry Calls U.S. Military Housing in Saudi Arabia Safe but Austere," *Washington Post*, 1 Dec 96, A–37; Saeed Al Ahmed conversation notes; Perry, Report to the President, 4.

40. Swope-Hawley Report, 1:57. Photographs taken by Capt. Jones, and others, contributed to this description of the Khobar Towers complex. On 23 Feb 99, the author showed Gen. Schwalier a map of the compound labeled "Khobar Towers"; the general immediately remarked that it represented only the American part of the complex.

41. Statement by Gen. J.H. Binford Peay, Central Command news release, 27 Jul 96; Perry, Report to the President, 1; Col. M. Perini to the Directors of the HQ Air Combat Command Staff, 26 Jun 96; Swope-Hawley Report, 1:57; Schwalier conversation notes, 23 Feb 99.

42. Schwalier conversation notes, 24 Feb 99. A nine-tenths of a mile distance can be established from a map in the Bomb Damage Survey Executive Summary, 2. Capt. Matthew Winker, a jogger, ran the perimeter and also put the distance at nine-tenths of a mile (Winkler interview).

43. Air Force Khobar Towers map; Schwalier conversation notes, 24 Feb 99. On the origin of the "Towers" in "Khobar Towers," it is noteworthy that Lt. Col. James J. Traister, the commander of the wing's security police squadron, used the noun "tower" interchangeably with "building" in his end of tour report (SP Commander EOTR).

44. Army Khobar Towers map; plan of a typical floor of a Khobar Towers dormitory, provided by Col. Robb; Robb interview. The photographs taken by Capt. Jones also contributed to this description of the Khobar Towers compound.

45. Schwalier comments on "Khobar Towers"; Grant, "Khobar Towers," 42; Schwalier interview, 23 Feb 99; Dick interview with author; AFHSO oral history interview 26. The Eastern Region map established the Khobar Towers-ARAMCO distance.

46. 4404th Civil Engineering Squadron, Five-Year Facilities Improvement Plan FY 96–FY 00, 24 May 96, in 4404th Wing History, vol. 7, supporting document IV–2, 8, 9.

47. Swope-Hawley Report, 1:57; Schwalier conversation notes, 24 Feb 99. Here again, the photographs taken by Capt. Jones, and others, contributed to this description of the area around the compound.

48. Undated "Dhahran Area Guide Map," provided by the Air Force Manpower and Personnel Center to the Air Force Chief of Staff's operations group; Eastern Region map; Winkler interview. Photographs taken by Capt. Jones

and others of the area around the compound again were helpful.

49. "Major Air Force deployments," *Air Force Times* 56:47 (24 Jun 96), 31.

Chapter Three

1. Atkinson, *Crusade*, 416–23; Donatella Lorch, "Twisted Hulk of Warehouse Tells a Grim Story of Death," *New York Times*, 27 Feb 91, A–18; Schwalier conversation notes, 23 Feb 99.
2. Howard Schneider, "Bombing in Saudi City Kills American," *Washington Post*, 7 Oct 01, A–1.
3. Lancaster, "Few See Saudi Stability Threatened."
4. Schwalier interview, 23 Feb 99. See also Grant, "Khobar Towers," 43.
5. Elaine Sciolino, "Blasts Wreck U.S. Military Aid Installation—35 to 40 Are Wounded in Attack," *New York Times*, 14 Nov 95, A–1; "Background: Terrorism in the AOR," an undated, unpaginated report written by SrA. Ronald J. Biggs, historian of the 4404th Composite Wing (Prov.); Perry, Report to the President, 2. "AOR" is an acronym for "area of responsibility"; in the title of SrA. Biggs's report, it refers to the U.S. Central Command's area of responsibility, Southwest Asia.
6. Grant, "Khobar Towers," 43; Sciolino, "Blasts Wreck U.S. Military Aid Installation," A–1; Steven Erlanger, "U.S. Commanders at Saudi Base Defend Efforts to Avoid Attack," *New York Times*, 28 Jun 96, A–1; message from the Office of the Secretary of State to all diplomatic and consular posts, and several other addressees, "Public Announcement—Saudi Arabia," 15 Nov 96, 2336 zulu time.
7. Lancaster, "Few See Saudi Stability Threatened," A–24; Philip Shenon, "Officials Say Size of Bomb Caught Military by Surprise," *New York Times*, 27 Jun 96, A–1.
8. Nelan, "Gulf Shock Waves," 23; Grant, "Khobar Towers," 43.
9. Grant, "Khobar Towers," 43.
10. Interview with Maj. Bennie L. Umstead II, executive officer to the commander of the Joint Task Force Southwest Asia, Andrews AFB, Md., 19 Aug 97.
11. Grant, "Khobar Towers,"43; "U.S. Commanders at Saudi Base," *New York Times*, 28 Jun 96, A–1; AFHSO Khobar Towers oral history interview 31.
12. Downing Report, 48; AFHSO Khobar Towers oral history interview 5. See also interview 23. Another 4404th Wing document also was used in writing this paragraph.
13. Grant, "Khobar Towers," 43.
14. Lt. Gen. James F. Record, "Independent Review of the Khobar Towers Bombing: Part A," 31 Oct 96, and "Part B, Accountability Review," 3 volumes, 20 Dec 96, B, I:71 (hereafter cited as the Record Report; this is a secretno foreign document, but all the material used from it is unclassified); Swope-Hawley Report, 1:33; Biggs interview; Grant, "Khobar Towers," 43. The base commander established the threatcon level on the basis of many sources; in the case of oversea installations, these included information from the US embassy in the country (Swope-Hawley Report, 1:86–87; Umstead interview). On the security measures taken at the Khobar Towers between the Riyadh bombing and 25 Jun 96, see also the 4404th Wing History, vol. 1, 68–70. This section is unclassified; one of its paragraphs is "for official use only." Wing documents show that the wing commander addressed the Battle Staff Directives to his group commanders, for them to implement.
15. Swope-Hawley Report, 1:6; "Explanation of Terrorist Threat Conditions," Appendix D of the HNSC Report, citing Air Force Instruction 31-210, 1 Jul 95. See also the Guerrero and Biggs interviews. In Aug 01 the Department of Defense, adopting a recommendation of the *USS Cole* Commission, replaced term "threatcon" with "force protection condition," or "FPCON" (SSgt. Amy Parr, "Changes made to force protection programs," *The Beam*, Bolling AFB, D.C., 59:31 (10 Aug 01), 1).
16. "Explanation of Terrorist Threat Conditions," Appendix D of the HNSC Report; 11th Wing office of public affairs, "Know Your Threatcons," 24 Aug 94. A commander declared Threatcon Charlie when either a specific incident or broader intelligence information indicated that a terrorist action was imminent. The additional measures at this level included increasing security police manning; reducing to a minimum the number of entrances to the

installation; checking the identification of every person entering the facility; prohibiting all parking next to structures; suspending all non-essential activities; and restricting the wearing of uniforms and operating of government vehicles in the local community. Threatcon Delta went into effect when a terrorist attack had occurred or when there was intelligence that one was about to take place against a specific target. Some of the additional measures that would be taken at this highest level represented classified information; unclassified ones included identifying all of the vehicles in the area and searching all packages and briefcases. Air Force Instruction 31-210 also recognized as the base level of its conditions a "Threatcon Normal," a routine security posture ("Explanation of Terrorist Threat Conditions," Appendix D of the HNSC Report). For an example of how one specific security measure—the numbers of security police manning posts—differed between Threatcon Bravo and Threatcon Charlie, see the Swope-Hawley Report, 1:32.

17. Swope-Hawley Report, 1:132; Guerrero interview; Biggs interview; interview with SSgt. Jefferson A. Craven, high-voltage electrician, 45th Civil Engineering Squadron, Patrick AFB, Fla., 6 Feb 97.

18. Grant, "Khobar Towers," 43; Biggs interview; Guerrero interview.

19. SP Commander EOTR; Grant, "Khobar Towers," 43; Central Command operating location of the Air Force Office of Special Investigations to the Deputy Commander in Chief, Central Command, 25 Jun 96 (hereafter cited as AFOSI OL, 25 Jun 96); HNSC Report, 6. See also Grant, "Khobar Towers," 45, and Record Report, B, I:71.

20. Record Report, B, I:71; HNSC Report, 6; Grant, "Khobar Towers," 43–44.

21. Record Report, B, I:72; Biggs, "Khobar Chronology," entries for safety, 2210, and SP squadron, 2215, 25 Jun 96; Schwalier conversation notes, 23 Feb 99; notes taken during conversations with SrA. Ronald J. Biggs, Jr., historian of the 4404th Composite Wing (Prov.), Nellis AFB, Nev., 8 Nov 96.

22. Record Report, B, I:72; Schwalier comments on "Khobar Towers."

23. Ibid. This Vulnerability Assessment remains classified. There are open-source discussions of it in the unclassified version of the Record Report; in the Downing Report, 3, 47, 49, 50; and a particularly good one in Grant, "Khobar Towers," 44–45.

24. Grant, "Khobar Towers," 44. See also Record Report, B, I:70–72.

25. Record Report, B, I:70–72. Like the Jan 96 AFOSI Vulnerabilities Assessment, the Jul 95 one remains classified. There are open-source discussions of it in the unclassified version of the Record Report, and the Downing Report, 3, 47, 50.

26. Grant, "Khobar Towers," 44. On the Vulnerability Assessment itself, see note 23.

27. Record Report, B, I:72.

28. Grant, "Khobar Towers," 44. On the Vulnerability Assessment itself, see note 23.

29. Record Report, B, I:74; Grant, "Khobar Towers," 44.

30. Grant, "Khobar Towers," 45; Royal Embassy of Saudi Arabia, *National Guide & Atlas of the Kingdom of Saudi Arabia* (Jeddah, Saudi Arabia, 1989), 106; "Transformation of the Dammam—Dhahran—Al-Khobar Triangle"; Robb interview.

31. Grant, "Khobar Towers," 45; AFHSO Khobar Towers oral history interview 8.

32. Commander, 4404th Wing (Prov.), Battle Staff Directive 96-6, 25 Jun 96, 0900 zulu time, in 4404th Wing History, vol. 12, supporting document U–16; Husted interview.

33. Biggs, "Background: Terrorism in the AOR"; HNSC Report, 11; Bradley Graham, "Bomb Kills 23 Americans at Saudi Base," *Washington Post*, 26 Jun 96, A–1.

34. "Previous Attacks and Threats in Saudi Arabia," *Washington Post*, 27 Jun 96, A–24; Commander, 4404th Wing (Prov.), Battle Staff Directive 96-2, 20 May 96, 1300 zulu time, in 4404th Wing History, vol. 12, supporting document U–16; Biggs, "Background: Terrorism in the AOR."

35. SP Commander EOTR.

36. Schwalier interview, 23 Feb 99; Record Report, B, I:106.

37. Schwalier interview, 23 Feb 99; SP Commander EOTR. See also HNSC Report, 6.

38. HNSC Report, 7; SP Commander EOTR.

39. SP Commander EOTR; Schwalier interview, 23 Feb 99; HNSC Report, 7; Grant, "Khobar Towers," 45; AFOSI OL, 25 Jun 96. The map on page 11 does not show tower dormitory 201; it stands off the area represented, to

the southwest. It appears on other maps, including the "Dhahran Area Guide Map," provided by HQ Air Force Manpower and Personnel Center to the Air Force Chief of Staff's operations group.

40. SP Commander EOTR; AFOSI OL-CENT to the Deputy Commander in Chief, USCENTCOM, 25 Jun 96. See also the Air Force Khobar Towers map.

41. Grant, "Khobar Towers," 45.

42. "Previous Attacks," *Washington Post*, A–24; HNSC Report, 11.

43. Philip Shenon, "Saudi Rebuffed U.S. Efforts To Interrogate 1995 Bombers," *New York Times*, 28 Jun 96, A–1; Youssef M. Ibrahim, "Terror Blast at Saudi Base," *International Herald Tribune*, 14 Nov 95, 1; Philip Shenon, "Saudi Bombers Got Outside Support, Perry Tells Panel," *New York Times*, 10 Jul 96, A–1.

44. Grant, "Khobar Towers," 46; Schwalier interview, 23 Feb 99; Swope-Hawley Report, 1:82.

45. Grant, "Khobar Towers," 46; Schwalier interview, 23 Feb 99; Schwalier conversation notes, 23 Feb 99; Swope-Hawley Report, 1:82. An unclassified portion of a classified intelligence report prepared for the Air Force Chief of Staff gives an exact date, in May.

46. Schwalier interview, 23 Feb 99. A document provided by the Joint Chiefs of Staff office of public affairs was used to date the Chairman's trip.

47. Text of speech [29 May 96] by Chairman of the Joint Chiefs of Staff Gen. John M. Shalikashvili, Office of the Special Assistant for Public Affairs of the Office of the Chairman, Joint Chiefs of Staff. Minor changes in punctuation were made in the Chairman's 29 May speech at Dhahran as quoted in this paragraph. Gen. Schwalier pointed out that the issue of terrorism was never raised during Gen. Shalikashvili's visit and that the Chairman evidently considered the region safe enough for his wife to accompany him on this tour (Schwalier interview, 23 Feb 99).

48. Swope-Hawley Report, 1:106–7; SSgt. Guy Renkel, "Threatcon Bravo: More than just long hours," *Gulf View* 7:16 (18 Apr 96), 3; see also Swope-Hawley Report, 1:106–7. A 4404th Wing document also was used to write this paragraph.

49. Biggs, "Background: Terrorism in the AOR." Checking cars for explosives was much on the minds of a number of people, in addition to the security police. See, for example, Robb and Husted interviews.

50. Swope-Hawley, 1:132. A wing "stand up" was the commander's meeting with his or her staff, typically held weekly. The group commanders and other subordinates would report briefly to the wing commander on their area of responsibility and receive his or her guidance on specific issues.

51. Schwalier interview, 23 Feb 99; Biggs, "Background: Terrorism in the AOR." On the security meetings, see also the Umstead interview.

52. AFOSI OL, 25 Jun 96.

53. Record Report, B, I:74; Schwalier conversation notes, 23 Feb 99; AFHSO Khobar Towers oral history interview 31; Grant, "Khobar Towers," 42; Schwalier comments on "Khobar Towers." On Gen. Schwalier's interest in security briefings, see also Biggs, "Background: Terrorism in the AOR."

54. Schwalier interview, 23 Feb 99; AFHSO Khobar Towers oral history interview 31.

55. Biggs interview; Schwalier interview, 23 Feb 99; "Saudi Bombers Got Outside Support," *New York Times*, 10 Jul 96, A–1; Biggs, "Background: Terrorism in the AOR." See also Husted interview.

56. AFOSI OL, 25 Jun 96; SP Commander EOTR; Air Force Khobar Towers map.

57. Commander, 4404th Wing (Prov.), Battle Staff Directive 96-4, 31 May 96, 1700 zulu time, in 4404th Wing History, vol. 12, supporting document U–16; Biggs interview; AFOSI OL, 25 Jun 96. On the distances, see Swope-Hawley Report, 1:106 and the Eastern Region map. Gen. Schwalier also confirmed them in a 23 Feb 99 conversation.

58. SP Commander EOTR; Record Report, B, I:106; AFOSI OL, 25 Jun 96.

59. SP Commander EOTR; AFOSI OL, 25 Jun 96.

60. Commander, 4404th Wing (Prov.), Battle Staff Directive 96-5, 4 Jun 96, 0700 zulu time; Schwalier interview, 23 Feb 99.

61. Burgess interview; interview with 1st. Lt. Stephanie Bronson, civil engineer, 45th Civil Engineering Squadron, Patrick AFB, Fla., 6 Feb 97; interview with SSgt. Boris Rudinski, 741st Maintenance Squadron, Patrick AFB, Fla., 5

Feb 97.

62. Interview with Capt. Russell D. Barile, pilot, 71st Rescue Squadron, Patrick AFB, Fla., 4 Feb 97; Capt. Jeff Prichard, 59th Fighter Squadron, quoted in Steven Komarow, "There was warning, but it still wasn't enough," *USA Today*, 27 Jun 96, 1A.

63. Grant, "Khobar Towers," 45; Record Report, B, I:26.

64. Nathan Alderman, 347th Wing public affairs, "Dhahran doctor details disaster," 12 Jul 96, memorandum copy of an Air Combat Command News Service story; Robb interview; roster of the 4404th Medical Group, 6 Jul 96; Biggs, "Khobar Chronology," entry for transportation squadron, 1000, 20 Jun 96, 1000.

65. Record Report, B, I:24; Schwalier interview, 23 Feb 99; SSgt. Richard Roberts, "Terrorism: Real threat exists in AOR; stay alert, be observant," *Gulf View* 7:25 (20 Jun 96), 3; Dick interview with author; Maj. Gen. Dan Dick (USAF, ret.), comments on "Khobar Towers: Tragedy and Response" manuscript, 17 May 05.

66. HNSC Report, 7; "Shaw wounded come home," *The Item*, Shaw AFB, S.C., 30 Jun 96, 7A; Philip Shenon, "Saudis Offer U.S. Full Cooperation In Bombing Inquiry," *New York Times*, 1 Jul 96, A–1. In writing this paragraph the author also used unclassified material from some summary papers and memoranda that remain classified.

67. HNSC Report, 7. On the Saudi reservations about moving the northern perimeter, see also press accounts such as Jack Kelley, "Warnings plentiful in Saudi bombing," *USA Today*, 26 Aug 96, 16A; and "U.S. General Didn't Tell Superiors of Saudi Refusal to Widen Buffer," *Washington Post*, 2 Jul 96, A–5.

68. Shenon, "Saudi Bombers Got Outside Support," A–1; "Shaw wounded," *The Item*, 30 Jun 96, 7A; transcript of U.S. Navy Capt. Michael Doubleday's Department of Defense news briefing, 2 Jul 96, 2:30 p.m. See also "Pentagon backs off assertion that Saudis refused tougher security," *Philadelphia Inquirer*, 3 Jul 96, 10.

69. "U.S. General Didn't Tell Superiors" A–5; "U.S. Commanders at Saudi Base," *New York Times*, 28 Jun 96, A–1.

70. "U.S. Commanders at Saudi Base," *New York Times*, 28 Jun 96, A–1; Graham, "Bomb Won't Deter U.S.," A–1.

71. Bomb Damage Survey Executive Summary, 8.

72. AFHSO Khobar Towers oral history interview 29; Dick interview with author.

73. AFOSI OL, 25 Jun 96.

Chapter Four

1. Umstead interview; Dick interview with author; Air Combat Command News Service to Air Combat Command unit public affairs officers and other addressees, 15 Jul 96. Gen. Dick was promoted to major general on 1 Aug 98 and retired on 1 Jul 03.

2. Umstead interview; Treadway interview; interview with Maj. Cynthia Coles, assistant chief, standardization and evaluation, 86th Operations Group, 86th Aeromedical Evacuation Squadron, Ramstein Air Base, Germany, 6 Mar 97.

3. Alderman, "Dhahran doctor details disaster"; Robb interview. Even after Dr. Robb and his companions returned to the Khobar Towers and learned from a security policeman at the gate about the bombing, Robb continued to believe there had been an explosion downtown: he assumed there must have been a multiple bombing.

4. HNSC Report, 1; Umstead interview.
5. Bruffy interview.
6. Shafer conversation notes.
7. Berry interview.
8. Barile interview; Berry interview.
9. Barile interview; Berry interview.
10. McCarthy interview.
11. Ibid.; Valencia interview; Cochran interview.
12. McCarthy interview; Treadway interview.
13. McCarthy interview.
14. Burgess interview; list of active duty personnel injured at Dhahran compiled by the Secretary of the Air Force's office of public affairs, 28 Jun 96 (hereafter cited as Secretary's list of injured personnel); list of hospitalized casualties prepared by the PERSCO office, Mission Support Squadron, 4404th Composite Wing (Prov.), 29 Jun 96 (hereafter cited as PERSCO's list of hospitalized casualties); Schwalier con-

versation notes, 24 Feb 99. Some sources, such as PERSCO's list of hospitalized casualties and PERSCO office messages, refer to the MODA complex as "MODA 1." Gen. Schwalier explained that there were several such facilities across Saudi Arabia and that the "1" identifed this one as being in Dhahran as opposed to, for example, MODA 3, in Riyadh (Schwalier conversation notes, 23 Feb 99). The MODA complex included King Abdul Aziz Air Base Hospital. Air Force personnel generally used the term "MODA Hospital" to mean the King Abdul Aziz Hospital (Dr. Kamal Shahab, chief of surgery, King Abdul Aziz Air Base Hospital, to Perry D. Jamieson, 10 Apr 99).

15. Burgess interview.
16. Ibid.
17. Ibid.; Ziegler interview. The exchange is quoted as Sgt. Burgess recalled it in his oral history interview: Ziegler did not quote himself in his interview, and Burgess is the better witness to his own words. Ziegler's memory of Burgess's reply was in fact very similar: "You sit right there, and I'll be up." As in many other instances where two or more interviewees discussed the same subject in their interviews, the accounts in these two interviews, given six months after that stressful night, are remarkably similar.
18. Burgess interview.
19. Ziegler interview.
20. Ibid.
21. Ibid.
22. Ibid.; William Matthews, "Most hurt in bombing return to duty," *Air Force Times* 57:13 (28 Oct 96), 31; Secretary's list of injured personnel.
23. Ziegler interview; Burgess interview.
24. Ziegler interview; Burgess interview.
25. Burgess interview. Sgt. Burgess provided SrA. Jerwoski's name in a subsequent conversation with SSgt. Yancy Mailes, historian, 33d Fighter Wing.
26. Burgess interview; Ziegler interview; list of confirmed deceased, compiled by the Secretary of the Air Force's office of public affairs, 1 Jul 96 (hereafter cited as Secretary's list of confirmed deceased).
27. Burgess interview; Treadway interview; Matthews, "Most hurt in bombing," 31. For a few of many references to the importance of shoes that night, see Aleson interview; Bronson interview; Winkler interview.
28. Burgess interview; Ziegler interview; Secretary's list of injured personnel.
29. Barile interview; Morelock interview; PERSCO's list of hospitalized casualties.
30. Morelock interview; Ziegler interview; Burgess interview.
31. Burgess interview. Many sources mentioned the uncertainty about the condition of the building, or the possibility of further attacks. For a few examples see Coles interview and Lt. Col. Thomas H. Shafer's undated nominations of Capt. Russell D. Barile, MSgt. Dwayne R. Berry, and others for the Airman's Medal; Morelock interview.
32. Guerrero interview; Watkins, "They didn't hesitate," 13; transcript of "Aftermath of Saudi Bombing," ABC World News Tonight, ABC Television, 27 Jun 96, 6:30 p.m.; Bryant, "Tested by terror," 5.
33. Guerrero interview.
34. Christopher Dickey, "Target: America," *Newsweek* 128:7 (8 Jul 96), 27; Watkins, "They didn't hesitate," 13.
35. Winkler interview; Morelock interview.
36. Winkler interview; Morelock interview. See also "25 Jun 96: Mike Morelock."
37. Winkler interview; Morelock interview; "25 Jun 96: Mike Morelock."
38. Winkler interview; Secretary's list of injured personnel; PERSCO's list of hospitalized casualties.
39. Morelock interview; Col. Shafer's undated nomination of Capt. Michael D. Morelock for the Airman's Medal; Friers interview.
40. Morelock interview; Winkler interview.
41. Morelock interview; "25 Jun 96: Mike Morelock."
42. Ibid.; Winkler interview.
43. Morelock interview; "25 Jun 96: Mike Morelock."
44. Morelock interview; Secretary's list of injured personnel; PERSCO's list of hospitalized casualties.
45. "25 Jun 96: Mike Morelock"; Morelock interview.
46. Morelock interview; "25 Jun 96: Mike Morelock."
47. Morelock interview; Col. Shafer's undated nomination of Capt. Morelock; Aleson interview. See also Berry interview. The day after the bombing, MSgt. Dwayne R. Berry, the first

sergeant of the deployed 71st Rescue Squadron, traveled with Col. Shafer to visit the wounded members of the 71st who were patients in Dhahran hospitals. Sgt. Berry characterized Col. Shafer as "severely injured."

48. Morelock interview.

49. Ibid.; Ziegler interview; Burgess interview.

50. Morelock interview; Graham, "Bomb Won't Deter U.S.," A–1; Col. Shafer's undated nomination of MSgt. William F. Sine for the Airman's Medal; Secretary's list of injured personnel.

51. Col. Shafer's undated nomination of SSgt. Matthew A. Wells for the Airman's Medal; Morelock interview; Winkler interview.

52. Morelock interview; Winkler interview.

53. Guerrero interview; Biggs interview; AFNS video tape, at the Khobar Towers exhibit in the Enlisted Heritage Hall, Gunter Annex, Maxwell AFB, Ala., 12 Dec 03.

54. Secretary's list of injured personnel; Guererro interview. A document written by SrA. Dick also was used to write this paragraph.

55. Col. Shafer's undated nomination of Capt. Lawrence H. Branch for the Airman's Medal; Secretary's list of injured personnel.

56. Schwalier conversation notes, 23 Feb 99; Secretary's list of injured personnel.

57. Biggs interview.

Chapter Five

1. Secretary's list of confirmed deceased; "Air Force clarifies status of Dhahran attack victims," *AFNS Review*, 3 Jul 96, 3. Biographical sketches of the deceased appear in the backmatter.

2. Secretary's list of confirmed deceased; "Air Force clarifies status," 3. Airman Morgera's unit and TSgt. Nguyen's nickname are given as they appear on the Khobar Towers memorial at Eglin AFB.

3. Secretary's list of confirmed deceased; "Air Force clarifies status," 3. This source lists Capt. Haun as Leland T. Haun, while the Khobar Towers memorial at Patrick AFB, Fla. has L. Timothy Haun. His full name was Leland Timothy Haun, and he went by Tim Haun. The 71st Rescue Squadron moved from Patrick AFB to Moody AFB, Ga., about a year after the Khobar Towers bombing (AFNS, "Air Force announces force structure change," 2 May 97).

4. Secretary's list of confirmed deceased. A1C. Lester's rank is given here as it appears on the Khobar Towers memorials at Eglin and Patrick AFBs.

5. Robb, "Medical Response"; McCarthy interview.

6. Robb, "Medical Response." Messages sent by the PERSCO office of the 4404th Mission Support Squadron state that Dr. Robb pronounced the nineteen dead on the scene. One example among the nineteen: message from the PERSCO office of the 4404th Mission Support Squadron to HQ Air Force Personnel Center and several other addressees, "Casualty Report, Initial Death Report, Hostile," 29 Jun 96, 0145 zulu time.

7. Message from the PERSCO office of the 4404th Mission Support Squadron to HQ Air Force Personnel Center, "Casualty Report, Abbreviated, Hostile," 22 Jul 96, 1435 zulu time. At least two factors give weight to these numbers. First, the PERSCO office was the personnel office of the deployed unit and its statistics were official ones. Second, by 22 Jul nearly a month had passed after the bombing and a reliable accounting became feasible. The two airmen very severely injured were SrA. Paul A. Blais and SrA. Roger K. Kaalekahi. The seven severely injured were: Capt. Sandra J. Beneway, SSgt. Manuel J. Carrasco, MSgt. George G. Dyer III, Capt. Thomas F. Edman, A1C. Shawn K. Hale, A1C. Jon C. Schamber, and A1C. Frank D. Sills.

8. Robb, "Medical Response." The Downing task force adopted Dr. Robb's numbers: Downing Report, 55. Gen. Schwalier, writing soon after the attack, gave a lower figure (148) for the number taken to hospitals in Dhahran, but a very similar one (69) for admissions (Brig. Gen. Terryl J. Schwalier, "Dhahran Bombing Fatality Accountability," 30 Jun [96]). The medical group's "Chronological Record of Medical Care," Standard Form 600 report for Jun 96 gave the same number as Dr. Robb for those hospitalized (202) and stated that the clinic saw 425 patients on 25 Jun. This figure presumably included the 20 or so airmen that the facility would treat during any given day. The "Chrono-

logical Record" puts the number hospitalized at 67 (4404th Wing History, vol. 7, supporting document V–4). Dr. Robb's figures, given in the text, represent the most mature, and best, statistics.

9. Treadway interview.

10. Robb interview; Treadway interview; notes taken during a telephone conversation with SMSgt. Fred Clark, Recognition Programs Branch, Directorate of Personnel Programs Management, HQ Air Force Personnel Center, Randolph AFB, Tex., 17 Nov 97; Julie Bird, "In the wake of disaster... Airmen injured in Dhahran will receive Purple Hearts," *Air Force Times* 57:11 (5 Aug 96), 7.

11. Graham, "Bomb Won't Deter U.S.," A–1; "4404th Medical Group (P) Events Chronology," entry for 1 Jul 96, 1000, chronology compiled by the 4404th Medical Group (Prov.), 22 Jul 96 (hereafter cited as "4404th Medical Group Chronology"); Robb interview. A report persisted that, somewhat later than the truck bombing at the Khobar Towers, a series of bombs exploded in a downtown Dhahran shopping mall frequented by Americans and other foreigners. Many of the Saudi casualties may have occurred there. (See the wing Operations Center Log of Events, entry for 25 Jun 96, 2311, in 4404th Wing History, vol. 8, supporting document VI–11; "Dhahran up close and Personal," an undated account written by SSgt. Darryl A. Parker, the noncommissioned officer in charge of the Small Computer Concept Center; McCarthy interview; Husted interview.) Dr. Robb and other medical professionals compiled the "4404th Medical Group Chronology" soon after the attack, and SrA. Biggs included material from it in his "Khobar Chronology."

12. Dick interview with author; Schwalier interview, 24 Feb 99; Graham, "Bomb Won't Deter U.S.," A–1. Gen. Dick stated that the Americans saw two deceased children in an emergency room. It is very unlikely that these were the two young people Secretary Christopher visited because on 26 Jun State Department representative Nicholas Burns predicted of the children whom the Secretary called on: "They're both going to make it, they're in pretty good spirits." (Graham, "Bomb Won't Deter U.S.," 1.) As Gen. Dick, Dr. Robb, and others emphasized, the Saudis would not discusss their casualties.

13. 4404th Wing History, vol. 1, 81.

14. Barile interview.

15. Morelock interview; Bomb Damage Survey Executive Summary, 1.

16. Bomb Damage Survey Executive Summary, 1; Defense Special Weapons Agency, "Dhahran Crater" briefing slide, n.d.; Burgess interview.

17. Bomb Damage Survey Executive Summary, 3.

18. Ibid., 2; McCarthy interview; Biggs interview.

19. Bomb Damage Survey Executive Summary, 4. Early press accounts put the yield much lower (Graham, "Bomb Won't Deter U.S.," A–1; Shenon, "Saudi Bombers Got Outside Support," A–1).

20. Robb, "Medical Response"; Defense Special Weapons Agency, "Murrah Building Oklahoma City" briefing slide, n.d.; Robert D. McFadden, "Blast Hits Trade Center, Bomb Suspected; 5 Killed, Thousands Flee Smoke In Towers," *New York Times*, 27 Feb 93, A–1; John Kifner, "At Least 31 Are Dead, Scores Are Missing After Car Bomb Attack In Oklahoma City Wrecks 9-Story Federal Office Building," *New York Times*, 20 Apr 95, A–1. The "Medical Response" briefing states that the explosive tonnage at Oklahoma City was greater than at the Khobar Towers, but the Defense Special Weapons Agency source, a stronger one on this point, shows that the opposite was the case.

21. Berry interview; Umstead interview; Schwalier conversation notes, 23 Feb 99; Husted interview; McCarthy interview.

22. Biggs, "Khobar Chronology," SP squadron entry for 25 Jun 96, 2154; Khobar Towers map.

23. Biggs, "Khobar Chronology," SP squadron entry for 25 Jun 96, 2155.

24. Schwalier comments on "Khobar Towers"; Schwalier conversation notes, 23 Feb 99; Biggs conversation notes. The SP squadron entry for 25 Jun 96, 2215, has the DCG "ordered to activate" at that time, but in his 21 Oct 04 comments, Gen. Schwalier stated he directed its activation "within the first few minutes" after the bombing.

25. Biggs, "Khobar Chronology," SP squadron entry for 25 Jun 96, 2157.

26. Ibid.; Guerrero interview; Tim Albritton to

U.S. Army, Central Command-Saudi Arabia G–2, 6 Nov 97.

27. Biggs, "Khobar Chronology," SP squadron entry for 25 Jun 96, 2201. At 6 a.m. the next morning, the security police released the two to the custody of Lt. Bader Dewish, the Royal Saudi Military Police commander in the area (Biggs, "Khobar Chronology," SP squadron entry for 26 Jun 96, 0600; unclassified portions of classified documents were used to identify Lt. Bader). Col. Traister said of Lt. Bader: "He is a true asset to our security enhancement. It is my pleasure to have known him and work with him. A true professional." (SP Commander EOTR.)

28. Biggs, "Khobar Chronology," SP squadron entry for 25 Jun 96, 2157.

29. Guerrero interview; Coles interview; Treadway interview. Many of those interviewed who were at the Khobar Towers that night mentioned this bogus alarm of a second attack. See also Biggs, "Khobar Chronology," SP squadron entry for 25 Jun 96, 2157.

30. Biggs, "Khobar Chronology," SP squadron entry for 25 Jun 96, 2155. The Army Khobar Towers map, which is labeled as a building evacuation plan, identifies the area immediately south of the Desert Rose Inn as "Rally Point 1," and the area south of the medical clinic as "Rally Point 2." *If* Army planners had decided before 25 Jun 96 to use the Desert Rose Inn and medical clinic as "rally points" in an emergency, their intentions had no effect on the events the night of the bombing. Gen. Schwalier later offered two points about these map designations. First, he pointed out that although he coordinated all of his battle staff directives with the Army, as well as the French and British, he remained unaware of any Army plans to use the clinic and dining hall as rally points. Second, he noted that as far as he knew, no Army personnel reported to either of these buildings that night (Schwalier conversation notes, 23 Feb 99). The Air Force Khobar Towers map has the medical clinic labeled incorrectly as Building 108. It was Building 111; 108 was just to the northeast (Air Force Khobar Towers map; Army Khobar Towers map). SSgt. Rudolph Grimm II, a dental technician who lived and worked in Building 111, brought this map error to the author's attention.

31. Biggs, "Khobar Chronology," SP squadron entry for 25 Jun 96, 2157, and transportation squadron entry for 25 Jun 96, 2205; Umstead interview.

32. "4404th Medical Group Chronology," entry for 25 Jun 96, 2202; Robb interview; testimony of MSgt. [Wayne] Mello, appendix to Secretary of Defense William S. Cohen, Report on Personal Accountability for Force Protection at Khobar Towers, 31 Jul 97, 14 (hereafter cited as Cohen Report); Lt. Col. Douglas Robb, Office of Health and Environment, Office of the Surgeon General, HQ USAFE, to Dr. Perry D. Jamieson, AFHSO, 8 Apr 98.

33. Col. Shafer's undated nomination of SSgt. Matthew A. Wells for the Airman's Medal.

34. Coles interview; Aleson interview.

35. Cochran interview; McCarthy interview; Treadway interview.

36. Aleson interview; Morelock interview.

37. Coles interview; interview with SSgt. Rudolph Grimm II, dental technician, 45th Medical Group, Patrick AFB, Fla., 6 Feb 97; Robb interview; Biggs, "Khobar Chronology," clinic entry for 3 Jul 96, 1400.

38. Schwalier comments on "Khobar Towers." The ellipses are Gen. Schwalier's.

39. MSgt. M. Lipparelli, HQ Air Combat Command Chaplains Office to [Lt. Col. T.] Wuerffel, HQ Air Education and Training Command Chaplains Office, 26 Jun 96. Col. (Chaplain) John Lundin, senior chaplain for the Kaiserslautern Military Community, which included Ramstein Air Base, Landstuhl Regional Medical Center, Kleber Kaserne, Vogelweh Complex, and other facilities, explained that during the 1990s, the Air Force had a shortage of Roman Catholic chaplains and it was fortunate that one happened to be available for Khobar Towers at its time of need (interview with Col. (Chaplain) John Lundin, senior chaplain for the Kaiserslautern Military Community, Ramstein Air Base, Germany, 3 Mar 97; Dan Cragg, *Guide to Military Installations* (Mechanicsburg, Pa., 1994), 357–58).

40. Aleson interview; Lt. Col. (Chaplain) S. Frick, HQ Air Combat Command Chaplains Office, to Col. (Chaplain) J. Blair, HQ USAF, Personnel, Materiel, and Readiness Division, Office of the Chief of the Chaplain Service, and other addressees, 27 Jun 96; Biggs, "Khobar Chronology," chaplain entry for 25 Jun 96, 2155. On the chaplains' response to the attack, see also the Chaplains Office Report, 1 May to

Notes to pages 60–63

1 Aug [96] and Lt. Col. (Chaplain) Dennis E. Aleson's Operation Southern Watch After Action Report, 27 Mar–4 Jul 96, in the 4404th Wing History, vol. 2, supporting documents I–10 and I–14.

41. Schwalier interview, 24 Feb 99; Schwalier comments on "Khobar Towers"; SP Commander EOTR.

42. Schwalier comments on "Khobar Towers."

43. Matt Labash, "The Scapegoat: How the Secretary of Defense Ended the Career of an Exemplary Air Force General," *The Weekly Standard* 3:11 (24 Nov 97), 20–21; Air Combat Command News Service to All Air Combat Command Unit Public Affairs Officers and other addressees, 15 Jul 96. An excerpt of Labash's article appeared in *Air Force Times* 58:18 (8 Dec 97), 12–16. On Gen. Schwalier's letter writing that night, see also Dick interview with author. Gen. Schwalier's end of tour report is in the 4404th Wing History, vol. 7, supporting document III–6.

44. Dick interview with author. During this interview, Gen. Dick produced a scrapbook and showed the author the original note, written in pen on Gen. Schwalier's stationery. Probably for greater clarity, the Labash article altered the text slightly, to: "Dan, Welcome to Dhah . . . " This work follows the original note: "Dan, Welcome to Dh—."

45. Schwalier interview, 24 Feb 99; Dick interview with author.

46. Schwalier interview, 24 Feb 99.

47. Umstead interview.

48. Ibid; Dick interview with author.

49. Schwalier interview, 24 Feb 99.

50. Ibid.; Schwalier comments on "Khobar Towers."

51. Schwalier interview, 24 Feb 99.

52. Ibid.

53. Ibid.; Biggs, "Khobar Chronology," operations group entry for 25 Jun 96, 2153. SrA. Biggs and SSgt. Guerrero identified the "Saber" call signs used on the brick radios.

54. Biggs, "Khobar Chronology," operations group entry for 25 Jun 96, 2215; Biggs conversation notes; Swope- Hawley Report, 1:121; Schwalier conversation notes, 23 Feb 99; USAF biography of Lt. Gen. Tad J. Oelstrom. Oelstrom was promoted to lieutenant general on 1 Aug 97, when he became superintendent of the USAF Academy. The author also found information about Tadtown in the unclassified portions of some classified documents.

55. Schwalier interview, 24 Feb 99.

56. Biggs, "Khobar Chronology," operations group entry for 25 Jun 96, 2215; Schwalier interview, 24 Feb 99.

57. Ibid.

58. Robb interview; "4404th Medical Group Chronology," entry for 25 Jun 96, 2225.

59. Dick interview with author.

60. Schwalier interview, 24 Feb 99; Biggs, "Khobar Chronology," operations group entry for 25 Jun 96, 2215; Burgess interview.

61. Biggs, "Khobar Chronology," SP squadron entry for 25 Jun 96, 2155.

62. "Talking Paper on Dhahran Bombing Fatality Accountability"; Biggs, "Khobar Chronology," operations group entry for 25 Jun 96, 2215; Schwalier interview, 24 Feb 99; Schwalier comments on "Khobar Towers."

63. "Talking Paper on Fatality Accountability"; "4404th Medical Group Chronology," entry for 25 Jun 96, 2240; "Khobar Towers Chronology of Events," clinic and JAG entries for 25 Jun 96, 2240; Col. Robb to Dr. Perry D. Jamieson, 8 Apr 98; Husted interview. The wing Operations Center Log of Events has Gen. Schwalier give Maj. Greenfield this tasking at the 2215 battle staff meeting and also has an entry for an hour later: "Moda Hospital—JAG sent for accountability" (entries for 25 Jun 96, 2215 and 2315, in the 4404th Wing History, vol. 8, supporting document VI–11). The "4404th Medical Group Chronology" covers Greenfield's assignment in a 2240 entry, which also relates some of the information that the major obtained. Gen. Schwalier gave the JAG this tasking shortly after 2215, and began to hear back from him by telephone at 2240. Asked on 23 Feb 99 if these times were approximately correct, Gen. Schwalier agreed.

64. "4404th Medical Group Chronology," entry for 25 Jun 96, 2240. King Fahd University Hospital was administered by King Faisal University Hospital. This fact, and their identical initials, introduced confusion about these two facilities in some Air Force documents (notes taken during an interview with Dr. Feher S. Alsharif, assistant medical attache, Medical Section, Royal Embassy of Saudi Arabia, 8 Apr 99; Dr. Kamal Shahab, chief of surgery, King

Abdul Aziz Air Base Hospital, to Perry D. Jamieson, AFHSO, 10 Apr 99).

65. "4404th Medical Group Chronology," entry for 25 Jun 96, 2240.

66. "Talking Paper on Fatality Accountability"; Biggs, "Khobar Chronology," operations group entry for 25 Jun 96, 2215; Dick interview with author.

67. Air Combat Command News Service to All Air Combat Command Unit Public Affairs Officers, and others, 15 Jul 96; Umstead interview; Dick interview with author.

68. Dick interview with author; Schwalier comments on "Khobar Towers."

69. Biggs, "Khobar Chronology," operations group entries for 25 Jun 96, 2318 and 2335; unclassified portion of a classified message sent by the 4404th Composite Wing Operations Center to HQ Air Combat Command and other addressees, 25 Jun 96, 2135 zulu time.

70. Interview with Col. (Dr.) Dan L. Locker, USAFE command surgeon, Ramstein Air Base, Germany, 4 Mar 97. On 1 Jul 97 Col. Locker was promoted to brigadier general and assigned to command the 81st Medical Group; he retired on 1 Aug 02 (USAF biography of Brig. Gen. (Dr.) Dan L. Locker, Jun 02). The use of daylight time in Europe but not Saudi Arabia sometimes created confusion, a point made by Lt. Col. Bruce Crow, USA, chief of psychology, LRMC, Germany during a 10 Mar 97 interview.

71. Locker interview; 39th Aerospace Medicine Squadron Commander to the USAFE Surgeon General, [Plans office], "39th Medical Group FAST (Flying Ambulance Surgical Team) medical response to the Dhahran, Saudi Arabia terrorist bombing, 26 Jun–3 Jul 96," 16 Jul 96. "FAST team" is a common Air Force useage, with a redundancy: the "T" in the acronym "FAST" stands for "team."

72. Interview with Col. (Dr.) James W. Bost, Commander, 86th Aeromedical Evacuation Squadron, Ramstein Air Base, Germany, 4 Mar 97; 86th Aeromedical Evacuation Squadron Surgeon General to the 86th Operations Group Commander and other addressees, "Medical After Action Report, Dhahran Bombing," 22 Jul 96 (hereafter cited as 86th AES After Action Report.)

73. Bost interview; 59th Medical Wing Critical Care Aeromedical Transport Team (Deployed) to the 86th Aeromedical Evacuation Squadron Commander and other addressees, "Medical After Action Report, Dhahran Bombing," 17 Jul 96 (hereafter cited as 59th Medical Wing After Action Report).

74. Bost interview; 86th Aeromedical Evacuation Squadron Surgeon General to the 86th Operations Group commander and other addressees, 22 Jul 96; Medical Group Chronology, entry for 25 Jun 96, 2350. The small Dhahran aeromedical staging flight referred to by Dr. Bost mustered three nurses and seven medical technicians that night (Robb, "Medical Response"; Coles interview).

75. Lundin interview.

76. Friers interview.

77. Ibid.; Bryant Jordan, "4,794 will add a stripe," *Air Force Times* 56:47 (24 Jun 96), 8. The line numbers of the technical sergeants who had been promoted had become available in Saudi Arabia the same day (interview with MSgt. Cedric Williams, first sergeant, 58th Fighter Squadron, Eglin AFB, Fla., 4 Dec 96).

78. Jozayt interview.

79. Ibid.

80. Ibid. All Khobar Towers telephone service, including the Defense Switched Network, went out immediately after the bombing (Downing Report, 47; point paper on the communications impacts from the Dhahran bombing, prepared by the Operations Division, Directorate of Mission Systems, Deputy Chief of Staff for Communications and Information, HQ USAF, 1 Jul 96).

81. Friers interview.

82. Ibid.; Jozayt interview.

83. Jozayt interview.

84. "Khobar Bombing Chronology," entry for 25 Jun 96, 1355 (chronology prepared by SSgt. Yancy Mailes, historian, 33d Fighter Wing, on 29 Jun 96); interview with Lt. Col. Stan Hill, Commander, 33d Operations Group, Eglin AFB, Fla., 5 Dec 96; Dylewski interview. For a survey history of the Air Force's AEF, see Richard G. Davis, "Immediate Reach, Immediate Power: The Air Expeditionary Force and American Power Projection in the Post Cold War Era," Air Force History and Museum Program pamphlet, 1998. In 2003, the Atlanta airport was renamed Hartsfield-Jackson Atlanta International Airport to honor former mayor Maynard H. Jackson.

85. Mailes, "Khobar Bombing Chronology,"

entry for 25 Jun 96, 1530; Hill interview; interview with Capt. Brenda L. Campbell, public affairs officer, 33d Fighter Wing, Eglin AFB, Fla., 5 Dec 96.

86. Hill interview; Campbell interview.

87. Mailes, "Khobar Bombing Chronology," entry for 25 Jun 96, 1615.

88. Ibid., 1800.

89. Interview of Air Force Chief of Staff Gen. Ronald R. Fogleman by Air Force historian Dr. Richard P. Hallion, 4 Nov 97; "Significant Event Notification Record," an undated summary paper found in the files of the Regional Plans and Issues office of the office of the Deputy Chief of Staff for Air and Space Operations, HQ USAF.

90. Gen. John M. Shalikashvili (USA, ret.) to [Brig. Gen. David A. Armstrong (USA, ret.)], 1 Jan 98, with a marginalia note by Gen. Armstrong, 7 Jan 98. A document prepared in the Office of the Chairman of the Joint Chiefs of Staff was also used in writing this paragraph.

91. Interview of Secretary of the Air Force Dr. Sheila Widnall by Dr. George Watson, historian, AFHSO, 27 Oct 97.

92. Graham, "Bomb Won't Deter U.S.," A–1; transcript of "Bombing in Saudi Arabia," CBS Evening News, CBS Television, 25 Jun 96, 7 p.m.

93. Fogleman interview; DOD photograph number 960626–N–00000–002; Biggs, "Khobar Chronology," entry for 26 Jun 96, 0919.

Chapter Six

1. Bryan E. Bledsoe, Robert S. Porter, and Bruce R. Shade, *Brady Paramedic Emergency Care* (Upper Saddle River, N.J., 1997), 1074. See also Daniel Limmer, Bob Elling, and Michael F. O'Keefe, *Essentials of Emergency Care: A Refresher for the Practicing EMT-B* (Upper Saddle River, N.J., 1996), 203. The "Response" section quotation is from the Robb interview.

2. Robb, "Medical Response"; Capt. Timothy Bailey with Nathan Alderman, "Buddies Cared," *Airman* XL:10 (Dec 96), 11.

3. Bailey, "Buddies Cared," 11.

4. Interview with SSgt. John C. Orlando, information management specialist, 58th Fighter Squadron, Eglin AFB, Fla., 4 Dec 96; AFHSO Khobar Towers oral history interviews 36 and 8.

5. McCarthy interview.

6. Robb interview; Treadway interview; Grimm interview; [a U.S. Army noncommissioned officer] to U.S. Army, Central Command-Saudi Arabia G–2, 6 Nov 97. Sgt. Grimm's superior, Lt. Col. (Dr.) Bruce Lauder, said of him in his monthly report: "SSgt Grimm was treated and released for minor injuries sustained in the 25 Jun 96 terrorist bombing. He had great presence of mind and was a major contributor in the ensuing mass casualty response." (4404th Wing History, vol. 7, supporting document V–5B.)

7. Dick interview with author.

8. Husted interview.

9. Barile interview; MSgt. William Sine, 41st Rescue Squadron/DOJ, to Dr. Perry D. Jamieson, AFHSO, 8 Sep 98.

10. Craven interview.

11. Parker, "Dhahran up close and Personal"; Aleson interview.

12. Robb interview.

13. Downing Report, 55; Robb interview; Treadway interview.

14. Robb interview; Cochran interview; Col. Shafer's undated nominations of SrA. Michael D. Atkins, SSgt. Matthew A. Wells, SrA. Gregory E. Randall, and MSgt. William F. Sine for the Airman's Medal; MSgt. William Sine, 41st Rescue Squadron/DOJ, to Dr. Perry D. Jamieson, AFHSO, 1 and 8 Sep 98.

15. Morelock interview; Col. Shafer's undated nomination of Capt. Michael D. Morelock for the Airman's Medal.

16. Morelock interview.

17. Parker, "Dhahran up close and Personal"; Bailey, "Buddies Cared," 11.

18. Robb interview.

19. Ibid.; "4404th Medical Group Chronology," entry for 3 Jul 96, 1400.

20. Robb interview; Schwalier comments on "Khobar Towers"; Bailey, "Buddies Cared," 9.

21. Robb interview; "4404th Medical Group Chronology," entry for 3 Jul 96, 1400.

22. Schwalier comments on "Khobar Towers."

23. On the designation of this building, see chapter five, note 30.

24. Biggs, "Khobar Chronology," SP squad-

ron entry for 25 Jun 96, 2153; Robb, "Medical Response."

25. Biggs, "Khobar Chronology," clinic entry for 25 Jun 96, 2202; Robb interview; "4404th Medical Group Chronology," entry for 25 Jun 96, 2202; testimony of MSgt. [Wayne] Mello, appendix to the Cohen Report, 14.

26. Biggs, "Khobar Chronology," SP squadron entry for 25 Jun 96, 2157, and transportation squadron entry for 25 Jun 96, 2205; Umstead interview.

27. "4404th Medical Group Chronology," entry for 25 Jun 96, 2202; Treadway interview.

28. "4404th Medical Group Chronology," entry for 25 Jun 96, 2210.

29. Ibid.; Robb interview.

30. William Matthews, "Stunning blast drew a swift medical response," *Air Force Times* 56:49 (8 Jul 96), 13; Robb, "Medical Response"; Robb interview.

31. Matthews, "Stunning blast," 13.

32. Robb, "Medical Response."

33. Treadway interview; Matthews, "Stunning blast," 13; Robb interview; Bailey, "Buddies Cared," 10. PERSCO's list of hospitalized casualties and the Bailey article refer to Dr. Goff as a captain; Dr. Treadway identified him as a major, as did a 17 Jul 96 caption on an official Air Force photograph of him receiving the Airman's Medal.

34. Robb, "Medical Response"; Bailey, "Buddies Cared," 10. The figure twenty-two is derived from Dr. Robb's briefing to Air Force Chief of Staff Gen. Ronald R. Fogleman, which puts the Air Force clinic total at twenty-six. Bailey's article in *Airman* gives the Air Force clinic total as twenty-five.

35. "4404th Medical Group Chronology," entry for 25 Jun 96, 2202; Robb, "Medical Response"; Coles interview. Members of the 4404th were justifiably proud of their efforts on the night of 25 Jun 96. *Airman* magazine's initial coverage of the bombing, an Aug 96 article, mentioned the Air Force and Army medical personnel who flew to Saudi Arabia, but not the members of the 4404th, 4410th, and others already on the scene. The periodical soon heard from readers in Dhahran who believed it had slighted the contributions of those already in place (Arana-Barradas, Johnson, and Norman, "Southern Watch Continues," 19; "Airmail," *Airman* XL:10 (Dec 96), 30).

36. Coles interview; "4404th Medical Group Chronology," entry for 25 Jun 96, 2202.

37. Coles interview.

38. Robb, "Medical Response"; Bailey, "Buddies Cared," 11; Burgess interview.

39. Bailey, "Buddies Cared," 11; Robb, "Medical Response."

40. Robb, "Medical Response"; Bailey, "Buddies Cared," 10.

41. "4404th Medical Group Chronology," entry for 25 Jun 96, 2225; Bailey, "Buddies Cared," 11; Robb, "Medical Response."

42. Robb interview; Grimm interview; Coles interview. Dr. Robb provided a floor plan of the clinic, which appears in the text.

43. Aleson interview; Treadway interview. The floor plan provided by Dr. Robb labels every room in the clinic, including those in the administrative wing.

44. Treadway interview; Grimm interview.

45. "Chronological Record of Medical Care," Standard Form 600 reports for May and Jun 96, in the 4404th Wing History, vol. 7, supporting documents V–3 and V–4; "4404th Medical Group Chronology," entry for 25 Jun 96, 2225; Bailey, "Buddies Cared," 9; Coles interview.

46. Coles interview.

47. Treadway interview.

48. J.E. Mansion, ed., *Heath's Standard French and English Dictionary*, 2 parts (Boston, et al., 1939), 1:859; Harvey D. Grant, Robert H. Murray, Jr., and J. David Bergeron, *Emergency Care* (Englewood Cliffs, N.J., 1986), 458.

49. Alderman, "Dhahran doctor details disaster." Air Combat Command News Service also transmitted at least one other version of this account, through the command's electronic mail service, on 11 Jul 96. These two news service stories are substantially the same. Another variant, co-authored and edited for publication, is Bailey "Buddies Cared."

50. Alderman, "Dhahran doctor details disaster"; Treadway interview.

51. Grant, Murray, and Bergeron, *Emergency Care*, 460; Robb interview.

52. Biggs, "Khobar Chronology," operations group entry for 25 Jun 96, 2215; Dick interview with author.

53. Grimm interview; Robb interview.

54. Rudinski interview; Grimm interview.

55. Robb interview.

Notes to pages 79–83

56. Ibid.; Treadway interview; Downing Report, 55.
57. Robb interview.
58. "4404th Medical Group Chronology," entries for 25 Jun 96, 2155 and 2215; Coles interview.
59. "4404th Medical Group Chronology," entry for 25 Jun 96, 2230; Dick interview with author.
60. "4404th Medical Group Chronology," entry for 25 Jun 96, 2230; Robb interview. Dr. Robb doubtless provided the figure which appears in the Downing Report: "20–30 ambulances making multiple hospital runs" (Downing Report, 55).
61. Robb interview; "4404th Medical Group Chronology," entries for 25 Jun 96, 2300 and 2330; Eastern Region map.
62. "4404th Medical Group Chronology," entry for 26 Jun 96, 0030; Eastern Region map; Robb interview.
63. "4404th Medical Group Chronology," entry for 26 Jun 96, 0030; Dr. Kamal Shahab, chief of surgery, King Abdul Aziz Air Base Hospital, to Perry D. Jamieson, AFHSO, 10 Apr 99; Eastern Region map. The Downing Report, 55, offers very slightly different statistics than this chronology about the Saudi doctors and nurses who reached the clinic before 1 a.m. The text follows the medical group's chronology because this source is more detailed than the Downing Report. The chronology identifies the hospitals and other organizations that contributed to the effort, states the number of M.D.s and R.N.s each sent, and gives their arrival times.
64. Downing Report, 55; "4404th Medical Group Chronology," entry for 25 Jun 96, 2300. See also point paper on the communications impacts from the Dhahran bombing, prepared by the Operations Division's Directorate of Mission Systems, Deputy Chief of Staff for Communications and Information, HQ USAF, 1 Jul 96.
65. "4404th Medical Group Chronology," entry for 25 Jun 96, 2245; point paper on communications impacts, 1 Jul 96; Dick interview with author.
66. Biggs, "Khobar Chronology," communications squadron entry for 26 Jun 96, 0300.
67. Robb interview.
68. Ibid.; Treadway interview; Downing Report, 55.
69. "4404th Medical Group Chronology," entry for 25 Jun 96, 2230; Robb interview; "4404th Medical Group Chronology," entry for 25 Jun 96, 2245. Dr. Treadway said the ambulances were designed to carry four passengers; the medical group's chronology stated that this first run transported five. The circumstances explain the extra patient (Treadway interview; "4404th Medical Group Chronology," entry for 25 Jun 96, 2230).
70. Robb interview; "4404th Medical Group Chronology," entry for 25 Jun 96, 2345.
71. Berry interview; "4404th Medical Group Chronology," entry for 26 Jun 96, 0100.
72. Morelock interview; Bronson interview; interview with Lt. Col. Sherry Conner, DSW, USA, chief, social work services, LRMC, 10 Mar 97.
73. Robb interview.
74. Ibid.
75. Ibid.; "4404th Medical Group Chronology," entry for 26 Jun 96, 0100.
76. Robb interview.
77. Ibid.; Dick interview with author.
78. Treadway interview.
79. Robb interview; "4404th Medical Group Chronology," entry for 26 Jun 96, 0100.
80. Treadway interview; Daniel Cude, "Shaw physician makes a difference," *The Item*, Shaw AFB, S.C., 29 Jun 96, 1A.
81. "U.S. Air Force Chief of Staff presents the Airman's Medal to Maj. Steven Goff," 17 Jul 96 description of a 3 Jul 96 Joint Photographic Experts Group photograph, in Kharmn.HTM, 29 Nov 97 file, "Khobar Files" computer disk, documents of Capt. Erik B. Pohlmann, assistant chief of staff, G–2, HQ U.S. Army Forces Central Command-Saudi Arabia; Robb interview; Treadway interview.
82. Robb interview; HNSC Report, 20; PERSCO's list of hospitalized casualties; Bailey, "Buddies Cared," 10; "U.S. Air Force Chief of Staff presents the Airman's Medal to Maj. Steven Goff," 17 Jul 96.
83. "4404th Medical Group Chronology," entry for 26 Jun 96, 0100; Robb interview.
84. Robb interview; Col. (Dr.) Douglas J. Robb, comments on "Khobar Towers: Tragedy and Response" manuscript, 27 Jun 05.
85. Robb interview.
86. "4404th Medical Group Chronology," entry for 26 Jun 96, 0530. Drs. Robb and

Treadway both recalled working until after 6 or 7 a.m. (Robb interview; Treadway interview).

87. Dick interview with author.

88. Robb interview; "4404th Medical Group Chronology," entry for 26 Jun 96, 0315. Col. Schafer was promoted to brigadier general on 1 Sep 97 (USAF biography of Brig. Gen. Klaus O. Schafer, Nov 97). Col. Roudebush was promoted to brigadier general on 1 Jul 98 and to major general on 24 May 01. On 4 Aug 06, he was promoted to lieutenant general and became the Air Force surgeon general (USAF biography of Lt. Gen. James G. Roudebush, Aug 06).

89. "4404th Medical Group Chronology," entry for 26 Jun 96, 0115; Cmdr. G.J. Hume, Public Affairs Office, HQ U.S. Navy Central Command, to Dr. Perry D. Jamieson, AFHSO, 16 Mar 98; Robb interview.

90. "4404th Medical Group Chronology," entry for 26 Jun 96, 0450.

91. Robb interview.

92. Locker interview; 39th Wing Public Affairs Office biography of Col. Carlisle Harrison, Jr., n.d.

93. Locker interview; European Theater Command Center and the Surgeon General's Office, HQ U.S. Commander in Chief, European Command to HQ USAFE and other addressees, "Medical Support to USCINCCENT—Dahahran, SA Bombing," 26 Jun 96, 0601 zulu time; 39th Aerospace Medicine Squadron Commander to the USAFE Surgeon General, [Plans office], 16 Jul 96. The activation time of 3 a.m. in Turkey is from the 39th Aerospace Medicine Squadron commander's memorandum. The "4404th Medical Group Chronology," entry for 26 Jun 96, 0330 has HQ USAFE alerting the FAST team at 3:30 a.m. in Dhahran, 1:30 a.m. at Ramstein Air Base, Germany.

94. Locker interview.

95. AES After Action Report; Bost interview; "4404th Medical Group Chronology," entry for 25 Jun 96, 2350.

96. Bost interview.

97. Ibid.

98. Ibid.

99. Ibid.; 86th AES After Action Report.

100. 86th AES After Action Report; Bost interview.

101. Bost interview.

102. 86th AES After Action Report. The Medical Group chronology has the two C-141s leaving Ramstein Air Base at 1505 Dhahran time, 1405 at Ramstein ("4404th Medical Group Chronology," entry for 26 Jun 96, 1505). The Landstuhl stress management team's after action report gives it as "approximately 1400" (Commander, Psychology Service, LRMC to Col. Kevin C. Kiley, Commander, LRMC, 27 Jun 96 (hereafter cited as Commander, Psychology Service, to Kiley) in Commander, Psychology Service, LRMC, "After Action Review: LRMC Stress Team Deployment to Saudi Arabia in Response to a Terrorist Bombing," 4 Sep 96, n.p. (hereafter cited as the LRMC After Action Review). The after action reports of the 59th Medical Wing's Critical Care Aeromedical Transport Team and of the 86th Aeromedical Evacuation Squadron, which are better sources on this point, put the departure at 1230 zulu time, 1430 local time at Ramstein (59th Medical Wing After Action Report; 86th AES After Action Report). The departure was delayed because the aircraft had to be reconfigured and because some supplies and pallets arrived late. Although the unit saved time by using the pallets built for the Central African Republic deployment, that mission did not involve mass casualties and additional equipment had to be added for the Khobar Towers mission (86th AES After Action Report; interview with Lt. Col. Bruce Crow, USA, chief of psychology, LRMC, and officer in charge, Dhahran stress management team, LRMC, 10 Mar 97; see also interview with TSgt. James B. Cooper, Jr., noncommissioned officer in charge of psychology services, 86th Medical Squadron, LRMC, 10 Mar 97). The overriding point is that the departure was remarkably expeditious: the unit left a little over twenty-four hours after receiving its first notice, by telephone (Bost interview).

103. "4404th Medical Group Chronology," entry for 26 Jun 96, 0330; 86th AES After Action Report; 59th Medical Wing After Action Report.

104. "4404th Medical Group Chronology," entry for 26 Jun 96, 0350; Cragg, *Guide to Military Installations*, 358, 361.

105. European Theater Command Center and the Surgeon General's Office of HQ U.S. Commander in Chief, European Command to HQ USAFE and other addressees, "Medical Support to USCINCCENT—Dhahran, SA Bombing,"

26 Jun 96, 0601 zulu time; Commander, Pyschology Service, to Kiley, 27 Jun and 31 Jul 96.

106. Notes taken during an interview with Col. (Dr.) Ney M. Gore, USA, deputy commander for clinical services, U.S. Army Europe Regional Medical Command and Landstuhl Regional Medical Center, 7 Mar 97. Col. Kiley was frocked to the rank of brigadier general on 12 Aug 96 (LRMC biography of Brig. Gen. Kevin C. Kiley, M.D., n.d.).

107. Crow interview; Conner interview. Col. Conner outranked Col. Crow, but deferred to Crow's Riyadh experience; the two officers agreed that Crow should head the team.

108. LRMC After Action Review; Cooper interview.

109. Interview with Col. Carolyn Bulliner, USA, deputy commander for nursing, LRMC, 11 Mar 97; Crow interview.

110. "4404th Medical Group Chronology," entry for 26 Jun 96, 0350; Robb interview; Web Administrator, Office of the Surgeon General, HQ US Central Command, to Dr. Perry D. Jamieson, AFHSO, 24 Mar 98.

111. Robb interview. See also Locker interview. This exchange was part of the first of many conversations between the these two officers. In Mar 97, Dr. Locker estimated that they conferred at least once a day for the next ten to twelve days.

112. Robb interview.

113. Treadway interview; "4404th Medical Group Chronology," entry for 25 Jun 96, 2355; Aleson interview.

114. "4404th Medical Group Chronology," entries for 26 Jun 96, 0230, 0315, 0530, and 2100. It is difficult to state the exact time when the count reached nineteen (see chapter seven, note 50).

Chapter Seven

1. Cochran interview.

2. Schwalier, "Dhahran Bombing Fatality Accountability"; Schwalier conversation notes, 23 Feb 99; Schwalier comments on "Khobar Towers."

3. AFHSO Khobar Towers oral history interviews 8, 9, and 10.

4. AFHSO Khobar Towers oral history interviews 8, 9, and 10.

5. Secretary's list of confirmed deceased. A document prepared by the wing's mission support squadron also was used in writing this paragraph.

6. Cochran interview. Col. Cochran estimated that he knew about half of the squadron members on sight. A message sent from the Eglin Command Post about 8 a.m. on 27 Jun put the total number of 33d Fighter Wing personnel then in Dhahran at 232 (message from the Eglin Command Post to the office of the Director for Operations, HQ Central Command, and several other addressees, "SitRep 33 FW, Eglin AFB, Fl," 27 Jun 96, 1255 zulu time).

7. Dick interview with author; Jones conversation notes, 7 Nov 96.

8. Berry interview; Husted interview; Dick interview with author.

9. AFHSO Khobar Towers oral history interviews 17 and 12. See also interview 10.

10. Cochran interview. Where rosters *were* available, they listed personnel by their room assignments. PERSCO officers also prepared a weekly listing (Jones conversation notes, 7 Nov 96).

11. Schwalier, "Dhahran Bombing Fatality Accountability." A document prepared by the wing's mission support squadron also contributed some of the information in this paragraph.

12. Interview of Linda Brown, director, Eglin AFB Family Support Center, by SSgt. Yancy Mailes, historian, 33d Fighter Wing, Eglin AFB, Fla., 16 Dec 96; Friers interview.

13. Cochran interview; Williams interview.

14. Morelock interview; Barile interview.

15. Barile interview; Col. Shafer's undated notes on the 71st Rescue Squadron's accounting; Friers interview.

16. Barile interview.

17. Ibid.; Berry interview.

18. Barile interview; Berry interview.

19. Ibid.

20. On the uncertain and dangerous condition of the buildings, see Coles interview; Col. Shafer's undated nominations of Capt. Russell D. Barile, MSgt. Dwayne R. Berry, and others for the Airman's Medal; Morelock interview. On the importance of prompt accounting, see

Notes to pages 92–97

AFHSO Khobar Towers oral history interview 8.

21. Burgess interview. Documents created by the 4404th Wing's services and civil engineering squadrons also were used to write this paragraph.

22. Burgess interview.

23. Ibid.

24. "4404th Medical Group Chronology," entries for 25 Jun 96, 2325 and 2355. See also Treadway and Aleson interviews.

25. Biggs, "Khobar Chronology," communications squadron entry for 25 Jun 96, 2330; Al Moyers, Air Force Communications Agency History Office to Dr. Perry D. Jamieson, AFHSO, 30 Nov 98. The later source refers to the Army unit as the 335th Signal "Company," but a HQ ARCENT-Saudi Arabia organization chart identifies it as a "Command."

26. Biggs, "Khobar Chronology," communications squadron entry for 25 Jun 96, 2330. SrA. Biggs provided information on Army-Air Force communications cooperation.

27. 4404th Civil Engineering Squadron, Five-Year Facilities Improvement Plan FY 96–FY 00, 24 May 96, page 19, in 4404th Wing History, vol. 7, supporting document IV–2; Biggs, "Khobar Chronology," communications squadron entries for 25 Jun 96, 2330, 2345; Biggs, "Khobar Chronology," SP squadron entry for 25 Jun 96, 2345; Biggs, "Khobar Chronology," clinic entry for 25 Jun 96, 2355. The wing's civil engineers and others were aware the conference room was inadequate to serve as a Site Recovery Center (SRC) in the aftermath of so major an event. The unit's Five-Year Facilities Improvement Plan, page 19, provided for constructing a new SRC (4404th Wing History, vol. 7, supporting document IV–2). A document prepared by the wing's mission support squadron identifies the officers who helped establish the SRC, and it puts the time of its activation slightly earlier than does the chronology cited here.

28. Biggs, "Khobar Chronology," first of three services squadron entries for 26 Jun 96, 0100–0130; Aleson interview; Dick interview with author.

29. "4404th Medical Group Chronology," clinic entry for 26 Jun 96, 0100; AFHSO Khobar Towers oral history interviews 8 and 18.

30. Biggs, "Khobar Chronology," communications squadron entry for 26 Jun 96, 0140; Schwalier, "Dhahran Bombing Fatality Accountability."

31. Biggs, "Khobar Chronology," communications squadron entry for 26 Jun 96, 0245.

32. Biggs, "Khobar Chronology," communications squadron entry for 26 Jun 96, 0145; Crow interview.

33. This praise appears in a report prepared in a personnel office of the wing's mission support squadron.

34. Aleson interview; Lt. Col. (Chaplain) S. Frick, HQ Air Combat Command Chaplains Office, to Col. (Chaplain) J. Blair, HQ USAF, Personnel, Materiel, and Readiness Division of the Office of the Chief of the Chaplain Service, and other addressees, 27 Jun 96; "4404th Medical Group Chronology," entry for 25 Jun 96, 2325.

35. Biggs, "Khobar Chronology," services squadron entry for 26 Jun 96, 0230–0300 and clinic entry for 0500; "4404th Medical Group Chronology," entry for 26 Jun 96, 0230; Dick interview with author.

36. Interview with Lt. Col. (Chaplain) Ray Hart, chief, chaplain readiness, office of the command chaplain, HQ Air Combat Command, Langley AFB, Va., 12 Sep 96.

37. Aleson interview; Schwalier conversation notes, 23 Feb 99.

38. McCarthy interview.

39. Ibid.; Schwalier conversation notes, 23 Feb 99.

40. Jones conversation notes, 7 Nov 96; Biggs interview; McCarthy interview.

41. McCarthy interview.

42. "4404th Medical Group Chronology," services squadron entry for 25 Jun 96, 2325; Biggs, "Khobar Chronology," entry for 26 Jun 96, 0400–0430; Schwalier, "Dhahran Bombing Fatality Accountability."

43. "4404th Medical Group Chronology," entry for 26 Jun 96, 0530; Biggs, "Khobar Chronology," services squadron entry for 26 Jun 96, 0530–0600; Dick interview with author. On the bulldozing near Building 131 mentioned here by Gen. Dick, see chapter twelve.

44. "4404th Medical Group Chronology," entry for 26 Jun 96, 0900. Gen. Dick's mention of remains being recovered at that time probably refers to the body that mortuary services personnel reported finding in room D, suite 1, on the ground floor of Building 131, sometime

Notes to page 97

between 7:30 and 8 a.m. on 26 Jun (Biggs, "Khobar Chronology," services squadron entry for 26 Jun 96, 0730–0800). The precise times that the eighteenth and nineteenth remains were found are difficult to establish. The clinic entry for 26 Jun 96, 0800, in Biggs's "Khobar Chronology," states there were "18 [remains] in morgue," according to a PERSCO list. This time may be a bit early; it is significant that the entry for this date and time in the medical group chronology, which the "Khobar Tower" chronology drew on, is nearly identical, but does not include the phrase "18 in morgue." The time that the nineteenth of the remains was located is even more difficult to establish; see note 50 below. The compilers of these chronologies should not be faulted for the omissions and inconsistencies of these sources, but rather they deserve great credit for keeping track of a large amount of information, under difficult circumstances.

45. Morelock interview; Col. Shafer's undated nomination of Capt. Michael D. Morelock for the Airman's Medal.

46. Morelock interview.

47. Aleson interview.

48. Ibid.

49. Ibid.

50. Sources offer a wide range of times for this event. The earliest one found, 7:30 a.m. on 26 Jun 96, can be inferred from the second of three "Khobar Chronology" services squadron entries for that date, 0730–0800: "19 casualties/injuries." It is extremely doubtful that nineteen fatalities had been established that early. The phrase "casualties/injuries" is ambiguous, and no comparable entry appears in the "4404th Medical Group Chronology." Moreover, both of these chronologies clearly state that eighteen remains had been found by 9 a.m., so that the locating of the nineteenth must have occurred later than that ("4404th Medical Group Chronology," clinic entry for 26 Jun 96, 0900; Biggs, "Khobar Chronology," entry for 26 Jun 96, 0900). The question of when the nineteenth of the remains was found is further clouded by a services squadron entry in the "Khobar Chronology" for 26 Jun 96, 0900–1930. It states that "at this point," which cannot be earlier than 9 a.m., there were "16 sets of remains in the refrigerator" at the AMC terminal. This number is low. By 9 a.m. there certainly were seventeen, and very likely eighteen, bodies at the MCP. See the citations in notes 43 and 44, above. The medical group chronology offers the *latest* time, 9 p.m. on 26 Jun, for locating the nineteenth body: "Per Mortuary Affairs, another deceased found in the bomb site rubble. Total count: 19 deceased" ("4404th Medical Group Chronology," entry for 26 Jun 96, 2100). Other sources contradict a time so late as this. A services squadron entry in the "Khobar Chronology" for 26 Jun 96, 1230–1300, for example, states that two NCOs located "one additional set of remains," doubtless the nineteenth, between 12:30 and 1 p.m. This source is convincing in its details: it identifies the NCOs and mentions that the body was taken to the MCP by an Army transport. In addition, the entry for 2100 on 26 Jun in the medical group chronology is very similar in wording to one for 0530 on that day, which suggests that the information given for 2100 was entered for an incorrect time. Giving "midday" as the time when the nineteenth body was found is based on three services squadron entries in the "Khobar Chronology" for 26 Jun 96: 1130–1200, which states that the "body count" at that time was "19 dead," and that eighteen of the nineteen remains had been processed; 1200–1230, which states that sometime between noon and 12:30 p.m. a mortuary services representative reported to HQ CENTAF that there were nineteen confirmed dead; 1230–1300, discussed above, which details the retrieving of the nineteenth body. While some readers might like to know the precise times when events took place, the remarkable fact is that, given the stress of the situation, the participants kept track of information as closely as they did.

51. Biggs, "Khobar Chronology," services squadron entry for 26 Jun 96, 1230–1300.

52. Ibid. The time is imprecise; see note 50 above.

53. Biggs, "Khobar Chronology," services squadron entry for 26 Jun 96, 0900–1930.

54. This follows Gen. Schwalier's accounting, written soon after the event, and the second of three "Khobar Chronology" services squadron entries for 26 Jun 96, 0730–0800, which lists by rank and last name eleven "preliminary identifications." When Col. McCarthy was interviewed, six months later, his recollection was very similar: "We viewed all nineteen that were dead.

I'd say, ten of them you could identify and the other nine, there was no way you could identify them." Gen. Dick stated that the unit commanders, first sergeants, and supervisors *eventually* identified fourteen of the remains.

55. Biggs, "Khobar Chronology," services squadron entry for 26 Jun 96, 0900–1930.

56. Biggs, "Khobar Chronology," chaplain entry for 26 Jun 96, 0300; Aleson interview.

57. Biggs, "Khobar Chronology," clinic entry for 26 Jun 96, 0215.

58. Biggs, "Khobar Chronology," second of three services squadron entries for 26 Jun 96, 0100–0130; Husted interview; Biggs, "Khobar Chronology," clinic entry for 26 Jun 96, 0215.

59. Biggs, "Khobar Chronology," clinic entries for 26 Jun 96, 0215, and 0515 and services squadron entry for 26 Jun 96, 0500–0530.

60. Biggs, "Khobar Chronology," services squadron entry for 26 Jun 96, 0300–0330. See also services squadron entry for 26 Jun 96, 0500–0530.

61. Biggs, "Khobar Chronology," first of three services squadron entries for 26 Jun 96, 0730–0800, and another services squadron entry for the same date, 1200–1230. That the French aircraft in fact left at 0700, and that its main cargo was medical supplies, see Biggs, "Khobar Chronology," clinic entry for 26 Jun 96, 0700.

62. SrA. Biggs provided information about the use of blankets. See also Biggs, "Khobar Chronology," third of three services squadron entries for 26 Jun 96, 0100–0130.

63. Biggs, "Khobar Chronology," mortuary services squadron entry for 26 Jun 96, 0500–0530, and the second of three services squadron entries for the same date, 0530–0600.

64. Biggs, "Khobar Chronology," mortuary services squadron entry for 26 Jun 96, 0500–0530; the second of three mortuary services squadron entries for the same date, 0530–0600 (flatbed truck transport); first of three mortuary services squadron entries for the same date, 0730–0800; services squadron entry for the same date, 1200–1230. That the transport in fact left at 0700, see clinic entry for 26 Jun 96, 0700.

65. Biggs, "Khobar Chronology," transportation squadron entry for 26 Jun 96, 0900, and services squadron entry for the same date, 1030–1100.

66. Biggs, "Khobar Chronology," services squadron entries for 26 Jun 96, 1100–1130 and 1130–1200.

67. "4404th Medical Group Chronology," entry for 25 Jun 96, 2240; Biggs, "Khobar Chronology," clinic entry for 25 Jun 96, 2240; Col. Robb to Dr. Perry D. Jamieson, AFHSO, 8 Apr 98. On the question of when Gen. Schwalier dispatched Maj. Greenfield, see chapter five, note 63.

68. Biggs, "Khobar Chronology," judge advocate entry for 26 Jun 96, 0800. Some Air Force documents obscure the identity of the fourth of these hospitals. The judge advocate entry in the "Khobar Chronology" just cited, for example, followed a JAG source and called this facility the "KKMMC," without translating the abbreviation. Details about this fourth hospital and its location were found on the web page of Helen Ziegler and Associates, Incorporated, and also are in Dr. Kamal Shahab, chief of surgery, King Abdul Aziz Air Base Hospital, to Perry D. Jamieson, AFHSO, 10 Apr 99.

69. Wing Operations Center Log of Events, entry for 26 Jun 96, 0320, in 4404th Wing History, vol. 8, supporting document VI-11. Virtually the same information appears, with the hospital names abbreviated, in the "4404th Medical Group Chronology," entry for 26 Jun 96, 0315.

70. Biggs, "Khobar Chronology," judge advocate entry for 26 Jun 96, 0345; Husted interview; SSgt. Selena P. Zuhoski (nee Husted) to Jamieson.

71. Husted interview; Biggs, "Khobar Chronology," mortuary services squadron entry for 26 Jun 96, 0630–0700; "4404th Medical Group Chronology," entry for 26 Jun 96, 0800.

72. "4404th Medical Group Chronology," entry for 26 Jun 96, 0800; Biggs, "Khobar Chronology," judge advocate entry for 26 Jun 96. Maj. Greenfield's estimate, at that early morning hour, was reasonably close to Col. Robb's later figure of seventy-one patients admitted (Robb, "Medical Response").

73. Husted interview; Biggs, "Khobar Chronology," SP squadron entry for 26 Jun 96, 0900.

74. Biggs, "Khobar Chronology," judge advocate entry for 26 Jun 96, 0800. This same entry shows that at 8 a.m. on the twenty-sixth the JAG representatives were still in place at the MODA, ARAMCO, and King Fahd University hospitals

and at the King Fahd Military Medical Complex. The accounting responsibility moved in a gradual and orderly transition. JAG entries in the "Khobar Chronology" note that "In late morning/early afternoon [of 26 Jun], we were able to hand this [accounting for the status of the injured] off to [the] med folks" (26 Jun, 0345); and that "Late in morning, hand off [of accounting for injured] was made to medical SRC rep" (26 Jun, 0800). The "4404th Medical Group Chronology" states: "MCC [medical clinic commander] takes over patient tracking from legal and SRC" (26 Jun, 1400).

75. Husted interview. Sgt. Husted's use of the phrase "status ... pending" makes her accounting of the unidentified compatible with those of Col. McCarthy and Gen. Dick. See note 54 above.

76. "4404th Medical Group Chronology," entry for 26 Jun 96, 1650; Biggs interview; Grimm interview.

77. Jones conversation notes, 7 Nov 96; Schwalier, "Dhahran Bombing Fatality Accountability."

78. An undated Patrick AFB map, "45th Services Squadron Facilities Map," shows the location of this and other major buildings on the installation. The arrival of the news of the bombing at Patrick is discussed in chapter five.

79. Friers interview; SSgt. J. Bowden, 1st Fighter Wing Command Post systems administrator, to Dr. Perry D. Jamieson, AFHSO, "Re: Col. Dupre," 16 Jul 98, 10:59 a.m. Col. Dupré was promoted to brigadier general in May 2000 and to major general in Jul 03. He retired in Jul 05. (USAF biography of Maj. Gen. Felix Dupré, Jul 05.)

80. Friers interview.

81. Ibid.

82. Jozayt interview.

83. Friers interview.

84. Ibid.

85. Ibid.; Jozayt interview. Brig. Gen. Robert C. Hinson was promoted to major general in Aug 98 and to lieutenant general in Jul 2000. He retired in Sep 03. (USAF biography of Lt. Gen. Robert C. Hinson, Sep 03.)

86. Friers interview; Jozayt interview. On the clock times involved, see also the Secretary's list of confirmed deceased.

87. Friers interview; "Air Force clarifies status of Dhahran attack victims," *AFNS Review*, 3 Jul 96, 3.

88. This paragraph summarizes events which are discussed in greater detail in chapter five.

89. Brown interview.

90. Dylewski interview; AFHSO Khobar Towers oral history interview 12.

91. Dylewski interview; Hill interview; Brown interview.

92. Hill interview.

93. Dylewski interview; Brown interview.

94. Hill interview.

95. Ibid.

96. Ibid.; Campbell interview; undated telephone script in the files of the 33d Fighter Wing History Office. Col. Hill may have written the script on his own, although he modestly avoided claiming so in an oral history interview conducted in Dec 96. Capt. Campbell praised his performance during the days after the bombing: "Lt. Col. Hill was amazing." The same could be said of the efforts of Capt. Campbell herself, and of many Air Force officers, airmen, and civilians during those late June days.

97. Brown interview.

98. Hill interview; Campbell interview.

99. Hill interview.

100. Dylewski interview.

101. Ibid.; Campbell interview.

102. Campbell interview. See also Hill interview. This phenomena represented the natural desire of survivors to communicate with their loved ones, and of course was not limited to Eglin personnel. In a number of the AFHSO oral history interviews about the Khobar Towers bombing, the subjects acknowledged making such calls or referred to others placing them.

103. AFHSO Khobar Towers oral history interviews 12 and 10.

104. Hill interview.

105. Ibid.

106. Ibid.

107. "Notification Officers," an undated note written by Col. David A. Deptula, Commander, 33d Operations Group, in the files of the 33d Fighter Wing History Office. Col. Deptula was promoted to brigadier general in Sep 99, to major general in Jan 02, and to lieutenant general in Oct 05 (USAF biography of Maj. Gen. David A. Deptula, Jan 07).

108. Dylewski interview. This interview men-

tions a lower number of teams than in "Chronological Sequence of Events After Terrorist Bombing in Dhahran, Saudi Arabia; Eglin AFB, Florida—25 Jun 96," an undated chronology prepared by Lt. Col. (Chaplain) Ray W. Hinch, chaplain, 33d Fighter Wing. The number of teams may have increased over time.

109. "Battle Staff: Khobar Towers Bombing," 26 Jun 96, 1300, briefing prepared by Lt. Col. Stan Hill, director, 33d Fighter Wing battle staff; Hinch, "Chronological Sequence," entry for 25 Jun 96, 1830; Mailes, "Khobar Bombing Chronology," entry for 25 Jun 96, 1830.

110. Hinch, "Chronological Sequence," entries for 25 Jun 96, 2100 and 2230. In Jun 98 the AFHSO commander, Col. Christine Jaremko, who had served a 94–97 tour at Eglin, provided information about the location of the MPF.

111. "Battle Staff: Khobar Towers Bombing," 26 Jun 96, 1300; Mailes, "Khobar Bombing Chronology," entries for 25 Jun 96, 2300, and 26 Jun 96, 0130. Messages from the PERSCO office of the composite wing in Dhahran also contain official information about the notifications, and the Secretary's list of confirmed deceased gives clock times that are consistent with the ones in this paragraph.

112. Hinch, "Chronological Sequence," entry for 25 Jun 96, 2230–[26 Jun 96] 0230. Messages sent from the theater also confirm the locations of the families.

113. Hinch, "Chronological Sequence," entry for 25 Jun 96, 2230–[26 Jun 96] 0230, seems to give the time as 2:30 a.m. on Wednesday morning, but Mailes, "Khobar Bombing Chronology," entry for 26 Jun 96, 0130, and the "Battle Staff: Khobar Towers Bombing," 26 Jun 96, 1300 briefing expressly state that the three teams completed the notifications at 3:20 a.m. It is likely that the 0230 time given in "Chronological Sequence" represents a mistaken reversing of the interior digits.

114. Hinch, "Chronological Sequence," entry for 25 Jun 96, 2230–[26 Jun 96] 0230.

Chapter Eight

1. Bruffy interview.
2. Berry interview. The Army Khobar Towers map and the Air Force Khobar Towers map, used together, identify Building 109 as the billeting office.
3. Berry interview.
4. Burgess interview.
5. Cochran interview; McCarthy interview; Dick interview with author; Schwalier comments on "Khobar Towers." See also Tim Albritton to ARCENT G2, 6 Nov 97.
6. 4404th Wing History, vol. 1, 81; McCarthy interview.
7. Cochran interview; AFHSO Khobar Towers oral history interview 29; correspondence provided by Capt. Erik R. Pohlmann, USA, deputy G–2, HQ ARCENT-Saudi Arabia.
8. Cochran interview; Burgess interview.
9. Cochran interview; Biggs interview; Biggs, "Khobar Chronology," services squadron entry for 28 Jun 96, 1000–1030.
10. Cochran interview; McCarthy interview.
11. Morelock interview; Aleson interview.
12. Jozayt interview.
13. Friers conversation notes.
14. Lt. Col. R. Hart to all assigned personnel at the Office of the Chaplain, HQ Air Combat Command, 26 Jun 96; Dick interview with author.
15. [A U.S. Army noncommissioned officer] to U.S. Army, Central Command-Saudi Arabia G–2, 6 Nov 97; SSgt. McCarthy's Khobar Towers attack account.
16. At least one published account implies a later time for the reassembly; the version here follows Col. Cochran's interview. See also Jason A. Smallheer, "Eglin mourns Nomads, Members of 33d Fighter Wing recount trip home from hell to honor comrades," *Leading Edge* (38:3) Aug 96, 2–3.
17. Cochran interview; McCarthy interview; Smallheer, "Eglin mourns Nomads," 3.
18. Cochran interview; AFHSO Khobar Towers oral history interviews 7 and 13.
19. Cochran interview; McCarthy interview.
20. A1C. Lavallee's Khobar Towers attack account.
21. SSgt. McCarthy's Khobar Towers attack account.
22. McCarthy interview; AFHSO Khobar Towers oral history interview 9; Cochran interview.
23. McCarthy interview; Burgess interview. See also interview with Lt. Col. Jacqueline

Notes to pages 113–118

Murdock, chief nurse, 86th Aeromedical Evacuation Squadron, Ramstein Air Base, Germany, 4 Mar 97.

24. Berry interview; Biggs interview. The locations of the two communities were found on the Eastern Region map and discussed with Gen. Schwalier on 23 Feb 99.

25. Robb interview; Berry interview. See also Husted interview.

26. MSgt. Dale Warman, "Community lends hand to Dhahran airmen," *AFNS Review*, 3 Jul 96, 7; Robb interview.

27. Undated note from an ARAMCO family to Lt. Col. (Dr.) Douglas J. Robb; photocopy of a child's hand-drawn card, provided by Col. Robb; Robb interview. See also Husted interview.

28. Shafer conversation notes.

29. Ibid.; Schwalier comments on "Khobar Towers"; Schwalier, "Dhahran Bombing Fatality Accountability." A document prepared by the 4404th Wing's mission support squadron also contributed some of the information in this paragraph.

30. Shafer conversation notes; Khobar Chronology," first of two services squadron entries for 27 Jun 96, 1030–1100. Here, too, a document prepared by the wing's mission support squadron contributed some of the information in this paragraph.

31. A document prepared by the wing's mission support squadron provided the information in this paragraph.

32. Robb interview. Air Force Chief of Staff Gen. Ronald Fogleman came to Dhahran on 3 Jul (an episode covered in chapter eleven) and visited the Saudi hospitals that had aided the American airmen. When he offered his heartfelt thanks to one senior Saudi health administrator, the official replied that it was a solemn medical duty to treat all patients: medicine knows no cultural boundaries (Robb comments on "Khobar Towers").

33. Guerrero interview; Orlando interview; Williams interview.

34. Robb, "Medical Response."

35. Bronson interview. The "44404th Medical Group Chronology," entry for 26 Jun 96, 0530, has the suturing completed by that hour. Drs. Robb and Treadway recalled working until after 6 or 7 a.m. (Robb interview; Treadway interview).

36. A1C. Lavallee's account of the Khobar Towers attack; Morelock interview.

37. Robb interview; "4404th Medical Group Chronology," entry for 26 Jun 96, 1400; interview with Col. (Dr.) Edward B. Freyfogle, USA, chief, department of surgery, LRMC, 7 Mar 97.

38. Ziegler interview; Morelock interview; Bronson interview.

39. Gore interview notes; Murdoch interview. Col. Conner cited the remarks of the Air Force patient at King Fahd University Hospital.

40. "4404th Medical Group Chronology," entry for 26 Jun 96, 0800; Robb interview; Coles interview. See also Treadway interview. After the 58th Fighter Squadron's 9 a.m. meeting, Dr. Treadway joined this team of care providers in making the hospital rounds. On the transition of the accounting responsibility, see chapter seven, note 74.

41. Robb interview. This estimate of casualties in the Ramstein air show tragedy was given by Col. Freyfogle, who at the time was assigned to the LRMC, which received 120 patients from the disaster.

42. "4404th Medical Events Chronology," entries for 26 Jun 96, 0800, 1410, 1455.

43. Ibid., 1730.

44. "4404th Medical Group Chronology," entries for 26 Jun 96, 1650; Biggs interview; Grimm interview; Jones conversation notes, 7 Nov 96; "Talking Paper on Dhahran Bombing Fatality Accountability."

45. "4404th Medical Group Chronology," entry for 26 Jun 96, 1930; Jones conversation notes, 7 Nov 96; Dick interview with author.

46. Jones conversation notes, 7 Nov 96; Schwalier, "Dhahran Bombing Fatality Accountability"; Biggs, "Khobar Chronology," second of three services squadron entries for 26 Jun 96, 0730–0800. See also A.J. Plunkett, "Hampton airman alive," *Daily Press*, Langley AFB, Va., 30 Jun 96, A–1.

47. Schwalier, "Dhahran Bombing Fatality Accountability"; Jones conversation notes, 7 Nov 96.

48. Schwalier, "Dhahran Bombing Fatality Accountability"; Dick interview with author; Biggs interview; Jones conversation notes, 7 Nov 96.

49. Dick interview with author; Biggs interview. Such observations are always subjective.

Contradicting the overwhelming testimony on this point, at least one airman adamantly contended that Blais and Lester looked *nothing* alike (AFHSO Khobar Towers oral history interview 27).

50. "4404th Medical Group Chronology," entry for 26 Jun 96, 1650; Biggs interview; Dick interview with author.

51. Plunkett, "Hampton airman alive," A–1; Dennis Thompson, Jr., "Patrick dealt another blow," *Florida Today*, 28 Jun 96, 1A; Jozayt interview.

52. Biggs interview; Jones conversation notes, 7 Nov 96. A document prepared by the wing's mission support squadron also was used in writing about the Blais-Lester case.

53. Dover Port Mortuary summary paper, "Dover AFB Significant Events—1996," n.d.; Jones conversation notes, 7 Nov 96.

54. Biggs interview. See also Jones conversation notes, 7 Nov 96.

55. AFHSO Khobar Towers oral history interview 4. A document prepared by the wing's mission support squadron also provided evidence of this.

56. AFHSO Khobar Towers oral histories 27 and 70.

57. "4404th Medical Group Chronology," entry for 26 Jun 96, 2235.

58. David E. Sanger, "Clinton Leads Rites for Dead In Saudi Blast," *New York Times*, 1 Jul 96, 1.

59. "4404th Medical Group Chronology," 25 Jun 96, 2202; Robb, "Medical Response"; Coles interview; Murdoch interview. On the 4410th's role in the immediate aftermath of the attack, see chapter six, note 35.

60. "4404th Medical Group Chronology," entry for 26 Jun 96, 1005; 86th AES Surgeon General to the 86th Operations Group Commander and other addressees, "Medical After Action Report, Dhahran Bombing," 22 Jul 96; Murdoch interview. The "4404th Medical Group Chronology," entry for 26 Jun 96, 1500, has AE teams setting up "aeromedical evacuation patient holding areas" in the GUTS hangar at that hour.

61. "4404th Medical Group Chronology," entry for 26 Jun 96, 1500; Coles interview.

62. Graham, "Bomb Won't Deter U.S.," A–1; Schwalier interview, 24 Feb 99; CBS, "Bombing in Saudi Arabia."

63. Biggs conversation notes; Schwalier interview, 24 Feb 99.

64. Grant Hales, Air Combat Command command historian, to Larry Benson, Office of the Air Force Historian, 10 Jul 96; Husted interview.

65. Biggs, "Khobar Chronology," judge advocate entry for 26 Jun 96, 1100.

66. Khobar Towers Air Force map; Hales to Benson, 10 Jul 96; Biggs, "Khobar Chronology," judge advocate entries for 26 Jun 96, 1100 and 1410; Husted interview.

67. Biggs, "Khobar Chronology," both judge advocate entries for 26 Jun 96, 1100; Husted interview.

68. Biggs, "Khobar Chronology," judge advocate entries for 26 Jun 96, 1400 and 1900; Husted interview.

69. Biggs, "Khobar Chronology," judge advocate entries for 26 Jun 96, 1300, 1500, 1520, 1845. Lt. Col. Dooley was the US Military Training Mission's judge advocate general and worked out of its Riyadh and Dhahran offices. He had been with Maj. Greenfield and Capt. Winnecke in Dhahran for dinner and shopping at the time of the attack, remained with them, and helped the 4404th's judge advocate personnel in the aftermath of the bombing.

70. Biggs, "Khobar Chronology," judge advocate entries for 26 Jun 96, 1515 and 1520; "Additional info for wing members: Claims and legal office," *Gulf View* 1:2 (28 Jun 96), 1.

71. Biggs, "Khobar Chronology," judge advocate entry for 26 Jun 96, 2030; 4404th Wing History, vol. 1, 10. Unclassified material from another source, not cited here, shows that the eventual total in individual property claims paid by the entire Defense Department significantly exceeded this $69,000.

72. Biggs, "Khobar Chronology," judge advocate entry for 26 Jun 96, 1415; Schwalier interview, 24 Feb 99; Dickey, "Target: America," 24.

73. Schwalier interview, 24 Feb 99; Army Forces Central Command-Saudi Arabia Historical Summary, Sep 97, 11 and unnumbered appendix page; Biggs, "Khobar Chronology," communications squadron entry for 26 Jun 96, 1415.

74. Graham, "Bomb Won't Deter U.S.," A–1. Information provided by Gen. Schwalier also was used in writing this section about Secretary Christopher's visit to Dhahran.

75. Dickey, "Target: America," 25; Paul Richter, "I Kept Finding Bodies—Not a Lot Of

Notes to pages 122–127

Them Breathing," *Washington Post*, 27 Jun 96, A–24. Press articles and photographs documented that a number of Saudi officials accompanied the Secretary of State. For two examples among many, see Brian Duffy and others, "Bombs in the desert," *U.S. News & World Report* 121:2 (8 Jul 96), 28, and Nelan, "Gulf Shock Waves," 23.

76. "4404th Medical Group Chronology," entry for 26 Jun 96, 1930; Schwalier interview, 24 Feb 99; Graham, "Bomb Won't Deter U.S.," A–1.

77. "4404th Medical Group Chronology," entries for 26 Jun 96, 1730 and 1930.

78. Steven Erlanger, "Survivors of Saudi Explosion Knew at Once It Was a Bomb," *New York Times*, 27 Jun 96, A–1; Secretary's list of injured personnel; Richter, "I Kept Finding Bodies," A–24.

79. Schwalier interview, 24 Feb 99; Erlanger, "Survivors of Saudi Explosion," A–1; Richter, "I Kept Finding Bodies," A–24.

80. 39th Aerospace Medicine Squadron Commander to the USAFE Surgeon General, [Plans office], 16 Jul 96; AFNS story 960657, "Incirlik team fills void after Dhahran bombing," 10 Jul 96. On the activation time of 3 a.m. in Turkey, see chapter six, note 93.

81. 39th Aerospace Medicine Squadron Commander to USAFE Surgeon General. The "4404th Medical Group Chronology," entry for 26 Jun 96, 1235, has the FAST team departing Turkey at 1235, Dhahran time, which matches with an 1130 boarding, Incirlik time.

82. 39th Aerospace Medicine Squadron Commander to USAFE Surgeon General.

83. This follows the unit's after-action report; the medical group chronology has the FAST team arrive at the clinic at 5:15 p.m. (39th Aerospace Medicine Squadron Commander to USAFE Surgeon General; "4404th Medical Group Chronology," entry for 26 Jun 96, 1715).

84. 39th Aerospace Medicine Squadron Commander to USAFE Surgeon General. The contribution of the ASU team is treated in chapter six. Its departure time is given in the "4404th Medical Group Chronology," entry for 26 Jun 96, 1700.

85. "4404th Medical Group Chronology," entry for 26 Jun 96, 1900. For the tie to the administrative staff, see "4404th Medical Group Chronology," 25 Jun 96, 2355.

86. Robb interview; "4404th Medical Group Chronology," entry for 26 Jun 96, 1900; AFNS, "Incirlik team fills void after Dhahran bombing," 10 Jul 96.

87. 39th Aerospace Medicine Squadron Commander to USAFE Surgeon General; "4404th Medical Group Chronology," entry for 26 Jun 96, 2200.

88. 39th Aerospace Medicine Squadron Commander to USAFE Surgeon General.

89. "4404th Medical Group Chronology," entry for 26 Jun 96, 2210; 86th AES After Action Report; 59th Medical Wing After Action Report; Bost interview. On the departure time of these units from Ramstein, see chapter six, note 102.

90. 86th AES After Action Report; Bost interview.

91. Murdoch interview.

92. 86th AES After Action Report; "4404th Medical Group Chronology," entry for 26 Jun 96, 2200; Coles interview.

93. 86th AES After Action Report; 59th Medical Wing After Action Report; Murdoch interview.

94. Bost interview.

95. 86th AES After Action Report; 59th Medical Wing After Action Report.

96. Treadway interview; Robb interview.

97. The formation and dispatch of the Landstuhl stress management team is discussed in chapter six.

98. Commander, Psychology Service, to Kiley, 27 Jun 96; Crow interview; Cooper interview.

99. Crow interview; Cooper interview; Commander, Psychology Service, to Kiley 27 Jun 96.

100. AFHSO Khobar Towers oral history interview 56; Crow interview. Most of the team evidently billeted on the fourth floor (Commander, Psychology Service, to Kiley, 27 Jun 96). Col. Conner, and perhaps others, had rooms on the fifth (Conner interview).

101. AFHSO Khobar Towers oral history interview 48.

102. Crow interview; Cooper interview.

103. Crow interview; Commander, Psychology Service, to Kiley, 27 Jun 96; Cooper interview. Sgt. Cooper mentioned Sgt. Stark's attendance at this meeting. Stark signed his full name to a letter published by *Airman* magazine ("Air-

mail," *Airman* XL:10 (Dec 96), 30).

104. Crow interview. On the location of the Ark, see Husted interview; Aleson interview; Air Force Khobar Towers map.

105. Crow interview; Aleson interview; Lt. Col. R. Hart, chaplains office, HQ Air Combat Command, to all chaplain personnel assigned to Air Combat Command, 26 Jun 96. The Riyadh chaplains, who belonged to the Air Education and Training Command, were sent to Dhahran at 7 a.m. that Wednesday morning (Lt. Col. T. Wuerffel, chaplains office, HQ Air Education and Training Command, to J. Blair and [B. Thomason], 26 Jun 96). This message mentions three "CS [chaplain service] personnel": the third member of the party was an NCO (CMSgt. J. Skoworn, chaplains office, HQ Air Combat Command, to Lt. Col. R. Hart, chaplains office, HQ Air Combat Command and all chaplain personnel assigned to Air Combat Command, 27 Jun 96). Lack of transportation prevented the Dhahran chaplain who had been visiting Taif Air Base at the time of the attack from making a prompt return to the Khobar Towers (Biggs, "Khobar Chronology," chaplain entry for 26 Jun 96, 1430). By midafternoon on Thursday 27 Jun in Dhahran, there were ten chaplains at the Khobar Towers and, as late as a day later, there were "still seven chaplains present" (Biggs, "Khobar Chronology," chaplain entry for 26 Jun 96, 1430; Col. H. Jones, chaplains office, HQ Air Combat Command, to all chaplain personnel assigned to Air Combat Command, 28 Jun 98).

106. Hart to all chaplain personnel, 26 Jun 96; Aleson interview.

107. Crow interview. As Col. Crow remembered the sequence of events, he "dropped off" Chaplain Minsky and "ran into" SSgt. Cooper on his way to the Desert Rose Inn. Sgt. Cooper's account suggests that he continually accompanied Crow from the Khobar Inn. Cooper gives details which make it certain that he attended the meeting with Dr. Robb and Sgt. Stark (Cooper interview). Both men were drawing on their memories of events that had taken place nine months earlier, in the dead of night, after a long flight, and under difficult circumstances, and both gave excellent interviews.

108. Crow interview; Cooper interview.

109. Ibid.

110. Crow interview; Commander, Psychology Service, to Kiley, 27 Jun 96.

111. Crow interview; Cooper interview.

112. Interview with MSgt. Kevin Smith, air traffic controller liaison, 45th Operations Support Squadron, Patrick AFB, Fla., 6 Feb 97; Morelock interview.

Chapter Nine

1. Gore interview notes. Col. Kiley was frocked to the rank of brigadier general on 12 Aug 96 (Kiley biography).

2. Gore interview notes; Plans, Operations, and Training Division of HQ U.S. Army Europe Regional Medical Command to the Commander of the U.S. Army Europe Regional Medical Center, 13 Sep 96 (hereafter cited as the ERMC After Action Report). That it was before 3 a.m.—probably just shortly before that hour—is evident from the logbook of the LRMC emergency operations center (hereafter cited as EOC logbook), provided by SSgt. Brian J. Peplinski, USA, the NCO in charge of the EOC, and from the Freyfogle interview.

3. Gore interview notes.

4. Freyfogle interview; homepage of the Bundeswehrzentralkrankenhaus, 15 Jul 99.

5. Gore interview notes.

6. Ibid.; interview with Lt. Col. Dawn M. Oerichbauer, Commander, 86th Aeromedical Staging Flight, LRMC, 11 Mar 97.

7. ERMC After Action Report; directory of key personnel of the U.S. Army Europe Regional Medical Command and the LRMC, Jan 97; EOC logbook.

8. See chapters six and eight.

9. Bulliner interview.

10. Notes taken during an interview with Marie Shaw, chief of the LRMC public affairs office, LRMC, 8 Mar 97.

11. Marie Shaw interview notes; ERMC After Action Report.

12. Marie Shaw interview notes; interview with Marie Shaw, chief of the LRMC public affairs office, LRMC, 8 Mar 97; ERMC After Action Report; Matthews, "Stunning blast," 13.

13. Marie Shaw interview notes; ERMC After Action Report; Marie Shaw interview.

14. Freyfogle interview; Oerichbauer interview.

15. Crow interview. Col. Crow's estimate of the flight time matched almost exactly with that of the first medevac aircraft carrying Khobar patients from Dhahran to Ramstein ("4404th Medical Group Chronology," entries for 27 Jun 96, 1735, and 28 Jun 96, 0125).

16. Freyfogle interview; AFHSO Khobar Towers oral history interview 60.

17. Bulliner interview.

18. Col. (Dr.) Kevin C. Kiley, USA, Summary of LRMC Prepartions for Receipt of 26 Jun 96 Dhahran Truck Bombing Casualties, a 26 Jun 96 memorandum for the record; Gore interview notes.

19. Gore interview notes; ERMC After Action Report. See also Bulliner interview.

20. Summary of LRMC Preparations, 26 Jun 96; Matthews, "Stunning blast drew a swift response," 13; ERMC- LRMC directory, Jan 97.

21. Bulliner interview.

22. Ibid.; Marie Shaw interview.

23. Interview with Captain Stephanie Shaw, executive officer, 71st Rescue Squadron, Patrick AFB, Fla., 4 Feb 97.

24. Friers interview.

25. Jozayt interview; Thompson, "Patrick dealt another blow," 1A.

26. Jozayt interview.

27. Friers interview; "In Memory Of Those Who Served: Memorial Service, Base Theater, Patrick AFB, Fla., Jun 30, 96," order of service, 45th Space Wing History Office working files.

28. Friers interview.

29. Mailes, "Khobar Bombing Chronology," entry for 25 Jun 96, 1530; Hill interview.

30. Dylewski interview; Hill interview. *Which* of the early battle staff meetings remains a question. The decision *may* be related to one which was made at the third one, held at 6 a.m. on 26 Jun, to assign a project officer to each injured airman who returned to Eglin, but this seems late (notes taken by SSgt. Yancy Mailes at the 33d Fighter Wing battle staff meeting, 26 Jun, 0600). The first and second meetings, held at 3:30 and 6 p.m. on the twenty-fifth, are strong candidates and, given the information available to the wing at the time of each, the second meeting is the more likely (Mailes, "Khobar Bombing Chronology," entries for 25 Jun 96, 1530 and 1800).

31. Dylewski interview; Brown interview. A list of these points of contact as of 28 Jun 96 shows that in all but one case, two NCOs were assigned to each family.

32. Col. Gary R. Dylewski, "A Message to all Nomads from the 33d Fighter Wing Commander," n.d.; Linda Brown, "Dhahran Bombing Lessons Learned: Eglin AFB Family Support Center, n.d. (hereafter cited as FSC AAR). There are difficulties in determing the time of the first discussion about establishing the People Place. The time given here is derived from the FSC AAR and from the Brown interview. The latter makes it clear that Ms. Brown learned about the attack from Col. Lee Weitzel during the interval between the first two battle staff meetings, 3:30 and 6 p.m. on Tuesday 25 Jun. The FSC AAR implies that the guidance to set up the People Place came at the initial battle staff meeting she attended, the 6 p.m. one. A further complication is that in the interview, Linda Brown stated that the FSC "got involved" in Khobar Towers "after the third battle staff meeting." Since that conference did not take place until 6 a.m. on the twenty-sixth, this remark can only be taken to mean that she and her staff began working on establishing the People Place that morning. The statement also sharpens the distinction between an active involvement by the FSC staff on Wednesday morning, in contrast to an earlier decision to have them make telephone notifications, late the previous afternoon, which was soon reversed. See the Brown interview and chapter seven. The People Place was Col. Weitzel's concept (Hill interview; notes taken at the 33d Fighter Wing battle staff meeting, 26 Jun 96, 1800).

33. Dylewski interview. Among those best placed to know about the choice of location, Col. Dylewski addressed the subject the most directly. Perhaps out of modesty, Linda Brown spoke of the choice of location in passive voice (Brown interview). It is possible to infer from Col. Hill's interview that the FTD site was Col. Lee Weitzel's idea, but he didn't directly say so.

34. Dylewski, "A Message to all Nomads"; Eglin AFB official map, 30 Aug 96. The author toured the FTD building on 5 Dec 96. In Linda Brown's after action report and an interview, she recommended that family support center directors should identify, in advance of emergencies, buildings on their bases like this one (FSC AAR; Brown interview).

Notes to pages 136–152

35. FSC AAR.

36. Mailes, "Khobar Bombing Chronology," entries for 26 Jun 96, 1200 and 1400; FSC AAR; Brown interview.

37. Dylewski, "A Message to all Nomads."

38. FSC AAR; Brown interview. Ms. Brown went on to point out that this thin manning resulted from the difficulty of estimating the work load during the days ahead and certainly not from anyone's unwillingness to help. She noted that Hurlburt Field, which stood nearby, and Tyndall AFB, which also was close, just east of Panama City, would have sent augmentees. Eglin's memoranda of agreement also would have brought help from the family-support units of other services on installations within Florida, like the Pensacola Naval Air Station, and also from beyond the state, such as the Coast Guard tenants of the New Orleans Naval Air Station.

39. Dylewski, "A Message to all Nomads"; Hill interview. From the context around Col. Hill's comments about the move to the fighter squadron's hangar on the flightline, it can be inferred that this relocation was intended to protect the privacy of the family members, if journalists became intrusive.

40. Brown interview.

41. Dylewski interview; Hill interview; FSC AAR; Brown interview.

42. FSC AAR.

43. Ibid.

44. Campbell interview; "Explosion in Saudi Arabia," Air Force Development Test Center press release number 96- 033, [25 Jun 96].

45. Campbell interview. Maj. Gen. Cranston was promoted to lieutenant general on 2 Dec 97 and retired on 1 Mar 2000 (USAF biography of Lt. Gen. Stewart E. Cranston, 1 Mar 2000).

46. Campbell interview; Arana-Barradas, Johnson, and Norman, "Southern Watch Continues," 18. A similar reporting of Gen. Cranston's remarks appeared in Rajiv Chandrasekaren, "Shock Waves Envelop Florida Bases, Families Around the Country," *Washington Post*, 27 Jun 96, A–24.

47. Freyfogle interview; Friers interview; Dylewski interview.

Chapter Ten

1. "4404th Medical Group Chronology," entry for 27 Jun 96, 0100; Aleson interview; Biggs, "Khobar Chronology," services squadron entry for 26 Jun 96, 2100–2130. A document provided by Gen. Schwalier also was used in writing these paragraphs about the departure ceremony.

2. Schwalier interview, 24 Feb 99; Swope-Hawley Report, 1:101. A document written by the commander of the 4404th Support Group was also used in writing this paragraph.

3. Shafer conversation notes; "Khobar Bombing," video tape provided by Lt. Col. Shafer, 4 Feb 97 (hereafter cited as "Lt. Col. Shafer's tape"); Aleson interview.

4. Aleson interview; Lt. Col. Shafer's tape; Biggs, "Khobar Chronology," services squadron entry for 26 Jun 96, 2330–2400. The counter on Lt. Col. Shafer's video tape established the times given in this section.

5. Shafer conversation notes; Morelock interview.

6. Schwalier interview, 24 Feb 99

7. Aleson interview; Lt. Col. Shafer's tape.

8. Lt. Col. Shafer's tape. This tape shows that the parties had six members. The services squadron entry for 26 Jun 96, 1930–2000, in Biggs's "Khobar Chronology," states that the original plan was to use 114 pall bearers and that this number was reduced to 58. Either a decision was made to revert to the original scheme, or this entry's 58 may refer to the number of individuals who participated, rather than the number of pall bearer positions—some people may have served with more than one party. The nighttime lighting of the video tape makes it impossible to identify individuals.

9. Biggs, "Khobar Chronology," second of two services squadron entries for 26 Jun 96, 2130–2200 and the third of three services squadron entries for 2300–2330; Lt. Col. Shafer's tape.

10. Aleson interview. The unit of the inbound personnel is identified in the Cochran interview and in the 4404th Wing History, vol. 1, 87.

11. Schwalier interview, 24 Feb 99. Very early that Wednesday afternoon, Gen. Schwalier announced his intention to address the newcomers on this flight. See Biggs, "Khobar Chronology," operations group entry for 26 Jun 96, 1224.

12. During a 24 Feb 99 interview, Gen. Schwalier characterized the ceremony as "very

245

Notes to pages 152–156

well done." He carried this praise further in the document referred to in note 1 above. See also Biggs, "Khobar Chronology," services squadron entry for 27 Jun 96, 0100–0130.

13. Biggs, "Khobar Chronology," services squadron entry for 27 Jun 96, 0100–0130; Shafer conversation notes; AFHSO Khobar Towers oral history interview 4. An interview with the deployed first sergeant of the squadron also mentions that relatively few members of the unit remained in Dhahran by the time of the ceremony (Berry interview).

14. Morelock interview.

15. Ibid.

16. Ibid.

17. Schwalier interview, 24 Feb 99. The search for a qualified pilot very likely led to more than one departure time being posted for this flight. A services squadron entry in the "Khobar Chronology," for 26 Jun 96, 2100–2130, has the departure scheduled for 0200. Another services squadron entry in the same source, for 27 Jun 96, 0130–0200, and the "4404th Medical Group Chronology," 27 Jun 96, 0130, both have the C–5A departing at 0130. The time almost certainly was later, at around 3 a.m. When Lt. Col. Frank Shealy, the deputy commander of the support group and its commander during the nighttime shift, called the flightline at 2:40 a.m. and asked about the aircraft's status, he was told it had neither taken off nor taxied (Biggs, "Khobar Chronology," transportation squadron entry for 27 Jun 96, 0240). When the author asked Gen. Schwalier about this point in Oct 99, the general replied: "Based on the timing of the flightline ceremony, the night support group commander's (Shealy's) status call, and my recollection of the next morning's discussion, I am confident that the C–5's departure was significantly later than 0130—again, more like 0300." Schwalier to Dr. Perry D. Jamieson, AFHSO, 10 Oct 99.

18. Morelock interview.

19. This estimated time of arrival adjusts the projected one found in Biggs, "Khobar Chronology," services squadron entry for 27 Jun 96, 0030–0100, and transportation squadron entry for 27 Jun 96, 0114, which assume a departure of 1:45 a.m. local time.

20. "4404th Medical Group Chronology," entry for 27 Jun 96, 0730. The arrivals of the FAST team, 86th AES, and Landstuhl stress management team are discussed in chapter eight.

21. 39th Aerospace Medicine Squadron Commander to the USAFE Surgeon General; "4404th Medical Group Chronology," entry for 27 Jun 96, 0730. A section in chapter eight describes how the 4410th Aeromedical Evacuation Flight established the ASF in the GUTS hangar; the disposition of the patients by hospital, as of the evening of the twenty-sixth, is also detailed in chapter eight.

22. "4404th Medical Group Chronology," entry for 27 Jun 96, 0730; Commander, Psychology Service, to Kiley, 27 Jun 96.

23. "4404th Medical Group Chronology," entry for 27 Jun 96, 1120. The figure of sixty-six is one higher than the last accounting, at 5:30 the previous afternoon ("4404th Medical Group Chronology," entry for 26 Jun 96, 1730).

24. "4404th Medical Group Chronology," entry for 27 Jun 96, 1120.

25. Ibid., 0730; Locker interview.

26. Craven interview.

27. Commander, Psychology Service, to Kiley, 27 Jun 96; Conner interview; Crow interview.

28. Conner interview.

29. Ibid.

30. "4404th Medical Group Chronology," entry for 27 Jun 96, 0800.

31. The "4404th Medical Group Chronology" gives the time of the meeting as 8 a.m. This time is supported by the LRMC After Action Review, which states that the team of four was dispatched at 7:30 a.m. (Commander, Psychology Service, to Kiley, 27 Jun 96).

32. This time is the one given in Commander, Psychology Service, to Kiley, 27 Jun 96. Interviewed in Mar 97, Col. Crow suggested a broad period of time that morning during which he dispatched the team, and his estimate was consistent with the 7:30 a.m. given in this document.

33. Commander, Psychology Service, to Kiley, 27 Jun 96; Crow interview.

34. "4404th Medical Group Chronology," entry for 27 Jun 96, 0900; Robb interview; Robb comments on "Khobar Towers."

35. Robb interview; Locker interview.

36. Robb comments on "Khobar Towers"; Robb interview.

37. Robb interview.

38. 39th Aerospace Medicine Squadron

Commander to USAFE Surgeon General. The 4404th Medical Group chronology has the first patients arriving at noon; the after action report of the 86th Aeromedical Evacuation Squadron puts the time somewhat later ("4404th Medical Group Chronology," entry for 27 Jun 96, 1200; 86th AES After Action Report).

39. Crow interview; Conner interview.

40. "4404th Medical Group Chronology," entry for 27 Jun 96, 1630; 86th AES After Action Report.

41. 39th Aerospace Medicine Squadron Commander to the USAFE Surgeon General; "4404th Medical Group Chronology," entries for 27 Jun 96, 1630, and 1735; 86th AES After Action Report.

42. Schwalier interview, 24 Feb 99.

43. "4404th Medical Group Chronology," entry for 27 Jun 96, 1735; 86th AES After Action Report.

44. "4404th Medical Group Chronology," entry for 27 Jun 96, 1735; Conner interview.

45. "4404th Medical Group Chronology," entry for 27 Jun 96, 1942; 86th AES After Action Report.

46. 86th AES After Action Report; Murdock interview.

47. 59th Medical Wing After Action Report; 86th AES After Action Report. Two more AE missions were flown to Landstuhl. At 12:01 p.m. on Sunday 30 Jun, a third C–141 left for Germany with fifteen patients, including SrA. Paul Blais, who been positively identified at King Fahd University Hospital the previous evening. It arrived at Ramstein Air Base at 8:15 p.m. The fourth and last AE C–141 mission left King Abdul Aziz at 9 a.m. on Wednesday 3 Jul and arrived in Germany at 5:10 p.m. the same day. It carried three patients from other stations in southwest Asia, whose transport was classified "routine"; its fourth passenger was the last of the Khobar airmen who had been hospitalized in Dhahran ("4404th Medical Group Chronology," entries for 30 Jun 96, 1201 and 2015; 3 Jul 96, 0800, 0900, and 1710).

48. 39th Aerospace Medicine Squadron Commander to USAFE Surgeon General; AFNS, "Incirlik team fills void after Dhahran bombing."

49. LRMC After Action Review.

50. Eglin Command Post to J3C, HQ Central Command, and several other addressees, "SitRep 33 FW, Eglin AFB, Fl," 27 Jun 96, 1255 zulu time; Biggs, "Khobar Chronology," logistics group entry for 27 Jun 96, 1430.

51. Eglin Command Post to J3C, HQ Central Command, and several other addressees, "SitRep 33 FW, Eglin AFB, Fl," 27 Jun 96, 2045 zulu time; "Aircraft Chronology" prepared by SSgt. Yancy Mailes, historian, 33d Fighter Wing, 28 Jun 96.

52. McCarthy interview; Cochran interview.

53. Cochran interview; message from the Eglin Command Post to J3C, HQ Central Command, and several other addressees, "SitRep 33 FW, Eglin AFB, Fl," 28 Jun 96, 2200 zulu time; "Notes from the arrival of the six F–15s (5C, 1D)," SSgt. Yancy Mailes, historian, 33d Fighter Wing, 29 Jun 96.

54. Cochran interview.

55. McCarthy interview.

56. Ibid.; Burgess interview; Smallheer, "Eglin mourns Nomads," 1.

57. McCarthy interview; Burgess interview.

58. Cochran interview; Treadway interview; Schwalier interview, 24 Feb 99.

59. "Khobar Towers Chronology of Events," services squadron entry for 27 Jun 96, 1400–1430, and transportation squadron entry for 27 Jun 96, 1430; Eglin Command Post to J3C, HQ Central Command, and several other addressees, 27 Jun 96, 1255 zulu time.

60. Schwalier interview, 24 Feb 99; message from the Eglin Command Post to J3C, HQ Central Command, and several other addressees, 27 Jun 96, 1255 zulu time.

61. Schwalier interview, 24 Feb 99; McCarthy interview.

62. Schwalier interview, 24 Feb 99.

63. AFHSO Khobar Towers oral history interview 8. In addition to this issue, Gen. Fogleman took a direct interest in the transportation of the wounded, as well. Col. (Dr.) Dan L. Locker, USAFE's surgeon general, summarazied the Chief of Staff's guidance on this subject: "He made it known that he wanted *more than enough* [aeromedical evacuation airlift]. Whatever the response is needed, make sure you've got that, plus a little [more]." (Locker interview.)

64. Eglin Command Post to J3C, HQ Central Command, and several other addressees, 27 Jun 96, 2045 zulu time; Mailes, "Aircraft Chronology"; McCarthy interview.

65. Eglin Command Post to J3C, HQ Central

Command, and several other addressees, 28 Jun 96, 2200 zulu time; Mailes, "Aircraft Chronology."

66. Shafer conversation notes; Jozayt interview.

67. Shafer conversation notes; Barile interview.

68. Shafer conversation notes.

69. Barile interview.

70. Berry interview; Barile interview. The departure date of the first group, of nineteen personnel, was established from these interviews and also the Morelock interview and the Shafer conversation notes.

71. Berry interview; Stephanie Shaw interview; Barile interview.

Chapter Eleven

1. Col. John P. Pope, HQ Air Combat Command Battle Staff Director, to the HQ Air Combat Command Battle Staff Operations Officer, 28 Jun 96, 4 p.m. On the C–5A's estimated time of arrival, see chapter ten, note 19.

2. Secretary of the Air Force's office of public affairs film, "Air Force Tribute to Fallen Comrades," Dover AFB, Del., 27 Jun 96; Col. John P. Pope to the HQ Air Combat Command Battle Staff Operations Officer, 28 Jun 96, 4 p.m.; MSgt. Louis A. Arana-Barradas, "Airmen's remains brought home," AFNS, 27 Jun 96; interview of Michael C. Tocchetti, chief mortuary officer, Dover Port Mortuary, by SSgt. C. Mike Sibley, 436th Airlift Wing historian, and the author, 12 Jun 97.

3. Audio tape recording of a tour of the Dover Port Mortuary, Dover AFB, Del., conducted by Michael C. Tocchetti, chief mortuary officer, for Dr. Perry D. Jamieson, AFHSO, and SSgt. C. Mike Sibley, historian, 436th Airlift Wing, 12 Jun 97; "4404th Medical Group Chronology," entry for 28 Jun 96, 2145.

4. Tocchetti interview.

5. "4404th Medical Group Chronology," entries for 29 Jun 96, 0030, 0100, 0200, 0250, 0330, 0430, 0500, 0615, 0800, 1430.

6. "4404th Medical Group Chronology," entries for 29 Jun 96, 1445, 1615, 1700, 1815. See also entries for 1945 and 2130, and Grimm interview. Lt. Col. (Dr.) Bruce Lauder stated in his monthly report: "The dental staff coordinated with AFIP [the Armed Forces Institute of Pathology] to assist with the positive identification of one of the hospitalized bombing casualties." (4404th Wing History, vol. 7, supporting document V–5B.) The AFIP was a tri-service Department of Defense agency, located on 16th Street Northwest in the District of Columbia.

7. "4404th Medical Group Chronology," entry for 29 Jun 96, 0315; Jordan, "A serious case," 4.

8. "4404th Medical Group Chronology," entry for 28 Jun 96, 0125; EOC logbook. This latter source shows that two busses transported patients from the first flight, and two from the second. On the ASF's operations, see Oerichbauer interview.

9. AFHSO Khobar Towers oral history interview 52.

10. "4404th Medical Group Chronology," entry for 28 Jun 96, 0245; Winkler interview. Traffic using the autobahn from Ramstein can conveniently enter Landstuhl's Gate 2. Vehicles could reach Gate 1 only after driving through downtown Landstuhl and then climbing a steep and winding street up Kirchberg Hill—encountering cars and pedestrians in both places. This emphatically was not a good route for ambulances. The author discussed these access patterns with Marie Shaw, chief of the LRMC public affairs office, on 11 Mar 97, and drove the challenging approach to Gate 1 several times during that same month.

11. Interview with SSgt. Brian J. Peplinski, USA, initial NCO in charge of the emergency operation center, LRMC, 11 Mar 97.

12. Freyfogle interview; interview with 2d Lt. Kate Van Arman, USA, nurse, 8–D medical unit, LRMC, 11 Mar 97.

13. Friers interview.

14. Ibid.; AFNS press release, "Air Force releases screening board results," Feb 96.

15. Friers interview.

16. Ibid.

17. Dylewski interview.

18. Hill interview.

19. Campbell interview. Commenting on a draft of "Khobar Towers" in Oct 04, Gen. Schwalier noted that unlike Eglin, Dhahran had received no additional public affairs officers. It "would have been *very* helpful," he stated.

20. Grant, "Khobar Towers," 47; 4404th Wing

History, vol. 1, 87; Robb interview. See also Dick interview with author.

21. "Honoring and Remembering: A Memorial Service of the 4404th Wing (P), King Abdul Aziz Air Base, Dhahran, Kingdom of Saudi Arabia," 28 Jun 96. Maj. Bennie L. Ulmstead II provided the author with a copy of this order of service.

22. Aleson interview.

23. Ibid.

24. Ibid.; "Honoring and Remembering."

25. Maj. Debbie Millett, "Nellis chaplain speaks of experience in Dhahran," *Bullseye*, 26 Jul 96, 8; Aleson interview.

26. "Honoring and Remembering." SrA. Biggs provided the author with two copies of Chaplain Kovalcin's prayer. One is titled "Memorial Prayer"; they are otherwise identical.

27. "Honoring and Remembering."

28. Ibid.; ABC television footage on Lt. Col. Shafer's tape. Chaplain Aleson commented that Col. Shafer's remarks were "the most poignant and the most moving part of that service. He, first of all, is a person of deep faith, and he talked out of his own faith experience."

29. Aleson interview; "Honoring and Remembering"; Isaiah 40:31.

30. "Honoring and Remembering."

31. Schwalier interview, 24 Feb 99; Aleson interview.

32. Freyfogle interview; Bulliner interview.

33. Winkler interview; Ziegler interview.

34. Gore interview notes. SrA. Paul Blais, who was positively identified on Saturday 29 Jun, remained at Landstuhl several more days, as did another ICU patient. Airman Blais later was medically retired and hospitalized at Tampa Veterans Hospital in Tampa, Fla. Matthews, "Most hurt in bombing," 31; Friers interview. A few patients with eye injuries went from Landstuhl to Walter Reed Army Medical Center, Washington, DC, rather than to their home stations (Gore interview notes).

35. Interview with MSgt. Janice M. Sjoberg, USA, superintendent of administrative services, 86th Aeromedical Staging Facility, LRMC, 11 Mar 97; Craven interview.

36. Freyfogle interview; interview with Capt. Robin F. Erchinger, ward 14 C/D nurse manager, department of nursing, LRMC, 10 Mar 97; Sjoberg interview; Winkler interview.

37. Stephanie Shaw interview; Jozayt interview; Friers interview. On the departure of the nineteen, see the last two paragraphs of chapter ten.

38. Friers interview; AFHSO Khobar Towers oral history interview 25.

39. Jozayt interview.

40. Local television news footage on Lt. Col. Shafer's tape.

41. Ibid.; Friers interview; AFHSO Khobar Towers oral history interview 25.

42. Local television news footage on Lt. Col. Shafer's tape; Bronson interview.

43. Jozayt interview.

44. Local television news footage on Lt. Col. Shafer's tape; Friers interview.

45. Local television news footage on Lt. Col. Shafer's tape.

46. Barile interview; Jozayt interview; AFHSO Khobar Towers oral history interview 21.

47. Smallheer, "Eglin mourns Nomads," 3; 46th Test Wing Multimedia Center, "58th Fighter Squadron Arrival 28 Jun 96." SSgt. Yancy Mailes provided the author a copy of this video tape; hereafter it is cited as "SSgt. Mailes's tape."

48. SSgt. Mailes's tape, "58th Fighter Squadron Arrival 28 Jun 96."

49. Ibid.

50. Burgess interview; AFHSO Khobar Towers oral history interview 8; Treadway interview.

51. Campbell interview; SSgt. Mailes's tape, "58th Fighter Squadron Arrival 28 Jun 96"; AFHSO Khobar Towers oral history interview number 13.

52. SSgt. Mailes's tape, "58th Fighter Squadron Arrival 28 Jun 96"; Smallheer, "Eglin mourns Nomads," 3; Campbell interview.

53. Mailes, "Notes from the arrival of the six F–15s"; SSgt. Mailes's tape, "58th Fighter Squadron Arrival 28 Jun 96."

54. Mailes, "Notes from the arrival of the six F–15s"; SSgt. Mailes's tape, "The Wounded Return Home"; Brown interview. The names of spouses sometimes can be found in official Air Force biographies but because of increased international terrorism, information about the families of senior officers is less widely published than it once was. Mr. Widnall appears in the entry about his wife in Marquis Who's Who, *Who's Who in America 1998*, 2 vols. (New Providence, N.J., 1997), 2:4617.

55. SSgt. Mailes's tape, "The Wounded

Notes to pages 169–172

Return Home"; Mailes, "Notes from the arrival of the six F–15s."

56. Brown interview.

57. "Memorial Service, King Hangar, Eglin AFB, Fla., Sunday 30 Jun 96"; undated Air Force map of Eglin AFB, Fla. The Federal News Service transcript shows that the president spoke at 11:15 a.m. (Federal News Service transcript, "Remarks by President Clinton at a Memorial Service for U.S. Bombing Victims in Saudi Arabia, Eglin AFB, Fla.," 30 Jun 96, 11:15 a.m.). SSgt. Yancy Mailes provided the author a copy of the order of service for the Eglin ceremony.

58. David E. Sanger, "Clinton Leads Rites for Dead In Saudi Blast," *New York Times*, 1 Jul 96, 1; SSgt. Mailes's tape, "A Memorial Service honoring those who died in the Defense of Freedom in Saudi Arabia, King Hangar, Eglin AFB, Fla., Sunday 30 Jun, 96."

59. SSgt. Mailes's tape, "A Memorial Service . . . Jun 30, 96"; Sanger, "Clinton Leads Rites," 1.

60. SSgt. Mailes's tape, "A Memorial Service . . . Jun 30, 96"; Smallheer, "Eglin mourns Nomads," 4.

61. SSgt. Mailes's tape, "A Memorial Service . . . Jun 30, 96."

62. AFHSO Khobar Towers oral history interviews 12 and 10.

63. "Memorial Service, King Hangar"; SSgt. Mailes's tape, "A Memorial Service . . . Jun 30, 96"; Col. LaVerne L. Schueller to Col. Chris Hallion and others, 21 Sep 01.

64. Final draft of Col. Dylewski's remarks at the 30 Jun 96 memorial service, 33d Fighter Wing History Office working files; SSgt. Mailes's tape, "A Memorial Service . . . Jun 30, 96."

65. SSgt. Mailes's tape, "A Memorial Service . . . Jun 30, 96"; Lt. Col. Shafer's tape; Federal News Service transcript, "Remarks by President Clinton," 30 Jun 96.

66. Federal News Service transcript, "Remarks by President Clinton," 30 Jun 96; SSgt. Mailes's tape, "A Memorial Service . . . Jun 30, 96"; See also the Office of the White House Secretary's transcript, "Remarks by the President at Memorial Service for Servicemen Killed in Dhahran, Saudi Arabia," 30 Jun 96.

67. "Memorial Service, King Hangar"; SSgt. Mailes's tape, "A Memorial Service . . . Jun 30, 96"; Dylewski interview.

68. SSgt. Mailes's tape, "A Memorial Service . . . Jun 30, 96"; Smallheer, "Eglin mourns Nomads," 4.

69. SSgt. Mailes's tape, "A Memorial Service . . . Jun 30, 96"; AFHSO Khobar Towers oral history interview 8; Valencia interview.

70. SSgt. Mailes's tape, "A Memorial Service . . . Jun 30, 96."

71. Friers interview; local television news footage on Lt. Col. Shafer's tape; notes taken at Patrick AFB, 23 Jun 04. It had been intended that Col. Friers would ride with President Clinton and Gen. Hinson, since he might be better able to answer some of the commander in chief's questions than the commander of the 45th Space Wing, who only recently had returned to Patrick. As it turned out, no embarassment followed from the two senior officers being separated (Friers interview).

72. Friers interview; 45th Services Squadron map of Patrick AFB, Feb 02; notes taken at Patrick AFB, 23 Jun 04.

73. Lt. Col. Shafer's tape, "1st Rescue Group, Dhahran Incident Memorial Service, Patrick AFB, June 30, 1996"; "Memorial Service, Base Theater, Patrick AFB, Fla., June 30, 1996." Mark Cleary, historian of the 45th Space Wing, provided the author with a copy of this order of service. A memorial service also was held for Airman Lester, in Hangar 148 of Wright-Patterson AFB on 1 Jul. Bruce Hess of the Aernautical Systems Center History Office sent the author a copy of the order of service for this ceremony. SSgt. King was recognized in a booklet published for the 55th Wing's 1999 Birthday Ball. TSgt. Tracy Reed of the 55th Wing History Office provided a copy of this booklet.

74. Lt. Col. Shafer's tape, "1st Rescue Group . . . June 30, 1996."

75. Friers interview; Rita Elkins, "Local services will remember the slain," *Florida Today*, 28 Jun 96, A–4.

76. Friers interview.

77. Lt. Col. Shafer's tape, "1st Rescue Group . . . June 30, 1996,"; SSgt. Mailes's tape, "A Memorial Service . . . June 30, 1996."

78. Lt. Col. Shafer's tape, "1st Rescue Group . . . June 30, 1996"; Col. Thomas R. Friers to Dear Patrick AFB Family and Local Communities, 1 Jul 96.

79. Bill Clinton, "Americans who made a dif-

Notes to pages 172–176

ference," *Air Force Times* 56:50 (15 Jul 96), 37; David E. Sanger, "Clinton Leads Two Memorials for Victims of Saudi Bombing," *New York Times*, 1 Jul 96, A–7.

80. AFHSO oral history interview 18.

81. Lt. Col. Shafer's tape, "1st Rescue Group . . . June 30, 1996"; Friers interview.

82. Friers interview; Lt. Col. Shafer's tape, "1st Rescue Group . . . June 30, 1996."

83. Cutline on photograph accompanying Thompson, "Patrick dealt another blow," A–1; Friers interview.

84. Friers interview; AFHSO Khobar Towers oral history interviews 19 and 23.

85. Friers interview; Col. Friers also provided a document used to write this paragraph.

86. Col. Friers to Patrick AFB and Local Communities, 1 Jul 96; "Editorials & Opinions," *Missileer*, Patrick AFB, Fla., 5 Jul 96, 2. The punctuation of Col. Friers's remarks was changed for clarity.

87. Dylewski interview.

88. Hill interview; McCarthy interview.

89. Richard H. Kohn, ed., "The Early Retirement of Gen Ronald R. Fogleman, Chief of Staff, USAF," *Aerospace Power Journal* XV:1 (Spring 01), 15; "Visit of the Secretary of Defense the Honorable William J. Perry to the Kingdom of Saudi Arabia, June 29–30, 1996," in 4404th Wing History, vol. 10, supporting document VI–17; Schwalier interview, 24 Feb 99; Schwalier comments on "Khobar Towers." Sec. Christopher's visit is discussed in chapter eight.

90. Schwalier interview, 24 Feb 99; Kohn, "Early Retirement," 15–16.

91. Schwalier interview, 24 Feb 99. A document provided by Gen. Schwalier mentions Gen. Fogleman's presentation of the plaques. Some sources have the chief of staff visiting five hospitals, another says six ("4404th Medical Group Chronology," entry for 3 Jul 96, 0800–1000). The three facilities mentioned in this paragraph treated the overwhelming majority of the American patients. Mohammed al Dosha Hospital treated six airmen and al Mana one ("4404th Medical Group Chronology," entry for 3 Jul 96, 0800–1000; "4404th Medical Group Chronology," "Casualty Summary Update" entry). A sixth hospital may well have received a visit from Gen. Fogleman. In any case, it is certain that more than six institutions aided the Americans. The 4404th Medical Group chronology, after listing the five hospitals mentioned in the text and this note, points out that approximately "60 more patients [were] treated and released [from] various hospitals; no available documentation due to overwhelming patient load/minimal administrative support availability."

92. Robb comments on "Khobar Towers."

93. Schwalier interview, 24 Feb 99. A document provided by Gen. Schwalier mentions Gen. Fogleman's presentation of the plaques. On the building designation of the medical clinic, see chapter five, note 30.

94. Biggs, "Khobar Chronology," Medical Group entry for 3 Jul 96, 1045; Schwalier interview, 24 Feb 99. Col. Robb also discussed this episode with the author in a lunchtime conversation on 6 Jun 97.

95. Schwalier interview, 24 Feb 99.

96. Video of Gen. Fogleman at the Desert Rose Inn, dated 3 Jul 96, 12:10 p.m., on Lt. Col. Shafer's tape; Schwalier interview, 24 Feb 99. A document provided by Gen. Schwalier mentions that the Air Force oath was Gen. Fogleman's main topic.

97. Video of Gen. Fogleman at the Desert Rose Inn, on Lt. Col. Shafer's tape; "U.S. Air Force Chief of Staff presents the Airman's Medal to Maj. Steven Goff," Defense Link photograph and caption 960703–F–2095R–005; "U.S. Air Force Chief of Staff presents the Airman's Medal to Staff Sgt. Alfredo R. Guerrero," Defense Link photograph and caption 960703–F–2095R–006; "U.S. Air Force Chief of Staff presents the Airman's Medal to SrA. Corey P. Grice," Defense Link photograph and caption 960703–F–2095R–007; "U.S. Air Force Chief of Staff presents the Airman's Medal to Airman 1st Class Christopher T. Wagar," Defense Link photograph and caption 960703–F–2095R–008. SSgt. Guerrero also later received the Noncommissioned Officer Association's 97 Vanguard Award (AFNS, "Edwards NCO earns Vanguard Award for actions," 29 Apr 97).

98. Schwalier interview, 24 Feb 99. A document provided by Gen. Schwalier also mentions this segment of Gen. Fogleman's visit.

99. Schwalier interview, 24 Feb 99; Gen. Ronald R. Fogleman, "Fogleman commends Air Force men and women," *The Flyer*, Langley AFB, Va., 19 Jul 96, 5. A document provided by Gen. Schwalier supplied a few of the details in this paragraph.

Chapter Twelve

1. Graham, "Bomb Won't Deter U.S.," A–1; Schwalier interview, 24 Feb 99; CBS, "Bombing in Saudi Arabia."
2. Biggs, "Khobar Chronology," SP squadron entries for 27 Jun 96, 1006 and 1030; Air Force Khobar Towers map.
3. Transcript of a Department of Defense news briefing by Lt. Gen. Howell M. Estes, director for operations (J–3), Joint Chiefs of Staff, 12 Jul 96; Schwalier interview, 24 Feb 99; Biggs interview.
4. Husted interview.
5. HNSC Report. The quotations are on pages 20 and 21.
6. HNSC Report, 8–9; Pexton, "Desert Moves," 3.
7. "Senate Select Committee on Intelligence Staff Report on the Khobar Towers Terrorist Attack," 11, attached to [Brig. Gen. Lansford E. Trapp, Jr.,] chief of the Secretary of the Air Force's office of legislative liaison, to Secretary of the Air Force Dr. Sheila Widnall, 12 Sep 96.
8. Downing Report, 1.
9. Ibid., 1–2; Department of the Army biography of Gen. Wayne Allan Downing, 1 May 96. The open literature about the "black world" of special operations is limited. Gen. H. Norman Schwarzkopf mentioned Gen. Downing in his memoir, H. Norman Schwarzkopf with Peter Petre, *It Doesn't Take a Hero* (New York, et al., 1992), 470; Gen. Downing's career during the Gulf War is discussed at greater length in Atkinson, *Crusade*, 140–43, 144, 174, 177–79, 360, 474; and in the revisionist work, Michael R. Gordon and Bernard E. Trainor, *The Generals' War: The Inside Story of the Conflict in the Gulf* (Boston, et al., 1995), 241–46, 340–42.
10. Draft of the Secretary of Defense to Gen. Wayne A. Downing, USA (ret), n.d., attached to a memorandum from HQ USAF's deputy chief of staff for plans and operation's directorate of plans to the Chief of Staff and other offices, 28 Jun 96; "Assessment of Khobar Towers Bombing: Charter," attached to Gen. John M. Shalikashvili, Chairman, Joint Chiefs of Staff to the Secretary of Defense, 28 Jun 96.
11. Gen. John M. Shalikashvili, Chairman, Joint Chiefs of Staff to the Secretary of Defense, 28 Jun 96; Downing Report, 2. A document provided by Gen. Schwalier also was used to write this paragraph.
12. Air Combat Command News Service release, "Dhahran Wing Changes Command"; Schwalier interview, 24 Feb 99.
13. Schwalier interview, 24 Feb 99.
14. Air Combat Command News Service release, "Dhahran Wing Changes Command"; Dick interview with author. A document provided by Gen. Schwalier also was used in writing this paragraph.
15. USAF biography of Maj. Gen. Daniel M. Dick, Jul 99; Air Combat Command News Service release, "Dhahran Wing Changes Command."
16. Dick interview with author.
17. Schwalier interview, 24 Feb 99; Schwalier biography. A document provided by Gen. Schwalier also was used in writing this paragraph.
18. This paragraph was based on interviews with the airmen it mentions, and on Matthews, "Most hurt in bombing," 31; Bryant, "Tested by terror," 4, 8.
19. "Change of Command Ceremony: 4404th Medical Group (Prov.), King Abdul Aziz Air Base, Kingdom of Saudi Arabia," 10 Jul 96, ceremony program, copy provided by Col. Conner; Robb interview.
20. MSgt. David P. Masko, "Coalition forces on the move in the desert," *Southern Watch* 5:32 (21 Aug 96), 1; Philip Shenon, "For Safety, Pentagon May Scatter G.I.'s Around Saudi Arabia," *New York Times*, 18 Jul 96, 1.
21. Dick interview with author; "22/06/1999: Prince Sultan at inauguration ceremony of Prince Sultan Air Base," Saudi Arabian Information Resource web site, 4 Jan 02.
22. Schwalier interview, 23 Feb 99; 4404th Wing History, vol. 1, 1.
23. "22/06/1999: Prince Sultan at inauguration ceremony"; Clancy and Horner, *Every Man a Tiger* (New York, 1999), 307. After the Gulf War, Lt. Gen. Horner was promoted to general, served as commander of Air Force Space Command, and retired on 1 Oct 94 (USAF biography of Gen. Charles A. Horner, Sep 93).
24. William T. Y'Blood, *Sharpening the Eagle's Talons* (Washington, DC, 1993), 102

and see 102n. This Air Force History and Museums Program monograph is classified secret-no foreign; the information used here is unclassified.

25. Bill Gertz, "Miracle in the Desert," *Air Force Magazine* 80:1 (Jan 97), 61; William T. Y'Blood, *The Eagle and the Scorpion* (Washington, DC, n.d.), 94n. This Air Force History and Museums Program monograph is classified secret-no foreign; the material used here is unclassified.

26. James P. Coyne, *Airpower in the Gulf* (Arlington, Va., 1992), 23; Gertz, "Miracle in the Desert," 60; Dick interview with author.

27. Dick interview with author; transcript of interview of Brig. Gen. Daniel M. Dick by SSgt. Richard Brink, historian, 4404th Composite Wing (Prov.), Prince Sultan Air Base, Saudi Arabia, 5 Feb 97, hereafter cited as the SSgt. Brink interview of Dick; Mask, "Coalition forces on the move," 1; John R. Anderson, "Troops adjust to life in the desert," *Air Force Times* 57:13 (28 Oct 96), 31.

28. Dick interview with author.

29. SSgt. Brink interview of Dick. See also Dick interview with author.

30. MSgt. David P. Masko, "Meeting the Southern Watch Standard," Air Force news release, Sep 96; SSgt. Brink interview of Dick. An unclassified briefing slide titled "Tent City Layout" in a classified 21 Jul 96 briefing, found in the files of the Regional Plans and Issues office of the office of the Deputy Chief of Staff for Air and Space Operations, HQ USAF, was also used in writing this paragraph.

31. SSgt. Brink interview of Dick.

32. TSgt. Miconna J. Boaldin, "RED HORSE builds tent city in Saudi Arabia," Air Force news release, Aug 96; Dick interview with author; SSgt. Brink interview of Dick.

33. SSgt. Brink interview of Dick.

34. Gertz, "Miracle in the Desert," 62; SSgt. Brink interview of Dick; Dick interview with author.

35. Grant, "Khobar Towers," 47; Gen. Schwailer to Dr. Perry D. Jamieson, AFHSO, 6 Nov 04. Capt. Erik B. Pohlmann, USA, assistant chief of staff, G–2, HQ U.S. Army Forces Central Command-Saudi Arabia, provided color transparencies of the demolition of Building 131.

36. Perry, Report to the President, 2; Bradley Graham and Dan Balz, "Iraqi Attack Raises U.S. 'Concern,'" *Washington Post*, 1 Sep 96, A–1; Bradley Graham, "U.S. Launches More Cruise Missiles Against Iraq," *Washington Post*, 4 Sep 96, A–1 and A–20; "U.S. forces launch cruise missiles at Iraqi facilities," *Southern Watch* 5:34 (11 Sep 96), 1; SSgt. Brink interview of Dick.

37. SSgt. Brink interview of Dick.

38. "U.S. forces launch cruise missiles," *Southern Watch*, 11 Sep 96, 1.

39. SSgt. Brink interview of Dick.

40. Gertz, "Miracle in the Desert," 62; Dick interview with author.

41. Gertz, "Miracle in the Desert," 61; Dick interview with author.

42. Secretary of Defense William J. Perry to the Secretary of the Air Force, 30 Aug 96; Air Force Chief of Staff Gen. Ronald R. Fogleman and Secretary of the Air Force Sheila Widnall to the Secretary of Defense and the Deputy Secretary of Defense, 23 Dec 96.

43. Air Force Chief of Staff Gen. Ronald R. Fogleman and Secretary of the Air Force Sheila E. Widnall to the Twelfth Air Force Commander, 4 Sep 96; William Matthews, "Will anyone be punished?," *Air Force Times* 57:9 (30 Sep 96), 13.

44. USAF biography of Lt. Gen. James F. Record, Jul 96. Lt. Gen. Record retired on 1 Feb 97.

45. Record Report, A: Tab B, 53–56; Federal News Service transcript of Defense Department special briefing, 16 Sep 96; Downing Report, 21.

46. Downing Report, 8–11.

47. Ibid., 11–13.

48. Ibid., 44–53; Steve Macko, "Report Says Pentagon Failed to Take Adequate Security Measures," Emergency Net News Service release, 18 Sep 96. See also William Matthews, "A Threat Not Met: A Report Blames a Commander and Lax Security Policies," *Air Force Times* 57:9 (30 Sep 96), 12.

49. Downing Report, 48. For examples of press reports, see Shenon, "Saudis Offer U.S. Full Cooperation," 1; Bradley Graham, "U.S. General Didn't Tell Superiors," A–1; Shenon, "Saudi Bombers Got Outside Support," A–1; R. Jeffrey Smith, "Intelligence Report Warned of Saudi Security Problems," *Washington Post*, 11 Jul 96, A–1.

50. Downing Report, 49. Commenting on "Khobar Towers: Tragedy and Response" in Oct 04, Gen. Schwalier called the last clause quoted here "blatantly false" and stated that his end of tour report graded the wing's logistical support from its numbered air force as unsatisfactory.

51. Downing Report, 52, 53.

52. Ibid., 52.

53. AFNS release, "Air Force issues statement on Downing Report," [16 Sep 96].

54. Patrick Pexton, "Responsibility... is mine alone," *Air Force Times* 57:9 (30 Sep 96), 13. Secretary Perry's testimony to the Senate committee that afternoon was similarly worded. See Office of the Assistant Secretary of Defense for Public Affairs News Release, Opening Statement by Secretary of Defense William J. Perry before the Senate Armed Services Committee, 18 Sep 96.

55. Lt. Gen. James F. Record to the Air Force Chief of Staff and the Secretary of the Air Force, 31 Oct 96, copy accompanying the Record Report; Bradley Graham, "Bomb Probe Spares Air Force Officers," *Washington Post*, 12 Dec 96, A–1; Eric Schmitt, "Air Force Inquiry Clears General In Saudi Bombing That Killed 19," *New York Times*, 12 Dec 96, A–1, A–12; Fogleman and Widnall to the Secretary of Defense and the Deputy Secretary of Defense; Record Report, A: vi–viii.

56. Record Report, B, I: 44 and 45.

57. Ibid., 37.

58. Ibid., 35.

59. Ibid., 32–33.

60. Ibid., 69.

61. Fogleman and Widnall to the Secretary of Defense and the Deputy Secretary of Defense.

62. Deputy Secretary of Defense John P. White to the Secretary of the Air Force, 29 Jan 97.

63. Air Force Chief of Staff Gen. Ronald R. Fogleman and Secretary of the Air Force Sheila E. Widnall to the Inspector General and the Judge Advocate General, 5 Feb 97.

64. USAF biographies of Lt. Gen. Richard T. Swope, Jul 96, and Maj. Gen. Bryan G. Hawley, Sep 98. Gen. Swope retired on 1 Oct 98; Gen. Hawley on 1 Mar 99.

65. Air Force Inspector General Lt. Gen. Richard T. Swope to Col. William J. Corbett III and others, 6 Feb 97; Air Force Judge Advocate General Maj. Gen. Bryan G. Hawley to H. Gordon Wilder and others, 4 Apr 97; Swope-Hawley Report, 3.

66. Fogleman and Widnall to the Inspector General and Judge Advocate General.

67. Swope-Hawley Report, cover page; Schwalier comments on "Khobar Towers."

68. Swope-Hawley Report, 150.

69. Ibid., 102.

70. Ibid., 149. For the inclusion of Mylar window coverings in the five-year plan, see 4404th Civil Engineering Squadron, Five-Year Facilities Improvement Plan FY 96–FY 00, 24 May 96, in 4404th Wing History, vol. 7, supporting document IV–2, pages 15, 18, and 23. Commenting on "Khobar Towers," Gen. Schwalier noted another factor in the Mylar decision: the wing had purchased heavy curtains for the dormitory windows during the previous year.

71. Swope-Hawley Report, 30, 31. For the inclusion of the alarm system in the five-year plan, see 4404th Civil Engineering Squadron, Five-Year Facilities Improvement Plan FY 96–FY 00, 24 May 96, in 4404th Wing History, vol. 7, supporting document IV–2, 15, 18, 23.

72. Swope-Hawley Report, 17–18.

73. William Matthews, "Fogleman: Don't Punish Dhahran Commander," *Air Force Times* 57:32 (10 Mar 97), 3.

74. Patrick Pexton, "Report says military had warnings of Saudi attack," *Air Force Times* 57:8 (23 Sep 96), 6, emphasis added.

75. Eric Schmitt, "Air Force Again Says Gen. Was Not Negligent in Saudi Bombing," *New York Times*, 14 Apr 97, A–13.

76. Matthews, "Don't Punish Commander"; Record Report, B, I:24, 43, and 89.

77. Matthews, "Don't Punish Commander"; Kohn, "Early Retirement," 15.

78. Eric Schmitt, "Citing Investigation, Top Gen. Seeks to Leave the Air Force," *New York Times*, 29 Jul 97, A–1. See also Bradley Graham, "Chief of Staff Of Air Force Resigns Post," *Washington Post*, 29 Jul 97, A–1.

79. Graham, "Chief of Staff Resigns," A–1; Office of the Secretary of Defense biography of William S. Cohen, n.d.

80. Graham, "Chief of Staff Resigns," A–1.

81. Kohn, "Early Retirement," 7.

82. Ibid., 23.

83. Bradley Graham, "Gen. Penalized in Saudi Bombing," *Washington Post*, 31 Jul 97, A–1;

Suzann Chapman, "Aerospace World: Khobar Report Delays Promotion," *Air Force Magazine* 80:4 (Apr 97), 13; Rebecca Grant, "The Second Sacking of Terryl Schwalier," *Air Force Magazine* 89:4 (April 06), 41.

84. Transcript of a Department of Defense news briefing on the Khobar Towers bombing by Kenneth H. Bacon, Secretary of Defense William S. Cohen, and Gen. John M. Shalikashvili, 31 Jul 97, 2 p.m. See also Secretary of Defense William S. Cohen, "Personal Accountability for Force Protection at Khobar Towers," 31 Jul 97.

85. See note above.

86. "Schwalier requests retirement," AFNS release, 31 Jul 97. Gen. Schwalier's executive officer gave his opinion of the general's conduct during the period between the bombing and late Jul 97, in a letter to the editor of *Air Force Times*: Lt. Col. Daniel Woodward, "Schwalier maintains 'the high ground,'" *Air Force Times* 57:51 (21 Jul 97), 23. In May 01 Gen. Schwalier himself wrote a letter to the editors of *Air Force Magazine*, in which he commented on an article in the publication's Mar 97 issue that had contrasted the actions taken in response to the Dhahran and the USS *Cole* attacks, and suggested that Secretary of Defense Donald Rumsfeld reopen the Khobar Towers case. Brig. Gen. Terryl J. Schwalier (USAF, ret.), "There's More to the Story," *Air Force Magazine* 84:5 (May 01), 4, 6.

87. Pierre Thomas, "Freeh to Advise Saudis on Probe," *Washington Post*, 4 Jul 96, A–24.

88. Biggs interview; Dick interview with author. See also "Khobar Towers Chronology of Events," operations group entry for 26 Jun 96, 0644. Unclassified material from another Air Force document also was used in writing this paragraph.

89. R. Jeffrey Smith, "U.S. Requests Access to Saudi Bomb Suspects," *Washington Post*, 13 Jul 96, A–15.

90. Ibid., A–1; R. Jeffrey Smith, "FBI Director Travels to Saudi Arabia," *Washington Post*, 23 Nov 96, A–17.

91. Smith, "U.S. Requests Access," A–1; Thomas, "Freeh to Advise Saudis," A–24.

92. John Mintz, "Saudis May Purchase U.S. F-16 Fighters; Bethesda's Lockheed Martin in Line for Multibillion-Dollar Deal," *Washington Post*, 31 Jan 97, A–1. See also Roberto Suro and Pierre Thomas, "Freeh Criticizes Saudis on Bomb Probe; Kingdom Has Withheld Important Evidence, FBI Director Says," *Washington Post*, 23 Jan 97, A–1.

93. DePalma, "Canada Links Pro-Iranian Group," A–1; DePalma, "Saudi Handed Over," A–1, A–8; "Canada Holds Saudi In Bombing of G.I.s," *New York Times*, 23 Mar 97, A–1.

94. DePalma, "Canada Links Pro-Iranian Group," A–1, A–6; DePalma, "Saudi Handed Over," A–8.

95. DePalma, "Canada Links Pro-Iranian Group," A–6; DePalma, "Saudi Handed Over," A–8. Canadian officials were said to have alleged that Sayegh drove a "signal car." (See chapter one, note 32.)

96. Anthony DePalma, "Judge Says Canada Can Deport Suspect in Lethal Saudi Bombing," *New York Times*, 6 May 97, A–7; DePalma, "Saudi Handed Over," A–1.

97. DePalma, "Saudi Handed Over," A–1, A–6.

98. David Johnston, "Suspect in 96 Saudi Bombing Says He Was in Iran at the Time," *New York Times*, 8 Jul 97, A–1, A–12; David Johnston, "Saudi Suspect Pleads Not Guilty, Disrupting Deal," *New York Times*, 31 Jul 97, A–18.

99. Roberto Suro, "Freeh Says Saudis Block Bomb Evidence," *New York Times*, 11 Sep 97, A–10; "U.S. Judge to Drop Charges Against Saudi," *New York Times*, 11 Oct 97, A–4; "Saudi Bombing Suspect Questioned," *Washington Post*, 31 Oct 99, A–34.

100. Thomas W. Lippman, "Gore Visits U.S. Unit In Saudi Desert," *Washington Post*, 3 May 98, A–25; John Lancaster, "Saudi Absolves Iran of 1996 Bombing That Killed 19 U.S. Soldiers," *Washington Post*, 23 May 98, A–26. See also John Daniszewski, "Saudis Find No Foreign Role In Blast," *Los Angeles Times*, 23 May 98, 4.

101. Norman Kempster, "U.S. Indictments In '96 Bombing Roil Saudi Arabia," *Los Angeles Times*, 24 Jun 01, 3; "Saudi Absolves Iran," *Washington Post*, 23 May 98, A–26. See also Daniszewski, "Saudis Find No Foreign Role," 1. Prince Nayef had visited the bomb site with Sec. Christopher, Gens. Anderson and Schwalier, and others, on the evening of 26 Jun 96. See chapter eight.

102. Philip Shenon and David Johnston,

Notes to pages 197–200

"U.S.-Saudi Inquiry Into 1996 Bombing Is Falling Apart," *New York Times*, 21 Jun 98, A–1. In Mar 01, Mr. Freeh persuaded the Justice Department to reassign the investigation from the Washington, DC, U.S. attorney's office to Federal prosecutors in Richmond, Va. ("Bomb Probe Reassigned," *Washington Post*, 25 Mar 01, A–6).

103. David Johnston, "14 Indicted By U.S. In '96 Saudi Blast," *New York Times*, 22 Jun 01, A–1. The Lebanese national, identified only as "John Doe," was alleged to have helped convert the truck for carrying explosives. Dan Eggen, "U.S. Trials Unlikely For Khobar Suspects," *Washington Post*, 23 Jun 01, A–22.

104. Johnston, "14 Indicted By U.S.," A–1.

105. Ibid.; USAF biography of Gen. Michael E. Ryan, Sep 01; AFNS, "Air Force officials respond to Khobar Towers indictments," 21 Jun 01.

106. Johnston, "14 Indicted By U.S.," A–1.

107. "U.S. Indictments In '96 Bombing," *Los Angeles Times*, 24 Jun 01, 3.

108. Eggen, "U.S. Trials Unlikely," *Washington Post*, 23 Jun 01, A–22.

109. Neil A. Lewis, "Judge Links Iran to '96 Attack in Saudi Arabia," *New York Times*, 27 Dec 06, A-13.

110. Robert D. McFadden, "Blast Hits Trade Center, Bomb Suspected; 5 Killed, Thousands Flee Smoke In Towers," *New York Times*, 27 Feb 93, A–1; Elaine Sciolino, "Bomb Kills 4 Americans in Saudi Arabia," *New York Times*, 14 Nov 95, A–1; James C. McKinley, Jr., "Bombs Rip Apart 2 U.S. Embassies In Africa; Scores Killed; No Firm Motive Or Suspects," *New York Times*, 8 Aug 98, A–1; John F. Burns and Steven Lee Myers, "Blast Kills Sailors on U.S. Ship in Yemen," *New York Times*, 13 Oct 2000, A–1.

111. Peter Slevin and Dan Eggen, "FBI Director Links Some Hijacking Suspects to al Qaeda," *Washington Post*, 28 Sep 01, A–18; Rowan Scarborough and Jerry Seper, "Pieces of Evidence Come Together As A Picture Of Bin Laden," *Washington Times*, 3 Oct 01, 1.

112. Winkler interview.

113. Interview with SSgt. MaryAnna Schuchman, cytotechnologist, LRMC, 7 Mar 97.

114. Interview with Capt. Lydia E. Vasquez, medical-surgical nurse, LRMC, 11 Mar 97.

Epilogue

1. Karen DeYoung, "Bush Urges U.N. to Stand Up to Hussein, Or U.S. Will Act," *Washington Post*, 15 Sep 02, A–3; Dana Milbank and Mike Allen, "President Tells Hussein to Leave Iraq Within 48 Hours or Face Invasion; Ultimatum Is Delivered After U.N. Effort Fails," *Washington Post*, 18 Mar 03, A–1.

2. Rick Atkinson, Peter Baker, and Thomas E. Ricks, "21 Days to Baghdad: Confused Start, Swift Conclusion," *Washington Post*, 13 Apr 03, A–1, A–34—A–35; Rajiv Chandrasekaran, "Hussein Captured: U.S. Forces Uncover Iraqi Ex-Leader Near Home Town," *Washington Post*, 15 Dec 03, A–1. Some noteworthy titles on the Baghdad campaign include: Michael R. Gordon and Bernard E. Trainer, *Cobra II:The Inside Story of the Invasion and Occupation of Iraq*, (New York, 2006); Rick Atkinson, *In the Company of Soldiers: A Chronicle of Combat* (New York, 2004); and Tommy Franks with Malcolm McConnell, *American Soldier* (New York, 2004).

3. Interview with Col. Charles Westenhoff (USAF, ret.), contractor, Checkmate Office, Headquarters United States Air Force, 19 Jul 05; Jim Garamore, "U.S. aircraft leaving Saudi Arabian base," Air Force Print News, 29 Apr 03; Eric Schmitt, "Saudis Are Said To Assure U.S. On Use of Bases," *New York Times*, 29 Dec 02, A–1; "Americans officially end era at Prince Sultan Air Base," *The Beam*, 5 Sep 03, 1. Unclassified material from the draft of a classified Air Force report on Operation Iraqi Freedom was also used in writing this paragraph.

4. "Americans officially end era," 5 Sep 03. In Dec 98 France stopped its sorties to enforce the southern no-fly zone and it later opposed the Iraq War, but the United Kingdom continued to help enforce the UN resolutions and it also contributed to Operation Iraqi Freedom. Military Analysis Network, "Operation Southern Watch," 13 May 03, available at http://www.fas.org; "U.S. aircraft leaving base," 29 Apr 03.

5. "U.S. aircraft leaving base," 29 Apr 03; "Americans officially end era," 5 Sep 03. See also Staff Sergeant A.J. Bosker, "Goodbye, Prince Sultan," *Airman* XLVII:10 (Oct 03), 24–29.

6. Invitation to the dedication ceremony, Khobar Towers memorial exhibit, Maxwell Air Force Base-Gunter Annex, Ala., 25 Jun [99]; Air Force News, "Khobar Towers: Exhibit memorializes fallen airmen," n.d.; notes and photographs taken by the author at the Enlisted Heritage Hall, Maxwell Air Force Base-Gunter Annex, Ala., 12 Dec 03.

7. Notes taken by the author at the Enlisted Heritage Hall, 12 Dec 03; "Gone, but not forgotten," *Airman* XLVII:10 (Oct 03), 27.

8. Notes and photographs taken by the author at the Enlisted Heritage Hall, 12 Dec 03.

9. Secretary of the Air Force F. Whitten Peters, Remarks at the Khobar Towers Memorial Dedication, Patrick Air Force Base, Florida, 25 Jun 2000; notes taken by the author at the Khobar Towers Memorial, Patrick Air Force Base, Fla., 23 Jun 04.

10. Notes and photographs taken by the author at the Khobar Towers memorial, Patrick Air Force Base, 23 Jun 04.

11. These three paragraphs, and the last one, are based on notes and photographs taken by the author at the Khobar Towers memorial, Eglin Air Force Base, Florida, 21 Jun 04.

Sources

The foundation of this book is a collection of oral history interviews. About seventy Air Force officers, airmen, and other individuals told me and other historians about their experiences with the Khobar Towers bombing. The list below gives the contributor; his or her rank at the time of the interview; the historian, if other than the author; where the session took place; and its date. Audio tapes of these interviews are held by the Air Force Historical Studies Office.

Lt. Col. (Chaplain) Dennis E. Aleson, Nellis Air Force Base, Nevada, November 7, 1996

Capt. Russell D. Barile, Patrick Air Force Base, Florida, February 4, 1997

U.S. Army SSgt. Robert H. Barrett, Landstuhl Regional Medical Center, Germany, March 8, 1997

U.S. Army SSgt. Todd M. Bentley, Landstuhl Regional Medical Center, Germany, March 10, 1997

MSgt. Dwayne Berry, Patrick Air Force Base, Florida, February 5, 1997

SrA. Ronald J. Biggs, Jr., Nellis Air Force Base, Nevada, November 8, 1996

Col. (Dr.) James W. Bost, Ramstein Air Base, Germany, March 4, 1997

1st Lt. Stephanie Bronson, Patrick Air Force Base, February 6, 1997

Linda Brown, by SSgt. Yancy Mailes, Eglin Air Force Base, Florida, December 16, 1996

SSgt. Jacques P. Bruffy, Patrick Air Force Base, Florida, February 5, 1997

U.S. Army Col. Carolyn Bullinger, Landstuhl Regional Medical Center, Germany, March 11, 1997

TSgt. George Burgess, by SSgt. Yancy Mailes and the author, Eglin Air Force Base, Florida, December 5, 1996

U.S. Army SSgt. Katsu Cannon, Landstuhl Regional Medical Center, Germany, March 7, 1997

Col. Douglas R. Cochran, by SSgt. Yancy Mailes, Eglin Air Force Base, Florida, December 20, 1996

Maj. Cynthia Coles, Ramstein Air Base, Germany, March 6, 1997

U.S. Army Lt. Col. Sherry Conner, Landstuhl Regional Medical Center, Germany, March 10, 1997

TSgt. James Cooper, Landstuhl Regional Medical Center, Germany, March 10, 1997

TSgt. Jefferson A. Craven, Patrick Air Force Base, Florida, February 6, 1997

U.S. Army Lt. Col. Bruce Crow, Landstuhl Regional Medical Center, Germany, March 10, 1997

Khobar Towers: Tragedy and Response

 Brig. Gen. Daniel M. Dick, Langley Air Force Base, Virginia, February 4, 1998
 Col. Gary R. Dylewski, by SSgt. Yancy Mailes, Eglin Air Force Base, Florida, December 18, 1996
 Capt. Robin F. Erchinger, Landstuhl Regional Medical Center, Germany, March 10, 1997
 U.S. Army Col. (Dr.) Edward B. Freyfogle, Landstuhl Regional Medical Center, Germany, March 7, 1997
 Col. Thomas R. Friers, Patrick Air Force Base, Florida, February 4, 1997
 Meryln T. Garcia, R.N., Landstuhl Regional Medical Center, Germany, March 7, 1997
 U.S. Army SSgt. Gina A. Green, Landstuhl Regional Medical Center, Germany, March 7, 1997
 SSgt. Rudolph Grimm II, Patrick Air Force Base, Florida, February 6, 1997
 SSgt. Alfredo R. Guerrero, private residence, November 9, 1996
 Lt. Col. (Chaplain) Ray Hart, Langley Air Force Base, Virginia, September 12, 1996
 Lt. Col. Stan Hill, Eglin Air Force Base, Florida, December 5, 1996
 SSgt. Selena P. Husted, Patrick Air Force Base, Florida, February 6, 1997
 Lt. Col. Donald R. Jozayt, Patrick Air Force Base, Florida, February 4, 1997
 U.S. Army SSgt. Alexis King, Landstuhl Regional Medical Center, Germany, March 8, 1997
 SrA. Daniel R. Koeppl, Landstuhl Regional Medical Center, Germany, March 7, 1997
 Col. (Dr.) Dan L. Locker, Ramstein Air Base, Germany, March 4, 1997
 Col. (Chaplain) John Lundin, Ramstein Air Base, Germany, March 3, 1997
 U.S. Army SSgt. Tyrone Lymos, Landstuhl Regional Medical Center, Germany, March 8, 1997
 Lt. Col. Thomas A. McCarthy, Eglin Air Force Base, Florida, December 4, 1996
 Capt. Michael D. Morelock, Patrick Air Force Base, Florida, February 4, 1997
 Lt. Col. Jacqueline E. Murdock, Ramstein Air Base, Germany, March 4, 1997
 Lt. Col. Dawn M. Oerichbauer, Landstuhl Regional Medical Center, Germany, March 11, 1997
 U.S. Army Corporal Donny P. Ong, Landstuhl Regional Medical Center, Germany, March 10, 1997
 SSgt. John C. Orlando, Jr., Eglin Air Force Base, Florida, December 4, 1996
 U.S. Army SSgt. Harold Patterson, Landstuhl Regional Medical Center, Germany, March 11, 1997
 U.S. Army SSgt. Brian Peplinski, Landstuhl Regional Medical Center, Germany, March 11, 1997
 SrA. Joseph J. Powell, Landstuhl Regional Medical Center, Germany, March 11, 1997

Sources

Lt. Col. (Dr.) Douglas J. Robb, Moody Air Force Base, Georgia, June 6, 1997

SSgt. Boris W. Rudinski, Patrick Air Force Base, Florida, February 5, 1997

SSgt. MaryAnna Schuchman, Landstuhl Regional Medical Center, Germany, March 7, 1997

Brig. Gen. (retired) Terryl J. (Terry) Schwalier, private residence, February 23 and 24, 1999

U.S. Army Sgt1C. Rito R. Serna, Landstuhl Regional Medical Center, Germany, March 10, 1997

Marie Shaw, Landstuhl Regional Medical Center, Germany, March 8, 1997

Capt. Stephanie Shaw, Patrick Air Force Base, Florida, February 4, 1997

MSgt. Janice Sjoberg, Landstuhl Regional Medical Center, Germany, March 11, 1997

MSgt. Kevin Smith, Patrick Air Force Base, Florida, February 6, 1997

SSgt. Darren M. Staggers, Landstuhl Regional Medical Center, Germany, March 11, 1997

U.S. Army Capt. Shajuanda D. Strickland, Landstuhl Regional Medical Center, Germany, March 10, 1997

SrA. David R. Thompson, Landstuhl Regional Medical Center, Germany, March 7, 1997

Michael Tocchetti, Dover Air Force Base, Delaware, June 12, 1997 (In addition to this oral history, Mr. Tocchetti gave the author and SSgt. C. Michael Sibley a tour of the Charles C. Carson Center for Mortuary Affairs, Dover Air Force Base, Delaware, on June 12, 1997.)

Capt. (Dr.) R. Morris Treadway, Jr., Eglin Air Force Base, Florida, December 5, 1996

Maj. Bennie L. Umstead II, Andrews Air Force Base, Maryland, August 19, 1997

A1C. Cielito (Lito) Valencia, by SSgt. Yancy Mailes, Eglin Air Force Base, Florida, February 11, 1997

U.S. Army 2d Lt. Kate Van Arman, Landstuhl Regional Medical Center, Germany, March 11, 1997

Capt. Lydia E. Vasquez, Landstuhl Regional Medical Center, Germany, March 11, 1997

U.S. Army Capt. Laura Wedel, Landstuhl Regional Medical Center, Germany, March 10, 1997

MSgt. Cedrick Williams, Eglin Air Force Base, Florida, December 4, 1996

Col. (Chaplain) J. Rick Wilson, Langley Air Force Base, Virginia, September 12, 1996

Capt. Matthew Winkler, Patrick Air Force Base, Florida, February 5, 1997

SSgt. Eric Ziegler, Eglin Air Force Base, Florida, December 4, 1996

Another valuable source for this work is SSgt. Eric O. Grzebinski's official history of the 4404th Composite Wing (Provisional) covering the crucial period May

Khobar Towers: Tragedy and Response

1–July 31, 1996. This narrative is supported by a particularly strong collection of documents. Sudden tragedies like the Khobar Towers bombing point up the value of having historians continually in place with field units.

There are several helpful articles about the Dhahran attack. The best introduction to the subject is a brief, but well written, account by Rebecca Grant: "Khobar Towers," *Air Force Magazine* (Volume 81, Number 6, June 1998, pages 41–47). There are several other useful articles on the bombing and related issues, most of them appearing in military publications. *Air Force Times* staff writer William Matthews compiled a series of stories, to mark the first anniversary of the attack: "One Year Later," *Air Force Times* (Volume 57, Number 48, June 30, 1997, pages 12–14, 16, 18). On the medical care that the young airmen gave one another, see Capt. Timothy Bailey and Nathan Alderman, "Buddies Cared," *Airman* (Volume XL, Number 10, December 1996, pages 8–11). A prominent military historian's interview of General Fogleman appears in Richard H. Kohn, ed., "The Early Retirement of Gen. Ronald R. Fogleman, Chief of Staff, United States Air Force," *Aerospace Power Journal,* (Volume XV, Number 1, Spring 2001, pages 6–23). The thesis of an article about Brig. Gen. Schwalier is stated in its title: Matt Labash, "The Scapegoat," *The Weekly Standard* (Volume 3, Number 11, November 24, 1997, pages 20–29). The move from Dhahran to Prince Sultan Air Base is recounted by Bill Gertz, "Miracle in the Desert," *Air Force Magazine* (Volume 80, Number 1, January 1997, pages 60–64). The newspapers of major American cities, and of several Air Force bases, published articles that give interesting details about Operation Southern Watch, the Khobar Towers bombing, and the aftermath of the attack. Many of these are cited in the endnotes. Unclassified versions of the official inquiries into the Dhahran tragedy are available on the internet.

Three important books were published while this manuscript was being reviewed. Written after Iranian responsibility for the Khobar Towers bombing was firmly established, Kenneth M. Pollock, *The Persian Puzzle: The Conflict Between Iran and America* (New York, 2004) puts the attack in its diplomatic context and weighs the merits of U.S. retaliation against Iran. Like Pollock's work, Bill Clinton, *My Life* (New York, 2004) and Louis J. Freeh, *My FBI* (New York, 2005) appeared too late to be used in this book.

Index

Numbers in ***bold italic*** indicate illustrations.

Abqaiq, Saudi Arabia: 80
Adams, Christopher J.: 13, 14, 50, 53, 55,
      164, 165, 201
Adams, Rita E.: 121
Advanced cadre teams: 86, 88, 124, 125, 126
Aeromedical Evacuation Coordination
      Center: 64, 86
Aeromedical evacuation crews: 85, 86, 124,
      125, 157
Aeromedical evacuation missions: 119, 130,
      157, 162
Aeromedical Staging Facility: 119, 124, 125,
      154, 155, 156
Aeromedical Staging Flight: 130, 162
Afghanistan: 198, 199
Air Combat Command: 18, 24, 43, 84, 95,
      111, 180, 187, 191
Aircraft types (Iraqi)
   Hind helicopter gunship: 16
   Hip helicopter gunship: 16
Aircraft types (Saudi Arabian)
   C–130:182
Aircraft types (U.S.)
   A–10 Thunderbolt II: 19
   B–52 Stratofortress: 185
   C–5 Galaxy: ***140***, ***142***, 151, 152, 153,
      159, 161, 168, 182, 183
   C–9 Nightingale: 85, ***142***, 166, 167
   C–12 Huron: 119, 125
   C–21 Learjet: 43
   C–130 Hercules: 18, 19, 85, 181, 185
   C–141 Starlifter: 85, 86, 87, 88, 123, 124,
      126, 153, 154, 155, 156, 157, 159,
      162, 169
   EF–111A Raven: 18
   F–4 Phantom II: 180
   F–4G Wild Weasel: 18
   F–15 Eagle: 9, 19, 67, 83, ***144***, 157, 159,
      160, 167, 169
   F–16 Fighting Falcon: 163, 180, 185
   F–16C: 18
   F–16CG: 185
   F–16CJ: 185
   HC–130P Combat Shadow: 5, 19, 44, 66,
      109, ***146***, 160, 163, 166, 167, 180
   KC–10A Extender: 153
   KC–135 Stratotanker: 88, 182
   L–1011 TriStar: 157, 158, 159
   MC–130 Combat Talon: 17
   RF–4C Phantom II: 18
Air Expeditionary Forces
   II: 102
   III: 67
Air Force Commendation Medal: 74
Air Force Development Test Center: 137,
      147, 163, 168
Air Force Instructions: 188
   Air Force Instruction 31–210: 25
Air Force Museum: 200
Air Force News: 132, 161, 200
Air Force Office of Special Investigations: 9,
      26, 27, 30, 31, 35, 58, 120, 177, 188,
      193
Air Force One: 171, 172
Air Force Operations Center: 68
Air Force Personnel Center: 54, 103, 117,
      118
   Casualty Center: 118
Air Forces (U.S.)
   Ninth: 18, 24, 191
   Thirteenth: 191
   Twelfth: 185, 186
Air Force Times: 192
Airman's Medal: ***40***, 74, 83, ***148***, 149, 176
Air Mobility Command: 63, 94, 95, 96, 97,
      98, 99, 117, 153, 155, 158, 159, 164,
      176
Air Staff: 188
Alabama: 140, 147, 200
Aleson, Dennis E.: 18, 58, 60, 73, 88, 94, 95,
      97, 98, 111, 127, ***140***, 151, 152, 164,
      165
Alexandria, Virginia: 197
Alfred P. Murah Building, Oklahoma City,
      Oklahoma: 56
"Al's Garage": 181
American Broadcasting Company: 83
American Embassy, Saudi Arabia: 23, 29
American Red Cross: 133, 135, 136, 163
Anderson, Kurt B.: 18, 34, 43, 60, 61, 122,
      128, ***148***, 151, 152, 165, 176, 180
Angelo, Frank: 68
Angelo, Thomas: 59, 60, 127, 165
Angelton, Texas: 53
Apalachicola River: 66
Arabian American Oil Company: 20, 21, 31,
      112, 113, 120
Arabian American Oil Company Hospital:

263

Index

50, 63, 66, 74, 80, 81, 91, 97, 98, 99, 103, 111, 115, 116, 117, 153, 154, 156, 167, 174
Arabian Gulf: 22, 30, *37*, 80, 185, 186
Arabic language: 20, 81
ARAMCO. *See* Arabian American Oil Company.
"Ark" (Khobar Towers Chapel): 120, 121, 127, 175, 176
Army Forces Central Command-Saudi Arabia: 121, 122
Ashcroft, John: 197
Ash Sharqiyah, Saudi Arabia: 18
Associated Press: 132
Atkins, Michael D.: 74
Atlanta, Georgia: 67, 103, 166, 167
Atlantic Ocean: 103, 133, 159, 162, 165, 171
Ayres, Paul K.: 18, 82, 151, 152
Azores: 85
Azraq, Jordan: 102

Baghdad, Iraq: 16, 17, 184, 199
Bahrain: 22, 27, 28, 32, 44, 84, 123, 127, 185
Bailey, Cynthia: 59
Baker, Andrew: 18
Bandar, Prince bin Sultan: 122
Bangladesh: 114
Barile, Russell D.: 44, 48, 55, 56, 73, 91, 92, 160
Barksdale Air Force Base, Louisiana: 185
Battle Creek, Michigan: 53
Battle Staff Directives: 24, 31
Bayliss, David: 71
Bedouins: 20, 21
Berry, Dwayne R.: 6, 44, 56, 81, 90, 91, 92, 109, 112, 113, 160, 180
Bible, Dale F.: 18, 32, 60, 61, 63, 158
Biggs, Ronald J., Jr.: 18
Billingsley, Van: 124
Bisby, Arthur: 6, 44
Blais, Paul, Jr.: 118, 119, 134, 161, 162
Blais, Paul, Sr.: 118, 134
Boll, Kevin: 59
Bosnia: 85, 131
Bost, James W.: 64, 65, 85, 86, 124, 125
Boyle, Gary S.: 18, 28, 33, 35, 61, 62, 92, 110
Branch, Lawrence: 51
Brevard County, Florida: 166
British forces: 21, 29, 30, 32, 110, 111, 113, 114, 127, 185, 199. *See also* Great Britain; United Kingdom.

Bronson, Donald: 167
Bronson, Stephanie: 81, 115, 116, 167
Brown, Linda: 90, 103, 104, 105, 135, 136, 137, 169
Bruffy, Jacques P.: 44, 109
Bulliner, Carolyn: 130, 131, 132, 133
Bundeswehzentralkrankenhaus: 129
Burgess, Andre: 18
Burgess, George: 7, 45, 46, 47, 48, 49, 55, 76–77, 92, 93, 109, 110, 158, 168, 169, 180
Burhite, Bradley K.: 18
Burns, Nicholas: 54
Bush, George: 15, 16, 17, 20, 23
Bush, George W.: 197, 198, 199

Cable News Network: 67, 68, 84, 134, 155, 164, 172
Cafourek, Daniel B.: 53, 201
Cairo, Egypt: 158
California: 9, 53, 181
Cambridge, Minnesota: 53
"Camelot" (slang): 181
Campbell, Brenda L.: 67, 105, 106, 137, 163, 169
Campbell, Millard D.: 53, 201
Canada: 196
Carr, Patrick J.: 162, 163
Cartrette, Earl F., Jr.: 53, 201
Castor, Eric: 74
Casualties: 53–55. *See also* Duty status, whereabouts unknown; Remains of the deceased; Wounded airmen.
Cayetano, Sylvia: 123
Central African Republic: 86
Central Command. *See* United States Central Command.
Central Command Air Forces. *See* United States Central Command Air Forces.
Central Intelligence Agency: 29
Cevallos, Diego: 123
Chairman of the Joint Chiefs of Staff: 30, 68, 161, 171, 179, 184
Channel 2 News, Brevard County, Florida: 166
Chapel (Khobar Towers). 120–21, 127, 175–76
 Used as JAG office: 120–21, 175
Chevrolet Caprice: 10, 12, 28, 196
Chiles, Lawton M., Jr.: 171
Christopher, Warren: 54, 121, 122, 123, 174
Chueikhat, Jaafar: 196

Index

Civil engineers: 55, 66, 76, 79, 81, 92, 93, 115, 117, 167, 189, 92
Clinic (Khobar Towers Building 111): 54, 57–60, 62, 74, 75, 76, 78, 79, 82–84, 94–96, 99, 109, 124, 127, 174
Clinton, William J.: 68, 120, 121, 134, *144, 145*, 166, 170, 171, 172, 177, 184, 197, 201
Clovis, California: 53
Cochran, Douglas R.: 6, 7, 44, 45, 58, 67, 74, 89, 90, 91, 95–96, 104, 105, 110, 111, 112, *149*, 155, 157, 158, 159, 169, 180
Cocoa Beach, Florida: 103, 173
Cohen, William S.: *150*, 193, 194
Cold War: 15
Coles, Cynthia D.: 43, 57, 58, 59, 77, 119, 125
Colorado Air National Guard: 18
Columbia Broadcasting System: 132
Combined Air Operations Center: 199
Congressional Research Service: 197
Connor, Sherry: 82, 87, 154, 155, 156
Cooper, James B., Jr.: 87, 126, 127, 128
Corning, California: 53
Cranston, Peggy: 169
Cranston, Stewart E.: 137, *142, 144*, 168, 169, 170, 171
Craven, Jefferson A.: 73
Critical Care Aeromedical Transport Team: 86, 87, 124, 125, 126, 130, 157
Crow, Bruce E.: 87, 126, 127, 128, 130, 154, 155
Cruise missile: 184

Daines, Michael: 131, 133
D'Amato, Roberto: 185
Dammam, Saudi Arabia: 20
Dammam Central Hospital: 80
Dammam Number 7 oil well: 20
Darwish, Marwan: 12, 62, 99, 120
Debary, Florida: 53
DeCook, Daniel: 123, 124
Defense Special Weapons Agency: 34, 55, 56
Defense Switched Network: 109
Delaware: 96, 117, 151, 161
Dendinger, William J.: 172
Department of Defense: 29, 34, 84, 87, 178, 181, 187, 188, 189, 196
Department of Justice: 196
Department of the Air Force: 188
Deptula, David A.: 107, 168

Deputy Chief of Staff, Air and Space Operations: 180
Deputy Secretary of Defense. *See* White, John P.
Desert Rose Inn (Khobar Towers Dining Hall): 57, 58, 61, 62, 75, 77, 78, 80, 82, 83, 89, 91, 94, 99, 101, 110, 115, 127, 128, 176
Desert Shield. *See* Operation Desert Shield.
Desert Storm. *See* Operation Desert Storm.
Al Dhafra Air Base, United Arab Emirates: 153
Dhahran, Saudi Arabia: 6, 7, 9, 10, 12, 15, 18–20, 22–24, 30, 32, 33, 43, 50, 54, 60, 62–68, 71, 72, 74, 75, 78–81, 83–90, 93, 94, 96, 98, 99, 101–3, 105, 106, 109, 112–14, 116–26, 129–34, 137, 151–61, 163–69, 172, 174, 175, 177–86, 188, 191, 193, 195–98, 200, 201
  Map, Dhahran and Vicinity: 100. *See also* Dhahran Air Base.
Dhahran Air Base, Saudi Arabia: 5, 19, 22, 25, 30, 31, *36*, 43, 44, 46, 61, 63, 83, 86, 92, 94, 98, 99, 109, 111, 112, 116, 122, 123, 124, 126, 151, 154, 157, 158, 160, 174, 176, 182, 184. *See also* Dhahran; King Abdul Aziz Air Base, Saudi Arabia.
Dhahran International Airport: 22, 46, 61
Diamanti, Stan S.: 93
Dick, Craig J.: 12, 51, 52
Dick, Daniel M.: 43, 60, 96, 121, 128, *150*, 159, 179, 180, 182, 195
  Introduced: 21
  Quoted: 21, 35, 63, 72, 78, 83, 95, 96, 111, 118, 183, 183–84, 184, 185
Dining Hall: *See* Desert Rose Inn.
Disaster Control Group: 26, 56, 57, 80, 93, 94, 101, 120, 121, 127, 128
Dittmer, Kurt B.: 18
Dixon, Rich: 73, 74
DNA (Deoxyribonucleic acid): 96, 123
Doha, Qatar: 67
Dolinar, Michael J., Jr.: 46, 47, 169
Dooley, Christomer: 12, 99, 121
Dormitory: typical floor plan, 8. *See also* Khobar Towers, Buildings, numbered.
Doubleday, Michael: 34
Dover Air Force Base, Delaware: 96, 98, 117, 151, 153, 161
  Remains transported to: 152–53, 161

265

Index

Dover Port Mortuary: 96, 97, 117, 118, 151, 152, 161, 162, 167
Downing, Wayne A.: 179, 180, 185–88, 189, 190, 192
Downing Report: 185–88, 189, 190, 192
Downing Task Force: 179, 180, 185–88, 189, 190, 192
Dudani, Mahender: 172
Dupre', Felix: 102
Duty status, whereabouts unknown: 117, 118, 135
Dye, Craig E.: 45
Dye, Lori: 45
Dylewski, Gary R.: 67, 103, 104, 106, 107, 135, 136, 137, 138, *144, 145,* 163, 169, 170, 171, 173

Eastern Province, Saudi Arabia: 18, 23, 151, 187
Edman, Thomas F.: 13, 49, 50, 51, 167
Edwards Air Force Base, California: 9, 181
Edwardsville, Illinois: 53
Eglin Air Force Base, Florida: 6, 20, 53, 54, 66, 67, 90, 101, 103, 105, 106, 107, 108, 122, 128, 138, *145,* 155, 157, 159, 167, 168, 169, 170, 172, 180. *See also* 58th Fighter Squadron.
   Air Force Development Test Center: 137, *147,* 163, 168
   Buildings, numbered
      1: 169
      205: 103, 104
      210: 108
      1312: 201
      1315: 201
      1363: 135–36. *See also* "People Place."
   Community support: 173–74
   Events after bombing: 134–37, 163
   Family Support Center: 90, 103, 104, 105, 135, 136
   Field Training Detachment Building: 135–36. *See also* "People Place."
   Hangar 130. *See* King Hangar.
   King Hangar: *145,* 169, 170, 171
   Main Base Eglin: 103, 104, 108, 135, 137, 163
   Memorial: *147,* 201–2
   Military Personnel Flight: 107, 108
   "People Place": 135, 136–37, 169
   Runway: *142, 144*
   Streets
      Eglin Boulevard: 10
      Eglin Parkway: 169
      Nomad Way: 135, 201
Egypt: 121, 158
11 September terrorist attacks: 23, 170, 198
Emergency medical technicians: 73, 74, 76, 83
Emergency Operations Center (Landstuhl Regional Medical Center): 130
English language: 20, 81
Enlisted Heritage Hall: 146, *147*
   Khobar Towers memorial: *147,* 200
Ertell, Mike: 131
Eskan Village: 20, 182
Europe: 85, 87, 88, 119, 155

Faisal, Prince Saud: 122
Family Support Center (Eglin Air Force Base, Florida): 90, 103, 104, 105, 135, 136
Farmer, Ken: 64, 84, 87
Federal Bureau of Investigation: 29, 31, 68, 120, 177, 178, 195, 196, 197
Fennig, Patrick P.: 7, 9, 53, 201
Ferrer, Cesario F., Jr.: 84, 85, 123, 124, 125
Field Training Detachment Building (Eglin Air Force Base, Florida): 135–36. *See also* "People Place."
58th Fighter Squadron: 6, 7, 46, 53, 54, 58, 67, 72, 74, 89, 90, 91, 92, 95, 96, 104, 105, 106, 110, 111, 112, 115, 128, 136, 149, 152, 155, 160, 167, 169, 174, 180, 201. *See also* Eglin Air Force Base, Florida.
   Returns to Eglin Air Force Base: 157–59
   Typical tour: 19–20
Fire chief: 58, 61, 75, 189
First aid: 71, 72, 73, 74, 75, 78
First Baptist Church, Cocoa Beach: 173
Five-Year Facilities Improvement Plan: 21–22, 189, 192
Flights
   86th Aeromedical Staging: 130, 162
   4410th Aeromedical Evacuation: 76, 119, 120, 125, 153, 155, 157
Floor plan (dormitory): 8
Florida: 6, 20, 53, 65, 66, 103, 155, 157, 162, 163, 166, 169, 171, 173, 180, 183, 201
Florida State Highway 1A1: 103, 171
Flying Ambulance Surgical Team: 64, 84, 87, 123–24, 124, 125, 126, 153, 154, 155,

Index

156, 157
Fogleman, Miss Jane: 169
Fogleman, Ronald: *40*, 68, 83, *148*, 159, 161, 169, 185, 186, 188, 189, 190, 191
   Early retirement: 192–94
   Meeting with Brig. Gen. Schwalier: 174, 179
   Visit to Khobar Towers: 174–76
Fort Bliss, Texas: 21
Fort Huachuca, Arizona: 21
4404th Composite Wing (Provisional): 6, 12, 24, 26, 27, 28, 29, 30, 31, 33, 43, 56, 59, 60, 61, 62, 71, 72, 76, 92, 111, 113, 120, 127, 150, 151, 159, 161, 163, 164, 165, 176, 177, 178, 179, 181, 183, 184, 185, 187, 189, 190, 191, 192. *See also* Terryl J. (Terry) Schwalier; Daniel M. Dick.
   Aircraft assigned: 18–19
   Change of command ceremony: 179–80
   Facilities improvement plan: 21–22, 189
   History of: 18
   Key personnel: 18
   Locations: 19
   Move to Prince Sultan Air Base: 181–85
   Organization: 18
   Personnel assigned: 19
   Rotation policy: 19
   Southern Watch operations: 18–19
   Wing Operations Center: 61, 62, 63, 64, 89, 99, 101, 159
   Battle Staff meeting in: 61–64
France: 17, 68, 98, 134. *See also* French forces.
Frankfort, Germany: 167
Franklin, Carl E.: 18, 179, 181, 185
Freeh, Louis J.: 196, 197
French forces: 21, 29, 30, 111, 113, 114, 185. *See also* France.
Freyfogle, Edward B.: 115, 129, 130, 132, 137, 165, 166
Friers, Thomas R.: 49, 65, 66, 91, 102, 111, 133, 134, 137, *149*, 162, 163, 166, 171, 172
Furniture Management Office: 177

Garner, Stephen: 123
General Motors Suburban ambulance: 154
Georgia: 181
Germany: 52, 64, 86, 87, 124, 129, 130, 153, 156, 157, 162, 165, 167, 169
Giant Voice: 187

Goff, Mike: 158
Goff, Steven P.: 76, 83, *148*, 176
"Golden Hour": 71, 78
Gore, Ney M.: 87, 116, 129, 130, 132, 157
Gration, Jonathan S. (Scott): 18, 62, 89, 151, 164
Great Britain: 17, 132. *See also* British forces; United Kingdom.
Greater USMTM Transportation Service: 119, 124, 125, 154, 155, 156
Greendale, Wisconsin: 53
Greenfield, Kevin C.: 12, 18, 62, 63, 99, 101, 120, 121
Grice, Corey P.: 9, 10, 12, *40*, 48, 49, 51, 176
Grimm, Rudolph II: 59, 72, 78, 79, 161
Grissom, Thomas E.: 86, 124, 125, 126
Group of Seven: 68, 134
Groups
   1st Rescue: 49, 65, 66, 91, 102, 111, 133, 134, 149, 161, 172, 173
   33d Logistics: 53
   33d Operations: 107, 168
   39th Medical: 84, 85, 86, 123, 153
   45th Mission Support: 201
   4404th Logistics: 18, 183
   4404th Medical: 18, 71, 76, 113, 119, 120, 154, 156, 161, 181
   4404th Operations: 18, 151
   4404th Support: 18, 189
   4409th Operations: 18, 19, 32, 60, 120, 158
Grover, Bob: 166
Guerrero, Alfredo R.: 9, 10, 12, 13, 14, *40*, 48, 49, 51, 56, 57, 62, 122, 176, 181
Gulf View: 30, 33
Gulf War: 16, 17, 18, 20, 21, 23, 107, 114, 179, 181
Gunther Annex, Alabama: 146, *147*, 200

Haines, Belinda: 123
Hamel, Bruce: 113
Hangar 130 (Eglin Air Force Base, Florida). *See* King Hangar.
Harrington, Dawn: 122
Harrison, Carlisle, Jr.: 64, 84, 85
Hart, Ray: 95
Hartman, Frank: 99
Hartsfield, Wayland: 18
Hartsfield International Airport: 67, 103, 166, 167
Haun, L. Timothy (Tim): 53, 201
Hawley, Bryan G.: 191–92

267

Index

Hayes, David: 67, 103, 169
Headquarters Pacific Air Forces: 191
Headquarters United States Air Force: 162, 180, 188, 191
Heaton auditorium: 132
Heidelburg, Germany: 87, 129, 132
Heidelburg University Hospital: 130
Heiser, Michael G.: 53, 200, 201. *See also* Michael G. Heiser Foundation.
Herlacher, Donald: 5, 180
Hezbollah: 195, 197
Hill, Stan: 104, 105, 106, 107, 135, 136, 163, 173
Hill Air Force Base, Utah: 180
Hinsch, Ray W.: 107, 108, 170
Hinson, Karen: 171, 172
Hinson, Robert C.: 103, 162, 171, 172
Hoffman, Dustin: 7
Holloway, Robert H.: 66, 102, 134
Hoopes, Troy R.: 123
Horner, Charles A.: 181
Hospitals. *See also* Arabian American Oil Company Hospital, Bundeswehzentralkrankenhaus; Dammam Central Hospital; Heidelberg University Hospital; King Fahd Military Medical Complex; King Fahd University Hospital; Landstuhl Regional Medical Center; Al Mana Hospital; Ministry of Defense and Aviation Hospital; Mohammed al Dosha Hospital; Walter Reed Hospital; Wilford Hall Medical Center.
    Map of Dhahran hospitals: 100
House National Security Committee: 68, 178, 188
Hurlburt Field, Florida: 108, 137, 163, 183
Husted, Selena P.: 72, 99, 101, 121

Incirlik Air Base, Turkey: 17, 64, 84, 85, 86, 87, 123, 124, 153
India: 114
Interstate Highway 95: 103
Investigations of the Khobar Towers bombing
    Downing Task Force: 179–80, 185–88, 189, 190, 192
    Federal Bureau of Investigation: 177–78
    House National Security Committee: 178
    Record Task Force: 186, 188–90
    Secretary of Defense-Chairman of the Joint Chiefs of Staff: 194
    Senate Select Committee on Intelligence: 178–79
    Swope-Hawley Team: 190–92
Iowa: 17
Iran: 16, 29, 195, 196, 197, 198
Iraq: 15, 16, 17, 18, 20, 23, 178, 184, 185, 199
Irbil, Iraq: 184
Isaiah, Book of: 165, 170
Islam: 20, 23, 27, 29. *See also* Muslims; Shi'ite Muslims; Sunni Muslims.

Janazzo, John: 107
Japan: 185
Jautakis, Harold R.: 122
Jerowski, Steve: 47
Jersey barriers: 10, 25, 26, 28, 29, 32, *37*, *38*, *39*, 53
John, Gospel of: 170
Johnson, Kevin J.: 53, 200, 201
Joint Chiefs of Staff. *See* Chairman of the Joint Chiefs of Staff.
Joint Forces Support Unit, Eastern Province, Saudi Arabia: 151
Joint Medical Regulating Office: 86
Joint Special Operations Command: 179
Joint Task Force Middle East: 186
Joint Task Force Southwest Asia: 17, 18, 24, 30, 34, 43, 44, 60, 63, 122, 149, 152, 165, 180, 182, 186
Jones, Bob: 93, 101, 114
Jordan: 28, 102
Jozayt, Donald R.: 65, 66, 102, 103, 134, 163, 166, 171
Judge advocate general: 63, 99, 101, 116, 120, 121, 177
Jumper, John P.: 18, 24

Kaiserslautern Military Community, Germany: 65
Katzman, Kenneth: 197
Al Kharj Air Base, Saudi Arabia: 18, 181
Al Khobar, Saudi Arabia: 10, 23
    History of: 20
"Khobar Konnection": 31, 56, 91
Al Khobar Park: 10, 22, 24, 34
Khobar Towers: 15, 19, *36*, *40*, 66, 67, 134, 137, 151, 152, 158, 161, 163, 167, 168, 171, 176, 177, 178, 179, 186, 189, 190, 193, 194, 195, 196, 197, 198. *See also* Dhahran, Saudi Arabia; Dhahran Air Base; 4404th Composite Wing (Provisional);

Index

Investigations of the bombing; King Abdul Aziz Air Base.
Accounting for personnel of: 89–108
Bombing of: 43–52
Buildings, numbered. *See also* T Building Typical Suite Floor Plan; U.S. Sector Khobar Towers Housing Complex.
   13: 120, 121, 127, 175, 176
   101: 29, 43, 55, 56, 60
   103: 55, 73, 80, 94
   104: 55
   107: 60
   109: 109, 114. *See also* Khobar Towers Inn.
   110: 94
   111. *See* Clinic.
   117: 29, 93, 94
   120: 56
   127: 6, 7, 29, *36*, 43, 44, 46, 47, 55, 57, 58, 90, 104, 110, 111, 112, 168, 180
   128: 55
   129: 55
   130: *36*, 55
   131: 7, 9, 10, 12, 14, 24, 29, 33, 35, *36, 40, 41*, 45–48, 51–53, 55, 56, 58, 61, 62, 62–63, 66, 68, 74–79, 83, 90, 92-97, 109–10, 110, 116, 122, ***139, 148***, 152, 158, 162, 165, 167–69, 171, 174, 176, 177, 180, 187, 189, 195, 200
     Razed, 184
   132: 55, 90, 113, 114, 120, 121
   133: 35, 43, 53, 54, 55, 66, 73, 110
   201: 29
Chapel:120–21, 127, 175–76
Clinic: 54, 57–60, 62, 74, 75, 76, 78,79, 82–84, 94–96, 99, 109, 124, 127, 174
Day after bombing: 109–28
Desert Rose Inn: 57, 58, 61, 62, 75, 77, 78, 80, 82, 83, 89, 91, 94, 99, 101, 110, 115, 127,128, 176
Dining hall: *See* Desert Rose Inn.
Description of compound: 20–22
History of: 20–21
Immediately after bombing: 53–64
Immediately before bombing: 5–14
Khobar Towers Inn: 109, 112, 114, 126, 127, 128

Map of: 11
Medical response to bombing: 71–88,
Move to Prince Sultan Air Base: 181–85
Northern perimeter fence: 187, 188, 191, 192
Responsibility for the bombing: 195–98
Security measures at: 23–35
Site Recovery Center: 57, 80, 93, 94, 99, 101, 119, 127, 128, 177
Streets
   Eighth: 6, 21, 31, *37*, 45
   Thirty-Fifth: 21, 29, 31
   Thirty-First: 21, 22, 31, 33, *38,* 53
   Thirty-Seventh: 29
   Thirty-Third: 31, 56, 57
   Twelfth: 21, 28, 29, 31, *38,* 53
Surrounding area: 22
Khobar Towers chapel: 120, 121, 127, 175, 176
Khobar Towers Inn: 109, 112, 114, 126, 127, 128
Al Khubar: 20
Kiley, Kevin C.: 87, 129, 132, 133
King, Ronald L.: 53, 171, 201
King Abdul Aziz Air Base, Saudi Arabia: 5, 15, 18, 22, 66, 91, 95, 98, 115, 123, 128, 151, 153, 157, 158. *See also* Dhahran Air Base.
King Fahd bin Abdul Aziz: 15, 184, 185
King Fahd causeway: 27, 84
King Fahd expressway: 22
King Fahd Military Medical Complex: 80, 99
King Fahd University Hospital: 50, 63, 80, 81, 83, 96, 99, 101, 111, 116, 117, 118, 154, 156, 161, 167, 174
King Hangar (Eglin Air Force Base, Florida): *145,* 169, 170, 171
Kirchberg Hill: 87, 162
Kitson, Kendall K., Jr.: 53, 201
Koblenz, Germany: 129
Kohn, Richard H.: 193, 194
Koury, Laura: 18
Kovalchin, John: 59, 164
Koza, Brian G.: 120
Kurds: 16, 17, 184
Kuwait: 15, 16, 20, 199

Ladtkow, Mark E.: 45
Lambeth, Royce C.: 197
Landstuhl Regional Medical Center, Germany: 52, 65, 82, 86, 87, 115, 116, 126, 127,

269

Index

128, 137, *141*, 154, 155,156, 157, 160, 162, 165, 166, 167, 169, 198
Emergency Operations Center: 130
Heaton auditorium: 132
On day after the bombing: 129–33
Ward 14: 133
Langley Air Force Base, Virginia: 102, 134, 152, 157, 163, 180
Lauder, Alfred B. (Bruce): 43, 161
Lavallee, Richard J., Jr.: 115
Lebanon: 195, 197
LeGrand, Ray: 123
Lester, Christopher B.: 53, 117, 118, 119, 161, 162, 171, 201
Levi's jeans: 113
Levy, Babe: 7
Locker, Dan L.: 64, 84, 85, 87, 88, 156
Lockheed Martin Corporation: 157
Looney, William R., III: 102
Louisiana: 185
Loyd, Ronald D.: 93, 113–14
Lucky Base, Saudi Arabia: 21, 98
Lundin, John: 65
Lyon, France: 68, 134

M–16 rifle: 57
M–60 machine gun: 25, 32, *38*
MacDill Air Force Base, Florida: 17, 33, 180
Madrigal, Luis: 33, 82
Malmstrom Air Force Base, Montana: 83
Al Mana Hospital: 80, 81, 117
Marathon Man: 7, 44
Marthaler, Brent E.: 7, 53, 201
M*A*S*H*: 21
Massapequa Park, New York: 53
Maxwell Air Force Base, Alabama: 146, *147*, 200
    Enlisted Heritage Hall: 146, *147*
    Khobar Towers memorial: *147*, 200
McCarthy, John: 112
McCarthy, Thomas A.: 6, 7, 14, 44, 45, 56, 58, 72, 95, 96, 111, 112, 157, 158, 159, 173, 180
McDonnell Douglas Corporation: 112, 113, 120
McVeigh, Brian W.: 53, 201
Meals Ready to Eat: 183
Meinders, Marvin D.: 64
Mellow, Wayne: 58, 61, 75
Memorials
    Eglin Air Force Base, Florida: *147*, 201–2
    Enlisted Heritage Hall, Maxwell Air Force Base, Alabama: *147*, 200
    Patrick Air Force Base, Florida: *146*, 200–201
    Prince Sultan Air Base, Saudi Arabia: *147*, 200
Memorial services
    Departure from Dhahran Air Base, Saudi Arabia: 151–52
    Dhahran Air Base, Saudi Arabia: 164–65
    Eglin Air Force Base, Florida: *145*, 169–71
    Patrick Air Force Base, Florida: 171–72
Mercedes-Benz tanker: 10
Michael G. Heiser Foundation: 200
Middle East: 87, 114, 197
    Map: xviii
Military Airlift Command: 191
Military Personnel Flight (Eglin Air Force Base Florida): 107, 108
Miller, William: 6, 7, 44, 45
Ministry of Defense and Aviation: 15, 181
Ministry of Defense and Aviation Hospital: 46, 48, 49, 51, 54, 62, 63, 80, 81, 98, 99, 101, 117, 122, 154, 155, 156, 169, 174
Ministry of Health: 79, 80
Mink, Allan L., II: 18
Minsky, Barry: 127
Misawa Air Base, Japan: 185
Missileer: 173
"Missing Man" formation: 169, 170
Mobile Aeromedical Staging Facility: 119
Modesto, California: 53
Mohammed al Dosha Hospital: 117, 154, 156
Montana: 83
Moody Air Force Base, Georgia: 181
Mooy, Peter R.: 18, 62, 78, 183
Morelock, Michael D.: 13, 14, 48, 49, 50, 51, 55, 59, 74, 81, 97, 115, 128, 152, 153
Morgera, Peter J.: 53, 201
Moron Air Base, Spain: 159, 169
Mortuary collection point: 92, 94, 95, 97, 99
Moschgat, James: 200
Al Mughassil, Ahmed Ibrahim Ahmad: 196
Murdoch, Jacqueline E.: 125
Muslims: 16. *See also* Islam; Shi'ite Muslims; Sunni Muslims.
Mylar: 187, 189, 192

Nam, Theodore S.: 133

Index

Naples, Italy: 64
National Broadcasting Company: 132
National Military Command Center: 68
National Museum of the United States Air Force: 200
National Naval Medical Center: 129
Nayef, Prince Ibn Abdul Aziz: 122, 196, 197
Nebraska: 171, 201
New Hampshire: 53
New Jersey barriers. *See* Jersey barriers.
Newman, Gary: 130
New York, New York: 56, 81, 198
New York Times: 119
Nguyen, Phillip D.: 134, 172
Nguyen, Thanh V. (Gus): 53, 171, 201
"Nomads": 104, 136, 157, 170
North Carolina: 118

O'Donnell, Michael: 59
Oelstrom, Tad J.: 61
Oerichbauer, Dawn M.: 130, 132, 162
Office of Program Management-Saudi Arabian National Guard: 15, 23, 24
Offutt Air Force Base, Nebraska: 171, 201
Ohio: 53, 117, 163, 171, 200, 201
Oklahoma: 53, 56
Oklahoma City, Oklahoma: 56
Olds, Sherry: 200
Olivier, Laurence: 7
Oman: 59, 109, 127
Operation Alysse: 17
Operation Desert Focus: 181–85
Operation Desert Shield: 15, 20, 21, 181
Operation Desert Storm: 16, 187. *See also* Gulf War.
Operation Enduring Freedom: 199
Operation Iraqi Freedom: 199, 200
Operation Jural: 17
Operation Just Cause: 179
Operation Northern Watch: 199
Operation Provide Comfort: 17, 18
Operation Provide Comfort Task Force: 18
Operation Southern Watch: 9, 15–22, 23, 30, 64, 65, 119, 134, 151, 160, 163, 164, 176, 178, 200, 199–200
Orlando, Florida: 118, 134
Orlando, John C.: 114, 168
Ottawa, Canada: 195
Overbay, Anthony: 24

Palm Coast, Florida: 53, 103
Panama: 68, 179

Panama City, Forida: 53
Paramount Pictures: 7
Pararescue jumpers: 51, 66, 73, 74, 76, 77, 83
Parker, Daryl A.: 73
Parkinson, Richard: 108
Pakistan: 114
Patrick Air Force Base, Florida: 6, 53, 65, 66, 76, 91, 101, 102, 103, 105, 137, 160, 166, 167, 169, 171, 172, 174, 180
  Buildings, numbered
    401: 171
    423: 102, 133
    425: 201
    431: 171, 201
    439 (Seaside Chapel): 171, 201
  Chapel choir: 172
  Community support: 173
  Events after bombing: 133–34, 162–63
  Memorial: *146*, 150, 202–201
  71st Rescue Squadron: 6, 13, 32, 49, 50, 51, 53, 55, 65, 66, 73, 74, 89, 91, 92, 97, 102, 103, 109, 110, 111, 112, 128, 133, 134, 151, 152, 163, 164, 166, 167, 171, 180, 198
    Returns to Patrick Air Force Base: 160
  South Patrick housing area: 167
  Streets
    Edward H. White Street: 201
    Falcon Avenue: 102, 201
    Thor Street: 201
    Titan Road: 201
  Wellness Center: 163
Patrick Pantry Organization: 173
Patriot missile: 21
Peay, J.H. Binford III: 17, 18, 33, 165
Pennsylvania: 178, 198
Pentagon: 23, 68, 170, 180, 194, 198
"People Place": 135, 136–37, 169
Performance Fitness Examination Study Guide: 73
Perry, William J.: 34, *148*, 149, 174, 181, 182, 183, 185, 188, 193
PERSCO. *See* Personnel Support for Contingency Operations.
Personnel Support for Contingency Operations: 54, 90, 93, 101, 113, 114, 117, 119, 120
"Person of the Week": 83
Peters, F. Whitten: *150*, 200
Philippines: 114
Pineville, West Virginia: 53, 117

271

Index

Pinkston, Terrance: 124
Pirmasens, Germany: 133
Plans, Operations, and Training Division (Landstuhl Regional Medical Center): 130
Pollert, Cinthia Y. (Cindy): 43, 128
Price, Roland: 80, 81, 82
Prichard, Jeff: 33
Prince Sultan Air Base, Saudi Arabia: 146, 199, 200
    Khobar Towers memorial: *147*, 200
    Move from Dhahran to: 181–85
Prince Sultan bin Abdul Aziz: 181, 182
Psalms, Book of: 164, 170
Purple Heart: 54, 74, 161

Al Qaeda: 198, 199
Al-Qahtani, Abdullah: 151
Qatar: 67, 103
Quinn, Jimmy M.: 93

Ralston, Joseph W.: 24
Ramstein Air Base, Germany: 63, 64, 65, 84, 85, 86, 87, 88, 116, 124, 125, 130, 132, 133, 153, 156, 157, 162, 167, 169
    Hoover Street: 64
    Tactical Air Control Center: 64, 85, 86
Ramstein air show disaster (flutag disaster): 116–17, 132
Randall, Gregory E.: 74
Randolph Air Force Base, Texas: 54, 103, 117, 118
Rapid Engineer Deployable Heavy Operational Repair Squadron Engineer (RED HORSE): 183
Rash, Kathryn: 170
Raths, David V.: 18
Record, James F.: 185, 186, 188–90, 192
Record Report: 188–90, 192
Record Task Force: 186, 188–90
Red, Dennis V.: 94
Red Crescent Society: 79
Red Cross. *See* American Red Cross.
"Red Hats": 12
Regional Security Officer: 188
Remains of the deceased, transported to Dover Air Force Base, Delaware: 152–53, 161
Reno, Janet: 195
Rice, Booker T.: 109
Richards, Andrea: 175, 176

"Right Start" briefings: 31, 56
Rimkus, Joseph E.: 53, 201
Riyadh, Saudi Arabia: 12, 15, 18, 19, 20, 23, 24, 31, 32, 43, 60, 63, 68, 87, 98, 121, 122, 127, 129, 176, 181, 182, 183, 184, 188
Riyadh bombing: 23, 24, 25, 26, 27, 28, 29, 32, 34, 87, 178, 198
Robb, Douglas J.: 18, 33, 43, 53, 54, 59, 62, 71, 72, 77, 101, 115, 116, 117, 120, 123, 124, 125, 127, *141*, 153, 154, 155, 157, 161, 181
    Quoted: 69, 73, 74, 75, 76, 78, 79, 80, 80–81, 82, 83, 84, 88, 113, 114, 115, 116, 117, 123–24, 126, 156, 163
Rosehill, Kansas: 53
Rota Naval Station, Spain: 159
Roudebush, James: 84, 87, 88
Royal Air Force: 127
Royal Air Force Lakenheath, United Kingdom: 64
Royal Canadian Mounted Police: 195
Royal Saudi Air Force: 151, 182
Rudinski, Boris: 78, 79
Ryan, Michael: *141*, 197

Saddam Hussein: 15, 16, 17, 23, 184, 185, 199, 200
Safwan Air Base, Iraq: 16
San Antonio, Texas: 113
Santa Ana, Rolando R.: 181
Saudi Arabia: 5, 6, 9, 12, 15, 16, 18–20, 23, 24, 27–31, 34, 54, 55, 57, 59–61, 63–65, 67, 68, 71, 80, 81, 83, 87, 93, 96, 102, 103, 109, 112, 114–16, 119, 120, 122, 123, 129, 133, 153–60, 165, 167, 173, 174, 177, 178, 180–87, 189, 195–98, 200, 201. *See also* Dhahran; Riyadh.
Saudi Embassy: 29
Saudi Ministry of Defense and Aviation: 15, 181
Saudi Ministry of Health: 79, 80
Saudi National Guard: 23
Saudi Rail Organization: 80
Al Sayegh, Hani Abdel Rahim: 195–96
Schaeffer, Joel: 5, 44
Schafer, Klaus O.: 84
Schellhous, Robbin: 189
Schofield, Wisconsin: 83
Schuchman, MaryAnna: 198

Index

Schueller, La Verne L.: 170
Schultz, Wayne L.: 18, 62
Schwalier, Terryl J. (Terry): 6, 19, 20, 24, 25, 26, 27, 28, 29, 30, 33, 35, 43, 51–52, 56, 60, 63, 75, 78, 79, 83, 89, 94, 95, 96, 99, 120, 121, 122, 128, *148*, 150, 152, 155, 158, 159, 164, 165, 174, 176, 177, 179, 180, 186, 187, 189, 191, 192, 195
   Introduced: 18
   Promotion: 193–95
   Quoted: 21, 24, 29, 31, 32, 34, 59, 61, 62, 95, 156, 175, 176
   Retirement: 194–95
Schwarzkopf, H. Norman: 16
Scott Air Force Base, Illinois: 65, 85
   Tactical Airlift Control Center: 65, 85
Scud missile: 23, 187
Search and Recovery teams: 92, 93, 96
Seaside Chapel: 171, 201
Secretary of the Air Force: 19. *See also* F. Whitten Peters; James G. Roche; Sheila Widnall.
Secretary of Defense. *See* Cohen, William S.; Perry, William J.
Secretary of State. *See* Christopher, Warren.
Security Forces. *See* Security Police.
Security Police: 9, 10, 12, 13, 14, 25, 29, 32, 33, 48, 51, 52, 56, 57, 58, 62, 74, 75, 80, 176, 178
   Desk blotters: 189
Seeb Air Base, Oman: 59
Self Aid and Buddy Care: 71, 72, 73, 74, 75, 78
Sellersburg, Indiana: 53
Senate Armed Services Committee: 188, 193
Senate Select Committee on Intelligence: 178
Senior Noncommissioned Officer Academy: 200
71st Rescue Squadron: 6, 13, 32, 49, 50, 51, 53, 55, 65, 66, 73, 74, 89, 91, 92, 97, 102, 103, 109, 110, 111, 112, 128, 133, 134, 151, 152, 163, 164, 166, 167, 171, 180, 198. *See also* Patrick Air Force Base.
   Returns to Patrick Air Force Base, Florida: 160
Shafer, Jane: 66
Shafer, Thomas H.: 13, 14, 44, 50, 55, 66, 91, 97, 102, 103, 111, 114, 115, 152, 153, 160, 164, 165, 167

Shaikh Isa, Bahrain: 185
Shalikashvili, John M.: 30, 68, 161, 171, 184, 194
Shannon, Ireland: 158
Shaw, Marie: 131, 132, 133
Shaw, Stephanie: 133
Shaw Air Force Base, South Carolina: 18, 180
Shealy, Francis W.: 93
Shi'ite Muslims: 16, 17, 195, 196. *See also* Islam; Muslims; Sunni Muslims.
Shreveport, Louisiana: 53
Simmons, Ben: 84
Sine, William F.: 51, 74, 167
Site Recovery Center: 57, 80, 93, 94, 99, 101, 119, 127, 128, 177
Smith, Ken: 5, 44
Smith, Kevin: 128
Smith, Roy: 76, 83
Souk's Supermarket: 23
South Carolina: 18, 68, 178, 180
South Dakota: 53
Southern Watch: *See* Operation Southern Watch.
Southwest Asia: 16, 20, 85, 102, 159
Southwest Asia service medal: 7
Space Coast: 166, 173
Spain: 159, 169
Spangdahlem Air Base, Germany: 64
Specter, Arlen: 178
Spence, Floyd: 68, 178
Squadrons
   27th Fighter: 152, 157
   33d Maintenance: 53
   33d Operations Support: 53, 122
   33d Tactical Fighter: 180
   41st Rescue: 66
   45th Civil Engineering: 167
   58th Fighter Squadron: 6, 7, 46, 53, 54, 58, 67, 72, 74, 89, 90, 91, 92, 95, 96, 104, 105, 106, 110, 111, 112, 115, 128, 136, 149, 152, 155, 160, 167, 169, 174, 180, 201. *See also* Eglin Air Force Base.
   Returns to Eglin Air Force Base, Florida: 157–59
   59th Fighter: 170
   60th Fighter: 53, 67, 201
   71st Rescue: 6, 13, 32, 49, 50, 51, 53, 55, 65, 66, 73, 74, 89, 91, 92, 97, 102, 103, 109, 110, 111, 112, 128, 133, 134, 151, 152, 163, 164, 166, 167,

273

Index

171, 180, 198. *See also* Patrick Air Force Base.
Returns to Patrick Air Force Base, Florida: 160
79th Fighter: 175
86th Aeromedical Evacuation: 64, 85, 86, 87, 88, 111, 124, 125, 126, 130, 153, 154, 155, 157
86th Medical: 87, 126
88th Civil Engineering: 53
95th Security Police: 181
96th Mission Support: 135
347th Aerospace Medical: 181
412th Operations Support: 48
555th Tactical Fighter: 191
741st Maintenance: 65
741st Rescue: 66
823d Rapid Engineer Deployable Heavy Operational Squadron Engineer: 183
4404th Civil Engineering: 189
4404th Communications Squadron: 93
4404th Mission Support: 54
Personnel Support for Contingency Operations (PERSCO): 54, 90, 93, 101, 113, 114, 117, 119, 120
4404th Security Police: 189
Stanton, Andre L.: 48, 51
Stark, Patrick R.: 127
State Department: 24, 29, 31
Steckel, Frederick A.: 133
Stratham, New Hampshire: 53
Stripes for Exceptional Performers promotion: 175
Stuttgart Air Base, Germany: 131
Sultan Hashim Ahmad: 16
Sunni Muslims: 16. *See also* Islam; Muslims; Shi'ite Muslims.
Swope, Richard T.: 191–92
Swope-Hawley Investigation: 190–92
Swope-Hawley Report: 190–92
Syria: 196
Szell, Christian: 7

Tactical Air Command: 18
Tactical Air Control Center (Ramstein Air Base, Germany): 64, 85, 86
Tactical Airlift Control Center (Scott Air Force Base, Illinois): 65, 85
"Tadtown": 61, 62, 99

Taif Air Base, Saudi Arabia: 59
Taliban: 198, 199
Talil Air Base, Iraq: 17
Taylor, Curtis: 118
Taylor, Jeremy A.: 53, 201
Taylor, Maria: 118
Taylor, Robert E.: 92, 101, 152
T Building, typical suite floor plan: 8
Thailand: 191
Theater Communications Management Cell: 93
Third-country nationals: 114, 115, 184, 195
39th Medical Group Hospital: 64, 84
Thompson, Donnell: 59, 60, 94, 95, 111
Threatcon Alpha: 24, 25
Threatcon Bravo: 25
Threatcon Charlie: 25
Threatcons (threatening conditions): 25
Tomahawk missile: 184, 185
Traister, James J.: 12, 28, 32, 35, 56, 60, 61, 62, 178
Travel Management Office: 160
Treadway, R. Morris (Mo): 43, 45, 47, 54, 57, 58, 72, 74, 75, 76, 77, 78, 81, 82, 83, 88, 126, *142*, *149*, 158, 168
Trushkowsky, Stewart: 172
Tuel, Timothy: 123
Turkey: 16, 17, 64, 84, 86, 123, 153
Tyndall Air Force Base, Florida: 163

Udorn Royal Thai Air Base, Thailand: 191
Umstead, Bennie L.: 24, 43, 56, 58, 60
Uniform Code of Military Justice: 189, 190
United Arab Emirates: 44, 153
United Kingdom: 17, 64. *See also* British forces; Great Britain.
United Nations: 15, 16, 178, 199
Resolutions: 16, 17, 199
United Service Organizations: 31
United States Air Forces in Europe: 64, 84, 85, 86, 88, 141, 156
Crisis Action Team: 130
United States Army: 19, 21, 23, 54, 93, 94, 98. *See also* Fort Bliss; Fort Huachuca; Lucky Base.
4th Infantry Division: 199
6th Battalion, 52d Air Defense Artillery: 21
54th Signal Battalion: 21
335th Signal Command: 93
Patriot Task Force: 19

Index

United States Army Corps of Engineers: 34, 55, 56
United States Army Europe: 129
   Crisis Action Team: 129, 130
   Regional Medical Command: 129
United States Army Forces, Central Command: 29, 30, 93
United States Army Medical Materiel Center, Europe: 133
United States Central Command: 16, 17, 24, 33, 63, 68, 84, 87, 93, 119, 165, 179, 182, 186, 188, 190
United States Central Command Air Forces: 18, 63, 97, 98, 179, 182, 187, 191
United States Congress. *See* United States House of Representatives; United States Senate.
United States Consul General (Dhahran, Saudi Arabia): 188, 191
United States Embassy bombings:
   Kenya: 198, 200
   Tanzania: 198
United States Embassy, Saudi Arabia: 63, 122, 188
United States European Command: 64, 84, 85, 86, 87, 131
   Commander in Chief: 131
   Headquarters Crisis Action Team: 130
United States House of Representatives: 178, 179, 188, 192
   National Security Committee: 68, 178, 188
United States Marines: 193
United States Military Training Mission: 12, 15, 63, 94, 117, 119, 151, 174
United States Naval Support Activity, Naples, Italy: 64
United States Navy: 64, 84, 123, 127, 185
United States Navy Administrative Support Unit, Bahrain: 84, 123
United States Navy, Central Command: 27, 28, 84
United States sector, Khobar Towers housing complex: 11
United States Senate: 178, 194
   Armed Services Committee: 188, 193
   Select Committee on Intelligence: 178
United States Southern Command: 186
United States Special Operations Command: 179
United States Transportation Command: 191

University of Hamburg Hospital: 129
USS Cole bombing: 198
Utah: 180

Vailhingen, Germany: 131
Valencia, Cielito: 171
Valor device: 74
Vasquez, Lydia E.: 198
Vietnam War: 179, 186, 191
Virginia: 134, 152, 157, 163, 180, 197
Vulnerability assessments: 26, 27, 188, 193

Wagar, Christopher T.: 9, 10, 12, 13, *40*, 48, 49, 51, 176, 181
Walsh, Ben: 167
Walter Reed Hospital: 129
Ward, James R.: 121
Ward 14 (Landstuhl Regional Medical Center): 133
Washington, D.C.: 68, 193, 194, 196, 198
Watertown, South Dakota: 53
Waylett, Suzanne M.: 183
Weather: 9, 10
Weems, Michael: 157
Weitzel, Lee: 103, 104, 135
Wellness Center (Patrick Air Force Base, Florida): 163
Wells, Matthew: 51, 58, 74
White, John P.: 186, 189, 190, 191
White House: 68, 120, 162, 170, 177
Widnall, Sheila: 68, *149*, 161, 169, 178, 185, 186, 188, 189, 190, 191
Widnall, William S.: 169
Wilford Hall Medical Center: 129
Williams, Cedric: 91, 92, 115
Williams, Dan: 74
Williams, Norman: 182
Wing Operations Center: 61, 62, 63, 64, 89, 99, 101, 159
   Battle Staff meeting in: 61–64
Wings
   1st Fighter: 102, 134
   2d Bomb: 185
   4th Tactical Fighter: 18
   33d Fighter: 19, 67, 90, 103, 104, 105, 107, 134, 135, 136, 137, 163, 168, 169, 170, 173, 201
   39th: 123
   45th Space: 65, 102, 103, 162, 171, 173
   58th Tactical Training: 180
   59th Medical: 86, 124

Index

96th Air Base: 103, 104
363d Air Expeditionary: 199
388th Fighter: 180
4404th Composite Wing (Provisional): 6, 12, 24, 26, 27, 28, 29, 30, 31, 33, 43, 56, 59, 60, 61, 62, 71, 72, 76, 92, 111, 113, 120, 127, 150, 151, 159, 161, 163, 164, 165, 176, 177, 178, 179, 181, 183, 184, 185, 187, 189, 190, 191, 192. *See also* Terryl J. (Terry) Schwalier; Daniel M. Dick.
    Aircraft assigned: 18–19
    Change of command ceremony: 179–80
    Facilities improvement plan: 21–22, 189
    History of: 18
    Key personnel: 18
    Locations: 19
    Move to Prince Sultan Air Base: 181–85
    Organization: 18
    Personnel assigned: 19
    Rotation policy: 19
    Southern Watch operations: 18–19
    Wing Operations Center: 61, 62, 63, 64, 89, 99, 101, 159
        Battle Staff meeting: 61–64
7440th Composite (Provisional): 17. *See also* 4404th Composite Wing (Provisional).
Winkler, Kim: 167
Winkler, Matthew: 13, 14, 49, 50, 152, 162, 165, 166, 167, 198
Winn, David: 33
Winnecke, Lisa A.: 12, 62, 63, 99, 120, 121
Wisconsin: 83
Wittman, David: 166
Wong, Normund: 87
Wood, Justin R.: 53, 200, 201
Woody, Joshua E.: 53, 201
World Trade Center: 23, 56, 198
Wounded airmen: 54, *139, 143*
    Arrive at Eglin Air Force Base: 167–69
    Arrive at Patrick Air Force Base: 166–67
    Medical care: 71–88
    Return to duty in U.S.: 180–81
    Transported to Landstuhl: 153–57, 162
    Transported to U.S.: 165–66
Wright-Patterson Air Force Base, Ohio: 53, 117, 163, 171, 200, 201
Würzburg University Hospital: 130

Yukon, Oklahoma: 53

Ziegler, Eric D.: 7, 9, 46, 47, 48, 51, 116, 165, 180–81